Nonprofit Organizations

This text provides a comprehensive overview of nonprofit and voluntary organizations, non-governmental organizations, philanthropic foundations, and civil society institutions. Taking an international perspective, *Nonprofit Organizations* details the background and concepts behind these organizations, examines relevant theories, and the central issues of nonprofit governance, management, and policy. Linking theory with practice, each chapter is illustrated with real life case studies.

Questions answered include:

- What is the history of the nonprofit sector?
- What is the scale and structure of the nonprofit sector?
- How can we explain the existence and behavior of nonprofit organizations?
- How do nonprofits obtain funding and how do they manage resources?

Nonprofit Organizations: Theory, Management, Policy is an invaluable core textbook for those studying nonprofit and voluntary organizations, as well as being of great interest to practitioners in the nonprofit sector.

Helmut K. Anheier is Professor and Director of the Center for Civil Society at UCLA's School of Public Affairs, and Centennial Professor of Social Policy at the London School of Economics.

Nonprofit Organizations

Theory, management, policy

Helmut K. Anheier

Routledge
Taylor & Francis Group

LONDON AND NEW YORK

First published 2005
by Routledge
2 Park Square, Milton Park, Abingdon, Oxon OX14 4RN

Simultaneously published in the USA and Canada
by Routledge
270 Madison Ave, New York, NY 10016

Reprinted 2006 (twice), 2007 (twice), 2008 (twice), 2010 (twice)

Routledge is an imprint of the Taylor & Francis Group, an informa business

Typeset in Perpetua and Bell Gothic by
Florence Production Ltd, Stoodleigh, Devon
Printed and bound in Great Britain by
TJ International Ltd, Padstow, Cornwall

British Library Cataloguing in Publication Data
A catalogue record for this book is available from the British Library

Library of Congress Cataloging in Publication Data
Anheier, Helmut K., 1954–
    Nonprofit organizations: theory, management, policy/Helmut K. Anheier.
        p. cm.
    Includes bibliographical references and index.
    1. Nonprofit organizations.   II. Title.
    HD2769.15.A538 2005
    060—dc22   2004011854

ISBN10: 0–415–31419–4 (pbk)
ISBN10: 0–415–31418–6 (hbk)

ISBN13: 978–0–415–31419–0 (pbk)
ISBN13: 978–0–415–31418–3 (hbk)

Contents

Illustrations

FIGURES

MAP

TABLES

BOXES

Preface

This book can be used as a general introduction to the study of nonprofit organizations and as a textbook for courses at the graduate and advanced undergraduate level. The lack of a multi-disciplinary textbook dedicated to the topic of nonprofit organizations, philanthropy, and civil society has long been a major complaint among faculty and students, as has been the absence of a general overview of current knowledge of the field. This book tries to meet both objectives.

The book grew out of over ten years of teaching nonprofit courses at various universities and in different curricular settings. First, between 1994 and 1998, for Master's students in public policy at the Johns Hopkins Institute for Policy Studies, I wrote the initial lectures that eventually developed very much the first part of this book, with a focus on theory and conceptual approaches. Between 1998 and 2002, I served as course tutor for the Master in Voluntary Sector Management and Administration at the London School of Economics, and put emphasis on lectures that became the governance and management-related parts of the book. Since moving to UCLA, I have continued to add to these sections, and also expanded the coverage of theory and policy. In addition, teaching as part of the European Summer Academy of Philanthropy, at various universities in Europe (University of Bologna, University of Freiburg in Switzerland, University of Oslo), and in executive education in countries as different as the UK, Germany, Spain, and China has added useful perspectives that are reflected in the structure and content of the book.

This textbook tries to cover the major areas of knowledge and expertise when it comes to nonprofit organizations. It follows a sequence of background–history–concepts–facts–theory–behavior–management–policy to cover the interests of academics, nonprofit leaders, and managers alike. Each chapter offers an overview of the topic covered and review questions at the end, with suggested readings for those who wish to explore topics in greater detail.

As a basic overview text, this book cannot cover all aspects of nonprofit studies; and even those addressed cannot be dealt with in the depth the subject matter frequently warrants. It is a testimony to the breadth and richness the field has achieved in recent years that an overview text such as this struggles to do justice to all aspects worth covering. A textbook must make choices—and this one is no different. One choice was to add comparative, international dimensions to the extent possible; another to introduce applied topics even though the book is primarily targeted at academic audiences.

As best as I can judge, this book is the first dedicated and comprehensive textbook on nonprofit studies. As such, it shows all the weaknesses that come with such an endeavor, and it is my hope that it will also show some of its promise of which future editions of this book can benefit, and on which others can build.

Acknowledgments

This book owes much to the effort of others. I would like to thank Regina List who carefully and creatively edited the chapters of this book not once but twice; Marcus Lam who has been a terrific and tireless research assistant and conducted numerous background researches; Laurie Spivak for managing the Center for Civil Society at UCLA so efficiently and graciously that I could find the time to work on this textbook even during very busy periods. Thanks are due to Hagai Katz who contributed to Chapter 4, and was influential in developing Chapter 15 on international issues.

Thanks are also owed to Francesca Heslop who first suggested the idea of this textbook to me, and to her and Rachel Crookes for encouragement and helping me across the finish line. Their patience is legendary.

I am indebted to various institutions and companies for granting permission to reproduce material. Every effort has been made to trace copyright holders, but in a few cases this has not been possible. Any omissions brought to my attention will be remedied in future editions.

Some of my most sincere thanks are reserved for the hundreds of students at UCLA, LSE, and Johns Hopkins, who patiently sat and sometimes suffered through my lectures over the last ten years. Their enthusiasm and feedback made this book possible, as did the pleasure of working with Sarabajaya Kumar at LSE in teaching the voluntary sector course in the Social Policy Department. I am also grateful to Jane Schiemann and Sue Roebuck.

I also wish to thank Lester Salamon, Stefan Toepler, Nuno Themudo, Avner Ben-Ner, Jeremy Kendall, and Lynne Moulton. I had the privilege of working with these excellent scholars on a number of projects and papers, and the result of our work has clearly influenced my thinking, which is amply reflected in the various chapters of this book. Specifically, Chapters 3 (definitions and concepts), 4 and 5 (on the contours of the nonprofit sector) benefited from my long-standing collaboration with Lester Salamon; Chapters 11 (management models) and 14 (foundations) from various projects and writings with Stefan Toepler; Chapter 15 on international aspects would not have been possible without my cooperation with Nuno Themudo; Chapter 6 on theoretical approaches shows the intellectual impact of Avner Ben-Ner; Chapter 16, the policy chapter, shows the influence of Jeremy Kendall; and Chapter 13, dealing with state-government relations, of Lynne Moulton. Of course, final responsibility for any faults and mistakes in this book is mine.

Part I

Introduction

Chapter 1

Studying nonprofit organizations

This introductory chapter presents an overview of the range of nonprofit institutions, organizations, and activities. The chapter briefly surveys the intellectual and political history of the study of nonprofit organizations, and states some of the key intellectual, practical, and policy-related issues involved. The chapter also discusses how the field relates to the various social science disciplines; shows its interdisciplinary nature; and presents a summary of the current state of the art. The chapter includes a description of the objectives and structure of the book by offering brief chapter summaries.

LEARNING OBJECTIVES

The study of nonprofit or voluntary organizations is a fairly recent development in the history of the social sciences. What has become one of the most dynamic interdisciplinary fields of the social sciences today began to gather momentum less than two decades ago. At the same time, the field is rooted in different traditions and approaches that each seek to come to terms with the complexity and vast variety of nonprofit organizations and related forms. After considering this chapter, the reader should:

- have an understanding of the wide range of activities and types of institution that come under the label of nonprofit organization;
- be able to identify key intellectual traditions of nonprofit sector research;
- have a sense of the major factors that influenced the field and that contributed to its development;
- be able to navigate through the book's various parts and chapters in terms of specific content and their thematic connections.

KEY TERMS

Some of the key terms introduced in this chapter are:

- charity
- civil society
- giving
- nongovernmental organization
- nonprofit organization
- nonprofit sector
- philanthropy
- social capital
- third sector
- voluntary association
- volunteering

A SECTOR RICH IN ORGANIZATIONAL FORMS AND ACTIVITIES

The nonprofit sector is the sum of private, voluntary, and nonprofit organizations and associations. It describes a set of organizations and activities next to the institutional complexes of government, state, or public sector on the one hand, and the forprofit or business sector on the other. Sometimes referred to as the "third sector," with government and its agencies of public administration being the first, and the world of business or commerce being the second, it is a sector that has gained more prominence in recent years—in the fields of welfare provision, education, community development, international relations, the environment, or arts and culture. The nonprofit or third sector has also become more frequently the topic of teaching and research, and this textbook seeks to offer students an overview of the current knowledge and understanding in the field.

Although we speak of the nonprofit "sector," which suggests clearly defined borders with the public sector and the forprofit sector, such sector distinctions are in reality quite blurred and fluid. Organizations "migrate" from one sector to another, e.g. hospitals change from public to nonprofit, or from nonprofit to forprofit status; others contain both profit and nonprofit centers within them, e.g. corporate responsibility programs, or businesses run by nonprofit organizations; and others yet are quasi-governmental institutions located somewhere between the private and the public realm, e.g. the Smithsonian Institute in Washington DC, or the BBC in the UK. Yet what many students of the nonprofit sector find as perplexing as fascinating is the sheer diversity of organizational forms, associations, and activities it encompasses. Here are some current examples of the rich variety of entities that make up the nonprofit sector in the US:

Museums: from major institutions such as the Metropolitan Museum of Art in New York, the Los Angeles County Museum of Art, the Getty Museum in Los Angeles, and the Chicago

Art Institute, to smaller institutions such as the Tyler Museum of Art in Texas, the Brevard Museum of Art and Science in Florida, the Peninsula Fine Arts Center in Virginia, and the Sheldon Swope Art Museum in Indiana.

Orchestras: from world renowned companies such as the Cleveland Symphony Orchestra, the Philadelphia Orchestra Association, and the Los Angeles Philharmonic Association, to smaller companies such as the Vietnamese American Philharmonics in California, the Peoria Symphony Orchestra in Illinois, and the Waterbury Symphony Orchestra in Connecticut.

Schools: from prestigious "academies" and "prep schools" in the New England countryside such as the Phillips Academy or the Exeter Academy to the many thousands of private elementary, middle, and high schools across the country (including institutions for special education such as the Morgan Center for Autism and the Conductive Education Center in California, and the Carroll Center for the Blind in Massachusetts).

Universities: from elite institutions such as Harvard, Yale, or Stanford, which have become multi-billion dollar nonprofit corporations, to smaller, local and regional colleges such as Scripps College and Humphreys College in California, Louisiana College, Sterling College in Kansas, and Rochester College in Michigan.

Adult education organizations: including schools for continuing studies, literacy programs, skills and vocational training such as Literacyworks and Opportunities Industrialization Center-West in California, Academy of Hope in Washington DC, the Hillsborough Literacy Council in Florida, and Second Chance Learning in Arizona.

Research institutions: including the RAND Corporation, the Brookings Institution, the Russell Sage Foundation, the Urban Institute, the Nuclear Policy Research Institute in San Francisco, the Center for Educational Research and the American Foundation for Chinese Medicine in New York, and the Tax Foundation and the Earth Policy Institute in Washington DC.

Policy think-tanks: from "Beltway" institutions such as the Cato Institute, the Center for Budget Priorities, or the Hudson Institute, to regional centers such as the California Budget Project or the Southern Poverty Research Center.

Health organizations: from major teaching hospitals such as Johns Hopkins Medical Corporation in Baltimore or the Mayo Clinic in Minneapolis to smaller local establishments such as Health Awareness Services of Central Massachusetts, or the Crisis Pregnancy Center of Ruston, Louisiana, and clinics and community health centers, rehabilitation centers and nursing homes, hospices, etc.

Mental health organizations: ranging from organizations serving specific ethnic communities, such as the Asian Community Mental Health Board in California or the Hawaii Community Health Services, to organizations that deal with specific issues, such as the Center for Grief Recovery and Sibling Loss in Illinois or the Mental Health and Retardation Services in

5

Massachusetts, and organizations that provide a broad spectrum of services, such as the East House Corporation in New York or Jane Addams Health Services in Illinois.

Human services: including day care for children, homes for the elderly, Meals on Wheels, social work organizations, YMCA, YWCA, counseling for youth, married couples, or people in financial debt, Big Brother/Big Sister programs, the Red Cross, and the Salvation Army.

Credit and savings: including Access to Loans for Learning Student Loan Corporation and the Consumer Credit Foundation in California, the Florida Community Loan Fund, the First State Community Loan Fund in Delaware, and the Henry Strong Educational Foundation in Illinois.

Environment and natural resources: including the Sierra Club, wetlands, urban parks, and organizations such as Campton Historic Agricultural Lands and Ducks Unlimited in Illinois, the Colorado Alliance for Environmental Education, the Captain Planet Foundation in Georgia, the Alaska Mineral and Energy Resource Education Fund, and the Tropical Reforestation and Ecosystems Education Center in Hawaii.

Local development and housing: from Habitat for Humanity International and Americorps to local and regional organizations such as Affordable Housing Associates in Berkeley, California, the Housing Assistance Corporation in Massachusetts, or the Southwest Neighborhood Housing Corporation in Colorado.

Humanitarian relief associations and international development organizations: from large organizations, such as CARE, Catholic Relief Services, World Vision, and Doctors without Borders, to regional organizations such as Assist International and India Relief and Education Fund in California, and ActionAid USA, Africare, and American Near East Refugee Aid in Washington DC.

Human rights organizations: including Amnesty International and Human Rights Watch to Anti-Slavery International, Kidsave International, International Campaign for Tibet (all in Washington DC), Afghanistan Relief and Global Exchange in California, and Grassroots International and the Human Rights Project in Massachusetts.

Rural farmers' associations: such as Minnesota Food Association, Ohio County & Independent Agricultural Societies, the American Society of Farm Managers and Rural Appraisers Colorado, Maryland Cattlemen's Association, and the Association of International Agricultural Research Centers in Virginia.

Religious organizations: from large institutional networks such as the Catholic Church, to local congregations of Lutheran, Baptist, Protestant, Hindu, Buddhist, Jewish, Muslim, and Islamic organizations.

Foundations: from large foundations such as the Ford Foundation, the Rockefeller Foundation, Charles Stewart Mott Foundation, John D. and Catherine T. MacArthur Foundation, and the William and Melinda Gates Foundation, to smaller endowments such as the McBean Family Foundation and the Nirenberg Foundation in California, or the Hitachi Foundation and Freed Foundation in Washington DC.

While these examples refer to organizations in the sense of corporate entities, others are primarily membership associations, for example:

Service organizations: such as the Rotary Club, the Lions, Kiwanis or Zonta International, or the Assistance League and its affiliate chapters, the Junior League and its affiliate chapters, or the Knights of Columbus Foundation.

Fraternities and sororities: such as the Alpha Omega International Dental Fraternity in Florida, numerous fraternity and sorority homes at universities across the country, the Elks, but also the Free Masons and similar societies.

Special interest associations and advocacy groups: such as the National Rifle Association Foundation, Mothers Against Drunk Driving, People for the Ethical Treatment of Animals, the American Association of Retired People, or the American Medical Association, to name a few.

Self-help groups: such as Alcoholics Anonymous, and countless local groups for divorcees, or the sharing of grief and loss, weight loss, or crime victims.

While Chapter 4 follows up the dimensions of the nonprofit sector in different countries more systematically, the following examples show the great diversity of nonprofit organizations around the world. Canada has over 66,000 organizations with charitable status, providing a range of services from education, youth programs, health, culture, and the arts, and serves all sectors of the population. Nonprofit organizations include labor unions, professional associations, managerial associations, business organizations, consumer organizations, ethno-cultural organizations, religious organizations, social clubs, and neighborhood groups, in addition to nonprofit service providers and foundations.

In Europe, the Charity Organisation Society, founded in 1883 in London, was at that time one of the largest formal organizations in the British Empire, and similar networks of private human service providers and charities began to form in Germany, France, Italy, Australia, and Japan. Today, two such networks, the Catholic and the Protestant Free Welfare Associations, are among the largest employers in Germany, with over 1,900,000 jobs; and UNIOPSS alone, a French social service and health care federation of nonprofit providers, employs over 350,000 people. ONCE, the Spanish organization for the blind, runs the largest lottery system in the country. And in Israel, nonprofit organizations serve large portions of the country's immigrant population as well as the elderly.

But it is not only in welfare and health care that nonprofit organizations are prominent in other countries. World-famous museums such as the Tate Modern in London or the Guggenheim in Bilbao, Spain, are nonprofit, as are other cultural institutions such as the Academy of St Martin's in the Field in London or the Scala Opera in Milan, Italy. In education, the French *Ligue d'Enseignement* (Education League) covers over 30,000 private schools, and Japan has a substantial number of *gakko hojin*, nonprofit school corporations. In terms of research and higher education, the nonprofit sector would include the London School of Economics, Oxford University, McGill University in Montreal, Canada, the *Wissenschaftszentrum* in Berlin and the various Max Planck Institutes in Germany, the Louis Pasteur Institute in Paris, the Institute for Social Research in Milan, and Keio University in Japan.

Among international humanitarian relief associations we find Doctors Without Borders, founded in France, in addition to the British nongovernmental organizations (NGOs) Oxfam and Amnesty International (the human rights organization), the German Bread for the World humanitarian assistance and development organization, and Greenpeace in the Netherlands. What is more, some of the largest and most influential foundations in the world are located in countries outside the US, such as the Canadian Alberta Heritage Foundation for Medical Research, the Foundation Compagnia di San Paolo in Italy, the Sasakawa Peace Foundation in Japan, the Bertelsmann Foundation in Germany, the J. R. Rowntree Foundation in England, the Myer Foundation in Australia, and the Open Society Institutes in Central and Eastern Europe.

Of course, the nonprofit sector is not limited to the developed countries of America, Asia-Pacific, and Europe. In Africa, Latin America, the Middle East, India, and Central and South East Asia, too, we find a rich tapestry of organizational forms and activities in the nonprofit field. Prominent examples include the Tara Institute and PRIA in India, the rural development NGOs in Thailand or Bangladesh, the countless rotating credit associations in West Africa, the associations among slum dwellers in Mumbai, the network of Catholic welfare associations in Brazil or Argentina, corporate foundations in Turkey, and the numerous *Al Wakf* foundations in Egypt and other Arab countries.

As the above examples from the US and other countries illustrate, when speaking of the nonprofit sector, we tend to refer to organizations, foundations, and associations first and foremost. Yet at the same time, the sector also covers individual activities and the values and motivations behind them, e.g. people's concerns, commitments to, and compassion for others outside their immediate family, respect for others, caring about their community, their heritage, the environment, and future generations.

Specifically, these aspects refer to related terms, such as:

Charity, i.e. individual benevolence and caring, is a value and practise found in all major world cultures and religions. It is one of the "five pillars" of Islam, and central to Christian and Jewish religious teaching and practise as well. In many countries, including the US, the notion of charity includes relief of poverty, helping the sick, disabled and elderly, supporting education, religion, and cultural heritage.

Philanthropy, i.e. the practises of individuals reflecting a "love of humanity" and the voluntary dedication of personal wealth and skills for the benefit specific public causes: while philanthropy, like the term charity, has deep historical roots in religion, its modern meaning emerged in early twentieth-century America and refers to private efforts to solve common social problems such as poverty or ignorance.

Volunteering, i.e. the donation of time for a wide range of community and public benefit purposes, such as helping the needy, distributing food, serving on boards, visiting the sick, or cleaning up local parks: over 50 percent of the US population volunteers on a regular basis, a figure somewhat higher than that for the UK, Australia, or Germany.

Giving, i.e. the donation of money and in-kind goods for charitable and other purposes of public benefit to organizations such as the Red Cross or religious congregations, or to specific causes such as HIV/AIDS, cancer research, or humanitarian relief. Over two-thirds of US households donate money, a number not too different from that of many other countries.

More recently, as we will see in more detail in Chapter 3, two additional concepts have entered the field of nonprofit studies—civil society and social capital:

Civil society: Many different definitions of civil society exist, and there is little agreement on its precise meaning, though much overlap exists between core conceptual components. Nonetheless, most analysts would probably agree with the statement that modern civil society is the sum of institutions, organizations, and individuals located between the family, the state, and the market, in which people associate voluntarily to advance common interests. The nonprofit sector provides the organizational infrastructure of civil society.

Social capital: This is an individual characteristic and refers to the sum of actual and potential resources that can be mobilized through membership in organizations and through personal networks. People differ in the size and span of their social networks and number of memberships. Social capital captures the norms of reciprocity and trust that are embodied in networks of civic associations, many of them in the nonprofit field, and other forms of socializing.

Although closely related, the terms nonprofit sector, social capital, and civil society address different aspects of the same social reality. Social capital is a measure of the individual's connection to society and the bonds of mutual trust it creates, the nonprofit sector refers to private action for public benefit, and civil society is the self-organizing capacity of society outside the realms of family, market, and state.

For a long time, social scientists and policymakers paid little attention to the nonprofit sector, social capital, and civil society, and perhaps even less to the question of what these different forms and activities might have in common. The focus of much social science thinking and policymaking was elsewhere, i.e. with markets and governments. By contrast to the world of government and business, analyzing the complex and varied landscape of nonprofit and civil society institutions seemed less important, and perhaps also too daunting a task, relative to its theoretical importance for understanding society and its policy relevance in fields such as employment, welfare, health, education, or international development. This attitude, however, began to change over the course of the last two decades of the twentieth century, as we will see in the next section.

9

AN EMERGING SECTOR, AN EMERGING FIELD OF STUDY

As we will see in Chapter 4, the nonprofit sector has become a major economic and social force. Parallel to the increase in economic importance is the greater recognition nonprofit organizations enjoy at local, national, and international levels. Prompted in part by growing doubts about the capacity of the state to cope with its own welfare, developmental, and environmental problems, political analysts across the political spectrum (see Giddens 1998; Dilulio 1998) have come to see nonprofits as strategic components of a middle way between policies that put primacy on "the market" and those that advocate greater reliance on the state. Some governments, such as the Clinton and Bush administrations, have seen an alternative to welfare services provided by the public sector in nonprofit and community organizations. This is most clearly the case in the so-called "faith-based initiative" in providing services and relief to the poor, or the school voucher program for both private and public schools. At the international level, institutions such as the World Bank, the United Nations, and the European Union, and many developing countries are searching for a balance between state-led and market-led approaches to development, and are allocating more responsibility to nongovernmental organizations (see Chapter 15).

A growing phenomenon

At the *local* level, nonprofit organizations have become part of community-building and empowerment strategies. Numerous examples from around the world show how policy-makers and rural and urban planners use nonprofit and community organizations for local development and regeneration. These range from community development organizations in Los Angeles or Milan to organizations among slum dwellers in Cairo or Mumbai, and from neighborhood improvement schemes in London or Berlin to local councils in Rio de Janeiro where representatives of local nonprofits groups sit next to political party leaders, business persons, and local politicians.

At the *national* level, nonprofit organizations are increasingly involved in welfare, health care, education reform, and public–private partnerships. Prominent cases include the expansion of nonprofit service providers for the elderly in the US, the establishment of private hospital foundations as a means to modernize the National Health Service in the UK, the transformation of state-held cultural assets into nonprofit museums in former East Germany, and the privatization of day care centers and social service agencies in former socialist countries more generally. In a number of countries, the greater role of nonprofits in welfare reform is aided by laws that facilitate their establishment and operation: for example, Japan and the nonprofit law passed in 1998 (Yamauchi *et al.* 1999; Itoh 2003), initial reforms in China (Ding *et al.* 2003), or policy innovations in Hungary (Kuti 1996) as among the most notable examples. In the course of the last decade, most developed market economies in Europe, North America, and Asia-Pacific have seen a general increase in the economic importance of nonprofit organizations as providers of health, social, educational, and cultural services of many kinds. On average, as we will see in more detail in Chapter 4, the nonprofit sector accounts for about 6 percent of total employment in OECD countries, or nearly 10 percent with volunteer work factored in (Salamon *et al.* 1999a).

At the *international* level (see Chapter 15), we observe the rise of international non-governmental organizations (INGOs) and an expanded role in the international system of governance. The number of known INGOs increased from about 13,000 in 1981 to over 47,000 by 2001. The number of INGOs reported in 1981 would make up just under 28 percent of the stock of INGOs twenty years later. What is more, formal organizational links between NGOs and international organizations such as the United Nations Development Program (UNDP), the World Health Organization (WHO), or the World Bank have increased 46 percent between 1990 and 2000 (Glasius *et al.* 2002: 330).

At the *global* level, recent decades have witnessed the emergence of a global civil society and transnational nonprofits of significant size, with complex organizational structures that increasingly span many countries and continents (Anheier and Themudo 2002; Anheier *et al.* 2001b). Examples include Amnesty International with more than one million members, subscribers, and regular donors in over 140 countries and territories. The Friends of the Earth Federation combines about 5,000 local groups and one million members. The Coalition against Child Soldiers has established partners and national coalitions engaged in advocacy, campaigns, and public education in nearly 40 countries. Care International is an international NGO with over 10,000 professional staff. Its US headquarters alone has income of around $450 million. The International Union for the Conservation of Nature brings together 735 NGOs, 35 affiliates, 78 states, 112 government agencies, and some 10,000 scientists and experts from 181 countries in a unique worldwide partnership.

All these developments suggest that nonprofit organizations are part of the transformation of societies from industrial to post-industrial, and from a world of nation-states to one of transnational, even global, economies and societies, where the local level nonetheless achieves greater relevance and independence. The full recognition of the immensely elevated position and role of nonprofit organizations at the beginning of the twenty-first century is the main difference to the latter part of the previous century, when nonprofits were "(re)discovered" as providers of human services in a welfare state context.

Nonprofit organizations are now seen as a part of the wider civil society and welfare systems of modern societies. Next to the institutional complexes of the state or public sector on the one hand, and the market or the world of business on the other, nonprofit organizations form a third set of institutions that are private, voluntary, and for public benefit. They thus combine a key feature of the public sector, i.e. serving public benefit, with an essential characteristic of the "forprofit" sector, i.e. its combined private and voluntary nature.

Even though they have been recognized as a distinct group or sector only in recent decades, nonprofit organizations have long been an integral part of the social, economic, and political developments in many countries—be it in the developed market economies of North America, Europe, or Japan, or in the transition economies of Central and Eastern Europe, or in the developing countries of Africa, Asia, and Latin America. What is more, this set of institutions has become more central to policy debates in most parts of the world, in particular since the end of the Cold War, and to attempts to reform welfare systems, government budget priorities, and labor markets. There are four main aspects that inform the chapters of this book:

1   The nonprofit sector is now a *major economic and social force* at local, national, and international levels. Its expansion is fueled by, among other factors, greater demands for human services of all kinds, welfare reform and privatization policies, the spread of democracy, and advances in information and communication technology with subsequent reductions in the cost of organizing.

2   Even though the *research agenda has expanded significantly* over the last decade, our understanding of the role of these institutions is still limited, and data coverage frequently remains patchy. Whereas theories of nonprofit institutions developed largely in the field of economics and organizational theory, social capital and civil society approaches have expanded the research agenda on nonprofits in important ways, and invited contributions from sociology and political science.

3   Whereas in the past, the nonprofit sector frequently constituted something close to the *terra incognita* of policymaking, it has now become the *focus of major policy initiatives*. These policy debates will undoubtedly have major implications for the future of nonprofits around the world; they could, ultimately, amount to a highly contradictory set of expectations pushing and pulling these institutions into very different directions.

4   Similarly, whereas in the past the *management of* nonprofit organizations was seen as esoteric and irrelevant, and organizational structures of nonprofits as trivial, there is now much greater interest in understanding how private institutions operating in the public interest ought to be managed and organized—not only bringing more attention to aspects of management models and styles appropriate to nonprofits but also questions of governance, accountability, and impact.

STUDYING NONPROFIT AND VOLUNTARY ASSOCIATIONS: A BRIEF HISTORY

When the foundations of nonprofit sector research were laid just over two decades ago, it would have been difficult to anticipate the significant growth that would take place, not only in the social, economic, and political importance of the nonprofit sector, but also in the advancement of research in this area. Indeed, until then, social scientists did not pay much attention to the nonprofit sector and related topics. This has changed, and a highly active research agenda has emerged since the early 1980s, in particular after a group of social scientists, loosely connected to the Program on Nonprofit Organizations at Yale University among others, began to address the role of nonprofit organizations in market economies in a systematic way.

The primary interest of the Yale Program at that time was to study American philanthropy, and to help shape its present and future role in US society. Yet, in a curious way, the renewed interest they encouraged soon connected with lines of inquiry first pursued during the founding period of modern social science in the nineteenth century—an intellectual trail that, though becoming thinner over time, can be traced to well into the mid twentieth century.

Indeed, there were promising beginnings in the way the social sciences examined aspects of the nonprofit sector and identified it as a central element of modern society. For example, the French sociologist Emile Durkheim (1933), in writing about the division of labor, suggested that voluntary associations serve as the "social glue" in societies with high degrees of professional specialization, economic competition, and social stratification. The German sociologist Max Weber (1924) focused on organizational development and saw the voluntary organization as a potentially unstable but highly dynamic and adaptable form, that tries to balance the "value-rationality" characteristic of religious or political organizations with the technocratic "means-rationality" of businesses or public agencies. The French writer Alexis de Tocqueville (1969), traveling the US in the 1830s, observed the highly decentralized nature of American government and society, and noted the prominent role of voluntary associations in the daily lives of citizens. Voluntary associations encouraged social participation and the inclusion of people from different backgrounds, with different preferences, in local societies. In de Tocqueville's terms, voluntary associations served as a remedy against the "tyranny of the majority." Writing a century later, Arthur Schlesinger (1944) spoke of the "lusty progeny of voluntary associations" in the US. What is more, sociologist Lewis Coser (1956) suggested that the overlap in associational membership reduces divisive social conflicts and class cleavages; with individuals being members of several groups and associations, conflicts in American society are less likely to coalesce around major cleavage lines such as class or religion.

But no "field" of nonprofit or voluntary sector studies as such emerged. Economics focused on markets and the business firm; political science on government and public administration; sociology on social classes, race, and gender; and policy studies on public policy and the welfare state. Crosscutting, interdisciplinary fields like organizational studies either focused on businesses or public agencies. Business schools as well as public policy schools rarely examined nonprofit organizations, and one prominent sociologist, Charles Perrow, declared nonprofits as "trivial" from the perspective of organizational theory and management (1986).

Yet while nonprofit topics were relegated to the background of social science theorizing and research, interesting work kept emerging, albeit without being considered in the context of a common framework or approach: urban studies began to identify the importance of community organizations for the success or failure of urban planning processes; historians learned of the important role foundations played in social innovation, research, and educational advances; social work emphasized the continued relevance of charities in health and social services despite the expansion of the welfare state; political science acknowledged the impact of interest associations in policymaking and the significance of political movements for the political process; and sociology examined the close connection between status seeking, membership in associations, and social stratification.

Generally, however, a "two-sector world-view" dominated, i.e. the "market vs. state model" of industrial society. It was an "either-or" perspective that was not challenged until the 1980s: the crisis of the welfare state, the limits of state action in dealing with social problems, the political challenge of neo-liberalism, and the end of the Cold War. Specifically, the greater interest in nonprofit organizations and the nonprofit sector can be attributed to:

- the increase in its economic importance in social services, health care, education, and culture (Salamon and Anheier 1999), and the emergence of nonprofit organizations that increasingly operated beyond local levels, even across national borders (Anheier

13

and List 2000; Anheier 2002), combined with a withdrawal of the state in providing welfare and related services;

■ an opening of political opportunities over and above conventional party politics at the national level; and also internationally, as a result of the end of the Cold War and the US favoring a minimalist liberal state;

■ the rise of a "New Policy Agenda," which emphasized the role of NGOs as part of an emerging system of global governance (Edwards and Hulme 1996);

■ major reductions in the cost of communication, in particular in telecommunications and internet access, which increased information sharing while reducing coordination costs overall (Clark 2001; Naughton 2001); the development of communications technologies has decreased the costs of organizing locally, nationally, as well as internationally;

■ generally favorable economic conditions in major world economies since the late 1940s, and a considerable expansion of populations living in relative prosperity (Hirschman 1982; Kriesberg 1997);

■ a value change over the last twenty-five years in most industrialized countries that emphasized individual opportunities and responsibilities over state involvement and control (Inglehart 1997);

■ a major expansion of democracy across most parts of the world, with freedom of expression and freedom to form associations granted in most countries (Linz and Stepan 1996); the "thickening" of the domestic and international rule of law since the 1970s has greatly facilitated the growth of civil society organizations (see Keck and Sikkink 1998).

For economists, as we shall see in Chapter 6, a basic argument for a greater nonprofit role in both developing and developed countries is based on an analysis of public administration (Salamon 1995), which suggests that nonprofits or NGOs are more efficient and effective providers of social and other services than governments. As a result, cooperative relations between governments and nonprofits in welfare provision have become a prominent feature in countries such as the US (Salamon 2002b), Germany (Anheier and Seibel 2001), France (Archambault 1996), and the UK (Plowden 2001; Strategy Unit 2002).

Salamon and Anheier (1996) suggest that the presence of an effective partnership between the state and nonprofits is one of the best predictors for the scale and scope of nonprofit activities in a country. Where such partnerships exist, e.g. the US (Salamon 1995), the Netherlands (Burger *et al.* 1999), Israel (Gidron *et al.* 2003), or Australia (Lyons 2001), the scale of the nonprofit sector is larger than in countries where no such working relationship is in place for the delivery of welfare, health, and education. The latter is the case in most developing countries as well as in Central and Eastern Europe.

Institutionalization

The modern field of nonprofit studies began in the US, and then quickly expanded and took roots in other countries (see Box 1.1). The Commission on Private Philanthropy and Public Needs (1973 to 1975), better known as the "Filer Commission" (after its chair John H. Filer),

BOX 1.1 TEACHING AND RESEARCH CENTERS ON NONPROFITS AND PHILANTHROPY

US (selection)

- Case Western Reserve University—Mandel Center for Nonprofit Organizations
- City University of New York—Center for the Study of Philanthropy
- George Mason University – Department of Public and International Affairs
- Georgetown University—Center for Voluntary Organizations and Service, Public Policy Institute; Center for Democracy and the Third Sector
- Harvard University, Hauser Center, John F. Kennedy School of Government
- Indiana University Center on Philanthropy
- Johns Hopkins University—Center for Civil Society Studies
- UCLA, Center for Civil Society, School of Public Affairs
- University of San Francisco—Institute for Nonprofit Organization Management
- University of Southern California, Center for Philanthropy and Public Policy
- University of Washington—Graduate School of Public Affairs

International (selection)

- Ben Gurion University, Israel
- El Colegio Mexiquense, Mexico
- Humboldt University/Maecenata Institute, Germany
- London School of Economics
- Queensland University of Technology, Brisbane, Australia
- Sokendai—The Graduate University for Advanced Studies, Hayama, Japan
- State University of Rio De Janeiro, Brazil
- Tiburg University, The Netherlands
- University of Bologna, Italy
- University of Economics, Vienna, Austria
- University of Fribourg, Switzerland
- University of Hong Kong
- University of Münster, Germany
- University of Natal, South Africa
- University of Osaka, Japan
- University of Paris, Sorbonne, France
- University of Technology, School of Management, Sydney, Australia
- Yonsei University, Seoul, Korea
- York University, Canada

produced the most far-reaching and detailed report of American philanthropy ever under-taken until then (see Brilliant 2000), and it became the stepping stone for further developments. Five volumes of specialized studies by scholars and other experts supplemented the discussions of the twenty-eight commissioners, whose report and recommendations were published under the title "Giving in America." The privately funded commission was the brainchild of John D. Rockefeller III and several of his closest advisers; they are also credited with being the source of a new conceptual framework of American society, a framework which added a "third sector" of voluntary giving and voluntary service alongside the first sector of government and the second sector of the private economic marketplace.

The scholarship produced by the Filer Commission also generated the intellectual interest that led to the establishment of the Program on Non-Profit Organizations at Yale University. The Program on Non-Profit Organizations (PONPO) at Yale University was founded in 1978 to foster interdisciplinary research on issues relevant to understanding nonprofit organizations and the contexts in which they function. Originally an initiative of then Yale president Kingman Brewster, PONPO was the first such center, and hosted many of the foremost scholars in the field today. John Simon of the Yale Law School and Charles Lindblom of Yale's Political Science Department first directed it, to be joined by Paul DiMaggio soon thereafter.

Since then, research and teaching programs have expanded greatly in the US and elsewhere, and have led to a veritable boom in dedicated centers in the US, Canada, Europe, Japan, Australia, and elsewhere (see Box 1.1). At present over 200 teaching programs exist in the US, Europe, and other countries, with thousands of students and a growing number of alumni.

The field of nonprofit studies has emerged as a fundamentally interdisciplinary field. Even though the initial theoretical thrust in the 1980s came predominantly from economics and other social sciences, intellectual bridges were quickly built. While much has been achieved in recent years both conceptually and empirically, as the following chapters will demonstrate, there remain major challenges that relate to the future role of nonprofit organizations in welfare reform, their relations with the state, increased competition and substitutability with forprofit corporations, and globalization, to name a but few.

OVERVIEW

This book is divided into four major sections and sixteen chapters, including this introductory chapter. The first section deals with background information and questions of definition, and offers an overview of the sector's dimensions in the US and other countries. The second section addresses theoretical issues, and the third looks at management topics. The fourth section deals with special topics as well as policy questions and future issues.

Part I Introduction

Chapter 2: Historical background   This chapter introduces the historical background to the development of civil society and the nonprofit sector in the US, and then compares the American experience with the experiences of other countries.

Chapter 3: Concepts   This chapter discusses the various types of activities, organizations, and institutions that make up the nonprofit sector (charities, foundations, associations, etc.), and looks at the various attempts to define the area between the market, state, and household sectors. The chapter also explores how the nonprofit sector relates to the concepts of civil society and social capital and their approaches.

Chapter 4: Dimensions I. Overview   In a first section, this chapter presents an overview of the size, composition, revenue structure, and role of the voluntary sector in the US. The chapter also considers the place of the nonprofit sector within the mixed economy of welfare. In a second section, the chapter presents an overview of the size, composition, revenue structure, and role of the sector in other parts of the world.

Chapter 5: Dimensions II. Specific fields   This chapter introduces the nonprofit sector in the context of selected fields of activity and examines in particular how nonprofit organizations compare in scale and scope to the other two major institutional complexes of modern society: the public sector and the market. The chapter also suggests a number of challenges and opportunities facing nonprofit organizations in each field of activity.

Part II Approaches

Chapter 6: Theoretical approaches   This chapter offers an overview of various economic, sociological, and political science approaches that address the origins and behavior of nonprofit organizations. It compares these approaches with one another, highlights their strengths and weaknesses, and points to new and emerging theoretical developments.

Chapter 7: Organizational theory and structure   This chapter looks at organizational theory and its contributions to understanding nonprofit organizations. The chapter also explores the factors involved in shaping the development of nonprofit organizations over time. It then examines more specific aspects of organizational structure and sets the stage for the presentation of different management approaches. Next, the chapter reviews the roles of power, authority, and leadership in nonprofit organizations. Finally, it looks at factors leading to alliances, partnerships, and mergers.

Part III Managing nonprofit organizations

Chapter 8: Nonprofit behavior and performance   This chapter looks at the behavior and performance of nonprofit organizations against the background of both nonprofit and organizational theory. The chapter also examines the functions and contributions of the nonprofit sector in different fields, and explores if, and under what conditions, the sector performs distinct tasks. This includes a discussion of performance measurement models and approaches.

Chapter 9: Resourcing nonprofit organizations   This chapter offers an overview of the financial and human resources nonprofit organizations use for achieving their objectives. The chapter

17

reviews various revenue strategies for nonprofits, including fund-raising, and then presents an overview of human resources in the nonprofit sector, with emphasis on both paid employment and volunteering.

Chapter 10: Stakeholders, governance, and accountability   This chapter is in three parts. First, the chapter explores the role of stakeholders in nonprofit organizations, and the special requirements that arise for governance and accountability from the multiple constituencies. Against this background, the chapter considers the governance of nonprofit organizations, the role of the board, and the relationship between the board and management. In a third part, the chapter examines the different forms of accountability in the third sector.

Chapter 11: Management I. Models   The chapter reviews the background to nonprofit management and introduces a normative–analytical management approach based on the notion that nonprofits are multiple stakeholder organizations.

Chapter 12: Management II. Tools   The chapter reviews a number of basic management tools and issues that reflect the normative–analytical management approach introduced in Chapter 11. More specifically, the chapter looks at human resource management and strategic management, presents a number of planning techniques appropriate for nonprofits, and concludes with a brief overview of financial management, business plans, and marketing.

Part IV Policy and special topics

Chapter 13: State–nonprofit relations   This chapter considers the different models and types of relationships nonprofit organizations have with the state in terms of funding and contracting, regulation, advocacy and campaigning, and consultation. The chapter also discusses the advantages and disadvantages of relations with governmental bodies and explores different forms of public–private partnerships.

Chapter 14: Foundations   This chapter first looks at the history of foundations and how the modern foundation evolved over the centuries, with a particular emphasis on the evolution of the grant-making and the operating foundation. The chapter then presents different types of foundations, and surveys their sizes, activities, and development over time, both in the US and other countries. The chapter also introduces theoretical perspectives on the role of foundations in modern society, and concludes with a brief overview of current developments in the field of philanthropy.

Chapter 15: International issues and globalization   The chapter examines the internationalization of the nonprofit sector in the context of globalization, and explores some of the reasons for the significant expansion of cross-border activities. Then the chapter focuses on the management of international nongovernmental organizations and other types of nonprofits that operate across borders. The chapter also covers policy issues related to globalization and cross-border activities in the fields of service delivery, humanitarian assistance, and advocacy.

Chapter 16: Policy issues and developments In this chapter, we first take an historical look at macro-level changes that have affected and will continue to affect the nonprofit sector over time. Next, the chapter discusses a number of critical policy issues related to the greater political salience of the nonprofit sector. In a closing section, the chapter returns to the broader, long-term issues and explores different scenarios for the future of nonprofit development.

REVIEW QUESTIONS

- What are some of the reasons why the nonprofit sector has become more relevant in recent years?

- What could be some of the reasons for the immense diversity of nonprofit organizations?

- Why did the social sciences pay less attention to nonprofit organizations and related topics such as civil society and social capital for much of the twentieth century?

RECOMMENDED READING

O'Neill, M. (2002) *Nonprofit Nation: A New Look at the Third America*, 2nd edition, San Francisco, CA: Jossey-Bass.

Ott, J. S. (ed.) (2001) *The Nature of the Nonprofit Sector*, Boulder, CO: Westview Press.

Powell, W. W. and Steinberg, R. S. (eds.) (forthcoming) *The Nonprofit Sector: A Research Handbook*, 2nd edition, New Haven, CT, and London: Yale University Press.

Salamon, L. M. (2003) *The Resilient Sector: The State of Nonprofit America*, Washington, DC: The Brookings Institution.

Chapter 2

Historical background

This chapter introduces the historical background to the development of civil society and the nonprofit sector in the US, and then compares the American experience to the experiences of other countries.

LEARNING OBJECTIVES

Historians argue that their craft is there to guide us in making decisions for the future, but, more often, a better role for historical analysis is to make the present meaningful. Looking at the historical development of the nonprofit sector helps us understand why certain cultural, social, and political features are the way they are, what they mean, and how they came about. After reading this chapter, the reader should:

■ be able to understand the historical development of the nonprofit sector in the US, the UK, and elsewhere;
■ be able to identify key patterns of nonprofit sector development;
■ know how the US pattern differs from that in other countries;
■ have a sense of how historical patterns influence current developments.

KEY TERMS

Some of the key terms covered in this chapter are:

■ American Exceptionalism
■ associationalism
■ charity
■ communitarianism
■ liberal model
■ self-organization
■ third-party government

INTRODUCTION

In this chapter we first consider the historical background to the development and understanding of civil society in the US to show how closely the notions of civil society and nonprofit voluntary activities are to the fundamentals of America as a society. In other words, to look at how the nonprofit sector emerged and developed in the wider context of American civil society is to take a look at the central social and political developments of the country as such. Indeed, the nonprofit sector/civil society "lens" is useful for understanding the critical and distinct aspects of American history and contemporary American society. For this purpose, in a second step, we set the US experience against the historical patterns and developments in other countries.

THE EMERGENCE OF THE NONPROFIT SECTOR IN THE US

While the concept of civil society as such is not common currency in the US, there is nonetheless a deep-seated cultural understanding that civil society finds its clearest expression in this country. Indeed a strong political as well as cultural current running through American history and contemporary society sees the US as an ongoing "experiment" in civility, community, democracy, and self-governance. Not only the country as a whole, but cities, such as New York, Chicago, Miami, and Los Angeles in particular, regard themselves as the "social laboratories" of modern urban life: they are among the most diverse in the world in ethnic, religious, and social terms, with large portions of immigrant populations, small local government, and high levels of community organizing and individualism.

A strong expression of this cultural self-understanding is that the US, in all its imperfections and injustices, is nonetheless regarded as the embodiment of human political progress. This ideological current assumes at times mythical dimensions, perhaps because it is so closely linked to, and rests on, major symbols of US political history. In countless political speeches as well as in popular culture frequent references are made to highly symbolic events and documents that provide deep roots of legitimacy to both nonprofit organizations and the notion of self-organization. Among the most prominent of such cultural-political icons:

- the *Declaration of Independence* of July 4, 1776 establishes legal equality and unalienable rights (life, liberty, pursuit of happiness), and that "to secure these rights governments are instituted . . ., deriving their just power from the consent of the governed";
- the US *Constitution* begins with the forceful sentence, "We, the people of the United States, in order to form a more perfect union . . .";
- the *Bill of Rights* (First Amendment to the Constitution) limits the power of government vis-à-vis society and declares that "Congress shall make no law respecting an establishment of religion, or prohibiting the free exercise thereof";
- in *The Federalist Papers* (volume 39), Madison speaks of the "great political experiment" and the "capacity of mankind for self-government"; in volumes 10 and 15, he argues that in a republic equipped with adequate checks and balances, special interests (economic, political, religious, etc.) should be encouraged to compete on equal terms and to lobby governments;

21

- President Lincoln's *Gettysburg Address* includes the emphatic wish "that government of the people, by the people, and for the people, shall not perish from the earth";
- Martin Luther King's speech "*I Have a Dream*" speaks about his vision of the US as a "table of brotherhood" and evokes strong biblical images—a not at all uncommon reference in US political discourse;
- President Reagan led the (still continuing) *roll-back of the federal government* by encouraging Americans "to take back from government what was once ours," referring back to the Declaration of Independence and reconfirming that the US is first a society of and for individuals and their communities, and only secondarily a national political entity defined by power.

Together, these cultural icons suggest a culturally and politically compelling portrait of the US as a self-organizing and self-governing civil society—a society of citizens based on the rule of law, and not on the power of the state. Indeed, the US political tradition reflected in the cultural icons listed above portrays government in a broad sense: not only government by a "state," but also social governance as an expression of formal political liberty, participation, and communal and individual obligations. Governance, the constitution of society, and the rights and obligations of citizens are interlinked and form part of the US political canon.

What are the historical roots of the cultural self-understanding fueled by these and other icons—an understanding that invites the popular notion among Americans from all walks of life that the US is a distinct and exceptional society, different from others, in particular different from its closest relative, Europe, as well as from Asia and Latin America? In the remainder of this section we identify some of the major factors involved (summarized in stylized form in Table 2.1), together with what are implied features of societies outside the US, in particular the "state-oriented" societies of Europe, as well as those of Canada and Australia. Of course, the distinctions made in Table 2.1 serve to emphasize what are tendencies in reality.

Civil society as associationalism

As a society, the development of the US—and its emergent civil society—is rooted in a profound and successful reaction against eighteenth-century European absolutism, the power of state–church relations, and the rigidities of what the "Founding Fathers," in the true spirit of the Enlightenment, saw as the dying political and social order of the "old world." In its place, the US sought to develop a complex political system of direct and indirect democracy based on checks and balances. The young republic put constraints on government, instituted clear separation of power at federal and state levels, allowed for a distinct economic class structure based on mobility that departed from the symbols of hereditary ranks, encouraged a religious system based on voluntarism with strict separation of church and state, and lodged educational, cultural, social, and welfare responsibilities at local community levels rather than with some form of central governmental structure.

Table 2.1 US civil society in comparative perspective

Factors encouraging civil society as associationalism in the United States	Factors discouraging civil society as associationalism elsewhere
Religious diversity with emphasis on local congregations rather than institutional hierarchy	Long history and legacy of dominant state religion with hierarchical institutional structures
Local elite do not rely on control of government for power; alternative spheres of influence exist	Weak local elites; few alternative power stratums
Concentrations of wealth and political power overlap but are neither identical nor dependent on each other	National political and economic elite networks overlap significantly
Ethnic, linguistic, and cultural heterogeneity as "default value"	Ethnic, linguistic, and cultural homogeneity as "default value"
Decentralized government, weak federal government with strong division of power at center, and primacy of rule of law	Centralized government and state apparatus; limited capacity for local taxation and policymaking
Bridging capital, higher interpersonal trust	High bonding capital, lower interpersonal trust
"Diversity in unity" creates social innovation	Homogeneity and political control stifles innovation

In the course of the next 225 years, many prominent observers—from A. de Tocqueville ([1835–40] 1969), E. Burke (1904), M. Weber ([1905] 1935), W. Sombart ([1906] 1976), and H. G. Wells (1906), to modern-day analysts such as Wuthnow (1998), O'Connell (1999) and Skocpol and Fiorina (1999)—have tried to come to terms with what G. K. Chesterton (1922) long ago identified as the "American Creed," a group of beliefs that sets this country apart from others. Similarly, social scientists such as Voss (1993) and Lipset (1996) use the term "American Exceptionalism" to suggest a profound departure of the US from its European origins and a qualitative difference in the development of US society from that of English, French, or German society.

Early on in US social and political history, philanthropy, democratic inclusion, and local civil society became closely linked to American Exceptionalism, and the very constitution of US society. Indeed, expanding on Chesterton's theme of the American Creed, McCarthy (2003) has shown how, during the nineteenth century, philanthropy became a factor in the abolitionist movement and in the struggle for social justice both in the broadest sense, and also in particular against the exclusion of women and minorities from effective political voice. According to Lipset (1996: 19), US society rests on the five basic ideological factors of classical liberalism, which together have provided American society with significant political stability despite profound changes in its social and economic structure:

■ The concept of *liberty* means freedom from arbitrary interference in one's pursuits by either individuals or government, as stipulated in the Bill of Rights and the 13th, 14th, and 15th Amendments to the US Constitution.

23

- *Egalitarianism*, as a formal legal principle, and *individualism* both originated from the ideas of Adam Smith and Jeremy Bentham, and were identified by Alexis de Tocqueville as fundamental elements of American society. Individualism includes a value system whereby the individual is of supreme value, and all people are morally equal. It opposes authority without consent and views government as an institution whose power should be largely limited to maintaining law and order.

- *Populism* is a seemingly non-ideological movement that combines elements of the political left and right, opposes corporate power and large financial interests, and favors "home-grown," "hands-on" local solutions. It was strongest in the late nineteenth century and arose from agrarian reform movements in the Midwest and South, but continues to surface in popular political movements such as the anti-tax sentiment in California or anti-federal government activities in states such as Alabama.

- *Laissez-faire* policies favor a minimum of governmental action in economic affairs beyond the minimum necessary for the maintenance of peace and upholding of property rights. It has been adopted as a basic principle of economic policy in the US throughout its history; laissez-faire assumes that individuals primarily pursuing their own preferences also contribute to society as a whole.

In a very profound sense, the US Constitution is the product of classical liberalism, as is US civil society itself, both historically and today. Only in the US, and not in Europe nor in countries such as Canada or Australia, did these factors come together to shape society and polity in such a clear and unchallenged manner. These factors are at the root of American civil society from the nineteenth century onward, and are also central for the development of the modern nonprofit sector in the twentieth century.

McCarthy shows how philanthropy helped shape the American Creed and, indeed, she succeeds in her argument that philanthropy is very closely related to the various ideological currents of early nineteenth-century America. McCarthy (2003) argues that in the early periods of US history many of the defining features of US civil society and nonprofit–government relationship evolved in a highly political and contested process that involved three distinct phases:

- The first spanned the last two decades of the eighteenth century and the first two decades of the nineteenth century, and saw a growing associational infrastructure for charity, the beginnings of American associationalism, a revival of missionary fervor, and the spread of religious organizations of many kinds.

- The second phase, partially described in de Tocqueville's travelogues, witnessed American associationalism and participatory democracy at its height, but the years between 1820 and 1830 were also a period of political tension (concerning social responsibilities for poverty and other social problems), violence, and racism. Jacksonian America held, as McCarthy shows, the beginnings of modern advocacy and political lobbying for diverse and conflicting interests by means of voluntary associations.

- The third period saw nascent US civil society severely tested by the growing tensions between North and South, and the ensuing Civil War, as well as concerns about the removal of Native Americans from vast areas of the country—all leading to a broader political mobilization of different population groups and, in particular, the beginning of the women's and civil rights movements.

It is, however, the complex mix of these five ideological factors that accounts for many of the seemingly contradictory patterns of American society, which, over the decades, have filled many pages of social analysis (e.g. Farley 1995; Bellah 1985). Central among these contradictions are: egalitarian social relations co-existing next to large inequalities in living standards across the population; deep-seated preferences for meritocracy despite persistent ethnic and religious discrimination; and high levels of tolerance for significant disparities in life chances combined with a deep-seated belief in individual advancement and responsibility (the "American Dream").

Wells, an Englishman, writing from a Fabian, socialist perspective, put it succinctly when he observed a century ago: "essentially America is a middle class . . . and so its essential problems are the problems of a modern individualistic society, stark and clear" (1906: 72, 76). Yet in contrast to England, in looking for political solutions American middle-class ideology was neither Tory (conservative) nor Labor (socialist); it was, as Wells concluded, simply "anti-State."

In today's parlance, the US developed a prototype of a *liberal* model of civil society and state–society relations, where a low level of government spending (social welfare, health, education, culture) is associated with a relatively large nonprofit sector engaged in both actual service provision and advocacy. This outcome, as Salamon and Anheier (1998b) argue, is most likely where broad middle-class elements are clearly in the ascendant, and where opposition either from traditional landed elites or strong working-class movements either has never existed or has been held at bay effectively. This leads to significant ideological and political hostility to the extension of government in scale and scope, and a decided preference for local, voluntary approaches instead—irrespective of effectiveness and equity considerations.

However, despite, or perhaps because of, these contradictory elements, US society has proved to be more resilient against some of the despotic, autocratic, or dynastic ills that have befallen many other countries. In fact, the sometimes arduous and even violent path of US history (displacement of indigenous populations; slavery and civil war; ethnic discrimination; extreme "moralist" policy measures such as Prohibition in the 1920s; McCarthyism in the 1950s; race riots in the 1960s; or the militia movements and domestic terrorism in the 1990s) has shown a remarkable capacity for "self-correction" or "self-mobilization." These processes typically happen through the electoral process and the system of checks and balances, or, failing that, through the mobilizing power of the numerous social movements that have shaped the political and social development of the country. Prominent examples are the progressive movement, the civil rights movement, the environmental movement, and the women's movement.

Much of this capacity for self-organization and self-correction is seen in the social power of associationalism, or what amounts to a perspective that features *local* civic society as a community of individuals who, through their actions, support a network of political, philanthropic, and voluntary associations in pursuit of specific interests. Early reference to this

25

capacity for self-organization was made in de Tocqueville's travelogue from the 1830s in now-famous passages such as:

> Americans of all ages, all stations of life, and all types of dispositions are forever forming associations . . . In every case, at the head of any new undertaking, where in France you would find the government or in England some territorial magnate, in the United States you are sure to find an association.
>
> (de Tocqueville 1969: 513)

After all, as Lipset (1996) reminds us, the US is the only Western country where government and voluntary associations did not have to deal with pre-existing, inert social formations and barriers to mobility, be they autocratic states (e.g. Germany), a centralized administration (France), or a rigid, quasi-aristocratic class system carried over from feudalism (England). Writing in the mid twentieth century, Schlesinger spoke of the "lusty progeny of voluntary associations," that he saw largely as a product of the religious voluntarism of the ante-bellum period, thereby keeping alive the Tocquevillian spirit of associationalism as a characteristic feature of American life:

> Traditionally, Americans have distrusted collective organizations as embodied in government while insisting upon their own untrammeled right to form voluntary associations. This conception of a state of minimal powers actually made it easier for private citizens to organize for undertakings too large for a single person.
>
> (Schlesinger 1944: 24)

The implicit comparison with Europe is also present in a variant of associationalism, i.e. its communitarian tradition rooted in some form of moral community of virtuous citizens (Etzioni 1996). Communitarianism is a social philosophy that views community as a voluntary grouping of individuals who come together to identify common goals and agree to rules governing the communal order. The community is created in part by recognizing common policies, or laws, that are set to meet legitimate needs rather than having been arbitrarily imposed from "above" and "outside" the groups. Members of such communities, e.g. neighborhood, city, or nation, accept responsibilities, both legal and moral, to achieve common goals and greater collective well-being.

Communitarianism is essentially a variant of the view that sees the US as a society of self-organizing communities. Again, frequent reference is made to another European thinker, this time Max Weber, who emphasized the close link between the Protestant (Puritan) ethic of capitalism, moral communities, and economic development. Religious congregations, and the voluntary associations they formed, provided the bonds that held early American society together; and, in political ideology, social structure, and economic behavior, complemented the five principles of American liberalism.

Following Weber's reasoning, Ladd (1994) suggested that the political and religious ethos reinforced each other most clearly in the case of Puritanism: since the Protestant congregations, in contrast to those of Catholicism, fostered individualism and egalitarianism, populist values that were pro-community but anti-state, and that favored local over central decision-making could take root. As Bellah (1985) argues, the American Protestant tradition again and again spawned movements for social change and social reform, most notable in the progressive era between 1893 and 1917, and in the civil rights movement in the 1950s and 1960s.

State–society relations

Of course, there is more to US society than associationalism, and analysts such as Skocpol *et al.* (2000) and others have challenged the voluntaristic, communitarian view of American social history. According to de Tocqueville's view of Jacksonian America, the inclusionary capacity of voluntary associations, the formal egalitarianism they espoused, and the prevention of tyrannical majority rule through the "art of association," facilitated both democratic and social development. Yet, as Skocpol *et al.* (2000) have shown, they were not isolated developments, as the potential for collective action was much greater if local groups came together and cooperated across local and state boundaries. In fact, many associations formed federated structures and assumed a regional and national presence early on.

Between the eighteenth century and the end of the nineteenth century, as Skocpol *et al.* (2000) and Skocpol (2002) show, nearly forty large-scale membership organizations emerged, most of them as federations of local and state groups, and each comprising at least one percent of the total US population at some time between 1800 and 1900. They became an instrument of social inclusion that cut across regional boundaries while expressing particular values and often religious preferences. Examples include:

- the American Temperance Society founded in Boston in 1826;
- the American Anti-Slavery Society, founded in Boston in 1833;
- the Young Men's Christian Association, founded in 1851 in Boston;
- the Benevolent and Protective Order of the Elks, founded in 1867 in New York;
- the Knights of Columbus, founded in 1882 in New Haven, Connecticut;
- the Women's Missionary Movement, founded in 1888 in Richmond, Virginia; and
- the National Congress of Mothers, founded in 1897 in Washington, DC.

The interplay between national polity and federated structures of civil society continued into the nineteenth and early twentieth centuries. In addition, alternative spheres of power developed, e.g. the Masonic movement and other "secret societies" and fraternities such as the Elks, the Rotarians, or alumni associations of many kinds.

The women's movement offers perhaps the clearest example of how the nonprofit sector and the wider civil society created opportunities for influencing policy (McCarthy 2003; Clemens 1993). In the US the women's suffrage movement emerged from the anti-slavery movement itself and as a result of the work of such leaders as Lucretia Mott and Elizabeth Cady Stanton, who believed that equality should extend to women as well as blacks and who, for example, organized the Seneca Falls Convention (1848). In 1850, Lucy Stone established the movement's first national convention. Stanton and Susan B. Anthony formed the National Women Suffrage Association in 1869 to secure an amendment to the Constitution, while Stone founded the American Women Suffrage Association to seek similar amendments to state constitutions; in 1890 the two organizations merged as the National American Women Suffrage Association. Following Wyoming's lead in 1890, states began adopting such amendments; by 1918 women had acquired suffrage in fifteen states. After Congress passed a women's suffrage amendment, a vigorous campaign brought ratification, and in August 1919 the 19th Amendment became part of the Constitution.

Hall (1992) argues that the late twentieth-century distinction between the public, forprofit, and nonprofit sectors did not apply to the US institutional landscape until the Great Depression. Civil and public governance intermingled and many hybrid organizational forms existed. This was the true institutional innovation of the US: a self-confident civil society works *with*, neither for nor against, government. Arendt gave this insight: "the true objective of the American Constitution was not to limit but to create more power, actually to establish and to duly constitute an entirely new power center" (1963: 152).

Large-scale institutional innovations brought the rise of philanthropic foundations, privately endowed universities, and think-tanks as independent centers of wealth, knowledge, and power. By the mid twentieth century, the density and diversity of civil society institutions were such that, in aggregate, civil society served to diffuse social conflicts by the very complexity of the institutional structure created. Indeed, this was the pattern sociologist Lewis Coser (1956) observed in his analysis of the question why American society did not follow the European class structure. In his answer, Coser pointed to the implications of multiple individual memberships in voluntary associations of many kinds. They create overlapping membership clusters that reach across many social boundaries, and thereby prevent the emergence of dominating social cleavages such as rigid class structures. The criss-crossing of membership patterns was not only beneficial for conflict diffusion, it also provided the organizational infrastructure for social movements, and facilitated the self-organizing capacity of US society. Indeed, the civil rights movement, the women's movement, and the environmental movement could develop in the context of the rich and varied networks of civil society institutions.

The aftermath of the Great Depression in the 1930s and the political responses to the mounting social and economic costs of World War II saw a period of greater involvement of federal government programs in welfare, most prominently in the fields of social security and health care, although welfare systems remained patchy and incomplete, with Medicare and Medicaid as the single largest initiatives. The reform movements of the previous twenty-five years had been fueled by "tax revolts" and a more conservative agenda aimed at reducing the role of government in social welfare. In some ways, the Filer Commission of the 1970s can be seen as part of a search for alternatives to the patchy American welfare state that had developed since World War II, probing into the capacity of nonprofit organizations to perform welfare and related functions.

The late twentieth century saw a revival of Tocquevillian perspectives of a "strong and vibrant civil society characterized by a social infrastructure of dense networks of face-to-face relationships that cross-cut existing social cleavages such as race, ethnicity, class, sexual orientation, and gender that will underpin strong and responsive democratic government" (Edwards *et al.* 2001: 17). Norms of reciprocity, citizenship, and trust are embodied in networks of civic associations. Sirianni and Friedland (2001) argue that these interpersonal and inter-associational networks are a key source of social, cultural and political innovation in the US, linking the future of American democracy to their constant "renewal," just as Putnam (2000) links them to the survival of community, and others, such as Fukuyama (1995), to economic prosperity.

Thus, the vibrancy of the US is ultimately the vibrancy of its civil society. For neo-Tocquevillians, civil society is not only a bulwark against a potential overly powerful state or a vehicle for democracy. It is much more than that: it is a general principle of societal constitution. Not surprisingly, political efforts to revitalize civil society either assume a voluntaristic tone that emphasizes social participation and mutual, interpersonal trust (see Putnam, 2000), or appeal to moralist, even religious, sentiments of civic virtue (Etzioni 1996; see also Council on Civil Society).

HOW THE HISTORY OF THE NONPROFIT SECTOR IN THE UNITED STATES DIFFERS FROM THAT OF OTHER COUNTRIES

Great Britain

In contrast to the US, the history of the nonprofit or voluntary sector in Great Britain is not one of associationalism, self-organization, and anti-statism; it is largely a history of how social welfare provision was organized in a liberal, yet traditionally class-based, society, in which the roles of voluntary action and the state changed over time in response to social, economic, and political needs. It is a rich history in terms of voluntary sector–government relationships and is characterized by profound changes: from a church-dominated system of welfare provision in the seventeenth and eighteenth centuries; to a system of "parallel bars" in the nineteenth and early twentieth centuries, with government and the voluntary sector performing separate but distinct roles; the "extension ladder" model of the British welfare state of the 1930s onward, where the voluntary sector acts as a complement to public provision; to the modernized "Third Way" approaches of the current Labour government (2004), which views market, government, and voluntary associations as being in a potentially synergistic relationship for solving social welfare problems of advanced market economies. To understand this development, and its different outcome when compared to the US case, it is useful to summarize the history of the voluntary sector in the UK (see Prochaska 1990; Kendall and Knapp 1996; Kendall 2003).

In Great Britain, as for the North American colonies that were to follow, the formalization and secularization of philanthropy began with the 1601 Elizabethan Statute of Charitable Uses. The Statute was part of the Poor Laws, a body of legislation for providing relief for the poor, including care for the aged, the sick, and infants and children, as well as work for the able-bodied through local parishes. Over time, the scope of the Poor Laws became limited more and more to the "deserving poor," especially during the Victorian period when poverty among the able-bodied, i.e. the undeserving poor, was considered a moral failing.

Throughout the Victorian era, the role of government in the administration and financing of the Poor Laws provisions expanded very gradually at first, with a parallel and related shift away from religious organizations as primary service providers. However, the Victorian model of philanthropy, i.e. the upper and middle classes voluntarily looking after the less fortunate, expanded as well, and cities such as London, Manchester, and Liverpool had, at the height of the industrial era between 1890 and 1915, vast networks of private charities in the fields of health care, social services, and education.

The system of charitable service provision had significant shortcomings in terms of coverage and access, and it faced increasing political opposition by a strengthening Labour Party in favor of socialist, i.e. state-financed and state-run, institutions. Within the Labour Party and among socialist groups generally, the Victorian approach to charity was seen not only as paternalistic, moralistic, and self-serving, but ultimately as pre-modern and inefficient. Charity was an obligation on behalf of the better off, but it carried no rights of entitlement for the poor. As such, it was part of the status quo and an instrument of oppression and injustice, irrespective of its moral underpinnings and good intentions.

In the 1930s and 1940s, and largely in reaction to the Great Depression and the two World Wars, the strong reliance on private charity was finally replaced by a comprehensive system of public welfare services, most prominently, in the early 1950s, in the form of universal national health care financed through general taxation and the central government budget. Large parts of the social service field, however, maintained a vital voluntary sector presence that has expanded significantly since the 1980s and the privatization policies of successive governments since those led by Margaret Thatcher.

In contrast to the US, the development of the nonprofit sector was not so much linked to the constitution of society, but more closely tied to the changing social needs and political constellations of the time. For example, when the Poor Laws were enacted in the early seventeenth century, Britain had suffered through the religious uncertainties of the Reformation. In addition, economic and social upheavals led to the emergence of a landless class of people. Industrialization in the eighteenth and nineteenth centuries brought a new set of problems, including urban poverty and population growth, and a significant problem of homeless children.

The government at that time, and in accordance with its ideology, felt that it did not have enough resources to meet increasing demands for social services and it encouraged voluntary organizations to fill this void. During the eighteenth and nineteenth centuries, the emergent class of industrialists and entrepreneurs formed most of the philanthropic organizations of the time. Some of these organizations were not only service providers but were also advocates for social justice, highlighting the inequities of the time. Some of the Victorian organizations became prototypes of modern-day professional voluntary service organizations such as Barnardo's, a major social welfare agency for children.

The working class also began to establish voluntary organizations during the Victorian period. In particular, this included mutual aid organizations such as friendly societies, trades unions, consumer cooperatives, building societies, and housing societies. The British government gave early formal recognition to friendly societies in 1793, and other mutual aid organizations were recognized by the Royal Commission of 1871–4 as important agents against "pauperism." In the nineteenth century, these voluntary associations were recognized as the "bulwark against poverty." The reform of the Poor Laws in 1834 delineated the state's responsibility toward the "undeserving poor" by establishing the "workhouse," while the voluntary sector provided for the "deserving poor."

The creation of the welfare state in the 1940s, in which government became the primary provider of education, health, social welfare, and income maintenance services, redefined the role of the voluntary sector. No longer was the sector responsible for serving one "group" of the population while the state was in charge of another. Rather, services of the voluntary sector played a more complementary and supplementary role. As expected, some organizations were marginalized, but others were invigorated by the reforms. For example, the National Association for Mental Health and the Mental Health Foundation were formed at this time.

We can take a closer look at state–society relations and the voluntary sector in Britain. Before the 1601 Statute, which provided a legal framework for charities, the informal sector and the Church were the main providers of social services. The Church dominated the delivery of social services from the early seventeenth century up to the early twentieth century, with the state only playing a minor role, but being increasingly joined by secular charities. By the mid nineteenth century, the government had established a permanent Charity Commission to oversee charitable trusts and administer the exemption of charities from certain taxes. Perhaps the most important development at this time was the recognition by the state that the public and voluntary sectors should operate in mutually exclusive spheres, as delineated by Poor Laws.

However, continued poverty, and the political challenges associated with it, prompted the government to replace voluntary organizations as the principal agents of social service provision in the early twentieth century. In the fields of health care, education, and social insurance, the public sector took over both funding and production. In the areas of social care activities, such as child care and care for the elderly, the voluntary sector remained the principal agent.

Once the welfare apparatus became established, government failures became apparent, and the voluntary sector, once again, was seen as filling the void. Government funding increased in the 1960s and 1970s. The influential Wolfenden Committee Report of 1978 emphasized the need for cooperation between the state and the voluntary sector and the need for "pluralism and partnership." However, an imbalance of power remained, with the voluntary sector as the junior, silent partner.

Throughout the 1970s, various factions of government—the Labour Party, the radical left, and the Conservative Party—defined the voluntary sector to suit their political ideologies and goals. The voluntary sector was used as a strategic weapon in the political struggle between central and local government. The realization of state limitations, emerging problems such as urban decay and racial tension, enhanced expectations from the public, the work of lobbying organizations to voice the rights of indigent peoples, and the growing notion that government agencies were ineffective prompted the Thatcher premiership in 1979 to roll back the "boundaries of state social provision." Privatization was a prominent term, and the Thatcher government replaced public sector activity with private sector activity whenever it could. In the 1990s the Major and Blair premierships continued this trend of contracting-out government activities and creating "quasi-markets." Since coming to power in 1997, the current Labour government has seen the voluntary sector as a partner in modernizing the welfare state and seeks to put in place private–public partnerships whenever possible (see Chapters 13 and 16).

Canada

Canada's nonprofit sector history is closer to that of Britain than to that of the US and signals not so much a break with the English model as a gradual development away from it. The origins of nonprofits and charities can be traced, as in most other countries, to the Church and other religious traditions. However, secularization of charity work occurred early in Canada's colonial period, when, in the late eighteenth century, the people in the town of Halifax raised 750 pounds to build a public school, and communities in Northern Canada established residences for the homeless.

Indeed, prior to the twentieth century, individuals and local groups were the main impetus for charity and mutual aid. In the twentieth century, however, the government began taking a more active role in formalizing income security and the social welfare system. Government-sponsored programs created in the last century included a universal pension system for workers, universal health care, and unemployment insurance. In contrast to Americans, as Lipset (1996) suggests, throughout the country's history, Canadians seem to have a stronger sense of social rights. They expect to see a more positive and proactive role of government in eliminating impediments to full social participation, such as poverty, and other inequalities.

Following the American Revolution, while the US successfully seceded, Canada remained part of the British Empire. Lipset describes the development of Canada's social economy as the "counter-revolution" to America's independence movement. According to Lipset: "Conservatism in Canada is descended from Toryism and monarchical statism; in the US, it is derived from Whiggism, classical anti-statist liberalism" (Lipset 1996: 91). Immediately following the Revolution, a migration occurred where 50,000 Tory Americans moved to Canada, with many Anglican priests moving north, although many Congregational ministers moved south. Lipset describes the consequence of this move northward:

> In Canada, the Tory tradition has meant support for a strong state, communitarianism, group solidarity, and elitism. Most provinces continue to finance church-controlled schools. Public ownership, much of it instituted under Conservative Party administrations, is considerably more extensive than in the United States. Canadian governments spend more proportionately on welfare. Canadians are more supportive of narrowing income differences, while Americans put more emphasis on equal opportunity or meritocratic competition.
>
> (Lipset 1996: 92)

As such, it is not surprising that Canada introduced major social programs earlier and more comprehensively than the US. Interestingly, the development of this welfare state in the decades following World War II did not diminish the growth of the nonprofit sector. In fact, between 1969 and 1996, the number of registered charities more than tripled, which can be attributed to strong government support and funding of the nonprofit sector (Jiwani 2000). Compared with the US, Canada developed a more highly pronounced and more comprehensive pattern of what Salamon (1995) identified as "third-party government," whereby the state subcontracts service delivery to nonprofit providers (see Chapter 13).

Australia

In contrast to the US, government has always played a highly visible role in Australia, but less so than in Canada.[1] Nonetheless, from the early days of the Australian Republic, the government was very active in building infrastructure and providing education, a tradition carried over from the nineteenth century, when Britain granted its Australian colonies limited self-government. With the passing of the Act federating the colonies into an independent Commonwealth in 1900, government assumed a positive stance toward voluntary associations. In social policy areas such as assisting the poor and the sick, the government encouraged the formation of organizations and provided subsidies for service delivery. At the same time, government regulation was positively related to the level of subsidy nonprofits received.

In the late nineteenth century, Australia's open democratic political system was an ideal environment for the formation of associations and voluntary organizations based on shared interests. In fact, the "bifurcation of parliamentary politics" that happened early on in Australian politics through the creation of the Liberal Party and the Labour Party can be traced to associations organizing for a common interest. The Labour Party was created by the Trades and Labour Council, and the Liberal Party was created by trade associations, women's groups, and Protestant religious groups.

During the 1920s and 1930s conservative business interests dominated Australian politics. Thus there was a growth of professional and trade associations, business groups, such as the Rotary Club, began to appear. However, the Great Depression ultimately weakened traditional charities and friendly societies and stunted the growth of business and professional associations. In response to growing social needs, the government encouraged new mutual finance institutions such as building societies and credit unions in the late 1930s, and increased its contribution to pensions, health care, and social services. Shortly after this, the government took over nonprofit hospitals, which, in turn, led to a diminution of philanthropy, as they were the main recipients of individual donations at that time.

From 1949 to 1972, the Conservative Party in power curtailed direct government services. Instead, it reverted to subsidizing nonprofits to provide an expanding range of services, and government became a funder rather than a provider for meeting social and health care needs. In education, support of Catholic and other private schools expanded, which proved vital for the timely expansion of secondary education in the 1970s and 1980s. Less pronounced than in Canada but more comprehensive than in the US, Australia developed a system of third-party government as the characteristic model for nonprofit sector–government relations.

In the 1970s, feminism, the community development movement, and the various rights movements influenced government thinking, encouraging the formation of new nonprofit and community-based organizations that provided a wide range of social services locally. What is more, for the first time the government also funded nonprofit professional arts organizations such as theater, opera, and ballet. In the latter decades of the last century, the demographics of the population changed with an increase in immigration from both Europe and Asia. Thus a wide range of nonprofits developed, including cultural and educational organizations, religious groups, and social welfare organizations.

France and Germany

Whereas the countries discussed thus far shared a common root, i.e. the 1601 Statute of Charitable Uses, France and Germany reveal a different starting point and evolution of the nonprofit sector (Anheier and Seibel 2001). This can be illustrated by way of comparison with the political role of voluntary associations, as described in Alexis de Tocqueville's *Democracy in America* ([1835] 1969, see above, p. 26). His analysis of American associations was also intended as a critique of France's post-revolutionary political order and society. Indeed, long before the Revolution of 1789 took place, France had been a centralized nation-state, and it was the very centralization of the state that had facilitated the Revolution's effectiveness. The *ancien régime* was replaced by a new ruling class that used the existing centralized state structure as a tool for rebuilding the country's political system and societal order. In accordance with the strict individualistic, anti-corporatist ideology of the Revolution, the influential *Loi Le Chapelier* (1791) stipulated that no "intermediary associations" were to exist between the individual as citizen and the state in order to allow the clearest expression of the *volonté générale* or public will.

As we have seen, individualism provided the basis of America's Revolution and subsequent political development. But in contrast to the French case, and with the exception of the slave-holding plantation system in the Southern states, American society was for much of the eighteenth and nineteenth centuries quasi-stateless and pragmatically oriented toward the maintenance of individual mobility and free choice, with a general mistrust of central state power. Accordingly, as de Tocqueville and others have argued, voluntarism and associational life evolved as an appropriate compromise between individualism and political collectivity. Whereas the French state had been conquered by a revolutionary regime that saw associationialism as a pre-modern element of the feudal and clerical order, the state in the US emerged only gradually, while local community and associational life remained the focus of democratic identity.

In both countries, *either* state *or* associational structures formed the basis of political progress and initial democratic identity. In this respect, the German case is fundamentally different. Politically, Germany's history of the eighteenth and nineteenth centuries is one of compromises between a "self-modernizing" feudal order on the one hand and the emergent civil society on the other. In contrast to France, Germany did not witness a successful anti-feudal revolution nor did it see the building of a central nation-state. Its 300 kingdoms, dukedoms, and baronies remained religiously and politically divided, with the Protestant Kingdom of Prussia and the Catholic Empire of Austria as two dominant autocratic powers. When elements of a civil society first evolved in the eighteenth century, government and state administration continued to remain under the exclusive control of the aristocracy. The new middle class, or *Bürgertum,* did not share political responsibilities.

In contrast to what happened in other European countries, the latent tension between the aristocratic and autocratic state on the one hand, and the emergent middle class with its political aspirations and associations on the other, did not lead to ultimate rupture (as it did in France or the US), despite serious conflicts during the nineteenth century. Especially in Prussia, where the state acted as the main driving force of modernization, an increasingly stable and later more widely applied pattern of cooperation provided the seed for what was to become a major aspect of the nonprofit sector in Germany. To a large extent, the German nonprofit sector did not develop in antithesis to the state, but in interaction with it.

Yet in both France and Germany, the history of the nonprofit sector is much more closely tied to the state than in the other countries reviewed above, in particular the US. As we will see in Chapter 6, France and Germany developed a corporatist nonprofit sector, where major components of the sector are in a subsidiary relationship to the state. This pattern was reinforced and expanded through the welfare state policies of the twentieth century that created some of the largest networks of nonprofit providers in the world. For example, the major nonprofit organizations providing social and health services in France and Germany are among the largest employers in their respective countries.

CONCLUSION

What these brief historical comparisons show is that the nonprofit sector is embedded in the broader political and social development of a country or region. Its development is shaped by political cultures and forms of government, but also by cultural and religious factors and sociological aspects of class structure. Salamon and Anheier (1998b) suggest that, cross-nationally, the nonprofit sector has different "moorings" in different countries that reveal different social and economic "shapes" and factors at work. They help create the diversity and the richness of the organizational forms and institutions located between the state and the market. In Chapter 3, we take a closer look at a complex terminology that has developed to depict the nonprofit or voluntary sector, including aspects of civil society and social capital.

The development of the US civil society was an arduous process, "a story of gains won, rescinded, and reclaimed . . . about the ebb and flow of democracy and the exercise of power: who wielded it, toward what end, and how Americans ultimately created a civil society" (McCarthy 2003: 9). But it is also a history that shows how unlikely such a successful outcome ultimately was, how many uncertainties were in its way, and how likely it was that developments could have turned out differently. This is indeed the lesson that we draw from for philanthropy in the early twenty-first century: as we try to "build" civil society and philanthropy in many parts of the world, the highly contingent and long-term prospect of any such endeavor becomes apparent. Building a sustainable civil society is not the work of single events or projects; it is not the work of a decade; but it is the work of generations.

REVIEW QUESTIONS

- What are some of the major patterns underlying the development of the US nonprofit sector?

- How does the history of the US nonprofit sector differ from the experiences of other countries?

- What is meant by the "embeddedness" of the nonprofit sector?

REFERENCES AND RECOMMENDED READING

Hall, P. D. (1992) *Inventing the Nonprofit Sector and Other Essays on Philanthropy, Voluntarism, and Nonprofit Organizations*, Baltimore, MD: Johns Hopkins University Press.

Hammack, D. C. (ed.) (1998) *Making the Nonprofit Sector in the United States*, Bloomington and Indianapolism, IN: Indiana University Press.

McCarthy, K. (2003) *American Creed: Philanthropy and the Rise of Civil Society 1700–1865*, Chicago, IL: University of Chicago Press.

Chapter 3

Concepts

This chapter discusses the various types of activities, organizations, and institutions that make up the nonprofit sector (charities, foundations, associations, etc.), and looks at different attempts to define the area between the market, state, and household sectors. The chapter also explores how the nonprofit sector relates to the concept of civil society and to social capital approaches.

LEARNING OBJECTIVES

Concepts are important tools for understanding and communicating. They are the building blocks of theories, and the meanings they convey become highly relevant in the policymaking process. Together, the concepts and terms introduced in this chapter are the key pillars of a new approach that goes beyond the state versus market perspective—a perspective that has dominated social science thinking and policymaking for much of the twentieth century. After reading this chapter, the reader should:

■ be able to point to the various definitions of nonprofit organizations;
■ be familiar with different types of nonprofit organizations and the various institutions located between state and market more generally;
■ have an understanding of the concepts of civil society and social capital, and how they relate to the nonprofit sector.

KEY TERMS

Some of the key terms covered in this chapter are:

■ charity
■ civil society
■ cooperative

- faith-based organization
- foundation
- independent sector
- mutual society
- nongovernmental organization
- nonprofit organization
- philanthropy
- public benefit organization
- social capital
- social economy
- voluntary association

THE NONPROFIT SECTOR

In the introductory chapter, we briefly reviewed the great diversity of organizational forms and activities in the nonprofit sector, be it in the US or elsewhere. Indeed, as Salamon and Anheier (1997c) argue, coming to terms with the diversity and richness of organizations located between the market and the state is the first challenge encountered in trying to gain a better understanding of this set of institutions. This task is complicated by the great profusion of terms: "nonprofit sector," "charities," "third sector," "independent sector," "voluntary sector," "tax-exempt sector," "nongovernmental organizations," "associational sector," "philanthropy," and, in the European context, "social economy" and "social enterprise," and many more. Clearly, each of these terms depicts one aspect of the social reality of the sector at the expense of overlooking or de-emphasizing other aspects. For example:

- The term *charity* emphasizes the support these organizations receive from private charitable donations and assumes a certain motivation on behalf of both donor and recipient. But private charitable contributions do not constitute the only, or even the major, source of their revenue; and many nonprofit organizations are not "charitable" but advocate special interests or seek to promote their members' interests through lobbying.
- The term *independent sector* highlights the role these organizations play as a "third force" outside of the realm of government (i.e. political power) and private business (i.e. the profit motive). But these organizations are far from independent, politically or financially. Politically, many are engaged in advocacy, and board membership is typically drawn from local, regional, and national elites; and in financial terms, they depend heavily on both government and private business for revenue.
- The term *voluntary organizations or sector* emphasizes both the significant input that volunteers make to the management and operation of this sector and the non-compulsory nature of participation in terms of membership. But a good deal of the activity of voluntary organizations is carried out by paid staff, and not by volunteers, and many nonprofits have no membership base at all.

- The term *NGO (nongovernmental organization)* is the term used to depict these organizations in the developing world and in international relations, but it tends to refer only to a portion of what elsewhere is considered to be part of this sector—namely, the organizations engaged in the promotion of economic and social development, typically at the grassroots level.

- The term *philanthropy* refers to the use of personal wealth and skills for the benefit of specific public causes and is typically applied to philanthropic foundations and similar institutions. Yet the sector also includes self-interested behavior, pecuniary or otherwise, and interest organizations that lobby on behalf of their members rather than for the common good.

- Even the term *nonprofit organizations/sector,* a term used by the UN System of National Accounts and, as we will see, economic theories, is not without its problems. This term emphasizes the fact that these organizations do not exist primarily to generate profits for their owners. But these organizations sometimes do earn profits, i.e. they generate more revenues than they spend in a given year. What is more, the terms suggest more about what the organization is not, than what it stands for, prompting one analyst to ask, "If not for profit—for what?" (Young 1983).

- The term *économie sociale* is the term used to depict a broad range of non-governmental organizations in France and Belgium, and increasingly within the European Community, but it embraces a wide variety of business-type organizations such as mutual insurance companies, savings banks, cooperatives, and agricultural marketing organizations that would be considered parts of the business sector in most parts of the world.[1] The definition used to delineate the organizations that form part of the social economy has four main components: (1) organizational purpose of service to members or some specified larger community rather than profit to shareholders; (2) independent management; (3) a democratic decision-making process; and (4) precedence of social aspects over capital in the distribution of income.

Different approaches

Behind these many terms are, of course, different purposes. Definitions are neither true nor false, and they are ultimately judged by their usefulness in describing a part of reality of interest to us. Specifically, a definition must be simpler than the reality it seeks to describe. In the social sciences, we are particularly interested in definitions that facilitate communication, generate insights, and lead to better understanding. In this respect, we can either use existing definitions, such as the legal and functional definitions reviewed below, or propose new ones, as is the case for the structural–operational definition, which, as we will see in some detail on pages 47–9, was inductively developed by comparing the terminologies used in a wide range of different countries (Salamon and Anheier 1997c; see the United Nations Handbook on Nonprofit Institutions 2002).

The legal definition

Perhaps the most certain and straightforward system for defining the nonprofit sector is the one provided in a country's laws and regulations. In the US, for example, nonprofit organizations are defined in the Internal Revenue Code, and for the most part in sections 501. As Table 3.1 shows, there are over twenty different categories of nonprofit or tax-exempt organizations, which cover a great diversity of entities. As the numbers in Table 3.1 make clear, however, there are basically two major types: 501(c)(3) and 501(c)(4) organizations. They account for about 70 percent of all nonprofit organizations registered under the classification of the Internal Revenue Service (IRS).

Most importantly, while both 501(c)(3) and (c)(4) organizations are exempt from income and other forms of taxation, only those categorized as 501(c)(3), the so-called public benefit organizations, can receive tax-deductible contributions from individuals and corporations. By contrast, contributions to 501(c)(4)s, the so-called social welfare organizations, do not qualify for tax deductibility for donors. Organizations falling into this category, 501(c)(4), include many civic leagues and advocacy organizations that support particular social and political causes.

To qualify for 501(c)(3) status, an organization must pass three tests: the organizational test, the political test, and the asset test. While nonprofits can be established for any lawful purposes, the organizational test for 501(c)(3) status requires that they operate exclusively in one or more of eight functional purpose areas:

- educational
- religious
- charitable
- scientific
- literary
- testing for public safety
- fostering certain national and international amateur sports competitions
- prevention of cruelty to children and animals.

The political test requires organizations with 501(c)(3) status not to participate in the political electoral process of promoting any specific candidates for office. This prohibition includes the preparation and distribution of campaign literature. The political constraints imposed on 501(c)(3) organizations go beyond actual elections and campaigning and extend to lobbying as well, and such organizations are prohibited from making substantial contributions to lobbying activities by third parties. Accordingly, a 501(c)(3) organization can spend up to 20 percent of annual expenditure on lobbying activities relating to the organization's mission. By contrast, 501(c)(4) organizations have no restrictions on their lobbying activities.

To pass the asset test, the nonprofit organization has to demonstrate procedures that prohibit assets or income being distributed to individuals as owners, managers, or their equivalents, except for fair compensation for services rendered. This also stipulates that the organization may not be used for the personal benefit of founders, board members, managers, staff, or associates.

Table 3.1 *Active entities on IRS business master file of tax-exempt organizations, 1998*

Tax code number	Type of tax-exempt organization	1998(b)
501 (c)(l)	Corporations organized under an act of Congress	14
501 (c)(2)	Title-holding companies	7,125
501 (c)(3)	Religious, charitable, and similar organizations (a)	733,790
501 (c)(4)	Social welfare organizations	139,533
501 (c)(5)	Labor and agricultural organizations	64,804
501 (c)(6)	Business leagues	79,864
501 (c)(7)	Social and recreational clubs	66,691
501 (c)(8)	Fraternal beneficiary societies	84,507
501 (c)(9)	Voluntary employees' beneficiary societies	14,240
501 (c)(l0)	Domestic fraternal beneficiary societies	21,962
501 (c)(11)	Teachers' retirement fund	13
501 (c)(12)	Benevolent life insurance associations	6,423
501 (c)(13)	Cemetery companies	9,792
501 (c)(14)	Credit unions	4,378
501 (c)(15)	Mutual insurance companies	1,251
501 (c)(16)	Corporations to finance crop operation	25
501 (c)(17)	Supplemental unemployment benefit trusts	533
501 (c)(18)	Employee-funded pension trusts	1
501 (c)(19)	War veterans' organizations	35,682
501 (c)(20)	Legal services organizations	56
501 (c)(21)	Black lung trusts	28
501 (c)(23)	Veterans' associations founded prior to 1880	2
501 (c)(24)	Trusts described in section 4049 of ERISA (c)	1
501 (c)(25)	Holding companies for pensions and so on	1,017
501 (d)	Religious and apostolic organizations	118
501 (e)	Cooperative hospital service organizations	43
501 (f)	Cooperative service organizations of operating educational organizations	1
521	Farmers' cooperatives	1,442
Total tax-exempt organizations		1,273,336

Source: Weitzman *et al.* 2002. © Independent Sector. Used by permission of John Wiley & Sons Inc.

Note: All figures are for the fiscal year ended September 30, 1998.
(a) Not all 501(c)(3) organzations are included because certain organizations, such as churches, integrated auxiliaries, subordinate units, and conventions or associatons of churches, need not apply for recognition of exemption unless they desire a ruling.
(b) Excludes state-sponsored high-risk health insurance organizations and workers' compensation reinsurance organizations, which were categories added to 1998 data. Figures are preliminary.
(c) ERISA = Employee Retirement Income Security Act.

RELIGIOUS CONGREGATIONS

The distinction between member serving and public serving reflected in US tax law in the distinction between 501(c)(3) and 501(c)(4) organizations is of course open to debate, and none is perhaps more controversial than the privileged treatment of religious congregations. In fact, of all private organizational entities in the US, they are the only type automatically entitled to tax exemption under Section 501(c)(3). What is more, religious congregations are exempt from the reporting requirements imposed on all other nonprofits with 501(c)(3).

The reasons for the privileged treatment are found in US constitutional law, the strict separation between state and church, and the limitations imposed on government to regulate the religious establishment, even for purposes of granting and supervising tax exemption. The special status of religion in American society is clear when we look at the vast network of religious institutions in the US. Americans are more religious in their value orientations and are more religiously active than the populations of all other developed countries (Lipset 1996; Wuthnow 2002). In recent years, the role of religious congregations has moved closer to the political agenda, as the discussion of faith-based organizations below will show.

CIVIL LAW SYSTEMS

In contrast to common law countries such as the US, Australia, or the UK, civil law countries such as France, Germany, and Japan have a different starting point for defining nonprofit organizations. The civil law system is based on the fundamental distinction between private law, regulating the rights and responsibilities of individuals and private legal personalities, and public law (e.g. administrative, fiscal, and ecclesiastical law), dealing with the relations between individuals and the state, public agencies, and public law corporations. The central point is that the state is regarded as a legal actor *sui generis* and in possession of its own legal subjectivity that requires laws and regulations qualitatively different from those addressing private individuals.

The civil law systems have two principal types of organizations: private law associations and corporations. To achieve legal personality, an association must be registered in some association registry which, depending on the country's administrative system, is typically maintained either locally at city or county courts or nationally at the Ministry of the Interior or an equivalent government department. To register, an association must pursue a non-commercial objective, have a specified minimum number of members, a charter, and a governing board. A non-registered association possesses no legal personality; the board legally represents it, and members are personally liable.

However, registration does not necessarily imply tax exemption for the organization. In most civil law countries, the distinction between public and private law equates the state with the public good and puts the burden of proof of public benefit on private law associations only. As a result, the law concerning public benefit is more complex than in common law countries and involves a legal act separate from registration. What is more, while many civil law countries have relatively simple registration procedures for associations and corporations, the achievement of public benefit status is much more demanding. In France and Japan, there are many more nonprofit organizations than tax-exempt nonprofit organizations.

The legal definition of what constitutes a nonprofit organization, however, makes clear the implicit assumptions about the purposes and objectives of nonprofit organizations. This points to the importance of what we call the functional definition, to which we now turn.

The functional definition

A second type of definition of the nonprofit sector emphasizes the functions or purposes that organizations in this sector carry out. Perhaps the most common type of function attributed to the nonprofit sector is the promotion of what is variously termed the "public interest," or "public purposes." Perhaps the most comprehensive statement of such a "public purpose" definition can be found, however, in the Preamble to England's Statute of Charitable Uses of 1601:

> . . . relief of aged, impotent and poor people . . . maintenance of sick and maimed soldiers and mariners, schools of learning, free schools, and scholars in universities . . . repair of bridges, ports, havens, causeways, churches, sea banks, and highways, education and preferment of orphans . . . relief, stock, or maintenance for houses of correction . . . marriages of poor maids . . . supportation, aid and help of young tradesmen, handicraftsmen . . . relief or redemption of prisoners or captives, . . . aid or ease of any poor inhabitant concerning payments of fifteens, setting out of soldiers, and other taxes.
>
> (cited in Hopkins 1987: 56; see Picarda 1977)

The functional definition also dominates the notion of charity in Britain, as specified in the case Income Tax Special Purposes Commission v. Pemsel 1891:

> Charity in its legal sense comprises four principal divisions: trusts for the relief of poverty; trusts for the advancement of education; trusts for the advancement of religion; and trusts for other purposes beneficial to the community, not falling under any of the preceding heads.

This now well over 110-years-old ruling and related legislation since then are to be modernized, according to a review conducted by the UK's Cabinet Office in 2002, and are to be replaced by ten purpose categories:

> A charity should be defined as an organization which provides public benefit and which has one or more of the following purposes:
>
> 1 The prevention and relief of poverty
> 2 The advancement of education
> 3 The advancement of religion
> 4 The advancement of health (including the prevention and relief of sickness, disease or of human suffering)
> 5 Social and community advancement (including the care, support, and protection of the aged, people with a disability, children and young people)

43

6 The advancement of culture, arts and heritage

7 The advancement of amateur sport

8 The promotion of human rights, conflict resolution and reconciliation

9 The advancement of environmental protection and improvement

10 Other purposes beneficial to the community.

The notion of public benefit is critical to the definition of charity. The *Charity Commission Guidelines* in the UK offer a useful set of criteria indicative of public rather than private benefit of organizational purposes:

- the organization benefits the public as a whole or a significant segment of it;
- the beneficiaries are not defined in terms of a personal or contractual relationship;
- membership and benefits should be available to all those who fall within the class of beneficiaries;
- any private benefit arises directly out of the pursuit of the charity's objects or is legitimately incidental to them;
- the amount of private benefit should be reasonable;
- charges should be reasonable and should not exclude a substantial proportion of the beneficiary class;
- the service provided should not cater only to the financially well off. It should in principle be open to all potential beneficiaries.

CIVIL LAW SYSTEMS

So far we have looked at the functional definition in the context of the common law countries, but what is the situation in civil law countries, where the state puts more onerous requirements on private actors that seek to work for the public good? In most civil law countries, the legal status of associations was at center stage in the emergence of civil society in the nineteenth century and became enshrined in the Civil Code, with the definition of what constitutes public benefit essentially defined by provisions in various tax laws.

Public benefit status today is foremost a fiscal term. Its definition and application serve to differentiate tax-exempt organizations from those liable to various forms of taxation. Using the German tax code as an example, the promotion of the following objectives are covered by the definition of public benefit:

- public well-being in material, spiritual and moral spheres;
- charitable and benevolent activities to support persons in need and unable to care for themselves;
- Church-related activities including the construction, maintenance, and administration of churches and church property, religious instruction, religious services, and training of the clergy.

Against the background of these general headings, the tax code lists the following types of activities as examples of public benefit:

- support of science and research, education and instruction, arts and culture, religion, international understanding and exchange, development aid, environmental protection, historical preservation, and local customs;
- support of youth welfare, the elderly, public health, welfare, and sport;
- the general support of a democratic state and community; and
- the support of animal husbandry, plant cultivation, and gardening (all non-commercial), traditional customs, veterans' affairs, amateur radios, model airplane clubs, and dog shows.

What is more, the tax code stipulates that private activities for public benefit must be carried out in a certain manner:

- *Selfless*, in the sense of altruistic, whereby members of the organization are neither allowed to receive profits nor other profit-like compensations: this strict non-distribution constraint excludes many mutual membership associations, as well as business and professional associations. It also implies that the cost behavior of nonprofits must be "reasonable" in terms of salaries and fringe benefits.
- *Exclusive*, in the sense that the organization pursues only purposes defined as public benefit: if an organization carries out other activities, it may lose the nonprofit tax status altogether. In practise, the organization may declare some of its activities as public benefit and others as "commercial." This has the effect that those activities classified as public benefit receive preferential tax treatment, whereas commercial activities may be subject to taxation.
- *Direct*, in the sense that the charitable purpose has to be served by the organization itself rather than through third parties. This provision contains many exceptions that basically relate to inter-organizational structures, financing, and special institutions, whereby a third party may provide services on behalf of a tax-exempt organization.
- *Timely*, in the sense that the organization has to spend its resources for the specified purposes within a certain time period, usually a given fiscal year. This implies that many nonprofit organizations are not allowed to build up financial reserves or accumulate capital for investment. Again, there are many exceptions to this rule.

The functional definition, under both common law and civil law, has at its core the notion that nonprofit organizations are identifiable by their financial behavior, in particular their lack of a financial profit motive or restriction of profit distributions. This is also the starting point for the economic definition.

The economic definition

According to this definition, the key feature that sets the nonprofit sector apart from the others is the revenue structure of nonprofits. According to economic definition, nonprofit institutions (or NPIs) do not receive the bulk of their income from the sale of goods and services in the market, or through taxation, but from the voluntary dues and contributions

45

of their members and supporters. Importantly, this basis for defining NPIs, which focuses on the common characteristic that they do not distribute their profits, is a central feature of most definitions of "the nonprofit sector" in legal (see above, p. 40) and social science literature, which we will review in Chapter 6.[2]

The economic definition is laid down in the System of National Accounts (or SNA) (United Nations 1993), the international economic standard used for economic reporting and forecasting purposes of many kinds.

Within this structure, the 1993 SNA distinguishes nonprofit institutions from other institutional units principally in terms of what happens to any profit that they might generate. In particular:

> Nonprofit institutions are legal or social entities created for the purpose of producing goods and services whose status does not permit them to be a source of income, profit, or other financial gain for the units that establish, control or finance them. In practise their productive activities are bound to generate either surpluses or deficits but any surpluses they happen to make cannot be appropriated by other institutional units.
>
> (UN 1993, para. 4.54)

National accounting groups similar kinds of economic entities into institutional sectors.[3] The SNA (1993) states that "corporations, NPIs, government units and households are intrinsically different from each other" and that "their economic objectives, functions and behavior are also different" (UN 1993, para. 4.17). The system groups NPIs into a specific institutional sector called "Nonprofit Institutions Serving Households" or NPISH.

Yet under SNA guidelines, as well as those of the European System of Accounts (ESA), national statistical offices are to identify separately, and collect data on, only a small subset of all nonprofit organizations, i.e. those that receive most of their income and support from households in the form of charitable contributions. Other nonprofit organizations, that is those that receive significant shares of their income from fees and service charges or government grants and contracts, are, under SNA guidelines, typically merged into either the business or government sector. SNA specialists have justified this treatment on the basis that these other nonprofit institutions are limited in both number and size. In this sense, the economic definition recognizes a large number of nonprofit organizations, but a more limited nonprofit sector.

Specifically, a series of stipulations addresses the allocation of NPIs to different sectors (see Figure 3.1). First, NPIs considered of minor economic importance, or deemed temporary and informal, are excluded from the NPISH and allocated to the Households Sector. Second, NPIs that sell most or all output at prices that are economically significant are treated as market producers and allocated to the Non-financial or Financial Corporations Sectors.[4] This leaves a group of non-market NPIs, which provide most of their output to others freely or at prices that are not economically significant. The SNA/ESA divides them into two further groups: NPIs controlled and mainly financed by government; and other NPIs. The first group is allocated to the Government Sector, while the second and residual group constitutes the NPISH Sector.

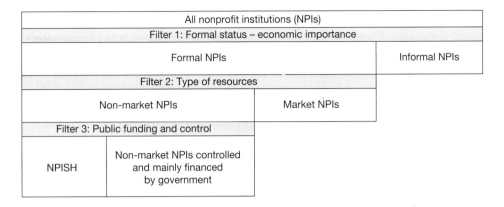

Figure 3.1 *The institutional sectoring of the nonprofit sector*
Source: Based on Anheier and Mertens 2003.

Thus, from an economic perspective, nonprofits are primarily defined by their revenue structure. As institutions barred from being a source of income to their owners or equivalents, they rely neither on sales and fees from market transactions nor do they depend on tax revenue. Within the logical framework of the SNA, they are defined as residual economic entities, i.e. as organizations that are left over once market firms, public agencies, and households have been identified.

The structural–operational definition

This definition does not emphasize the purpose of the organization or its sources of income but its basic structure and operation. According to this definition, which was first introduced by Salamon and Anheier in 1992a, an organization is defined as a nonprofit entity if it shows the following five characteristics:

1 *Organized, i.e. institutionalized to some extent*
What is important is that the organization has some institutional reality. In some countries a formal charter of incorporation signifies this, but institutional reality can also be demonstrated in other ways where legal incorporation is either not chosen or not readily available, such as having regular meetings, officers, rules of procedure, or some degree of organizational permanence. By contrast, purely ad hoc and temporary gatherings of people are not considered part of the nonprofit sector under this definition. Otherwise the concept of the nonprofit sector becomes far too amorphous and ephemeral to grasp and examine.

This criterion also requires meaningful organizational boundaries, e.g. some recognized difference between members and non-members; an awareness of the distinction between organizational and individual responsibilities; and an understanding of the difference between the organization and other entities such as family, friendship circles, and loose networks among individuals.

47

many countries once the right of association had become established. Examples of such turning points are the Law of 1901 in France and civil law legislation in other European countries. Associations became an important source of political mobilization (e.g. working-class movement, women's rights movement), and a platform for status competition in formally egalitarian societies, in particular at the local level. Being a member of the right club or association came to signal social distinction and prestige.

Regardless of the strikingly different political and social contexts in which voluntary associations developed historically, recent decades have witnessed a significant expansion in the number of associations and memberships. The number of voluntary associations in the US is well over 1.5 million, with 57 percent of the population being a member of at least one association (see Chapter 4). In France, an associational boom has increased the number of associations to 700,000–800,000 (Archambault, Gariazzo, Anheier, and Salamon 1999). Associational density in Germany has tripled since 1960, and nearly two-thirds of Germans belong to associations (Anheier and Seibel 2001). Social democratic countries such as Sweden have among the highest membership rates among developed societies, with over 80 percent of the population organized in voluntary associations (Lundström and Wijkström 1997).

In the developing world, this proportion is somewhat lower in regard to formal (i.e. registered) associations. Estimates of membership in indigenous forms of associations are very incomplete, as many of these organizations are informal and not registered. Moreover, the legacy of authoritarian rule in many developing countries over the last fifty years also contributed to somewhat lower membership rates in formal associations. In former state socialist countries, mass organizations linked to political parties accounted for very high membership rates; in the transformation process, however, many have lost a significant number of members or otherwise faced dissolution. As a result, the membership structure in such societies is reorganizing and remains at lower levels than in the West.

FOUNDATIONS

Foundations, which we will review in more detail in Chapter 14, have a long history, reaching back to antiquity, and with equally long traditions in most world cultures. Despite this heritage, the modern foundation is often associated with the rise of the large grant-making foundation in the US in the early twentieth century, and its replication in other parts of the world, in particular in Europe after World War II. In terms of numbers and material wealth, the foundations of most developed market economies are a product of the last three decades of the twentieth century, having benefited from prolonged economic prosperity, political stability, and, in many countries, more favorable legislation. In this sense, as is the case for nonprofit institutions, foundations are both old and recent phenomena.

The various legal systems define foundations rather differently; and registration, legal practices, and accountability and governance regimes vary accordingly. Despite these legal differences, the basic concept of a foundation shares common images: a separate, identifiable asset (the root meaning of the Latin-based *fund* or *fond*) donated to a particular purpose, usually public in nature (implying the root of charity or philanthropy). In fact, most legal systems incorporate the ancient Roman law differentiation between foundations based on some core asset (*universitas rerum*) and associations (*universitas personarum*) based on membership.

Working from the structural–operational definition, foundations are private assets that serve a public purpose, with five core characteristics:

1. *non-membership-based organization* based on an *original deed*, typically signified in a charter of incorporation or establishment that gives the entity both intent of purpose and permanence;
2. *private entity* institutionally separate from government, and "nongovernmental" in the sense of being structurally separate from the public sector;
3. *self-governing entity* equipped to control its own activities in terms of internal governance procedures;
4. *non-profit-distributing* by not returning profits generated by either use of assets or the conduct of commercial activities to their owners, members, trustees, or directors; and
5. *serving a public purpose* that goes beyond a narrowly defined social group or category, such as members of a family, or a closed circle of beneficiaries.

The nature of the assets can be stock and other shares in business firms, financial, real estate, patents, etc. There are basic categories that group the most common types of foundations according to type of activity:

- *grant-making foundations*, i.e. endowed organizations that primarily engage in grant-making for specified purposes;
- *operating foundations*, i.e. foundations that primarily operate their own programs and projects;
- *corporate foundations* such as the company-related or company-sponsored foundation based on corporate assets, which vary by the closeness to the parent corporations in terms of governance and management;
- *community foundations*, i.e. grant-making and operating foundations that pool revenue and assets from a variety of sources (individual, corporate, public) for specified communal purposes; and
- *government-sponsored or government-created foundations*, i.e. foundations that are either created by public charter or enjoy high degrees of public sector support for endowment or operating expenditures.

Over the past two decades, following a decline in the 1960s and 1970s, foundations have experienced a kind of renaissance. While the US, with over 60,000 foundations, has the largest foundation sector, Germany (about 9,000), Great Britain (about 9,000), Spain (about 6,000), and Italy (3,000) have seen significant increases in both numbers and assets throughout 1990s as well.

FAITH-BASED ORGANIZATIONS
As will be discussed in more detail in Chapters 5 and 13, faith-based nonprofit organizations (FBOs) are particularly important in the social policy debate of the 1990s and the beginning of the twenty-first century because they are being called upon to play an even

Handbook on Nonprofit Institutions (United Nations, 2002). Table 3.2 shows a summary of the major groups and subgroups of the ICNPO, and Appendix I offers a fuller description.

Civil society

The term civil society has a long intellectual history, reaching back to the Enlightenment period in eighteenth-century Europe. It played an important role in intellectual debates about the role of the state and its citizens until the early twentieth century, but it was then caught in the ideological battles of the times between authoritarianism and liberalism, and fell into disuse, seemingly relegated to the history of ideas with little contemporary relevance. In many ways, the term civil society suffered from the same intellectual neglect as the voluntary or third sector, largely as a consequence of dominant "state vs. market thinking" in the social sciences as well as in the world of politics.

Civil society, as a term, was rediscovered in the 1980s among Eastern European and Latin American intellectuals and civil rights activists, who were looking for an alternative public sphere outside that of a dominant autocratic state. The basic insight of these Eastern European and Latin American intellectuals was that society needs "space" for citizens to engage with each other, and that this space or sphere should be respected and not controlled by the state. The term brought to the forefront the idea that society is more than government, markets, or the economy, and more than individual citizens and their families. There had to be society—a civil society—where citizens, under the rule of law but otherwise self-organizing and self-directed, could come together to pursue their interests and values (see Keane 1998 for an overview).

The term became a successful shorthand for the broader context of civic actions for the common good and of values such as tolerance, respect for others, and philanthropy. It also came to be seen as the context in which nonprofit organizations operate and in which organized citizen interests are expressed, and sometimes clash with each other. Above all, the term became increasingly used in the social sciences and in political discourse alike, and definitions multiplied.

As in the nonprofit field more generally, many different definitions of civil society exist, and there is little agreement on its precise meaning, though much overlap exists between core conceptual components. While civil society is a somewhat contested concept, definitions typically vary in the emphasis they put on certain characteristics of civil society over others; some definitions primarily focus on aspects of state power, politics, and individual freedom, and others more on economic functions and notions of social capital and cohesion. Nonetheless, most analysts would probably agree with the statement that modern civil society is the sum of institutions, organizations, and individuals located between the family, the state, and the market, in which people associate voluntarily to advance common interests.

As in the case for nonprofit organizations, some definitions, such as Gellner's, are akin to what we called functional definitions and see civil society as a countervailing force keeping the forces of market and state in check:

> That set of nongovernmental institutions, which is strong enough to counterbalance the state, and, whilst not preventing the state from fulfilling its role of keeper of

peace and arbitrator between major interests, can, nevertheless, prevent the state from dominating and atomising the rest of society.

(Gellner 1994: 5)

Similarly, Keane defines civil society as:

> a complex and dynamic ensemble of legally protected nongovernmental institutions that tend to be non-violent, self-organising, self-reflexive, and permanently in tension with each other and with the state institutions that "frame," constrict and enable their activities.

(1998: 6)

By contrast, Anheier *et al.* propose an abstract definition similar to the structural–operational definition of nonprofit organizations to facilitate cross-national comparisons: "a sphere of ideas, values, institutions, organizations, networks, and individuals located between the family, the state and the market" (2001).

Civil society is primarily about the role of both the state and the market relative to that of citizens and the society they constitute. The intellectual history of the term is closely intertwined with the notion of citizenship, the limits of state power, and the foundation as well as the regulation of market economies. The prevailing modern view sees civil society as a sphere located between state and market—a buffer zone strong enough to keep both state and market in check, thereby preventing each from becoming too powerful and dominating, as suggested in Gellner's definition above. Civil society is not a singular, monolithic, separate entity, but a sphere constituted in relation to both state and market, and indeed permeating both.

Civil society is the self-organization of society outside the stricter realms of state power and market interests. For Habermas (1991), civil society is made up of more or less spontaneously created associations, organizations, and movements, which find, take up, condense, and amplify the resonance of social problems in private life, and pass it on to the political realm or public sphere. Dahrendorf (1991) sees the concept of civil society as part of a classical liberal tradition and as characterized by the existence of autonomous organizations that are neither state-run nor otherwise directed from the center political power.

As a concept, civil society is essentially an intellectual product of eighteenth-century Europe, in which citizens sought to define their place in society independent of the aristocratic state at a time when the certainty of a status-based social order began to suffer irreversible decline. The early theorists of civil society welcomed these changes. For Adam Smith, trade and commerce between private citizens created not only wealth but also invisible connections between people, the bonds of trust and social capital in today's terminology. Others, such as John Locke and Alexis de Tocqueville, saw civil society less in relation to the market but more in political terms, and they emphasized the importance of democratic association in everyday life as a base of a functioning polity. Friedrich Hegel sounded a more cautionary note about the self-organizing and self-regulatory capacity of civil society and emphasized the need for the state to regulate society. For Hegel, state and civil society depended on each other, yet their relation was full of tensions and required a

57

complicated balancing act. The role of the state relative to civil society was also empha-sized in the writings of Montesquieu, von Stein, and other thinkers, who saw the rule of law as the essence of state–society and society–market relations.

In the twentieth century, civil society became associated with notions of civility (Elias 1994), popular participation and civic mindedness (Putnam 2000), the public sphere (Habermas 1991), culture (Gramsci 1971), and community in the sense of communitari-anism (Etzioni 1996). The various concepts and approaches emphasize different aspects or elements of civil society: values and norms such as tolerance in the case of civility; the role of the media and the intellectual; the connections between people and the trust they have in each other; the moral dimensions communities create and need; and the extent to which people constitute a common public space through participation and civic engagement.

The complexity of civil society and the many relations and intersections it has with the economy, the state, and institutions such as the family, the media, or culture, make it not only possible but almost *necessary* to examine the concepts from different perspectives and orientations. Some analysts adopt an abstract, systemic view and see civil society as a macro-sociological attribute of societies, particularly in the way state and society relate to each other. Others take on a more individualistic orientation and emphasize the notions of indi-vidual agency, citizenship, values, and participation, using econometric and social network approaches in analyzing civil society. There is also an institutional approach to studying civil society by looking at the size, scope, and structure of organizations and associations and the functions they perform. Note that the different perspectives of civil society are not neces-sarily contradictory, nor are the various approaches to understanding it necessarily rival; on the contrary, they are often complementary as they differ in emphasis, explanatory focus, and policy implications rather than in principle.

SOCIAL CAPITAL

Whereas civil society provides the wider context for the nonprofit sector, the concept of social capital speaks to its micro-sociological foundation at the individual level. According to this line of thinking, economic growth and democratic government depend critically on the presence of "social capital," on the existence of bonds of trust and norms of reciprocity that can facilitate social interaction (Coleman 1990: 300–21). Without such norms, contracts cannot be enforced or compromises sustained. Hence markets and democratic institutions cannot easily develop or flourish.

The notion of trust embedded in interpersonal and institutional relations has become one of the most topical issues in current social science, and, as we will see in Chapter 6, forms a critical component in nonprofit theories. In many Western countries, this higher profile may stem, in part, from the seeming erosion of popular trust held in institutions such as the government, the media, the churches, or the family, frequently documented in public opinion polls in recent years. For example, general interpersonal trust levels in both the US and Britain were lower in the 1990s than they were in the 1980s, as was confidence in government, the press, and large corporations (see Pharr and Putnam 2000; Putnam 2002). What is more, the experience of widespread popular distrust in the political and economic systems of Eastern and Central Europe, and their ultimate breakdown in the late 1980s, may have contributed to a general sentiment that trust is a fragile element in modern societies (Beck 1992). Although we could add many more examples—from political scandals to fraudulent business deals and professional malpractise—contemporary "cultural diagnoses" suggest that trust is a problematic element of the modern Zeitgeist (Habermas 1985).

Three widely cited recent publications have further increased the attention social scientists pay to trust. In contrast to the problematic notion of trust in cultural discourse, these books try to show how the vibrancy and developmental potential of society is rooted in everyday mechanisms that generate and maintain trust. In *Making Democracy Work*, Putnam (Putnam *et al.* 1993) suggests that dense networks of voluntary associations are the main explanation for Northern Italy's economic progress over the country's Southern parts. In *Bowling Alone*, Putnam (2000) looks at participation in voluntary associations in the US and argues that a dramatic decline in both membership rates and other forms of civil engagement led to lower levels of trust in society and, consequently, to general increases in social ills such as crime. Fukuyama (1995) shows that differences in economic success among the US, Germany, and Japan are predicated on reservoirs of "sociability" and social trust, which, in turn, depend on some kind of "associational infrastructure."

Such recent formulations tend to be suggestive of a significant relationship between voluntary associations and trust—be it in Putnam's analysis of Italy, his diagnosis of current US culture, Fukuyama's study of major industrial economies, or other current work on social capital (for example, Dasgupta and Serageldin 2000; Halpern 1999). According to this thinking, voluntary associations form part of the social infrastructure of society that makes the generation of trust possible, and that at least makes it easier for trust relations and trusting attitudes to develop and to reinforce themselves within the population.

More generally, research has examined social capital as a resource from two perspectives: as an individual resource with aggregate effects at the group or community level, and as an emerging structural phenomenon. The individual perspective on social capital suggests that ties of trust and social cohesion are beneficial to members and groups alike. The argument made by Coleman that "connectivity and trust" among members of a given group, or society more generally, increases aspects associated with cohesive groups: lower delinquency, more collective action, and better enforcement of norms and values. Putnam *et al.* (1993) and Putnam (2000) applied this kind of thinking to economic development and social inclusion, and linked it to the realm of civil society. This is related to what we called the neo-Tocquevillian perspective in which norms of reciprocity, citizenship, and trust are embodied in networks of civic associations.

By contrast, Burt (1992) has argued that the absence rather than the presence of ties among individuals accounts for the true value of social capital at the individual level. The value of social capital is therefore in its unequal distribution, with some people in a society having more than others. The uneven distribution of social capital, measured as the number and reach of social ties, creates "structural holes" between unconnected individuals. These gaps in social ties allow the *tertius gaudens*, i.e. the person who benefits, to identify the "structural hole" and to make the connection among otherwise disconnected individual actors. This "gap-filling" social capital becomes the bridging material of modern society, and a key task for social entrepreneurs and voluntary associations as they try to bridge different groups of society.

59

REFERENCES AND RECOMMENDED READING

Center for Charitable Statistics, www.urban.org/content/PolicyCenters/NonprofitsandPhilanthropy/ Overview.htm.

Charity Commission Guidelines, www.charity-commission.gov.uk/supportingcharities/default.asp.

Hodgkinson, V. A. and Foley, M. (eds.) (2003) *The Civil Society Reader*, Hanover, NH, and London: University Press of New England.

Putnam, R. D. (ed.) (2002) *Democracies in Flux*, New York and Oxford: Oxford University Press.

Salamon, L. M. and Anheier, H. K. (1997) *Defining the Non-profit Sector: A Cross-National Analysis*, Manchester: Manchester University Press.

Chapter 4

Dimensions I: overview

In the first section, this chapter presents an overview of the size, composition, revenue structure, and role of the nonprofit sector in the US. The chapter also considers the place of the nonprofit sector within the mixed economy of welfare. In the second section, the chapter presents an overview of the size, composition, revenue structure, and role of the nonprofit sector in other parts of the world and places the US nonprofit sector in comparative perspective. The final section introduces data demonstrating the link between nonprofit organizations and notions of social capital and trust.

LEARNING OBJECTIVES

Having a good understanding of the scale of nonprofit activities is important for theory building and policymaking alike. After reading this chapter, the reader should:

- be able to understand the major contours of the US nonprofit sector;
- be able to understand how the US nonprofit sector differs from that of other countries in terms of its scale, scope, and revenue structure;
- be familiar with the dimensions of the nonprofit sector in different countries and regions of the world;
- recognize the empirical link between the nonprofit sector and social capital/trust.

KEY TERMS

This chapter is primarily about facts, and less concentrated on introducing new concepts. Nonetheless, some of the key terms covered in this chapter are:

- interpersonal trust
- membership
- mixed economy
- operating expenditure
- revenue types (e.g. third-party payments, statutory transfers)
- volunteering

DIMENSIONS OF THE NONPROFIT SECTOR IN THE US

For a long time, the dimensions of the US nonprofit sector remained among the most "uncharted territories" of the American institutional landscape in standard social and economic statistical reporting. Since the Filer Commission of the 1970s, however, this has changed and the data situation today, while far from perfect, continues to improve, reflecting in part the greater policy relevance of the sector itself, which brings with it a need for more comprehensive and better data. Of course, nonprofit sector statistics remain much less developed and are much less detailed than business and public sector statistics, and data on many important facets on nonprofit activities are not systematically collected, or even collected at all. Nonetheless, it is possible to present a portrait of the US nonprofit sector and its major dimensions, which we will summarize under ten headings.

Ten key facts about the US nonprofit sector

1 Scale: a vast and diverse set of organizations

In 1998, nearly 28 million organizations existed in the US, of which business accounted for 93.8 percent and government entities 0.3 percent. The balance of 1.6 million organizations, or 6 percent of the total, was nonprofit entities. This translates into roughly 1 nonprofit organization per 150 Americans.

There are different ways in which the organizational universe of US nonprofit organizations can be presented. One way is to look at tax status and the various types of tax-exempt entities (see Table 3.1). According to this way, there are over 730,000 501(c)(3) organizations, 140,000 (c)(4) welfare organizations, and over 65,000 social and recreational clubs, etc. Similarly, Salamon (1999: 22) uses the distinction between (c)(3) and (c)(4) organizations as a starting point to show the relative weight of nonprofits that are typically public serving, i.e. benefiting third parties other than members and supporters, versus those that are member serving, i.e. contributing primarily to the welfare of those supporting the organization through membership fees, dues, or other contributions. As Figure 4.1 shows,[1] of the approximately 1.6 million entities in the US nonprofit sector, about 1.2 million are primarily public serving (service providers making up the largest share with over 655,000 organizations) and 400,000 member serving, of which mutual benefit and cooperative societies dominate with 160,000 entities.

The distinction established in Figure 4.1 is one of tendency, of course, and while it conveniently summarizes a basic principle of US legal treatment of nonprofit organizations (i.e. public-serving organizations receive more beneficial tax treatment than member-serving organizations), it also opens up questions. Why are the 350,000 plus religious organizations classified as public serving, and the 6,100 political organizations as member serving? The reasons for this treatment are found in US history as well as tax law, which allocates a special status to religious organizations and a stricter set of rules for political organizations.

Table 4.1 shows the immense diversity of religious organizations in the US, and we should keep in mind that the figures reported there are incomplete, include formally

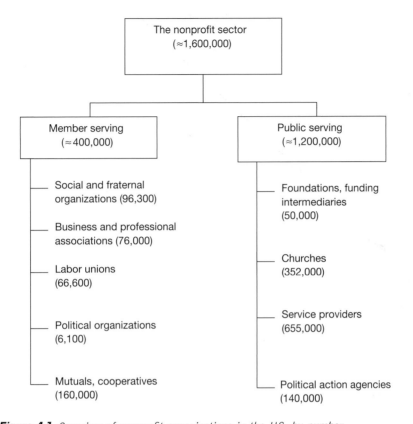

Figure 4.1 *Overview of nonprofit organizations in the US, by number*

Source: Salamon 1999: 22. © The Foundation Center. Used by permission of the Foundation Center, 79 Fifth Ave, New York, NY 10003, www.fdncenter.org.

recognized congregations only (by their respective religious body), and probably underestimate non-Christian religions, in particular Islam, Buddhism, and Hinduism. Even though the list and the data are incomplete, they underscore the long-standing importance of religion and religious organizations in US society, a point we made when discussing the history of the American nonprofit sector in Chapter 2.

2 Scale: a major economic force

The nonprofit sector employs an estimated 11 million people, or 7.1 percent of total employment in the US. The share of jobs in the nonprofit sector is three times that in agriculture and larger than that in wholesale trade, in construction, and in finance, insurance, and real estate (Salamon 2002a: 8) (Figure 4.2). One out of every twelve paid employees in the US worked in the nonprofit sector (Weitzman *et al.* 2002: 22–3). Paid earnings in the forprofit sector accounted for 80 percent, and government for 14 percent (Figure 4.3). In other words, nonprofit sector paid earnings represent about 8 percent of that for total business employment, and just under half of that for public sector employment.

Table 4.1 *Religious bodies in the US*

Religious body	Year	Churches reported
Advent Christian Church	1998	305
African Methodist Episcopal Church	1999	6,200
African Methodist Episcopal Zion Church	1998	3,098
American Baptist Association	1998	1,760
American Baptist Churches in the USA	1998	3,800
Apostolic Episcopal Church	1999	225
Assemblies of God	1998	11,937
Associated Reformed Presbyterian	1997	238
Association of Free Lutheran Congregations	1997	243
Baptist General Conference	1998	876
Baptist Missionary Association of America	1999	1,334
Brethren in Christ Church	1998	210
Christian and Missionary Alliance	1998	1,964
Christian Brethren (aka Plymouth Brethren)	1997	1,150
Christian Church (Disciples of Christ)	1997	3,818
Christian Churches and Churches of Christ	1988	5,579
Christian Congregation, Inc.	1997	1,438
Christian Methodist Episcopal Church	1983	2,340
Christian Reformed Church in North America	1998	733
Church Christ in Christian Union	1998	226
Church of Christ Scientist	1998	2,200
Church of God (Anderson, IN)	1998	2,353
Church of God (Cleveland, TN)	1995	6,060
Church of God in Christ	1991	15,300
Church of God Prophecy	1997	1,908
Church of Jesus Christ of Latter-Day Saints	1997	10,811
Church of the Brethren	1997	1,095
Church of the Nazarene	1998	5,101
Church of the United Brethren in Christ	1997	228
Churches of Christ	1999	15,000
Churches of God, General Conference	1998	339
Conservative Baptist Association of America	1998	1,200
Conservative Congregational Christian Conference	1998	236
Cumberland Presbyterian Church	1998	774
Episcopal Church	1996	1,390
Evangelical Covenant Church	1998	628
Evangelical Free Church of America	1995	1,224
Evangelical Lutheran Church in America	1998	10,862
Fellowship of Grace Brethren Churches	1997	260
Free Methodist Church of North America	1998	990
Friends General Conference	1998	620
Friends United Meeting	1997	501
Full Gospel Fellowship of Churches and Ministers International	1999	896
General Association of General Baptists	1997	790
General Association of Regular Baptist Churches	1998	1,415
General Conference Mennonite Brethren Churches	1996	368
Greek Orthodox Archdiocese of America	1998	523

Hutterian Brethren	1997	428
Independent Fundamental Churches of America	1999	659
International Baptist Bible Fellowship	1997	4,500
International Church of the Foursquare Gospel	1998	1,851
International Council of Community Churches	1998	150
International Pentecostal Holiness Church	1998	1,716
Jehovah's Witnesses	1999	11,064
Korean Presbyterian Church in America	1992	203
Lutheran Church—Missouri Synod	1997	6,218
Mennonite Church	1998	926
Mennonite Church, General Conference	1998	313
Missionary Church	1998	335
National Association of Free Will Baptists	1998	2,297
National Baptist Convention of America, Inc.	1987	2,500
National Baptist Convention, USA, Inc.	1992	33,000
National Congregational Christian Churches	1998	416
National Organization of the New Apostolic Church of North America	1998	401
North American Baptist Conference	1997	268
Old Order Amish Church	1993	898
Open Bible Standard Churches, Inc.	1998	386
Orthodox Church in America	1998	625
Pentecostal Assemblies of the World, Inc.	1998	1,750
Pentecostal Church of God	1998	1,237
Presbyterian Church in America	1998	11,260
Presbyterian Church (USA)	1997	1,340
Progressive National Baptist Convention, Inc.	1995	2,000
Reformed Church in America	1998	902
Religious Society of Friends (Conservative)	1994	1,200
Reorganized Church of Jesus Christ of Latter-Day Saints	1998	1,236
Roman Catholic Church	1998	19,584
Salvation Army	1998	1,388
Seventh-Day Adventist Church	1998	4,405
Southern Baptist Convention	1998	40,870
Sovereign Grace Believers	1998	300
United Church of Christ	1998	6,017
United Methodist Church	1998	36,170
United Pentecostal Church International	1995	3,790
Universal Fellowship of Metropolitan Community Churches	1998	300
Wesleyan Church (USA)	1998	1,590
Wisconsin Evangelical Lutheran Synod	1997	1,240
Number of churches 200 or more		343,050
Plus number of churches less than 200		6,456
Total Churches		**349,506**
Synagogues	1999	2,900
Mosques	1999	1,200
Total number of religious bodies reported		**353,606**

Source: Weitzman *et al.* 2002: 10–11. © Independent Sector. Used by permission of John Wiley & Sons Inc.

Note: Religious bodies that have 200 or more churches are identified in this table.

67

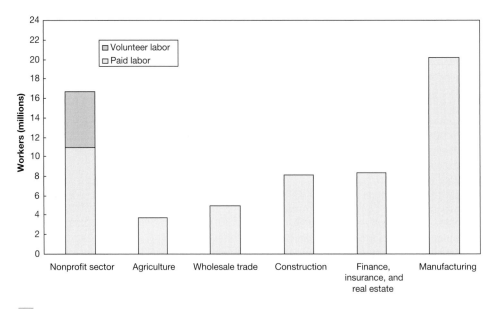

Figure 4.2 *Nonprofit employment in relation to employment in major US industries, 1998*

Source: Salamon 2002a: 8. Used by permission of The Brookings Institution.

Three out of four jobs in the nonprofit sector are in the field of public benefit service, 10 percent in each of member-serving activities and religion, and just around 1 percent in funding intermediaries such as foundations and federated funders such as United Way or the American Cancer Society.

Nonprofit sector expenditures, including the total wage bill and other operating expenditures, amounted to nearly $500 billion in the late 1990s (Weitzman *et al.* 2002: xxix), and represented a share of nearly 7 percent of national income. By comparison, as Figure 4.4 shows, the forprofit sector accounts for 80 percent of national income, and the public sector for more than 13 percent.

3 Composition: economic dominance of health, education, and social services

The nonprofit sector maintains a sizable presence in a number of fields that range from arts and culture to health care and education (Salamon 2002a: 9). As Figure 4.5 shows, in the field of health care, nonprofits represent about one-half of all hospitals, one-third of all health clinics, and one-quarter of nursing homes. In social services, they make up one-third of day care centers, 80 percent of individual and family service agencies, and 70 percent of vocational rehabilitation facilities. In education, nonprofits account for about half (46 percent) of higher education institutions. In culture, we find that nine out of ten orchestra and opera companies are nonprofit.

In economic terms, the service-providing component of the nonprofit sector accounts for the great majority of expenditure: health care accounts for over 60 percent (Figure 4.6),

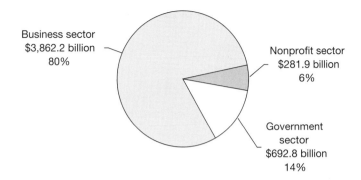

Figure 4.3 *Distribution of paid earnings by major sector, 1998*

Source: Weitzman *et al.* 2002: 24. © Independent Sector. Used by permission of John Wiley & Sons Inc.

mostly in hospitals; education for more than 16 percent; human services for 13 percent; and arts and culture for 2.4 percent. Religious organizations make up 1 percent of total expenditure and public, societal benefit organizations, 8 percent.

The dominance of the traditional welfare fields of health, education, and social services is borne out in Figure 4.6 (estimates are for 1996) when we compare share of expenditure to the relative number of organizations in a particular field (Boris and Steuerle 1999: 12). For example, hospitals account for less than 3 percent of all nonprofit organizations, but nearly half of total expenditure. By contrast, human service organizations represent about one in three nonprofits, and make up only 12.6 percent of expenditure. Arts and culture, religion, and public, societal benefit organizations show a similar pattern. In essence, the civil society component of the nonprofit sector is more pronounced when it comes to the number of organizations, and the social and health service-providing aspects are dominant in economic terms.

4 Revenue: the mixed economy

Nonprofit organizations can vary greatly in terms of their reliance on different types of support:

- *public sector payments*, which include grants, contracts, and transfers, and third-party payments;
- *private giving*, which includes foundation grants, business or corporate donations, and individual giving; and
- *private fees and charges ("program fees")*, which essentially include fees for service, dues, proceeds from sales, and investment income.

As reflected in Figure 4.7, private giving turns out to be the least important source of nonprofit revenue, with 10 percent of the total $670 billion in revenues in 1996 (Salamon 1999: 37). Of this share, most of it (77 percent) comes from individuals, with founda-tions (10 percent), corporations (5 percent), and bequests (8 percent), providing the rest

69

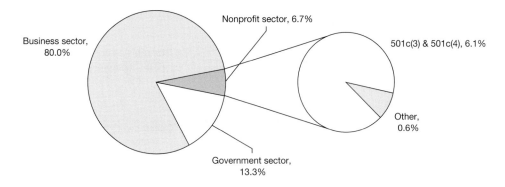

National income = $7.266 trillion (including assigned values for volunteers and unpaid family workers)

Figure 4.4 *Distribution of national income by major sector, 1998*

Source: Weitzman *et al.* 2002: xxix. © Independent Sector. Used by permission of John Wiley & Sons Inc.

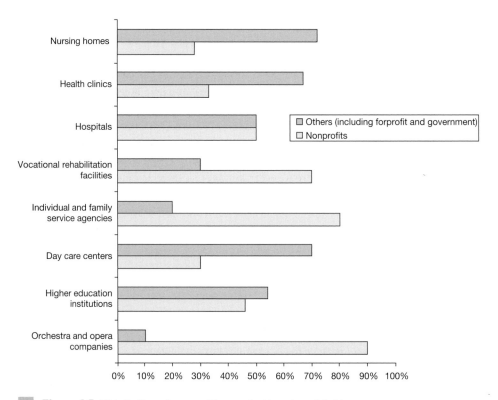

Figure 4.5 *Distribution of nonprofit organizations by subfield*

Source: Salamon 2002a: 9–10. Used by permission of The Brookings Institution.

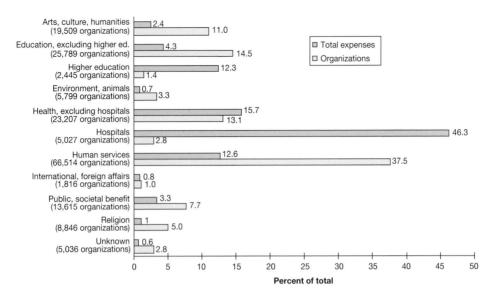

Figure 4.6 *Distribution of nonprofits and total expenses by activity, 1996*

Source: Boris and Steuerle 1999: 12. Used by permission of Urban Institute Press.

Note: Only operating public charities are included.

(Salamon 1999). By contrast, over half (54 percent) of all nonprofit income is derived from fees and sales. Finally, a significant 36 percent of nonprofit income is received from government.

As Figure 4.7 shows, the various fields of nonprofit sector activity vary greatly as to the importance of each revenue source, but they show clearly how government, private sector, and philanthropy come together in contributing to nonprofit revenue. Significantly, it may be wrong to think about the nonprofit sector as a part of the economy supported by philanthropy and charity. While both are important, in revenue terms private giving is the least important, and in the economically most central field, i.e. health care services, it accounts for only 5 percent of revenue. It is more useful to think of the nonprofit sector as a mixed economy that draws in revenue from philanthropy, government, and the private commercial sector.

5 Foundations

There are over 60,000 foundations in the US, and while these numbers may seem small in relation to the over 1.6 million nonprofit organizations, they play an important role in that they have, in the aggregate, a sizable endowment that provides for a relatively independent source of funding for the sector in the form of grants. In 2001, foundation assets were $476.8 billion, and grants disbursed amounted to $30.5 billion, i.e. 2 percent of the sector's total revenue or 10 percent of all philanthropic giving in the country. If we exclude giving to religious congregations, the share of foundation support to the nonprofit sector doubles to 20 percent of all giving, or 4 percent of total nonprofit revenue.

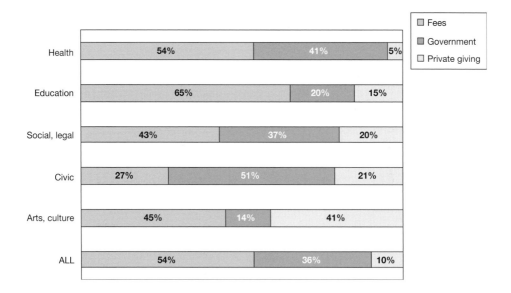

Figure 4.7 *Sources of nonprofit organization revenue, by type of agency, 1996*

Source: Salamon 1999: 37. © The Foundation Center. Used by permission of the Foundation Center, 79 Fifth Ave, New York, NY 10003, www.fdncenter.org.

As we have seen in previous chapters, there are several types of foundation. In the US, independent grant-making foundations account for nearly 90 percent of the total number of foundations (Figure 4.8) and 85 percent of total assets; corporate foundations are less numerous with just over 2,000 foundations and 3 percent of all assets. There are approximately 600 community foundations with $30.3 billion in assets, and a relatively small number of operating foundations as well.

6 Individual giving

The US has a well-developed system of individual giving that ranges from religious contributions in churches and synagogues and federated giving campaigns such as the United Way, United Jewish Appeal, or the American Heart Association, to the work of professional fundraisers. Together, individual giving amounted to nearly $180 billion at the end of the 1990s (Weitzman *et al.* 2002: 54), with 78 percent (Weitzman *et al.* 2002: 58) of all US households making contributions. On average, giving represents about 1.9 percent of personal income, or $503 per capita per year, or $1,075 per contributing household (Weitzman *et al.* 2002: 59).

As Figure 4.9 shows, nearly half of all American households contribute to religion, followed by health (27 percent), human services (25 percent), youth development (21 percent), and education (20 percent) (Weitzman *et al.* 2002: 71). In terms of dollar amount, Figure 4.10 shows that religion remains the top recipient (44 percent), with education second (14 percent), health (10 percent), human services (9 percent), and the arts (6 percent) (Weitzman *et al.* 2002: 56).

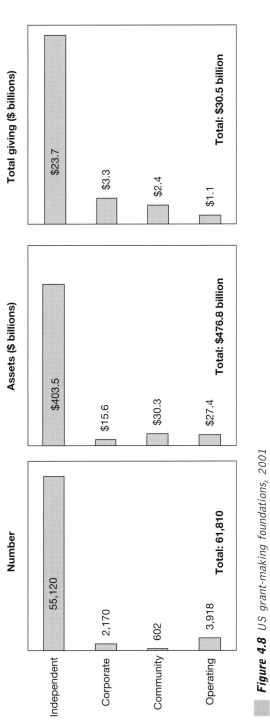

Figure 4.8 *US grant-making foundations, 2001*

Source: Based on data reported in Foundation Center 2003.

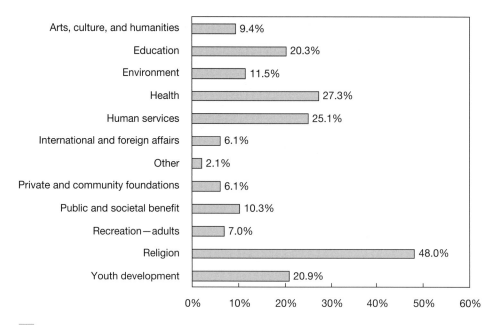

Figure 4.9 *Percentage of households contributing by area of activity, 1995*

Source: Weitzman *et al.* 2002: 71. © Independent Sector. Used by permission of John Wiley & Sons Inc.

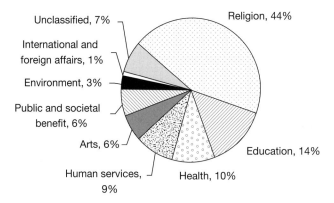

Figure 4.10 *Distribution of private contributions by recipient area, 1998*

Source: Weitzman *et al.* 2002: 56. © Independent Sector. Used by permission of John Wiley & Sons Inc.

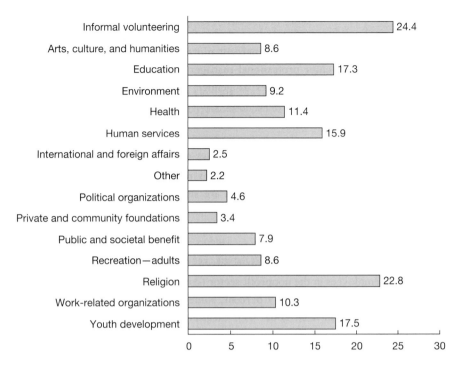

Figure 4.11 *Percentage of population eighteen years and older volunteering by areas of activity, 1998*

Source: Weitzman *et al.* 2002: 75. © Independent Sector. Used by permission of John Wiley & Sons Inc.

7 Volunteering

To some extent these giving patterns are reflected in volunteering as well. An estimated 110 million Americans over the age of 18 volunteer, representing 55.5 percent of the adult population. The average weekly number of hours volunteered was 3.5 hours in 1998, amounting to an estimated number of volunteer hours of 15.8 billon per year for the US as a whole, or the equivalent of 9.3 million jobs (Weitzman *et al.* 2002: 73).

As Figure 4.11 shows, other than informal volunteering among neighbors and local communities, the most frequent fields volunteered for are religion (23 percent), youth development (18 percent), education (17 percent), human services (16 percent), and health (11 percent). Many people volunteer for more than one organization, and the average number of assignments was 1.7 per volunteer.

8 Workforce

Wages in the nonprofit sector are lower than in both the public and the forprofit sectors, although significant differences exist within and across fields. Studies by Preston (1989), using the 1979 Census survey and the 1980 survey of job characteristics, show a 20 percent

In summary, the nonprofit sector represents a major and expanding part of the American economy and society (figures in the following list are for 1998 unless specified otherwise; source: www.independentsector.org/PDFs/inbrief.pdf):

- 1.6 million organizations;
- share of employment: 7.1 percent;
- share of national income: 6.1 percent;
- composition in terms of expenditure: 62 percent health (including hospitals); 17 percent education (including higher education); 13 percent human services; 1 percent religion; 2 percent arts and culture; 3 percent public, societal benefit (1996 figures from Boris and Steuerle, 1999);
- total revenues: nearly $670 billion;
- 70 percent of US households give to charity;
- 55 percent of Americans volunteer.

CANADA

Although the US is frequently seen as the prototype of the modern nonprofit sector, the nonprofit sector is important in other countries as well, and plays significant roles. In Canada, for example, the nonprofit sector appears to be larger—in relative terms—than in the US. In fact, as shown in Figure 4.13, nonprofits account for 8 percent of all entities in Canada (vs. 6 percent in the US). Furthermore, as shown in Figure 4.14, 8 percent of all workers are employed by nonprofits (vs. 7 percent in the US).[2]

The importance of nonprofit organizations in Canada goes well beyond their economic strength. For instance, the Health Charities Council of Canada (HCCC) represents national health charities that invest approximately CAN$300 million (see www.healthcharities.ca/

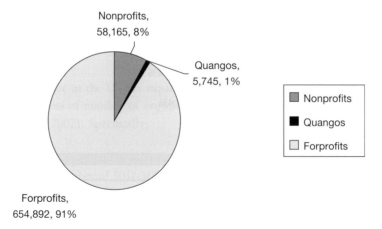

Figure 4.13 *Distribution of organizations across sectors, Canada, 1999*

Source: Based on McMullen and Brisbois 2003: 11.

Note: Does not include religious organizations.

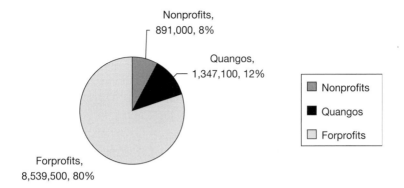

Nonprofits,
891,000, 8%

Quangos,
1,347,100, 12%

Forprofits,
8,539,500, 80%

Nonprofits

Quangos

Forprofits

Figure 4.14 *Distribution of employees across sectors, Canada, 1999*

Source: Based on McMullen and Brisbois 2003: 11.

Note: Does not include religious organizations.

en/science_research.htm) annually in health research. In addition, the HCCC was chosen by the Canadian government as one of two nonprofit organizations to host a capacity-building project and act as a voice for the voluntary health sector in national policy discussions. The Canadian government recognized the importance of the sector by approving, in 2000, its *Partnering for the Benefit of Canadians: Government of Canada-Voluntary Sector Initiative.*

However, over the last decades of the twentieth century, the nonprofit sector has been taking on more of the responsibility of these once government-sponsored social programs as various governments have cut programs and the social welfare system started to "unravel." Other shifts in Canadian social and economic life over the past few decades that have impacted the nonprofit sector include: changes in the characteristics of the Canadian family, in which two income earners are more typical with families relying more on professional child care services; the decline of fertility rates; increase in life expectancy; rising standards of living; increased leisure time; rising levels of educational attainment; and shifts in attitude among elected officials about the role the nonprofit sector (McMullen and Brisbois 2003). As a result, the nonprofit sector is not associated with any specific group of people or one type of service. As in the US, nonprofit organizations are active in the fields of health, education, culture, etc.

Most scholars, including Hall and Banting (2000), agree that government "retrenchment" in the 1990s has reduced many publicly funded community and social services, which has led to a renewed interest in the nonprofit sector in filling this service gap, while at the same time the government is not providing support to the sector. One of the watershed events of government "retrenchment" was the government's 1995 Canada Health and Social Transfer (CHST) program, which consolidated the Established Programs Financing Plan (EPFP) and the Canada Assistance Plan (CAP). Through CHST, the government remained committed to health and education, but, in actuality, this was a way for the government to reduce social spending and offset the deficit by "off-loading" discretionary power for program delivery to the provinces while replacing shared funding arrangements with block

79

grants (Beaudry 2002). The result of similar policies has left the nonprofit sector in Canada in a difficult position. More is expected of the sector while at the same time support and public sector funding has been cut.

On the positive side, charitable giving to nonprofit organizations seems to be increasing. In fact, nine out of ten Canadians made financial or in-kind contributions to nonprofits in 2000, up 3 percent from the figure in 1997 (Leslie 2002).[3] Direct financial contributions totaled CAN$4.94 billion, 11 percent more than the CAN$4.44 billion donated in 1997.

As in the US, religion received the highest value of donations, nearly half (49 percent) of all giving, followed by health organizations (20 percent) and social services (10 percent). However, in terms of the number of donations, health organizations rather than religious ones received the largest share (41 percent), with social services second (20 percent) and religion third (14 percent).

In terms of volunteering, on the other hand, fewer Canadians volunteered in 2000 than did in 1997 (McKeown, 2002: n. 2). In 2000, one in four Canadians (27 percent) worked on a volunteer basis for a nonprofit organization, down from 31 percent in 1997. Nevertheless, the average number of hours contributed per volunteer increased from 149 hours in 1997 to 162 hours in 2000.

As noted above, in 2000, the government established a joint, five-year $94.6 million initiative with the third sector called the Voluntary Sector Initiative (VSI). The goal is to help third sector organizations build capacity and improve their service capabilities. It remains to be seen, however, if this marks a new era of government–third sector partnership. From the objectives of the initiative and taking account of the scholars and officials involved with it, the future seems positive.

COMPARATIVE PERSPECTIVES[4]

As recently as the mid 1980s, the nonprofit sector was as much an "uncharted territory" for research and statistics in the rest of the world as it was in the US. However, in the intervening years the data situation has improved considerably, thanks to the efforts of individual researchers, umbrella organizations, and pioneering collaborative research efforts such as the Johns Hopkins Comparative Nonprofit Sector Project (Salamon and Anheier 1996; Salamon et al. 1999a; Salamon et al. 2003; www.jhu.edu/~ccss 2004). As a result, we can place the American nonprofit sector in a comparative perspective by focusing on a number of key dimensions used to describe the nonprofit sector in other countries and regions.

Size: wide variations among countries and regions

In the first place, as documented by the Johns Hopkins project, the nonprofit sector's scale differs considerably from place to place. The nonprofit sector workforce—both paid and volunteer—varies from a high of 14.4 percent of the economically active population in the Netherlands to a low of 0.4 percent in Mexico (see Figure 4.15) (Salamon et al. 2003). Interestingly, when using this measure of nonprofit sector size, the US ranks only fourth, behind the Netherlands, Belgium, and Ireland, among the thirty-five countries examined in the Johns Hopkins project.

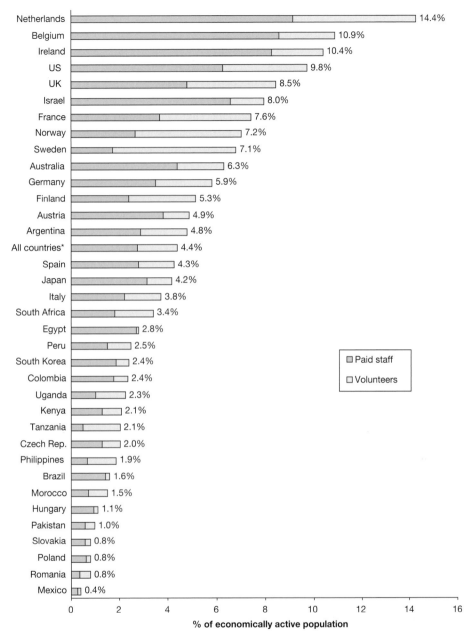

Country	%
Netherlands	14.4%
Belgium	10.9%
Ireland	10.4%
US	9.8%
UK	8.5%
Israel	8.0%
France	7.6%
Norway	7.2%
Sweden	7.1%
Australia	6.3%
Germany	5.9%
Finland	5.3%
Austria	4.9%
Argentina	4.8%
All countries*	4.4%
Spain	4.3%
Japan	4.2%
Italy	3.8%
South Africa	3.4%
Egypt	2.8%
Peru	2.5%
South Korea	2.4%
Colombia	2.4%
Uganda	2.3%
Kenya	2.1%
Tanzania	2.1%
Czech Rep.	2.0%
Philippines	1.9%
Brazil	1.6%
Morocco	1.5%
Hungary	1.1%
Pakistan	1.0%
Slovakia	0.8%
Poland	0.8%
Romania	0.8%
Mexico	0.4%

☐ Paid staff
☐ Volunteers

% of economically active population

* 35-country unweighted averages

Figure 4.15 Nonprofit workforce as percentage of economically active population, by country

Source: Based on Salamon *et al.* 2003.

Among the countries studied by the Johns Hopkins project, developed countries tend to have relatively larger nonprofit sectors than do less developed and transition countries. This is so even when the work of volunteers is factored in. In fact, the nonprofit workforce in the developed countries averages proportionally three times larger than that in the developing countries (7.4 percent vs. 1.7 percent of the economically active population) (Salamon *et al.* 2003).

Several reasons have been suggested to explain why the nonprofit sector in developing countries is generally smaller in economic terms than in developed market economies—a difference that seems to hold up despite likely underestimations due to the informal nature of organizational life in much of the developing world (Anheier and Salamon 1998a): low per capita income; low levels of government social welfare spending; the inability of the state to raise tax revenue to support nonprofit institutions; smaller urban middle classes; the legacy of authoritarian political regimes; and the different roles of religion in institution building (see Chapter 6 and, in particular: James 1987, 1989; Rose-Ackerman 1996).

In Central and Eastern Europe, the lower scale of nonprofit activities is largely attributable to the prolonged impact of state socialism. In particular, four factors seem to have discouraged a greater expansion of nonprofit activities after 1989: a centralization of society and polity that severely weakened civil society and reduced the capacity of citizens for self-organization; a lack of entrepreneurial talent and organizational skills; the absence of a working relationship between state and the nonprofit sector in the fields of education, social welfare, and health care; and weak legal frameworks for private nonprofit activity.

Composition: social welfare services dominate

The roles that nonprofit organizations play and the activities in which they engage are multiple—in the US and elsewhere. Figure 4.16 provides a rough approximation of the composition of this set of organizations by grouping organizations according to their principal activity and then assessing the level of effort each such activity absorbs, as measured by the share of nonprofit employment devoted to it. Generally speaking, nearly two-thirds of nonprofit activities in the thirty-two countries for which data were available are concentrated in service-oriented fields, in particular the traditional social welfare services of education (23 percent of the workforce), social services (19 percent), and health (14 percent) (Salamon *et al.* 2003). At the same time, at least one-third of the effort is absorbed by the sector's more expressive activities such as culture and recreation (19 percent), business and professional representation (7 percent), civic advocacy (4 percent), and environmental protection (2 percent).

While the dominance of service functions holds for most countries—both developed and developing, it is by no means uniform. For one thing, development and housing activities absorb a substantially higher proportion of the nonprofit workforce in developing countries than in developed ones (16 percent vs. 5 percent); and in African countries this figure reaches an average of 25 percent of the nonprofit workforce. This suggests a focus on community and economic development among nonprofit organizations in these developing regions, particularly in Africa.

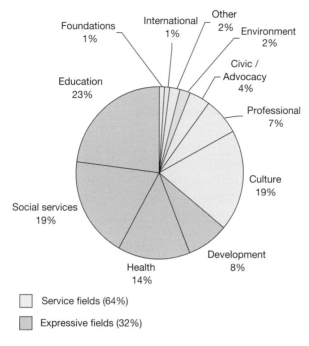

Figure 4.16 *Nonprofit workforce by field and type of activity*
Source: Based on Salamon *et al.* 2003.

Among developed and transition countries, as well, significant differences exist. For example, Western European nonprofit organizations tend to concentrate their efforts on providing social services, whereas nonprofits in the US, as well as Japan, Australia, and Israel, are concentrated in health services. Furthermore, in the Nordic countries and in the transition societies in Central Europe the expressive functions of the nonprofit sector are far more prominent than the service ones. This is most likely a reflection of the more dominant role of the state in providing social welfare services in these countries and, in the Scandinavian context, the vibrant heritage of citizen-based social movements and citizen engagement in advocacy, sports, and related expressive fields.

Volunteering

Not only do countries vary in the size and role of their nonprofit sectors, but they also vary in the extent to which these organizations rely on paid as opposed to volunteer labor. This reflects in part the important variations that exist across countries in notions of what a volunteer is, and these notions are closely related to aspects of culture and history (see Anheier *et al.* 2003a). In Anglo-Saxon countries, for example, the notion of voluntarism has its roots in Lockeian concepts of a self-organizing society outside the confines of the state, and is strongly associated with democratic concepts. In other countries, however, the notion of volunteering puts emphasis on communal service to the public good rather than on democracy.

A 1995 survey of volunteering in Europe found that 27 percent of the adult population in the nine countries studied (Belgium, Bulgaria, Denmark, Germany, Great Britain, Ireland, Netherlands, Slovakia, and Sweden) had volunteered in the previous year (Gaskin and Smith 1997). The level of volunteering among the adult population in the nine countries varied significantly from a high of 43 percent in the Netherlands to a low of 12 percent in Slovenia. The most common area of volunteering was sports and recreation (28 percent of all volunteers) followed by social services (17 percent) (Gaskin and Smith 1997: 28–31).

Researchers in the Johns Hopkins Comparative Nonprofit Sector Project mentioned earlier went a step further, collecting information not only on the number of volunteers but also on the number of hours volunteered, by field (Salamon *et al.* 2003). It was thus possible to express volunteer time in terms of the full-time equivalent workers that it represented. The researchers working with the Johns Hopkins project identified volunteer effort equivalent to 16.8 million full-time workers, or some 40 percent of the total 39.5 million full-time equivalent nonprofit jobs in the thirty-five countries covered (Salamon *et al.* 2003). Clearly, nonprofit organizations are able to mobilize significant human resources working on a voluntary basis. However, behind the average volunteer reliance level of 40 percent of the combined nonprofit workforce lies a wide range of variation: from a high of more than 75 percent in Sweden to a low of under 3 percent in Egypt.

Contrary to common belief, at the macro-level, paid nonprofit work does not seem to displace volunteers. In fact, there appears to be a general tendency for volunteer involvement to increase as paid staff involvement increases. Figure 4.17 shows that countries with liberal nonprofit regimes and larger nonprofit sectors such as the US, the UK, and Australia or the corporatist countries (France and Germany) also have larger volumes of volunteer input, whereas other countries or regions where the nonprofit sector is smaller (Africa or Eastern Europe) also rank lower in terms of volunteering (Salamon *et al.* 2003). This may reflect the fact that volunteering is a social, and not just an individual, act: people volunteer at least in part to join together with others. To be more effective, volunteers must be mobilized and their involvement structured, and this often requires permanent staff. This may also help to explain why the overall scale of volunteering tends to be higher on average in the developed countries (2.7 percent of the economically active population) than in the developing ones (0.7 percent).

Still, this pattern is by no means universal, as is also shown in Figure 4.17. The Nordic countries present the major deviations, with high levels of volunteering but relatively lower levels of paid staff. As noted previously, this reflects the strong social movement tradition in the Nordic countries.

The level of volunteer effort varies as well among different nonprofit activities. Thus, as a general rule, paid staff are even more heavily involved in the service functions of the nonprofit sector than are volunteers (72 percent vs. 52 percent respectively). Particularly noticeable is the role that volunteers play in cultural, recreational, civic, and environmental protection activities. Even in their service functions, moreover, volunteers appear to concentrate their efforts in different fields than paid staff do. In particular, volunteers focus disproportionately on social service and development activities. In fact, nearly half of all the work effort in these two fields is supplied by volunteers. Chapter 9 will address volunteering in more detail.

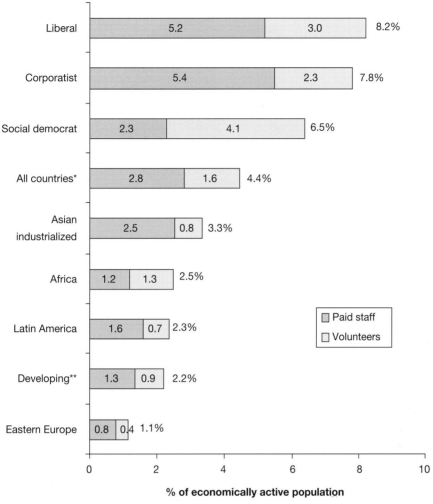

* 35 countries, unweighted
** Latin America, Africa, and other developing

Figure 4.17 *Civil society organization workforce as percentage of economically active population, by country cluster*

Source: Based on Salamon *et al.* 2003.

Revenue: a mixed economy

Among none of the thirty-two developed and developing countries on which comparable revenue data are now available is private philanthropy the principal source of income for the nonprofit sector. Rather, over half of all revenue on average comes from fees and charges (see Figure 4.18) (Salamon *et al.* 2003). By comparison, public sector payments amount to 35 percent of the total, and private philanthropy—from individuals, corporations, and foundations combined—a much smaller 12 percent.

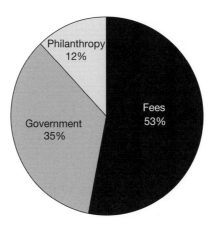

Figure 4.18 *Sources of revenue for nonprofit sector, average over 32 countries*
Source: Based on Salamon *et al.* 2003.

This basic pattern holds for most countries in Latin America, Africa, and Central and Eastern Europe, as well as the US, Australia, and Japan, in which fee income is a particularly important source of nonprofit sector. By contrast, public sector support—grants and third-party payments, primarily from public social insurance funds—is the most important source of income for the nonprofit sector in Western Europe. South Africa is the only developing country where fee income is less important than government funding, probably reflecting the post-apartheid policy of supporting nonprofit institutions as a means of strengthening civil society.

When volunteer time is factored into the equation and treated as a part of philanthropy, the picture of nonprofit sector finance changes significantly. In fact, philanthropy, whose share of total revenue increases from 12 percent to 30 percent, becomes the second most important source of nonprofit sector income, displacing public sector support (Salamon *et al.* 2003). This is an indication of how important contributions of time are to the support base of third sector institutions. This is particularly true in less developed regions, where financial resources are limited. But it also holds in the Nordic countries, where volunteer work is particularly marked, as well as in the US.

Growth

Since the 1980s in particular, both the scale and presence of the nonprofit sector appear to be expanding, and to be doing so quite substantially. One indicator of this is the growth in the recorded number of such organizations: the number of associations formed in France, for example, increased from approximately 10,000 per year in the 1960s and early 1970s to 40,000–50,000 per year in the 1980s and 1990s (Archambault 1996). Similarly striking growth was recorded in the number of nonprofit sector institutions in Italy in the 1980s, as new forms of "social cooperatives" took shape to supplement strained state social welfare institutions (Barbetta 1997). Developments in Central and Eastern Europe, and in much of the developing world, were even more dramatic since they often started from a smaller base (see, for example: Landim 1997; Fisher 1993; Ritchey-Vance 1991: 28–31).

The number of organizations is a notoriously imperfect variable through which to gauge the growth of this sector, however, since organizations vary so fundamentally in size and complexity. Looking at a different set of variables, the Johns Hopkins Comparative Nonprofit Sector Project documented a striking increase in the scale of the nonprofit sector in the early 1990s. Focusing on seven countries for which time series data could be assembled for 1990 and 1995 on a consistent range of organizations, researchers within the project found that employment within the nonprofit sector increased from an average of 3.5 percent of all nonagricultural employment in 1990 to 4.5 percent in 1995 (see Table 4.3) (Salamon *et al.* 1999a). Put somewhat differently, employment in the nonprofit sector grew by an average of 29 percent in these seven countries between 1990 and 1995 whereas overall employment grew by only 8 percent. At the same time, as also shown in Table 4.3, volunteering and membership rates expanded as well. In fact, despite talk of increased "bowling alone" in the US and the UK, all of the countries reported increases in volunteering and membership affiliation rates.

More generally, the growth in nonprofit employment evident in these figures was made possible not by a surge in private philanthropy or public sector support, but by a substantial increase in fee income. In fact, in these seven countries, fees accounted for 58 percent of the real growth in nonprofit income between 1990 and 1995 (Salamon *et al.* 1999a). By comparison, the public sector accounted for 34 percent and private giving a mere 8 percent. This means that the fee share of the total increased over time, whereas both the philanthropic and public sector shares declined.

There were certainly some exceptions to this general trend. In Israel, Hungary, and the UK, for example, the levels of public sector support for nonprofit organizations increased

Table 4.3 Indicators of nonprofit sector growth, 1990–5 (%)

Country	Indicator					
	Total paid non-agricultural employment		Percentage of population volunteering		Percentage of population holding memberships	
	1990	1995	1990	1995	1990	1995
Hungary	0.8	1.3	5	7	44	–
Japan	2.5	3.5	12	n/a	27	46
Sweden	2.5	2.6	36	51	84	91
Germany	3.7	4.9	13	26	64	77
UK	4.0	6.2	34	48	47	53
France	4.2	4.9	19	23	36	43
US	6.9	7.8	37	49	59	79
Average	3.5	4.5	24	29	53	65

Source: Based on Anheier and Salamon (forthcoming, in Powell and Steinberg).

substantially. In the four other countries, however, such support, while growing in absolute terms, declined as a share of total nonprofit revenue, with nonprofit organizations turning more extensively to fees and other commercial income. Moreover, this marketization trend was not only apparent in the US and Japan, where it has long been in evidence, but also in Western Europe. Thus in both France and Germany as well, fees and service charges grew faster than overall nonprofit income and thus boosted their share of total income.

The record of private giving during this period was varied. Some growth in private giving occurred in every country, and in at least three (Japan, Hungary, and France) the growth was substantial, exceeding 25 percent. In the case of Japan, this was probably due to the Kobe earthquake in 1995, which stimulated an outpouring of charitable activity, whereas in France the general increase in awareness of the nonprofit sector may have played a role. Because of the small base from which such growth is measured, however, it still did not add very much to overall nonprofit revenue, even in Japan where the percentage change exceeded 200 percent. Indeed, in five of these seven countries, the philanthropy share of total nonprofit income actually declined during this period.

SOCIAL CAPITAL

According to neo-Tocquevillian thinking, the nonprofit or voluntary sector is to form the social infrastructure of civil society. Nonprofits are to create as well as facilitate a sense of trust and social inclusion that is seen as essential for the functioning of modern societies (see for example Putnam 2000; Anheier and Kendall 2002; Halpern 1999; Offe and Fuchs 2002; Fukuyama 1995). As noted previously in Chapter 3, the link between nonprofits and social trust was first suggested in Putnam *et al.*'s 1993 book *Making Democracy Work*, where Putnam shows that dense networks of voluntary associations are the main explanation for Northern Italy's economic progress over the country's Southern parts.

Other works by Putnam (2000) and Fukuyama (1995) argue along lines that correlate participation and associations with social trust. Indeed, as Anheier and Kendall (2002) report, the relationship between interpersonal trust and membership in voluntary associations is a persistent research finding cross-nationally. The 1999–2000 wave of the European Values Survey[5] shows for twenty-eight of the thirty-two participating countries a positive and significant relationship between the number of associational memberships[6] held and interpersonal trust.[7] The summary of results from the European Values Survey, presented in Table 4.4, reveals a striking pattern. Respondents with three or more memberships were twice as likely to state that they trusted people than those holding no memberships. Overall, there is almost a linear relationship between increases in membership and the likelihood of trusting people.

Nor is this finding limited to the specific question about interpersonal trust used in the European Values Survey. In the US, a similar pattern emerges in relation to the question, "Do you think that most people would try to take advantage of you if they got a chance, or would you say that most people try to be fair?"[8] Results show that every second (46 percent) respondent with no memberships felt that people would try to take advantage, as opposed to every third (37 percent) for those with three memberships, and nearly every fourth (29 percent) for those with five and more memberships. Vice versa, 70 percent

Table 4.4 *Interpersonal trust by membership in voluntary associations (%)*

	Number of memberships held			
	None	One	Two	Three or more
Statements about trust				
Most people can be trusted	23	30	40	51
Cannot be too careful	77	70	60	49
Total N = 36,261	18,661	9,114	4,056	4,930
	(100%)	(100%)	(100%)	(100%)

Source: Based on data of *European Values Survey* 2000.

of respondents with five or more memberships felt that people tend to be fair, compared to only 54 percent of those holding no membership.[9]

The main argument is that participation in voluntary associations creates greater opportunities for repeated "trust-building" encounters among like-minded individuals, an experience that is subsequently generalized to other situations such as business or politics. Thus, the neo-Tocquevillian case for nonprofits is largely an argument based on the positive and often indirect outcomes of associationalism. The genius of Putnam (2000) was to link de Tocqueville's nineteenth-century description of a largely self-organizing, participatory local society to issues of social fragmentation and isolation facing American and other modern societies today (Hall 1992). This is what made his work so attractive to policymakers in the US and elsewhere: it identified a problem (erosion in social capital) and offered a solution from "the past" (voluntary associations, community), suggesting tradition and continuity to an unsettled presence. This connection "clicked" not only in the US (Sirianni and Friedland 2001), but also in Britain (e.g. the establishment of a social capital working group in the Cabinet Office) (Giddens 1999; Mulgan 2000) and countries such as Germany (Enquettekommission 2002).

Social capital at the local level

Los Angeles offers an instructive study for exploring the close link between social capital and nonprofit organizations. It is a vast and highly diverse metropolitan area of over 18 million people who are highly segregated by economic and ethnic lines.[10] Trust levels among LA citizens are lower than those for the US as a whole, and also lower than for other major cities (Table 4.5). Only 39 percent of Angelinos feel that most people can be trusted, while 53 percent fear that one cannot be too careful. For the national sample, we find that 46 percent are trusting, and 48 percent are not. When compared to other large cities in the US, LA shows the lowest trust levels except for Houston, Texas, where 36 percent of respondents indicated that most people can be trusted, yet 55 percent felt that one cannot be too careful.

89

Table 4.5 *Generalized trust, Los Angeles and the US (%)*

Can most people be trusted or can you not be too careful?	Los Angeles	US
Most people can be trusted	39	46
Depends	8	6
You cannot be too careful	53	48
Total	396	2,492
	(100%)	(100%)

Source: The Saguaro Seminar Social Capital Community Benchmark Survey 2000.

The low level of generalized trust is not uniform across the LA population. Trust levels among lower income groups and the less educated are lower than for the well-to-do and the better educated. Ethnicity plays an important role, however, which is closely associated with differences in income and education. For Latino respondents, who represent the largest ethnic group in LA, only 22 percent felt that people could be trusted, as did 27 percent of African American respondents, while 45 percent of Asian Americans and 54 percent of white respondents reported trusting others. Trust levels in LA, it seems, are closely linked with ethnic background, and two sets of groups seem to co-exist in the county: whites and Asians with relatively high trust levels close to the national average, and Latinos and African Americans with lower trust levels.

Trust levels are higher for longer-term residents of Los Angeles than for recent arrivals. For respondents having lived in Los Angeles less than five years, trust levels are 31 percent and for longer-term residents who have lived there five years or more, generalized trust is 43 percent, approaching the national average of 46 percent. Similarly, only 23 percent of recent arrivals trust people in their neighborhood, but 44 percent of longer-term members of the community do. Los Angeles has a higher proportion of respondents who have lived in the city for less than five years (10 percentage points higher than the national sample). Possibly, the low levels of trust in Los Angeles are related to this, and are a result of the transience of the population in Los Angeles and the large share of immigrants in the county's population. The higher trust levels among longer-term residents suggest that the experience of living in Los Angeles creates and reinforces rather than reduces trust in others. As we will see, these increases are greatest for those residents that participate in voluntary activities and become involved in community affairs.

Not only are trust levels lower among LA's population, so are levels of participation, involvement, and volunteering, although this profile is similar to that of other large cities. Nearly one-quarter of respondents are not involved in any nonprofit and community organizations; by contrast the figure for the US is just over 15 percent not involved. With a greater portion of "unaffiliated" among the community, the overall density of associational membership in LA is lower than that for the national sample. The unaffiliated, while present across all of LA's ethnic groups, are disproportionately found among the Latino community. Ten percent of white, 7 percent of African American, and 13 percent of Asian respondents are unaffiliated, as opposed to one in three Latinos (33 percent).

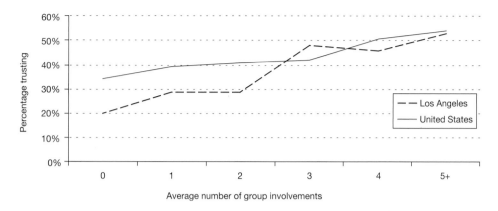

Figure 4.19 *Percent reporting "Most people can be trusted" by average number of group involvements, Los Angeles County and US, 2000*

Source: The Saguaro Seminar Social Capital Benchmark Survey 2000.

The interplay between involvement and trust is central for the healthy functioning of the region's civil society. As Figure 4.19 shows, generalized trust in others increases with the number of group involvements. Respondents with lower affiliation rates tend to report lower trust levels as well. Trust is lowest for those with no involvement in voluntary and community associations, and highest for those involved with five and more. The pattern for LA is similar to the US as a whole, but starts off at a lower level and then "catches up" for respondents with two and more involvements. The relationship between involvement and trust is similar across ethnic groups,[11] educational standards, age, and gender.

Involvement is also closely related to feelings of empowerment and the sense of having an impact on community affairs. Table 4.6 indicates that those respondents with higher levels of involvement are also more likely to feel that they can have an impact on making their community a better place to live (42 percent for LA, and 50 percent for the US), whereas those with no affiliations with voluntary associations report much lower levels of perceived impact (25 percent for LA, 24 percent for US).

Comparing social capital and nonprofit organizations: Sherman Oaks and Lynwood

Los Angeles is a region of extremes: the affluence of Beverly Hills on the one hand contrasts with the destitution of South-Central LA on the other. We looked into the correspondence between the spatial dispersion of a compound social capital indicator (created from the social involvement and social trust indicators discussed above) and the density of nonprofit organizations across Los Angeles County. Generally we found higher densities of nonprofit organizations where levels of social capital are higher. However, there are large areas in downtown LA and the main commercial core of the Wilshire Corridor, where high organizational densities coincide with low levels of social capital. Organizations in commercial areas are often headquarters and provide services elsewhere, and thus need less local social

Table 4.6 *Perceived individual impact by number of involvements, Los Angeles and the US (%)*

How much of an impact can you have to make your community a better place to live?

Los Angeles	0	1 to 2	3 to 5	6 or more
Big impact (%)	25	25	27	42
Moderate impact (%)	50	43	44	43
Small or no impact (%)	25	31	30	15
Total	95	99	101	110
	(100%)	(100%)	(100%)	(100%)
US	0	1 to 2	3 to 5	6 or more
Big impact (%)	24	30	36	50
Moderate impact (%)	43	43	45	38
Small or no impact (%)	33	26	19	13
Total	420	651	781	635
	(100%)	(100%)	(100%)	(100%)

Source: The Saguaro Seminar Social Capital Community Benchmark Survey 2000.

capital to develop, and may also contribute less to the social capital of the communities where they are based. It seems important to analyze the patterns of social capital and nonprofit organizations in more residential areas, comparing the presence of social capital and nonprofit organizations for rich and poor communities.

The two cities we chose for our comparison are not at the extremes of the spectrum, but they do differ considerably. Lynwood dates back to a farm settlement in 1810, but it was mostly urbanized by the beginning of the twentieth century. It is a lower-/lower-middle-class city, located in the southern part of LA, with 70,000 residents and a median annual household income of $36,000. Sherman Oaks dates back to 1911, but it was mostly developed after 1940. It is a middle-/upper-middle-class suburb in the San Fernando Valley, and the median household income of its 53,000 residents is $62,000 a year.

As Map 4.1 shows, Sherman Oaks has a very high level of social capital, and a correspondingly large number of nonprofit organizations. We counted sixty-six nonprofit organizations in Sherman Oaks (including organizations within a quarter-mile buffer around it, which are very likely to serve Sherman Oaks residents as well), which translates to 12.3 organizations per 10,000 population. By contrast, in Lynwood levels of social capital were among the lowest in the county, and correspondingly the number of nonprofit organizations was low: 17 organizations in Lynwood (plus the quarter-mile buffer)—a ratio of 2.4 organizations per 10,000 population.

Since Ventura Boulevard in Sherman Oaks is a predominantly commercial area, it can be argued that most of the nonprofits there do not necessarily serve local residents and that

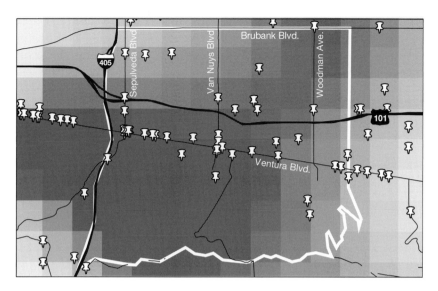

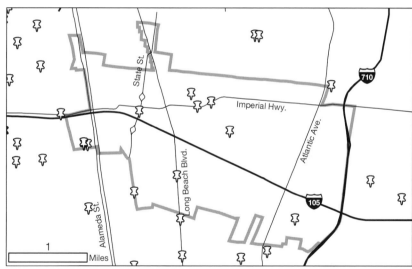

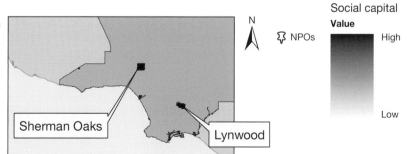

Map 4.1 *Social capital and nonprofit organizations: comparing two cities in the Los Angeles metropolis*

Source: Center for Civil Society, UCLA.

organizations located there should be excluded from the comparison. Yet, even after keeping only those Ventura Boulevard nonprofits that are unequivocally local, the prevalence of nonprofits in Sherman Oaks greatly exceeds that in Lynwood. Also, Imperial Highway in Lynwood is the central commercial street of the area, but it is not as filled with nonprofits as Ventura Boulevard.

Thus, comparing social capital and nonprofit organizations in LA with those of the US, as well as comparing different cities within LA County on these issues contributes to our understanding of social capital, nonprofit organizations, and their relationship with each other and with other factors, such as ethnicity, poverty, age of community, and land use types. It is clear that sociological and demographic factors play an important role in the development of social capital and nonprofit organizations and that there is strong link between them.

REVIEW QUESTIONS

- What are some of the major contours of the scale and revenue structure of the nonprofit sector in the US, and how do they differ from other countries?

- What are some of the reasons for the reported growth of the nonprofit sector?

- What policy implications follow from the observed relationship between social capital and the nonprofit sector at the local level?

REFERENCES AND RECOMMENDED READING

Salamon, L. M. (1999) *America's Nonprofit Sector: A Primer*, 2nd edition, New York: Foundation Center.

Salamon, L. M., Sokolowski, S. W., and List, R. (2003) *Global Civil Society: An Overview*, Baltimore, MD: Johns Hopkins Center for Civil Society Studies.

Weitzman, M. S., Jalandoni, N. T., Lampkin, L. M., and Pollak, T. H. (2002) *The New Nonprofit Almanac and Desk Reference: The Essential Facts and Figures for Managers, Researchers, and Volunteers*, 1st edition, San Francisco, CA: Jossey-Bass.

Chapter 5

Dimensions II: specific fields

This chapter introduces the nonprofit sector in the context of selected fields of activity and examines in particular how nonprofit organizations compare in scale and scope to the other two major institutional complexes of modern society: the public sector and the market. The chapter also identifies a number of challenges and opportunities facing nonprofit organizations in each field of activity.

LEARNING OBJECTIVES

Having presented the major contours of the nonprofit sector in the US and internationally, it is useful to take a closer look at the empirical profile of some of its major component parts such as health care, education, social services, and culture and the arts. After considering this chapter, the reader should:

- have a basic understanding of the nonprofit sector's role in the mixed economy of care and service provision in selected fields;
- understand the position of nonprofit organizations in different fields;
- have a sense of the challenges and opportunities facing nonprofit organizations in particular fields.

KEY TERMS

Some of the key terms introduced or reviewed in this chapter are:

- advocacy
- Charitable Choice
- community development
- faith-based organization
- lobbying
- third-party payers

INTRODUCTION

So far we have looked at the US nonprofit sector in the aggregate only. Of course, there are major differences across different fields such as health care, education, social services, and arts and culture. The brief summaries below demonstrate that the nonprofit sector does not exist in isolation from other institutions in society but is part of a mixed economy of care and service provision, typically alongside forprofit and public entities.

The health care field, which we will consider first, is a good illustration of how different sectors or actors are called upon to meet social and health care needs. Based on Roemer (1993), we can distinguish three types of health care system:[1]

- *Entrepreneurial health care systems* are characterized by limited roles allocated to government in the provision and financing of services, an emphasis on private provision, and the absence of compulsory health insurance coverage. Even though government takes on some responsibility, private insurance and provision remain dominant. The US offers the best and perhaps only example of this type of system among developed market economies.
- *Welfare-oriented regimes*, such as the national health insurance schemes of Germany, Japan, France, and Italy, allocate greater overall responsibility to the public sector and allow for plurality in both health care financing and provision. Typically, health care coverage depends on employment-based contribution schemes primarily, and on direct government funds only secondarily. As part of a general welfare approach, health care is closely linked to other benefits, in particular social services.
- *Comprehensive health care systems* allocate the largest share of responsibility to government. Financing of health care is tax-based, with service provided by public health bodies such as the National Health Service in the UK or the system of local county councils in Sweden. The choice of provider is usually somewhat limited, and health care access and coverage nearly universal.

In the following presentation of different fields, it is useful to keep in mind that the US generally tends to follow an entrepreneurial approach to public policy, with limited government involvement, and uses a multiplicity of organizational forms, funding schemes, and providers, loosely coordinated by various federal, state, and local public agencies. Specifically, we will examine nonprofit activities in:

- health care
- social services
- education
- housing
- arts and culture
- civic participation and advocacy
- religion.

96

Because of their unique role within the nonprofit sector as well as society, foundations are the subject of Chapter 14, and international issues are treated in Chapter 15.

SPECIFIC FIELDS

Health care

The health care industry in the US accounts for 14 percent of GDP. Not only does the health care industry represent a major part of the economy as a whole, it is, in both relative and absolute terms, larger than that of any other country. Only Switzerland (11 percent) and Germany (11 percent) come close to the share of GDP allocated to health care (OECD 2003). Health care is also the most important part of the US nonprofit sector, accounting for nearly two-thirds of its total operating expenditure, with 5.8 million paid and volunteer workers (Salamon 2002a).

However, the share of nonprofit organizations varies across different parts of the health care industry. In the late 1990s, subsectors of the health care industry in which nonprofit organizations were especially prominent included: outpatient mental health clinics (1,007 nonprofit vs. 322 forprofit entities); hospices (1,365 vs. 593); community health centers (641 vs. zero); multi-service mental health organizations (590 vs. 69 forprofits and 211 public); residential facilities for mentally handicapped children (590 vs. 69); and acute care hospitals (3,000 vs. 797 forprofits and 1,260 public) (Gray and Schlesinger 2002).

Medicare and Medicaid programs pay for a combined 28 percent of all medical care (Gray and Schlesinger 2002), and overall, as Figure 5.1 shows, total government expenditure accounts for just under half of all health care spending in the US (Salamon 1999). However, for hospital care and nursing homes, the share is much higher (60 percent or more). In other words, even though the role of the public sector is limited in terms of actual provision, it is a major contributor to health care finance. Private payments make up 49 percent of the total, accounting for an increasing share over time. By contrast, the role of philanthropy and charitable donations, while 4 percent overall, never reaches above 7 percent for any of the health subsectors.

The US health care industry is undergoing profound changes that are triggered by a complex set of factors such as demographic shifts, technological developments, and health care policies. They affect both the financing and the provision of services, and the access and choices different population groups have, and at what cost. With no system equivalent to national health care insurance in place, the US has a complex mix of various governmental finance mechanisms, such as Medicare and Medicaid, and a multitude of competing "third-party payers," such as insurance companies, health maintenance organizations (HMOs), and managed care organizations.

When the system of third-party payment developed in the mid 1960s, only rudimentary monitoring mechanisms for cost control were put in place. As a result, health care providers, whether nonprofit, forprofit or public, faced major "cost disease problems," and continued to pass on cost increases to third-party purchasers, and ultimately to either government or consumers. Since the 1980s, however, more comprehensive oversight and accountability

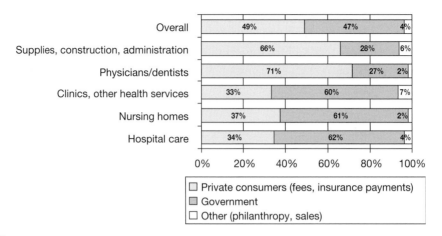

Figure 5.1 *Sources of health care spending, 1996*

Source: Salamon 1999: 80. © The Foundation Center. Used by permission of the Foundation Center, 79 Fifth Ave, New York, NY 10003, www.fdncenter.org.

methods have taken hold, and new organizational forms such as HMOs have come into being. This has had several consequences for the actual health care providers: for example, they lost much of their power to pass along cost increases. What is more, care and cost decisions were increasingly turned into management decisions and decided by those with no direct health care role; as a result, obtaining payment for health care service became a more complex administrative process, thereby increasing transaction costs, and reducing the professional autonomy of physicians. Finally, the ability of health care providers to finance community activities and pro bono treatment of the uninsured from patient dollars weakened.

Changes in health care financing also affect investments. Health care requires large capital investments for equipment, new technologies, and start-up costs. Since the 1980s, government funds and philanthropic contributions have been accounting for less of both operating and investment revenue. As a result, nonprofit health care organizations rely more on fees and charges for operating costs, and on the financial markets for investment funds. However, financial markets react to profit expectations and rarely value community service and treating the uninsured as an indicator of creditworthiness, which puts nonprofit health care organizations at a distinct disadvantage.

In certain health care fields, such as dialysis centers and rehabilitation hospitals, forprofit providers have expanded more quickly than nonprofit organizations since the mid 1980s, a process that gathered momentum in the 1990s. Nonprofits have to compete not only with profit-oriented management and marketing styles, but also with the advent of large investor-owned facilities and the possibility of takeovers. Evidence also suggests that investor-owned health care corporations have been more effective in lobbying for favorable public policies (Gray and Schlesinger 2002). Prominent examples are legislation for repealing tax exemptions under certain conditions to make it easier for health care businesses to acquire smaller nonprofits, and the 2003 health care reform legislation, which encourages a greater role for forprofit hospitals.

98

Indeed, the rationale for tax exemption of nonprofit health organizations has been increasingly challenged in recent years. This is due, to some extent, to findings that have shown only modest and frequently inconsistent differences between forprofit and nonprofit hospitals regarding the amount of uncompensated care provided (Clotfelter 1992; Gray and Schlesinger 2002). In fact, a congressional study (General Accounting Office 1990) questioned the value of their tax exemption relative to the amount of charity care provided. All this has led to allegations made by forprofit hospitals of unfair competition and calls for more stringent accountability measures.

Nonprofits have responded to these and other challenges in three ways. First, they have tried to emulate the behavior of forprofit health care providers to the greatest extent possible. Second, they have adapted to the changed accountability requirements by changing organizational practise and culture, thereby losing some of their professional autonomy to insurance companies and similar financial intermediaries. Finally, they have sought to maintain a distinctive nonprofit role, in particular in terms of charitable and community service.

Social services

To some extent the situation in the social services is similar to developments in the health care field, although the former is less "corporate" and includes many smaller establishments and associations. In fact, the social services field includes three general types of organizations:

- *informal organizations* that lack legal status and depend on small cash and in-kind donations and volunteers; examples are Alcoholics Anonymous, soup kitchens, and informal mutual assistance networks among poor immigrant communities;
- *traditional agencies* that have a diversified base of services and funding, e.g. the Salvation Army, YWCA, American Red Cross, etc.;
- *recent additions* to respond to current social needs and issues; some organizations are small, others are large; examples include domestic violence counseling and protection, rape crisis assistance, HIV/AIDS groups or community care networks, etc.

Social service nonprofits account for 17.5 percent of nonprofit sector paid employment and for 12 percent of total operating expenditures (Weitzman *et al.* 2002).[2] As Table 5.1 shows, individual and family services and child day care make up the largest share of nonprofit social service establishments,[3] with over 60 percent of all agencies. In terms of employment, however, five fields are important: individual and family services, with about one-third of all jobs; child day care; job training and rehabilitation; residential care; home health and social care—each with between 12 and 14 percent of all nonprofit social service jobs. Between 1977 and 1997, employment in the nonprofit social service industry nearly tripled, from 676,473 in 1977 to 1,969,586 in 1997. If we combine volunteers and paid employees, the number increases to approximately 2.6 million employees (1998 estimates from Salamon 2002a).

The social services field, like health care, is a mixed economy of private and public actors; and like health care, it relies heavily on government funding. Overall, nonprofit social

99

Table 5.1 *Nonprofit social services, 1997*

Service field	Establishments		Employment	
	Number	%	Number	%
Child day care	18,099	18.0	239,981	12.2
Individual and family services	42,427	42.2	692,454	35.2
Job training and vocational rehabilitation	5,668	5.6	269,738	13.7
Residential care	10,869	10.8	240,732	12.2
Miscellaneous social services	15,093	15.0	143,281	7.3
Home health and social care	3,375	3.4	267,484	13.6
Family planning	1,365	1.4	13,820	0.7
Outpatient mental health and substance abuse centers	3,646	3.6	102,096	5.2
Total	100,542	100.0	1,969,586	100.0

Source: US Census Bureau, *Census of Service Industries* (as reported by Salamon 2002a: 155). Used by permission of The Brookings Institution.

services in the US receive 37 percent of their funding from various public sector sources, 43 percent from earned income (fees, dues, and charges), and 20 percent from private giving. Indeed, the social services field has among the highest shares of philanthropic contribution, and it is also one of the major areas in which people volunteer. However, private donations to social service organizations have stagnated in relative terms in recent years, while the number of nonprofits seeking funding has tripled. Many agencies have increased their private fund-raising efforts by hiring professional development employees and appointing board members with fund-raising experience. What is more, organizations are also expanding ways to increase fees and earned income and actively pursue government contract opportunities.

Like health care, the social services field is undergoing major changes, with frequent calls for greater accountability and improved management. Policymakers and foundation executives alike have encouraged nonprofit executives to become more "entrepreneurial" and to diversify their funding base, typically by seeking income-generating services to support charitable activities. Not surprisingly, boundaries between traditional social services and other service activities have become blurred. A good example is a Boston child welfare agency that took over a forprofit health care management firm to help finance its child service provision.

As part of "reinventing government," state and local public agencies have restructured their approach away from direct cash benefits to services provided by intermediaries such as nonprofit organizations. This has also meant a diversification in government support for nonprofits, such as tax credits, loans, and tax-exempt bonds. The 1996 welfare reforms gave states more flexibility in spending federal allocations for social and welfare services. Moreover, state governments, often with the support of federal officials and nonprofit executives, refinanced social services by tapping into other sources of federal financing, especially Medicaid, the federal/state health insurance program for the poor and disabled.

The 1996 Welfare Reform Act encouraged state and local officials to use faith-based organizations to provide welfare-related services. Faith-based organizations, usually defined as organizations with a clear religious creed, mission, or religious institution, have received much attention due to policies such as the 1996 Charitable Choice provision and President Bush's Faith-Based Initiative. These initiatives assume that FBOs have a significant and largely unrealized potential to combat social problems at the local level. As a result, rules about government contracting with non-religious bodies are to be increasingly extended to religious organizations. Proponents of the initiatives argue that FBOs have a special role to play in enhancing the American welfare system, which will allow for a more compassionate and thorough confrontation of the unresolved problems of poverty and related social ills such as drugs, teen pregnancy, and family deterioration (Olasky 1992). Proponents also argue that FBOs have been historically discriminated against in the allocation of government funds for nonprofit human service provision. Opponents of these measures point to the lack of empirical evidence to warrant the claims that FBOs are indeed better than other service providers. What is more, opponents believe that funding explicitly religious organizations violates the constitutionally mandated separation of church and state (Chaves 2003).

Education

Education is the second most economically significant field of nonprofit activity in the US, following only health care. In fact, educational activities, including elementary, secondary, and higher education, as well as research, account for about 18 percent of total nonprofit operating expenditures and revenue and nearly 22 percent of nonprofit paid employment[4] (Weitzman et al. 2002).

The 27,400 nonprofit elementary and secondary schools educate approximately 11 percent of all students in the US between kindergarten and 12th grade. Of these more than 5 million private school students, 83 percent attend religious, mostly Catholic, schools (Stewart et al. 2002).

Nonprofit institutions play a larger role in the US market for higher or post-secondary education. Nearly 1,700 (42 percent) of the more than 4,000 higher education institutions in the US are nonprofit. These institutions have a combined enrollment of 3 million, representing 20 percent of all students enrolled (Stewart et al. 2002).

More so than in either health or social services, nonprofit organizations providing education and research services are heavily dependent on fees and other forms of commercial income, which account for 65 percent of revenue (Salamon 1999; see also Figure 4.7). In the case of higher education, in particular, nonprofit institutions receive some 70 percent of their total revenue from fees, primarily tuition and related fees (see Figure 5.2). This heavy reliance on tuition to cover escalating costs due to "competitive battles among elite institutions for the best faculty, top students, and research funding, as well as library costs and the heavy expense of technology" has made private schooling less and less affordable for middle-class families (Stewart et al. 2002: 114).

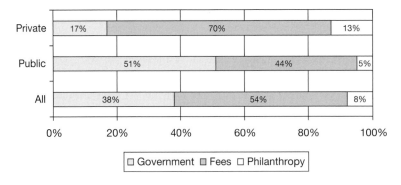

Figure 5.2 *Revenue of public and private higher educational institutions, 1994/95*
Source: Salamon 1999: 99. © The Foundation Center. Used by permission of the Foundation Center, 79 Fifth Ave, New York, NY 10003, www.fdncenter.org.

Nonprofit institutions of higher learning face a number of other challenges to their financial stability. Forprofit entities, including virtual universities and franchise-based institutions, such as the University of Phoenix, compete for part-time adult students. Moreover, private nonprofit universities must compete more and more with public universities for fund-raising dollars. As nonprofit universities have done traditionally, public entities have increasingly sought to generate additional revenue by seeking alumni as well as corporate and foundation donations.

Elementary and secondary schools face similar sets of challenges, in particular rising costs due to technology and faculty recruitment in the face of teacher shortages. However, recent public school reform efforts, including vouchers and charter schools, are opening new opportunities.

Housing and community development

Before discussing the distinctive position of nonprofit organizations in the field of housing and community development, a few definitions are in order. In the first place, housing development and management is a large industry of which nonprofits constitute a small niche. The industry is stratified along three dimensions: (i) ownership status (owner-occupied vs. rental); (ii) type of structure (single family, duplex, multi-family); and (iii) subsidy status (housing available at market rate, public, or assisted). Nonprofits engage primarily in assisted housing. In the second place, whereas housing refers to basic "bricks and mortar," community development is a far less tangible concept. It involves assets— including physical, human, intellectual, social, financial, and political assets—and the development of such assets in a community that will generate a stream of benefits over time. According to Ferguson and Dickens (1999), "Community development is asset building that improves the quality of life among residents of low- to moderate-income communities, where communities are defined as neighborhoods or multi-neighborhood areas" (as cited in Vidal 2002: 222).

In addition to the numerous small community development associations, there are at least three types of nonprofit housing organizations: (i) community development corporations

(CDCs), which engage not just in housing development but also in general community improvement; (ii) nonprofit housing providers that operate across a larger region (e.g. the Metropolitan Boston Housing Partnership), or in many communities across the country (e.g. Habitat for Humanity); and (iii) nonprofit financial intermediaries, such as the Local Initiatives Support Corporation (LISC) and the Enterprise Foundation, which also provide training, technical assistance, and other types of support to CDCs. A 1998 census of CDCs (www.ncced.org) counted some 3,600 spread throughout the US. CDCs seem to be widespread in Canada as well.

As alluded to above, the segment of nonprofit focus, i.e. assisted housing, accounts for only a modest share of the entire housing development industry. It is estimated that since the late 1960s, "nonprofits have developed about 14 percent of the housing built or preserved with federal support . . . Since assisted housing units are a relatively modest portion of the nation's overall housing, nonprofits are responsible for less than 2 percent of the nation's housing stock, despite the dramatic growth in the past two decades" (Vidal 2002). Nevertheless, the 550,000 units of affordable housing created through CDCs and the units built by area-wide nonprofit housing organizations such as BRIDGE in California (8,500 units), Mercy Housing in California (more than 10,000), Habitat for Humanity (50,000 in the US alone), and organizations associated with the Roman Catholic Church (more than 50,000) fill a gap in the dwindling supply of housing for low income residents. Furthermore, nonprofit organizations, especially CDCs, also engage in housing renovation and improvement, housing counseling, strengthening of community and neighborhood associations, financing, job creation, and workforce development.

Housing and community development nonprofit organizations—especially those involved in housing—are, of necessity, textbook examples of public–private partnerships. Few, if any, nonprofits control sufficient assets on their own to develop and maintain housing offered at below market rates, much less do this in addition to providing other community development and support services. As a result, nonprofits involved in housing and community development rely for their revenue on public sector support (37 percent of the total) as well as private philanthropy (20 percent), with the remainder (43 percent) derived from fees, including membership fees, rents paid, and similar fees (Salamon 1999).

In fact, nonprofits are the only sponsors eligible for certain federal government funding and receive the majority of other federal funding for housing and related programs. These include Section 202 (elderly housing), funds for housing services for homeless persons, the HOME program, and the low income housing tax credit (LIHTC). Two programs, HOME and LIHTC, set aside 15 percent and 10 percent of their funds respectively for nonprofits.

Furthermore, many banks and other financial institutions use CDCs and other nonprofits as vehicles to fulfill their Community Reinvestment Act requirements. Most channel financial resources and expertise to nonprofit organizations in the communities where they have branches or other types of operations. Some even create their own CDCs, as did SunTrust and National City Bank.

Such partnerships and multiple objectives present a number of organizational challenges. In the first place, in large part because of the funding mix, nonprofit developers are involved with much more complex financial arrangements than their forprofit counterparts. What is more, the specialized skills required to develop and manage assisted housing developments make these nonprofits hard organizations to staff and put them constantly at risk of becoming alienated from the communities they are seeking to serve.

In addition to these basic organizational challenges, nonprofits also face an increase in forprofit competition. Given the limits often inherent to nonprofit organizations, i.e. lack of capital, broader mission, etc., it will be hard to compete without the preferential treatment that has been traditionally provided by the public sector. At the same time, shifts in public policy from supply-side subsidies (which support housing production) to demand-side subsidies (i.e. Section 8 vouchers and certificates) create greater uncertainties for developers in general and for nonprofits in particular because they already tend to be more vulnerable.

Arts and culture

The field of arts and culture comprises an expansive industry as well, especially if Hollywood movies, television, and pop music are included along with, for example, visual art galleries, artists' organizations, museums, performing arts organizations in dance, theater, opera, music and historical societies, and cultural heritage organizations. But nonprofits have a special role in this industry. Art, when associated with forprofit corporations, sponsored by forprofit companies, or originating from Hollywood, is viewed as mere entertainment and not taken seriously as true or meaningful "art." When associated with government, art is viewed as bland, censored, and not fully expressing the perspectives of the artist. However, art from the community channeled through nonprofit organizations is seen as "true" art and the voice of the respective communities.

In relation to the rest of the nonprofit sector, the field of arts and culture is a relatively small one. The 2.1 million workers employed by nonprofit arts and culture organizations represent less than 2 percent of total nonprofit employment in the US (Weitzman *et al.* 2002). These organizations account for about 2 percent of all nonprofit revenue and 2 percent of operating expenditures, but attract 3 percent of individual charitable giving dollars and account for 5 percent of volunteer assignments (Weitzman *et al.* 2002).

Nonprofit activity in the arts and culture field differs significantly in many ways from the traditional welfare service fields described above. More specifically, most of the estimated 19,500–24,000 nonprofit arts, culture, and humanities organizations in the US[5] rely relatively little on government sources of funding and more on private sources, both commercial and philanthropic. In fact, Americans for the Arts estimates that nonprofit arts organizations, on average, receive 50 percent of their income from ticket and related sales, 45 percent from private philanthropy, including individual donations, corporate support, and foundations, and just over 5 percent from government, mostly local government (as cited in Wyszomirski 2002).[6] These figures do vary by type of organization, with museums receiving some 20 percent of their revenues from the public sector and theaters taking in as little as 8 percent from government sources (Listening Post Project 2003).

Given this revenue mix, most arts and culture nonprofits seem to be less sensitive to federal public policy shifts (e.g. the reduction of funding for the National Endowment for the Arts and the National Endowment for the Humanities after 1995). However, state and

104

local funding priorities are relevant. Fortunately, state and local government funding for the arts has been on the rise, although the differences among state arts agency appropriations range from $5.12 per person in Hawaii to $0.24 per person in Texas (Wyszomirski 2002).

Private giving for the arts is rising following decreases in individual giving and foundation dollars throughout the 1990s. Total contributions to the arts increased from $10 billion in 1995 to $11.1 billion in 1999. The proportion of charitable donations benefiting the arts increased from 9 percent of total charitable giving in 1995 to 11 percent in 1998. Foundation giving ranged from 12 percent of total foundation giving in 1995 to 13 percent in 1999 (Wyszomirski 2002).

Despite these relatively positive trends in government funding and private giving, arts and culture organizations face continued pressure to expand earned income and focus more on cultivating new audiences and new donors. Many organizations have also begun to invest their efforts in ancillary activities such as restaurants or gift shops. Although in theory commercial activities are intended to cross-subsidize an organization's mission, such activity often becomes an end in itself, diverting attention from artistic objectives.

Aside from these funding challenges, nonprofit arts and culture agencies face a leadership challenge (see Chapter 7 for more on leadership). Since many arts organizations rose to prominence in the 1960s and 1970s, their long-standing directors are aging. The challenge is to recruit new leaders who can cope with the multiple administrative concerns of marketing and audience development, fund-raising, programming, facilities, and volunteer management. To cope with this challenge, many arts organizations have instituted leadership programs.

Civic participation and advocacy

In a sense, the field of civic participation and advocacy represents the essence of civil society and the nonprofit sector. Organizations such as Mothers Against Drunk Driving (MADD), Kiwanis, the National Association for the Advancement of Colored People (NAACP), and the National Organization for Women (NOW) provide opportunities for individual citizens to become involved in community and public affairs and, in most cases, give voice to minority or particularistic interests. Providing opportunities for involvement builds civil society and social capital (see Chapter 3), while giving voice is one of the key roles nonprofit organizations are expected to play in society (see Chapter 8).

As might be expected, many nonprofit organizations promote civic participation and engage in some form of advocacy work, but few have these activities as their primary focus. In fact, civic, social, and fraternal organizations combined account for only 3 percent of total nonprofit operating expenditures and 4 percent of total nonprofit employment. "Public and societal benefit" organizations attract just 2 percent of private individual giving dollars, but nearly 5 percent of volunteer assignments (Weitzman *et al.* 2002).

For organizations focusing on advocacy as well as other more service-oriented nonprofits, there are legal restrictions to the advocacy work of those having 501(c)(3) status. As such, the distinction between advocacy and lobbying, in particular, is significant:

- Advocacy, as defined by Bruce Hopkins (1992: 32), is: "the act of pleading for or against a cause, as well as supporting or recommending a position . . . Advocacy is active espousal of a position, a point of view, or a course of action." This activity can be on behalf of individuals or groups such as Mothers Against Drunk Driving, or the NRA, and is carried out by both 501(c)(3) and (c)(4) organizations.
- Lobbying is a specialized form of advocacy and is described by Hopkins (1992) as largely the domain of 501(c)(4) organizations that seek to impact the policy- and issue-making functions of an administrative, regulatory, or legislative body.

Nonprofits can engage in unlimited advocacy involving education, research, and dissemination of information about an issue, but they are permitted to lobby only on a limited basis. Currently, the lobby limit is set at 20 percent of the first $500,000 of exempt purpose expenditures up to a cap of $1 million on total lobbying expenditures (Alliance for Justice 2000 as quoted in Boris and Krehely 2002). The fine line drawn between advocacy and lobbying ultimately appears to depend on the federal administration in office (Jenkins, forthcoming).

What is more, it appears that most organizations stay well within the limits. As shown in Table 5.2, of the 1,725 entities classified as "civil rights, social action, advocacy" organizations, only 115 reported any lobbying expenditures and these amounted to only 1.2 percent of their total expenses, or an average of less than $23,000 per organization. Not surprisingly, environmental nonprofits spend the next largest share (0.79 percent) of total expenses on lobbying. While organizations in the health and educational industries invest the largest dollar amounts in lobbying ($53.6 million and $24.4 million, respectively), these activities take up only a tiny portion of their budgets.

A crucial challenge for organizations in the civic participation and advocacy field is maintenance and development of their membership base. Organizations such as NOW and NAACP depend for a significant portion of their revenue on membership fees and other types of earned income. According to estimates by Salamon (1999), fees account for 57.7 percent of the total revenue of nonprofit advocacy organizations, with only 5.1 percent from government sources and 37 percent from individual giving.[7] The challenge is even greater for the growing number of "professional social movements" and "movements without members," which advocate broad public interests and do little to promote civic engagement during an era in which civic participation and trust in public institutions has declined (Jenkins, forthcoming).

Religion

Religion is the one field of activity that resides entirely within the nonprofit sector, with no comparable activity conducted by the forprofit or governmental sectors. Even so, and even with the separation of church and state, religious congregations do not exist in isolation of other institutions in society. What is more, as we will see below, religious congregations and related faith-based organizations are being called on today to take on an even larger role in attending to social needs in the broader community, well beyond the spiritual needs of their own members.

Table 5.2 Total lobbying and organizational spending, 1998

Type of organization	Number of organizations reporting	Total organizations reporting (%)	Number of organizations with lobbying expenses (%)	Total organizations with lobbying expenses	Organizations in category that lobby (%)	Total lobbying expenses Amount (1998 US$)	As a percentage of total expenses	Total lobbying expenses (%)
Arts, culture, and humanities	23,935	10.5	184	5.2	0.8	5,878,446	0.24	4.4
Education	37,928	16.7	576	16.4	1.5	24,411,841	0.07	18.1
Environmental and animal related	7,497	3.2	345	9.8	4.6	12,418,277	0.79	9.2
Health	33,623	14.7	934	26.7	2.8	53,619,362	0.06	39.7
Human services	78,448	34.4	824	23.5	1.1	15,969,938	0.23	11.7
International, foreign affairs, and national security	2,118	0.9	59	1.7	2.8	3,555,999	0.38	2.6
Public, societal benefit Civil rights, social action, advocacy	1,725	0.8	115	3.3	6.7	2,602,109	1.2	1.9
Community improvement, capacity building	9,687	4.3	138	3.9	1.4	4,186,015	0.47	3.1
Philanthropy and voluntarism	12,525	5.5	102	2.9	0.8	2,645,775	0.18	2
Research institutes/services	2,333	1.0	77	2.2	3.3	3,706,028	0.15	2.7
Public, society benefit, multi-purpose, and other	1,827	0.8	77	2.2	4.2	3,407,385	0.64	2.5
Religion-related, spiritual development	11,477	5.0	28	0.8	0.2	1,619,769	0.1	1.2
Mutual or membership benefit organizations	672	0.3	5	0.14	0.7	463,616	0.01	0.34
Unknown	3,936	1.7	51	1.5	1.3	743,468	1.5	0.55
Total	227,731	100.0	3,515	100.0	1.5	135,228,028	0.08	100

Source: NCCS Core files 1999 (Boris and Krehely 2002: 306). Used by permission of The Brookings Institution.

Table 5.3 *Denominational distribution of US congregations, 1998 (%)*

Denominational affiliation	Attendees in congregations with listed affiliation	Congregations with listed affiliation
Roman Catholic Church	29	6
Baptist conventions/denominations	18	25
None	10	18
Methodist denominations	10	14
Luther/Episcopal	10	9
Reformed tradition	8	8
Other Christian	6	9
Pentecostal	6	8
Jewish	2	1
Non-Christian and non-Jewish	2	3
Total	101	101

Source: National Congregations Study 1998 (as reported in Chaves 2002: 278). Used by permission of The Brookings Institution.

Whether congregations should or could assume additional roles is, at least in part, a question of their capacity. Of the over 350,000 religious congregations in America in 1998, including churches, synagogues, mosques, and temples (Weitzman *et al.* 2002): "forty percent of congregations, containing 15 percent of religious service attenders, have no full-time staff; 24 percent, with 7 percent of people, have no paid staff at all. Only 25 percent of congregations have more than one full-time staff person, but 65 percent of the people are in those congregations" (Chaves 2002: 276). The majority are small congregations with modest budgets compared to the relatively small number of very large congregations with sizable budgets. As shown in Table 5.3, 29 percent of churchgoers affiliate with the Catholic Church, but only 6 percent of congregations affiliate with the Catholic denomination. This indicates that the average Catholic congregation is fairly large. By contrast, Baptist denominations account for 25 percent of the congregations but only 18 percent of the attendees, indicating the likely smaller size of the Baptist congregations.

As a group, religious congregations tend to be relatively precarious financially. Approximately 80 percent of all the funds going to religious congregations come from individual donations. For some three-quarters of congregations this source constitutes at least 90 percent of their revenues. Fortunately, according to Chaves (2002), "overall giving in 29 denominations, adjusted for inflation, increased 63 percent between 1968 and 1998." Still, Chaves also found that the median congregation had only about $1,000 in its savings account, while the median person's congregation had savings of only $20,000. Furthermore, only 5 percent had endowments or savings that total twice their annual operating budget. Some congregations (23 percent) supplemented individual giving by renting or selling property or space and another 16 percent received income from other denominations or foundations.

With such a heavy reliance on individual giving, a significant concern for congregations is maintenance or expansion of membership. Generally speaking, membership in religious congregations has not declined significantly since the early 1970s (Cadge and Wuthnow, forthcoming). However, the balance of membership among the various denominations has changed. Cadge and Wuthnow (forthcoming) report that during the 1970s and 1980s, membership in mainline denominations, including Jewish congregations, declined by as much as a quarter while membership in evangelical denominations increased. This trend reversed during the late 1990s when the rate of decline in mainline denominations slowed to near zero and the rate of growth in evangelical denominations also showed significant decline from previous decades.

As mentioned above in the discussion of social services, government support now appears to be a carrot dangling in front of congregations' faces. The Charitable Choice provision (Section 104) of the 1996 welfare law (The Personal Responsibility and Work Reconciliation Act of 1996) was passed with the intention to expand the involvement of community and faith-based organizations in public anti-poverty efforts. For years religious denominations and orders have been involved in such activities through separately organized nonprofit organizations such as Catholic charities, Lutheran social services, etc. and have received significant sums of government funding, with a number of stipulations that ensure the non-religious and non-discriminatory nature of the services offered, as well as their providers. Meanwhile, congregations have engaged in service activities that are by and large informal and involve mainly volunteers. These activities may be accompanied by religious instruction or prayer, or they may be limited to denomination members. In any case, such congregational activities were not previously eligible for government funding on the grounds of church–state separation.

The Charitable Choice provision attempts to lay out a middle ground. While congregations and other faith-based organizations retain the right to discriminate in hiring, for example, only members of their own denomination, they may not discriminate against individuals receiving the service on the basis of religion. Furthermore, while the state cannot require the congregation to remove religious symbols from the buildings in which the service is being provided, funds received from the government cannot be used for worship or proselytizing. Most sources indicate that it is "too early to tell" whether the provision has succeeded, or will succeed, in increasing congregational involvement in social services (Chaves 2002; Cadge and Wuthnow, forthcoming).

CONCLUSION

The preceding pages have shown the complex and different roles nonprofit organizations play in American life. While the scale and scope of the nonprofit role varies by field, we can nonetheless draw three general conclusions. First, in fields of service provision (health, social services, education, housing), the sector is part of public–private partnerships that rest on the notion of third-party government. Second, in fields that are primarily advocacy-related, the sector finds itself close to the policymaking arena with its organizations in different alliances and coalitions with each other and government. Third, the nonprofit sector is experiencing a rapidly changing economic and policy environment that challenges many health and social services organizations particularly. Yet before we can step deeper into such organizational and policy analysis, it is important to ask a more basic question first: why do nonprofit organizations exist in market economies in the first place? This is a central topic of the next chapter.

REVIEW QUESTIONS

- What are some of the common themes in policy development in different fields?

- What is the distinction between advocacy and lobbying?

- Which field of nonprofit activity is experiencing most changes, and why?

REFERENCES AND RECOMMENDED READING

Listening Post Project (2003) "Communique No. 1," Baltimore: Johns Hopkins Center for Civil Society Studies, June 25. Available at www.jhu.edu/listeningpost/news/pdf/comm01.pdf

Salamon, L. M. (ed.) (2002a) *The State of the Nonprofit America*, Washington, DC: The Brookings Institution, in collaboration with the Aspen Institute.

Weitzman, M. S., Jalandoni, N. T., Lampkin, L. M., and Pollak, T. H. (2002) *The New Nonprofit Almanac and Desk Reference: The Essential Facts and Figures for Managers, Researchers, and Volunteers*, 1st edition, San Francisco, CA: Jossey-Bass.

Part II

Approaches

Chapter 6

Theoretical approaches

This chapter offers an overview of various economic, sociological, and political science approaches that address the origins, behavior, and impact of nonprofit organizations. It compares these approaches with one another, highlighting their strengths and weaknesses, and points to new and emerging theoretical developments.

LEARNING OBJECTIVES

The task of theory is to explain, and to help us understand, the world around us. The nonprofit field is rich in theories that offer important insights into the role of nonprofit organizations, and the functioning of modern economies and societies more generally. After considering this chapter, the reader should be able to understand:

- why nonprofit organizations exist in market economies, and what the demand and supply conditions are that encourage their growth;
- the conceptual foundations of the major theories, including their assumptions and implications;
- the strengths and weaknesses of the theories presented in this chapter;
- how the various theories relate to each other;
- what some of the theoretical potentials and current developments in the field are.

KEY TERMS

In contrast to the previous two chapters, this one is primarily concerned with conceptual issues. Consequently, a number of new and important terms are introduced throughout this chapter:

- demand heterogeneity
- entrepreneurs
- externalities

- free-rider problem
- government failure
- information asymmetry
- market failure
- median voter
- moral hazard
- non-distribution constraint
- (non-)excludability
- (non-)rivalry
- path dependency
- private goods
- product bundling
- public goods
- quasi-public goods
- stakeholder
- transaction costs
- trust
- voluntary failure

WHAT IS TO BE EXPLAINED? THE NONPROFIT RESEARCH AGENDA

In a 1990 article in the *Annual Review of Sociology*, DiMaggio and Anheier suggested a "road map" for nonprofit sector research that remains useful today. It is a simple map, and indeed the agenda proposed has only a few points or areas in it. When we think of the range of research topics that come within the compass of nonprofit organizations, three basic questions come to mind:

- Why do nonprofit organizations exist? This leads to the question of organizational origin and institutional choice.
- How do they behave? This addresses questions of organizational behavior.
- What impact do they have and what difference do they make? This points to the famous "So what?" question.

We can ask these questions at three different levels:

- that of the organization or case, or for a specific set of organizations;
- that of the field or industry (education, health, advocacy, philanthropy); and
- that of the economy and society.

The proposed agenda was organization-based and took the unit "nonprofit organizations" as its starting point. Wider institutional questions such as civil society, and individual aspects such as social capital, entered the explanatory concerns of nonprofit theories only later, as

114

we have seen in Chapter 1. The proposed agenda, while interdisciplinary in intent, invited economic models first and foremost—the majority of available theories of nonprofit organizations are economic in nature, i.e. they involve some notion of utility maximization and rational choice behavior.

The last years have been fruitful ones for theories of nonprofit organizations, and a number of answers have been worked out for the "why" questions in Table 6.1. Research is currently concentrating on questions of organizational behavior and impact, and available results and theories are less "solid" in the second and third row than in the upper left corners of the table, in large measure due to immense measurement problems. While we will deal with questions of behavior and impact in subsequent chapters, we will focus, for the time being, on theories that seek to answer *why* nonprofit organizations exist in market economies. After all, if market economies are about profit, why do some organizations elect *not* to make profit? Of course, in Chapter 2, we have already pointed out that the correct way to refer to nonprofit would not be "non-profit-making" but rather "non-profit-distributing." Therefore, we ask: why do some organizations in market economies choose not to distribute residual income as profit?

Before presenting the range of theories proposed in response to this question, it is useful to introduce some fundamental concepts of economic and sociological theory. We will do so by way of a famous example of social policy suggested by Richard Titmus in his famous treatise on the "Gift Relation" (1973). In this ground-breaking book, Titmus explores a seemingly perplexing question: if the value of goods and services in market economies are mediated through the price mechanism that balances supply and demand, how is it possible that some of the most valuable things have no market price and are not exchanged via market mechanisms? His example was the giving of blood, and he asked: why is blood not collected via markets, but by a voluntary system of individual gifts? Although Titmus worked through this example before the impact of the HIV/AIDS crisis on blood donations, it is still useful to explore his reasoning as he introduced much of the relevant terminology needed for economic theories of nonprofit organizations.

In essence, Titmus suggests that the voluntary supply of blood is a response to actual and assumed market failures in the supply of transfused blood. Specifically, six aspects are important to suggest that a free market system for blood may lead to "failures," i.e. unfair outcomes (see also Young and Steinberg 1995: 196–8):

- *Information asymmetry*: potential donors with contaminated blood may conceal this fact in order to receive money. Information asymmetries exist when either the seller or the buyer knows more about the true quality of the product or service offered. Under market conditions, there would be strong incentives to "conceal" such knowledge and use it to one's advantage, a phenomenon economists call moral hazard, i.e. to cheat and reap individual benefits from other people's ignorance.
- *Trust*: for blood collectors and ultimate recipients, inherent information asymmetries require some level of trust in the purity of the donated blood. They seek assurances that, due to their relative ignorance of the true quality of the blood, money-seeking contributors or careless altruists are not taking advantage of them. As we will see below, trust goods such as donated blood, child care, social services, and also cultural

115

Table 6.1 Basic third sector research questions

Basic question	Level of analysis and focus		
	Organization	Field/industry	Economy/country
Why?	Why is this organization nonprofit rather than forprofit or government?	Why do we find specific compositions of nonprofit, forprofit, government firms in fields/industries?	Why do we find variations in the size and structure of the nonprofit sector cross-nationally?
	Organizational choice	*Field-specific division of labor*	*Sectoral division of labor*
How?	How does this organization operate? How does it compare to other equivalent organizations?	How do nonprofit organizations behave relative to other forms in the same field or industry?	How does the nonprofit sector operate and what role does it play relative to other sectors?
	Organizational efficiency, etc.; management issues	*Comparative industry efficiency and related issues*	*Comparative sector roles*
So what?	What is the contribution of this organization relative to other forms?	What is the relative contribution of non-profit organizations in this field relative to other forms?	What does the nonprofit sector contribute relative to other sectors?
	Distinct characteristics and impact of focal organization	*Different contributions of forms in specific industries*	*Sector-specific contributions and impacts cross-nationally*

performances and used cars, are prone to market failures unless market-correcting mechanisms such as prohibition of profit distribution, government oversight, insurance coverage, or liability laws are in place.

■ *Externalities*: transmission of infection from donor to recipient in a market situation can yield "negative" externalities, and others not party to the initial blood transaction might get infected. Externalities exist when either a benefit or a cost is not directly accounted for by the market price but passed on to third parties. Air pollution is an example of a negative externality, as the sales price of a car does not include the car's lifetime contribution to lowering air quality. A private arboretum in a densely populated urban area would be an example of a positive externality, as the costs for maintaining the park would be borne by the owner but the fresher, cleaner air would benefit a much wider group of residents in the area.

■ *Transaction costs*, i.e. the costs of exchange, doing business, and contracting: of course "bad" or contaminated blood can be detected, but this could be expensive and, in fact, a procedure for this was only introduced in the wake of the HIV/AIDS crisis in the

1980s. However, if possible, markets seek to minimize such costs, as they take away from the efficiency of market exchange by adding to the cost of transactions. As economists have argued, consumer trust in the assumed quality of the good or service being provided can reduce transaction costs under conditions of information asymmetry.

- *Limitation of market*: this arises from a combination of information asymmetries, moral hazard, and transaction costs, and it is important to appreciate that market failure would likely lead to an oversupply of blood: if donors are paid, the blood supply will contain the blood of untainted altruists and both tainted and untainted money-seekers. Yet this oversupply would not be associated with a drop in the price of blood, as expensive screening and testing would increase transaction costs that would be passed on to consumers.
- *Limitation of a voluntary system* of blood donation is the mirror image of market failure. If all blood is donated through voluntary individual action, a *free-rider problem* arises that creates a potential undersupply of blood. As blood would be available to anyone in emergencies and time of need regardless of actual contributions to available blood banks, individuals have no incentive to donate blood themselves to what is de facto a public reserve bank of blood. As a result, a voluntary system may not be efficient from a societal perspective.

The tension between private and public benefits and individual incentives to contribute to some common good relative to moral hazards and free-riding potentials come together in a basic distinction between public goods and private goods:

- *pure public goods* are goods to which no property rights can be established and which are available to all irrespective of contribution; whereas
- *pure private goods* are goods with individual property rights, and their production, exchange, and consumption generates no externalities.

Pure public goods have two essential characteristics inherent in the nature of the good or service in question:

- *non-excludability*, i.e. once produced consumers cannot be prevented from benefiting except at great cost: for example, it is very costly, if not impossible, to exclude non-taxpayers from benefiting from national defense, public art, or urban green belts; and
- *non-rivalry*, i.e. individual use does not reduce the amount available for use by users or potential customers: for example, the presence of other people in the audience of a symphony hall typically does not diminish a person's enjoyment of a Mozart piano concerto.

However, only if non-excludability and non-rivalry are *both* present in the nature of the good or service do economists speak of pure public goods. Conversely, excludability and rivalry become the essential characteristics of a pure *private* good:

117

- *excludability*, i.e. once produced only consumers with property rights can benefit, and others can be prevented from benefiting at no or little cost: for example, food purchased in a supermarket is typically consumed by household members; others are easily excluded unless invited for lunch or dinner; and
- *rivalry*, i.e. individual use does limit and can even exhaust potential use by others: for example, only one person can wear a particular piece of clothing at a time, and food items are consumed by one person only, even if they share the same meal.

Excludability and rivalry are often a matter of degree, and they may not necessarily be manifest at equal levels in the same good or service. If only one of the characteristics of a public good is present, and the other either not at all or much less so, we are dealing with what are called quasi-public goods. As Table 6.2 shows, they come in two basic varieties:

- Non-excludable quasi-public goods are also referred to as common-pool goods or congestion goods. These goods are rival, but exclusion is possible only at a certain price. For example, the fish in the village pond are rival, and exclusion becomes an issue only if overfishing should occur; a dramatic example is the world's oceans, where fish stock is rival and mechanisms for exclusion and controlling overfishing are costly and difficult to enforce.
- Excludable quasi-public goods or toll goods are basically non-rival goods where exclusion of non-payers is possible, i.e. associated with lower transaction costs, and enforceable. For example, museum exhibitions, theater performances, or symphonies are typically toll goods. Patrons, once admitted, can enjoy the show or performance irrespective of others being admitted to the same event.

A basic tenet of economic theory is that markets best provide pure private goods, and that pure public goods are best provided by the state or public sector (see Table 6.3). The state has the power to set and enforce taxation and thereby counteracts free-rider problems associated with the supply of public goods through private mechanisms. Markets can handle individual consumer preferences for private goods efficiently, and thereby avoid the high transaction costs associated with the public sector provision of rival, excludable goods. Finally, nonprofit organizations are suited for the provision of quasi-public goods, i.e. where exclusion is possible and significant externalities exist.

By implication, markets, governments, and nonprofit organizations are less suited to supply some other types of goods. Economists refer to such situations as "failures."

Table 6.2 Types of goods

	Excludable	Non-excludable
Rival	Pure private good, e.g. food	Common-pool good, e.g. air, fishing
Non-rival	Excludable public good or toll good, e.g. museum	Pure public good, e.g. defense, lighthouse

Table 6.3 Types of goods and providers

	Private goods	Quasi-public goods	Public goods
Markets	Yes	Contested	No, due to market failure
Nonprofit organizations/sector	Contested	Yes	No, due to voluntary failure
State/public sector provision	No, due to government failure	Contested	Yes

Specifically:

- *Market failure*: this situation is characterized by a lack of perfect competition, where markets fail to efficiently allocate or provide goods and services. In economic terms, market failure occurs when the behavior of agents, acting to optimize their utility, cannot reach a Pareto optimal allocation. Sources of market failures include: monopoly, externality, and asymmetrical information.
- *Government failure*: this is a situation in which a service or social problem cannot be addressed by government. In economic terms, government failure occurs when the behavior of agents, acting to optimize their utility in a market regulated by government, cannot reach a Pareto optimal allocation. Sources of government failure include private information among the agents.
- *Voluntary failure*: this refers to situations in which nonprofits cannot adequately provide a service or address a social problem at the scale necessary for its alleviation. In economic terms, voluntary failure results from the inability of nonprofits to marshal the resources needed over prolonged periods of time. Since they cannot tax and cannot raise funds on capital markets, nonprofits rely on voluntary contributions that in the end may be insufficient for the task at hand.

While there is general agreement among economists and public policy analysts that markets are to provide private goods, and the public sector public goods, the situation for quasi-public goods is more complex, even though many nonprofits operate to provide such goods and services. The key point is that the area of quasi-public goods allows for multiple solutions: they can be provided by government, by businesses, and, prominently, by non-profit organizations. For example, health care and social services can be offered in a forprofit clinic, a hospital owned and run by a city or local county, or by a nonprofit organization, perhaps a nonprofit hospital.

Indeed, one of the key issues of nonprofit theory is to specify the supply and demand conditions that lead to the nonprofit form as the institutional choice, as opposed to a public agency or a business firm, and the theories we review next look at this very topic.

Even though economic reasoning presents a very useful classification of goods and services, it also becomes clear that, to some extent, the dividing line between quasi-public and private goods is ultimately political, in particular when it comes to the treatment of quasi-public goods. In this sense, economic theories imply important policy issues: depending on whether we treat education, health, culture, or the environment as a private, quasi-public, or public good, some institutional choices will become more likely than others.

For example, if we treat higher education more as a public good, we assume that its positive externalities benefit society as a whole, and, by implication, we are likely to opt for policies that try to make it near universal and funded through taxation. If, however, we see higher education as primarily a private good where most of the benefit incurs to the individual, with very limited externalities, then we would favor private universities financed by tuition and other charges, and not through taxation.

Many of the policy changes affecting nonprofit organizations are linked to political changes in how goods and services are defined, and how policies set guidelines on excludability and rivalry of quasi-public goods, whether in welfare reform, education, or arts funding.

THE MAJOR THEORIES

Against the background provided by Titmus's reasoning, we will now present each of the major theories that have been proposed over the last three decades. In each case, we will focus on the key elements of the theory, including important assumptions made, and highlight strengths and weaknesses. Even though we will look at the theories as "stand alone" bodies of thought, they tend to relate to each other and are more complementary than rival. In other words, even though when taken by itself, a particular theory may have major shortcomings, its explanatory power is significantly strengthened when combined with other approaches.

Three additional aspects are worth considering. First, the theories address primarily the "why" questions in Table 6.1, i.e. the origins of nonprofit organizations and the institutional choices involved. At the same time, they lead to expectations about organizational behavior and impact, and insights into the role of nonprofits more generally—topics which we will cover in Chapters 7 and 8.

Second, most of the economic theories presented below were developed against the backdrop of the US, which means that they apply to developed, liberal market economies first and foremost, and have limited applicability in other economic systems such as developed welfare states, developing countries, or transition economies. Nonetheless, they help us understand the different roles of nonprofit organizations in various parts of the world, as the social origins theory presented below shows. Table 6.4 offers a synoptic presentation of major nonprofit theories.

Public goods theories

In 1975, the economist Burton Weisbrod was among the first to publish a theory that attempted to explain the existence of nonprofit organizations in market economies. The paper entitled "Toward a theory of the voluntary nonprofit sector in a three-sector economy" became very influential and laid the groundwork for what became known as the "public goods theory of nonprofit organizations"—a theory that has been expanded and revised and, perhaps most importantly, influenced the development of other theories in the field (Kingma 2003).

Weisbrod's theory of nonprofit organizations is an extension of the public choice theories where public good problems are resolved by the collective action of the individuals affected (1977, 1988). Similarly, the public good theory of nonprofit organizations provides an economic rationale for the formation of nonprofit organizations to provide public goods. Although the theoretical background and terminology involved in the basic model refer to public goods and assume altruistic donors will compensate for any undersupply, the key policy relevance of the theory applies typically not to the pure public goods we discussed above but to quasi-public goods primarily.

The Weisbrod model explains the existence of nonprofit organizations with the help of two basic concepts: "demand heterogeneity" for the provision of public goods and "median voter." Demand heterogeneity refers to the demand for public and quasi-public goods, and the extent to which this demand is, broadly speaking, similar across the population (demand homogeneity) or if different population groups have divergent demands for such goods in both quality and quantity (demand heterogeneity). The median voter represents that largest segment of the demand for public and quasi-public goods within the electorate. Another way to define the median voter is to think of the statistically average person and the demands she would make on governmental spending policies.

In a competitive liberal democracy, government officials, in seeking to maximize their chances of re-election, will strive to provide a given public good at the level demanded by the median voter. This strategy of public goods provision, by which the government satisfies the demand of the median voter, would leave some demands unmet, for example demand by consumers who require the public good at quantitative and qualitative levels higher than expressed by the median voter. This unfilled demand for the public good may be satisfied by nonprofit organizations, which are established and financed by the voluntary contributions of citizens who want to increase the output or quality of the public good. In other words, nonprofit organizations are gap-fillers; they exist as a result of private demands for public goods not offered by the public sector. By implication, due to market failure, the public good would be unlikely to be supplied by forprofit organizations.

The basic model of nonprofit organizations considers the production of a single public good in situations of demand heterogeneity. In reality, of course, the situation is more complex, as quasi-public goods vary in quality and come in different versions or models. For example, there is not solely one health care or one education service, but many different kinds. But the important point Weisbrod identifies applies to the basic as well as the more elaborate models of public good provision: in a heterogeneous society, one would expect more nonprofit organizations than in homogeneous societies where the median voter segment of the demand curve for public goods would be much wider. Thus, the number of nonprofit organizations is positively related to the increase in the diversity of a population: diversity not just in terms of ethnicity, language or religion, but also in age, lifestyle preferences, occupational and professional background, income, etc.

Proponents of this theory point to the US as a "living example" of Weisbrod's theory (Kingma 2003). The vast array of nonprofit organizations in existence in the US can be

121

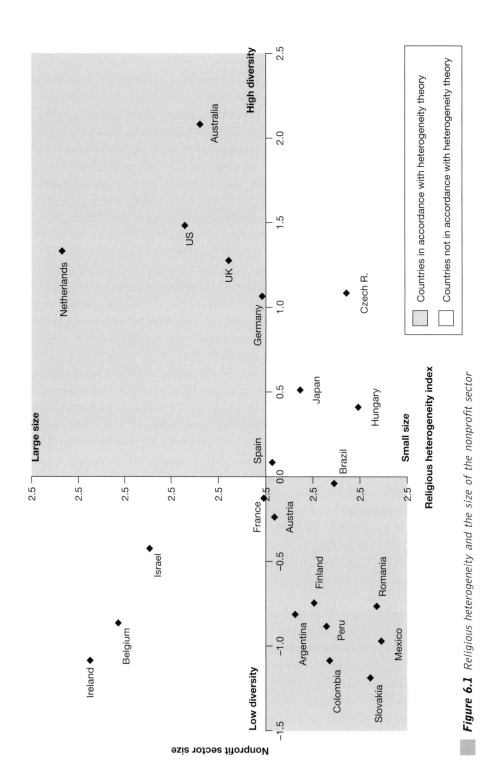

Figure 6.1 *Religious heterogeneity and the size of the nonprofit sector*

Sources: Based on Salamon *et al.* 1999b: 57.

attributed to its mixture of religious, political, ethnic, and racial backgrounds. Feigenbaum (1980) and Chang and Tuckman (1996) show that the heterogeneity in a population is related to the increase in size of the nonprofit sector in terms of number of organizations. Salamon and Anheier (1998b) provide cross-national evidence for the theory for some countries but not for others. As Figure 6.1 shows, there is a general tendency for the size of the nonprofit sector to increase with the religious heterogeneity of countries, although there are important exceptions, e.g. Ireland, Belgium, Israel, and the Czech Republic. We will follow up on the limited cross-national applicability of the heterogeneity theory below, as this point is taken up by the social origins theory.

Hansmann (1987: 29) argues that Weisbrod's theory works best when applied to near public goods, for example, the services provided by the American Heart Association or the National Trust in the UK. In such situations, nonprofit provision is substituted for government provision under conditions of demand heterogeneity for the public good in question. But how would the theory deal with the many nonprofit services that are quasi-public goods and allow for exclusion and rivalry? For Hansmann (1987: 29), the critical weakness in Weisbrod's theory when applied to quasi-public goods is that it "stops short of explaining why nonprofit, rather than forprofit, firms arise to fill unsatisfied demand for public goods." As we will see below (pages 124–6), Hansmann's trust-related theory, or contract failure theory, picks up on precisely this point.

Ben-Ner and Van Hoomissen address a related issue. They argue that it is not just enough to have a heterogeneous society; the actions of groups of "stakeholders" who care enough about the public good to assume control over its production and delivery are needed. Importantly, these stakeholders require common preferences distinct from governmental preferences or market interests to create sufficient "social cohesion" for the formation and operation of nonprofit organizations. This line of thinking becomes important in the stakeholder theory, which we will review below.

Weisbrod's pure public good theory states that nonprofit organizations provide public goods through donor support, which otherwise would have been provided by the government. Following this reasoning, donor support should change if the government either begins to supply the good itself or begins to fund nonprofit organizations for its provision. In other words, government spending will "crowd-out" donor contributions. However, studies reviewed by Steinberg (2003) reveal that the "crowd-out" may not be dollar for dollar but influenced by other incentives such as tax considerations, inertia, or information asymmetries. The important point to keep in mind is that the crowd-out effect, however partial, rests on some notion of a trade-off relation between public sector and nonprofit provision: an increase in government services in response to non-median voter demand will affect the scale of private nonprofit activities.

Major extensions of Weisbrod's model concentrate on the output or the goods produced by the nonprofit sector. These models incorporate the preferences of stakeholders other than donors, such as managers, volunteers, and employees. They also allow for more than one type of good produced. The result of adding other stakeholders and other goods into the model is an explanation of why certain nonprofit goods and services differ from those of government-provided goods and services. Indeed, the power of Weisbrod's model derives, in part, from its ability to offer a basis for other theorists to build upon.

123

commercial firm. Yet are consumers aware of differences in ownership among the organizations that provide them with services? If so, do consumers expect nonprofit organizations to behave in a more trustworthy manner than their forprofit counterparts? Studies show that people have an idea of the ownership of the services they use, but their impressions are not always reliable. And depending on the industry, people do indeed tend to view nonprofit providers as more trustworthy, as we will see in Chapter 8.

The trust-related theories point to an important set of factors concerning why nonprofit organizations might exist in market economies. At the same time, critics have pointed out two major shortcomings. First, Salamon (1995) points to the failure of trust-related theories to take account of government and the possibility that information asymmetries may find a response through public sector rather than nonprofit sector action. In this sense, the theory complements the heterogeneity or public goods theory, which answered the question: why private, and not government; whereas the trust-related theories help us understand why non-market rather than market solutions. In this sense, the two theories are complementary rather than rival.

Another criticism of trust-related theories was suggested by Estelle James (1987, 1989) who argues that the centrality of the non-distribution constraint finds no corresponding weight in the legal and tax systems of most countries. In fact, she finds that the non-distribution constraint may be overstated as organizations can cross-subsidize (i.e. use surplus revenue from one line of activities to support another, to effect an internal profit distribution to cover deficits) or engage in indirect profit-taking by increasing costs (e.g. lush offices, generous travel budgets, and personal accounts). Moreover, many legal systems have fairly light oversight regimes in place to monitor adherence to non-distribution, and penalties for violations tend to be relatively mild.

Despite these and other criticisms (see Ortmann and Schlesinger 2003), the trust-related theories have influenced many subsequent developments in the field. The basic tenet is that the nonprofit form emerges when it is more efficient to monitor financial behavior, in particular the treatment of potential profits, than it is to assess the true quality of output. The non-distribution constraint serves as a proxy-insurance signaling protection from profiteering.

Entrepreneurship theories

In contrast to the heterogeneity and trust-related theories, which emphasize aspects of the demand for services, entrepreneurship theories try to explain the existence of nonprofit organizations from a supply-side perspective. An entrepreneur is defined as an individual with a specific attitude toward change, whose function is to "carry out new combinations." According to the classic formulation by Joseph Schumpeter, the Austrian-American economist, entrepreneurs are the innovative force in capitalist economies (see Badelt 2003). They are part of the "creative destruction" that drives the capitalist system: they innovate by introducing new ways of seeing and doing things, and thereby displace old ones. Thus, if entrepreneurs drive missions and objective functions (and their inputs and outputs), one would expect to see not only innovations in goods and service delivery arise from nonprofit organizations, but also competition between alternatives.

In classical economic terms, the entrepreneur is understood as the one who assumes the risk of organizing and managing a new business venture or enterprise. Psychologists who have analyzed entrepreneurs argue that entrepreneurs have a persistent *opportunity* orientation and think in terms of *how* things can be done instead of *why* things *can't* get done. Dees *et al.* define entrepreneurs as: "Entrepreneurs are innovative, opportunity-oriented, resourceful, value-creating change agents" (2001: 4).

Social entrepreneurs differ from business entrepreneurs in that, instead of creating monetary value or economic value for the firm, they create social value, behaving in the following ways: adopting a mission to create and sustain social value; recognizing and relentlessly pursuing new opportunities to serve that mission; engaging in a process of continuous innovation, adaptation, and learning; acting boldly without being limited to resources currently in hand; exhibiting a heightened sense of accountability to the constituencies served and for the outcomes created (Dees *et al.* 2001).

Even though entrepreneurship approaches to understanding economic behavior and developments have a long history in the social sciences, with frequent reference made to Schumpeter and also to the economist Leibenstein, the most influential supply-side theorists in the nonprofit field have been Estelle James (1987), Susan Rose-Ackerman (1996), and Dennis Young (1983). In a series of papers in the 1980s and 1990s, they laid out the basic argument for what became known as the entrepreneurship theory of nonprofit organizations.

To appreciate entrepreneurship approaches, one has to understand that they take a very different starting point from the theories we reviewed so far. They question the emphasis trust-related theories place on non-distribution and the way heterogeneity theories emphasize demand for public and semi-public goods. While these aspects are acknowledged as important, they also, in the eyes of entrepreneurship theorists, miss two critical points. First, nonprofit organizations may not be interested in profits in the first place; in fact, their objective function may lie elsewhere and assume non-monetary forms. Second, the provision of services may not at all be the real, underlying reason for the organization's existence, and these activities may serve only as the means for achieving some other goal as the ultimate *raison d'être* or objective.

According to James (1987, 1989), nonprofits try to maximize non-monetary returns such as faith, or numbers of believers, adherents, or members; they are primarily interested in some form of immaterial value maximization, and the non-distribution constraints of monetary profits are only secondary to their organizational behavior. This reasoning points to the importance of religion and other value bases and ideologies. Indeed, James suggests that entrepreneurs, or ideologues in Rose-Ackerman's terms, populate nonprofit fields eager to maximize non-monetary returns.

The various types of entrepreneurs drive the mission, goals, and outputs of the organization. The motives of the entrepreneur play an important role in the organization's development, outputs, and mission. This role is most pronounced in the field of religion, as James writes (1987: 404):

> Universally, religious groups are the major founders of nonprofit service institutions. We see this in the origins of many private schools and voluntary hospitals

127

in the US and England, Catholic schools in France and Austria, missionary activities in developing countries, services provided by Muslim wacfs [religious trusts] and so on.

Indeed, James points out that nonprofits are strategically located in areas of taste formation: in primary socialization (day care, nurseries, schools), but also in critical life situations (hospitals, hospices, homes for the elderly), and situations of special need (disability, divorce, and other major life events). Entrepreneurship theories argue that during such phases and situations, we are more open to questions relating to religion than we would be under "normal" circumstances. Hence, nonprofit entrepreneurs seek out such opportunities and combine service delivery with religious or otherwise ideologically colored "messages" in an effort to garner adherents, believers, or recruits.

Whether nonprofit entrepreneurs try to maximize quantifiable aspects (such as members) or abstract concepts (such as "salvation" or some ideology) is irrelevant; what matters is that they often seek to combine such maximization efforts with service delivery. In this sense, many value-based nonprofits bundle products: one product that is the true and preferred output (e.g. salvation) and the other the necessary or auxiliary co-product, a means rather than the ultimate objective. Rose-Ackerman (1996) suggests that value-based or ideology-based nonprofit organizations tend to develop into multiple-product firms, and Weisbrod (1998c) argues that the product bundling is a key aspect of the revenue behavior of many nonprofit organizations.

In a sense, entrepreneurship approaches complete demand-side theories because nonprofits always need an actor or a group of actors to create the organization. Yet it is often difficult to differentiate between entrepreneurship and nonprofit management. This has consequences when trying to test the validity of the theory and may cause confusion with terminology. Moreover, it may be difficult to tell if the cause of innovations is from the entrepreneurship or from other factors. The problem with the innovation argument is that it can be applied and observed in entrepreneurs in almost all other types of organizations—a critique picked up by the stakeholder theory reviewed below.

As Badelt (2003) comments, original entrepreneurship theories tried to explain the existence of nonprofits; modern theories of organizational development try to extend this approach by describing and explaining the process of institutional change, in particular product bundling, thus ending up with a *behavior* theory of organizations. In other words, entrepreneurs create and react to demand heterogeneity, and thus become a critical element of the institutional dynamics of modern society.

The stakeholder theory

The stakeholder theory, associated primarily with the work of Avner Ben-Ner, is rooted in organizational economics and economic theories of institutions. The theory builds on Hansmann's trust argument, in which a variety of problems might make it difficult for the consumers of a particular commodity to police the conduct of producers by normal contractual or market mechanisms, thus resulting in contract or market failure. According to this reasoning, as we have seen, nonprofits exist because some demand for trust goods in market situations are not met by private firms.

Ben-Ner and Van Hoomissen (1991) also acknowledge the supply side and recognize that nonprofits are created by social entrepreneurs, religious leaders, and other actors who are not motivated by profit primarily. They refer to these and all other interested parties on both the demand side and the supply side as "stakeholders." The theory Ben-Ner and Van Hoomissen develop is built upon the interests and behaviors of stakeholders in the provision of trust-related goods.

The stakeholder theory begins with Hansmann's reasoning: the trade of trust-related goods typically entails a conflict of interest between seller and buyer. The buyer wants the lowest possible price at the best quality, while the seller wants the highest possible price at the lowest quality in order to maximize profits. In a perfect market with perfect information flows, the buyer knows how much it costs to produce the product and other relevant information, and firms know consumer preferences, therefore both parties maximize their utility and transactions occur at the most efficient price. Unfortunately, under conditions of information asymmetry, consumers are at a disadvantage and subject to profiteering by profit-seeking firms. Because of the non-distribution constraint, nonprofits can resolve this conflict, because they are not motivated by profit and therefore are less likely to downgrade their products to maximize profits.

The stakeholder theory also relates to Weisbrod's theory of public goods and demand heterogeneity in which limits to government provision drive demand-side stakeholders to seek institutions to fill their needs. Similar to Hansmann's approach, Ben-Ner argues that nonprofits are created by consumers and other demand-side stakeholders in order to "maximize control over output in the face of informational asymmetries."

The key demand-side stakeholders are those who feel so strongly about the quality of the service provided and protection from moral hazard that they decide to exercise control over the delivery of service themselves. They thus become demand- and supply-side stakeholders at the same time. For example, parents may decide to start a day care center for their children to achieve greater control over day care services. The situation for stakeholder control applies to non-rival goods primarily, as providers cannot selectively downgrade the services provided. Ben-Ner suggests that the combination of information asymmetry, non-rivalry, and stakeholder control sends much stronger signals of trustworthiness than the "milder" formulation by Hansmann. In this sense, Ben-Ner's argument is a stricter theory than the trust-related theory and describes a narrower range of demand- and supply-side conditions under which nonprofits emerge.

The interdependence theory

Whereas the approaches reviewed so far establish some notion of conflict between governmental provision and nonprofit provision, most clearly in the case of the heterogeneity theory, the interdependence theory takes a different starting point and begins with the fact, supported by the data presented in the previous chapter, that government and the nonprofit sector are more frequently partners rather than foes. We saw this most clearly in the significant portion of public funding that is made available to nonprofit organizations not only in the US but also in many other countries. We also see it in the increasingly frequent use of public–private partnerships.

The thrust of Salamon's (1995) argument is that government does not "supplant" or "displace" nonprofit organizations; rather, in line with the empirical evidence in Chapter 4, he argues that government support of the third sector is extensive and that government is a "major force underwriting nonprofit operations." He outlines the scope and extent of government support for nonprofits in terms of direct monetary support, indirect support, and variations in support with regard to where the nonprofit is located (regional) and the type of service it provides.

Salamon criticizes economic theories in their failure to describe this symbiotic relationship between the nonprofit sector and government, in particular Weisbrod's public goods theory and Hansmann's trust theory, which view nonprofits as institutions apart from government and perhaps even better than government—in essence, picking up the pieces in areas where government fails. In reality, the extensive government support of the third sector can be understood if we consider what Salamon labels the "third-party government." As Salamon describes it, "the central characteristic of this pattern is the use of nongovernmental, or at least non-federal governmental, entities to carry out governmental purposes, and the exercise by these entities of a substantial degree of discretion over the spending of public funds and the exercise of public authority."

The voluntary failure theory, the opposite of the market failure theory (in which nonprofit organizations exist where the public sector fails), argues that voluntary action exists because of people's natural tendencies for collective action and sense of social obligation. People volunteer out of choice, which thus explains the vibrancy and sustainability of the sector. Because of lower transaction costs, at least initially, voluntary organizations based on collective action typically precede government programs and other activities in addressing social problems of many kinds. For example, this was the case with the HIV/AIDS crisis, but also with domestic violence, drug abuse, and social welfare services more generally.

However, voluntary action is limited, sporadic, unorganized, and at times inefficient. Government may step in to assist the voluntary sector in areas of weakness. There are four main areas of weakness in the voluntary sector:

- *Philanthropic insufficiency* (resource inadequacy) suggests that the goodwill and charity of a few cannot generate resources on a scale that is both sufficient and reliable enough to cope with the welfare and related problems of modern society. A reason for this insufficiency, aside from the sheer size of the population in need, is the fact that third sector goods are quasi-public goods, and thus subject to the free-rider problem whereby those who benefit from voluntary action have little or no incentive to contribute.

- *Philanthropic particularism* refers to the tendency of voluntary organizations and their benefactors to focus on particular subgroups or clients while ignoring others. This leads to problems such as: addressing only the needs of the "deserving" poor; inefficiency due to duplication of effort whereby each particular subgroup wants their "own" agency or service; service gaps in the population; and those who control the organization's resources having particular groups they favor.

■ *Philanthropic paternalism* means that voluntary associations may lack sufficient accountability, and discretion on behalf of donors may lead to activities that benefit issues or needs close to the donors' interests but not necessarily reflective of wider social needs. After all, voluntary contributions and charitable giving depend on individual good will; they do not represent a right or entitlement.

■ *Philanthropic amateurism* points to the fact that voluntary associations frequently do not have professional teams of social workers, psychologists, etc., since they can ill afford to pay for such expertise. Therefore, they rely disproportionately on volunteers, who may not possess professional skills, in dealing with social problems.

In short, the voluntary sector's weaknesses correspond well with the government's strengths, and vice versa. Government can provide a more stable stream of resources, set priorities through a democratic process, discourage paternalism by making access to care a right and not a privilege, and improve quality of care by setting benchmarks and quality standards. The interdependence theory moves away from the zero-sum thinking that characterizes some of the economic theories presented above, and shows nonprofit–government relations in a less competitive light, emphasizing collaboration instead. Government and the nonprofit sector complement each other and compensate each other's strengths and weaknesses—a theme to which we will return in Chapter 13.

Summary assessment of economic theories: the supply and demand conditions

We have looked at a range of economic theories that try to explain the existence of nonprofit organizations in developed market economies (see Table 6.4). To a large extent, the various theories are complementary rather than rival, and, taken together, offer a convincing answer in terms of demand and supply conditions.

Suppose that we begin from the hypothetical situation of a developed market economy in which production is based on unregulated forprofit firms. Consider first the interface between consumers and forprofit sellers. Forprofit provision is problematic for consumers when goods and services are not purely private but have public attributes and are provided under conditions of asymmetric information. Public attributes include *non-rivalry* in consumption—one user's welfare is not affected by the use of others—and *non-excludability* in consumption—not all users can be compelled to pay for their use. Asymmetric information exists when consumers do not know all that they may care about with respect to the goods and services they wish to obtain until after payment takes place.

Under conditions of asymmetric information consumers may pay for goods and services that are of lower quality (or hold less of other desirable attributes) than that which is implied by the seller—unless there is an effective market for reputation whereby the discovery that a firm has taken advantage of its customers would damage the firm's future profits more than the gain from taking advantage of them. With non-excludability, forprofit firms cannot charge for their goods or services and will therefore not provide them. And with

Table 6.4 Synoptic presentation of major third sector theories

Theory/Summary	Key terms	Key strengths	Key weakness
Heterogeneity theory aka Public goods or governmental failure theory Unsatisfied demand for public and quasi-public goods in situations of demand heterogeneity leads to emergence of nonprofit providers	Demand heterogeneity; median voter; government; quasi-public goods	Explains part of government–private institutional choice dynamics in liberal democracies in the context of public fund shortages; why nonprofits become "gap-fillers"	Assumes inherent conflict between government and private nonprofit provision
Supply-side theory aka Entrepreneurship theory Nonprofit organizations are a reflection of demand heterogeneity served and created by entrepreneurs seeking to maximize non-monetary returns	Social entrepreneurship; non-monetary returns; product bundling; demand heterogeneity	Explains close link between value base of many nonprofits and choice of service field such as health and education (to maximize value impact and formation)	Assumes neutral state; equates religious and secular value-based behavior; what about non-value-based nonprofits?
Trust theory aka Contract or market failure theory Non-distribution constraint makes nonprofits more trustworthy under conditions of information asymmetry, which makes monitoring expensive and profiteering likely	Non-distribution constraint; trustworthiness; information asymmetry	Explains part of nonprofit–forprofit institutional choice from supply-side perspective, with focus on inherent problems in "nature" of good or service	Other institutional responses possible (government regulation); non-distribution constraint weakly enforced; indirect profit distribution possible (forprofits in disguise)

Theory				
Stakeholder theory	Given information asymmetries between provider and consumer, stakeholders decide to exercise control over delivery of service	Non-rival goods; information asymmetry; trust	Introduces tripartite relation as basic theoretical problem and goes beyond simple principal–agent issues: stakeholder–provider–recipient	Scope of theory limited to experience of informational problems faced by deeply concerned stakeholders—what about more conventional nonprofits?
Interdependence theory aka Voluntary failure or third-party government theory	Because of (initially) lower transaction costs, nonprofit organizations precede government in providing public benefit goods, but due to "voluntary failures" develop synergistic relations with the public sector over time	Philanthropic insufficiency, particularism, paternalism, and amateurism; third-party government	Moves away from zero-sum, competitive relation between voluntary sector and government; explains frequent pattern of public–private partnerships	Assumes neutral, yet well-meaning state; equates value-based and non-value-based behavior; when will synergies develop and when not—conditions unclear
Social origins	The size and structure of the nonprofit sector are a reflection of its "embeddedness" in a complex set of relationships, classes, and regime types	Comparative–historical approach; path dependency; state–society relations	Moves away from emphasis on microeconomic models and puts interdependence theory in context	Difficulty in testing counter-factual as nonprofit form varies significantly over time and across countries/cultures

Table 6.5 Government social expenditure and nonprofit sector size

Government social spending	Nonprofit sector economic size	
	Small	**Large**
Low	Statist (Japan, most developing countries)	Liberal (US, UK)
High	Social democratic (Sweden, Norway, Denmark, Finland)	Corporatist (France, Germany)

and the policymaking style associated with them, help account for cross-national differences in the nonprofit sector scale and structure.

Table 6.5 differentiates these regimes in terms of two key dimensions—first, the extent of government social welfare spending and, second, the scale of the nonprofit sector.[1] Thus, in the *liberal model*, represented by the US and the UK, a lower level of government social welfare spending is associated with a relatively large nonprofit sector. This outcome is most likely where middle-class elements are clearly in the ascendance, and where opposition from either traditional landed elites or strong working-class movements has either never existed or has been effectively held at bay. This leads to significant ideological and political hostility to the extension of government social welfare protections and a decided preference for voluntary approaches instead. The upshot is a relatively limited level of government social welfare spending and a sizable nonprofit sector.

The *social democratic model* is very much located at the opposite extreme. In this model, exemplified by Sweden, state-sponsored and state-delivered social welfare protections are extensive and the room left for service-providing nonprofit organizations quite constrained. Historically, this type of model was most likely to emerge where working-class elements were able to exert effective political power, albeit typically in alliance with other social classes. This is particularly true in the case of Sweden, where working-class political parties were able to push for extensive social welfare benefits as a matter of right in a context of a weakened, state-dominated Church and a limited monarchy. While the upshot is a limited service-providing nonprofit sector, however, it is not necessarily a limited nonprofit sector overall. Rather, the nonprofit sector performs a different function in social democratic regimes—one of advocacy and personal expression, rather than service-providing. In Sweden, a very substantial network of volunteer-based advocacy, recreational, and hobby organizations turns out to exist alongside a highly developed welfare state. In this kind of setting, in fact, the nonprofit sector may actually come closest to the ideal of a "civil society" sector functioning to facilitate individual and group expression.

In between these two models are two additional ones, both of which are characterized by strong states. However, in one, the *corporatist model* present in France and Germany, the state has been either forced to or induced to make common cause with nonprofit institutions, so that nonprofit organizations function as one of the several "pre-modern" mechanisms that are deliberately preserved by the state in its efforts to retain the support of key social elites while pre-empting more radical demands for social welfare protections. This was the pattern, for example, in late nineteenth-century Germany, when the state, confronting radical demands from below, began to forge alliances with the major churches and the landed elites to create a system of state-sponsored welfare provision that, over time, included a substantial role for nonprofit groups, many of them religiously affiliated (Anheier and Seibel 1998; Seibel 1990).

The *statist model* is the fourth possible model. In this model, the state retains the upper hand in a wide range of social policies, but not as the instrument of an organized working class, as in the social democratic regimes. Rather, it exercises power on its own behalf, or on behalf of business and economic elites, but with a fair degree of autonomy sustained by long traditions of deference and a much more pliant religious order. In such settings—in our analysis, Japan—limited government social welfare protection does not translate into high levels of nonprofit action, as in the liberal regimes. Rather, both government social welfare protection and nonprofit activity remain highly constrained.

Because of the complexity and relative amorphousness of the factors it identifies as important, the social origins theory is even more difficult to test empirically than the other theories discussed above, in particular the microeconomic theories. It lacks the parsimony of economic theories and calls for difficult qualitative judgments about the relative power of broad social groupings such as the commercial middle class or landed elites. Even then the resulting consequences establish only "propensities" and "likelihoods" rather than fully determined results (Young and Steinberg 1995; Ragin 1998). What is more, the four patterns identified by this theory are really archetypes, and many of the actual cases may in reality be hybrids that encompass features from more than one pattern.

CONCLUSION

This chapter reviewed major theoretical approaches to explain the existence of nonprofit organizations in market economies. Two aspects are worth emphasizing. First, the complementarity of the microeconomic approaches is a great strength of the field of nonprofit theorizing. Further steps in the theoretical development of the field should include better links between the microeconomic approaches such as the public goods or trust-related theory on the one hand, and the macro-level approach of the social origins theory—at present, they remain somewhat unconnected. More generally, the next major task is to come up with theories that not only explain the existence of nonprofits but their behaviors, impacts, and life cycle as well.

However, before we look at organizational behavior, we should briefly mention the second important aspect of the theories presented in this chapter: simplicity. We should recall that all social science theories are abstractions, and therefore simplifications of reality. Indeed, parsimony, i.e. the capacity to explain the essential characteristics of a phenomenon in simple terms, is a major sign of quality in theories. As we have seen, parsimony applies to all of the theories presented above. They typically operate with a rather limited number of key terms and concepts to explain the existence of nonprofit organizations in market economies. But by being parsimonious, they cannot by themselves take account of the full richness and variety of the third sector. However, other and future theories can build on the fundamentals of the approaches presented here and branch out into more specific aspects of nonprofit activity.

REVIEW QUESTIONS

- Explain the statement: "Nonprofit theories are complementary rather than rival."

- What are some of the major strengths and weaknesses of social origins theory?

- What are the supply and demand conditions for nonprofit organizations?

REFERENCES AND RECOMMENDED READING

Anheier, H. K. and Ben-Ner, A. (eds.) (2003) *The Study of the Nonprofit Enterprise: Theories and Approaches*, New York: Kluwer Academic/Plenum.

Hansmann, H. (1996) *The Ownership of Enterprise*, Cambridge, MA: The Belknap Press of Harvard University Press.

Young, D. R. and Steinberg, R. S. (1995) *Economics for Nonprofit Managers*, New York: Foundation Center.

Chapter 7

Organizational theory and structure

This chapter looks at organizational theory and its contributions to understanding nonprofit organizations. The chapter also explores the factors involved in shaping the development of nonprofit organizations over time. It then examines more specific aspects of organizational structure and sets the stage for the presentation of different management approaches. Next, the chapter reviews the role of power, authority, and leadership in nonprofit organizations. Finally, it looks at factors leading to alliances, partnerships, and mergers.

LEARNING OBJECTIVES

What is the contribution organizational theory can make to our understanding of the voluntary or nonprofit sector? How do organizations behave, how are they structured, what are their component parts, and what dynamics and factors are involved in shaping their development over time? Using a variety of examples, this chapter reviews the theory of bureaucracy, human relations, contingency theory, neo-institutionalism, and population ecology approaches, and looks at power and leadership to set the stage for the presentation of governance and management issues in the chapters which follow. After considering this chapter, the reader should:

- have a basic understanding of organizational theory;
- know some of the major phases of organizational development;
- understand the importance of the organizational task environment;
- be familiar with the specific aspects of organizational structure;
- understand the role of power, authority, and leadership in nonprofit organizations;
- be familiar with the factors involved in choosing alliances, partnerships, or mergers.

KEY TERMS

Some of the key terms introduced in this chapter are:

- bounded rationality
- bureaucracy
- charismatic leadership
- contingency theory
- coupling/interaction
- economies of scale/scope
- environmental carrying capacity
- environmental uncertainty
- human relations school
- isomorphism
- neo-institutionalist
- niche
- population ecology
- power, authority, leadership
- resource dependency
- task environment
- Taylorism
- transactional leadership
- transformational leadership

INTRODUCTION

While nonprofit organizations make up a separate institutional sector of modern societies, and are treated as such in national and international economic statistics (UN, 2002), they share some characteristics with business firms and public agencies (Young and Steinberg, 1995: 19–20):

- Like any business firm, nonprofit organizations have to "balance their books" so that revenues and expenditures match over time. Of course, nonprofits can make losses and profits in a given year but over a period of time discrepancies between the two items must be reasonable.
- Like businesses, nonprofit organizations are private initiatives and rely on the participation and contributions of citizens for their establishment and ongoing operation. They are voluntary entities, not demanded by law.
- Like governments, the mission, objectives, and activities of nonprofits are not to benefit a narrow group of owners but a broader public, and serve the public interest rather than the pecuniary interests of owners or their equivalents.
- Like government, nonprofits, as we have seen in economic theory, have to observe the non-distribution constraint in the treatment of financial and other surplus.

At the same time, nonprofit organizations are different not only because of the non-distribution constraint but also because values (religious, political, humanitarian, moral) are a distinct feature of many. We should recall that, according to one prominent theory, nonprofits try to maximize non-monetary returns such as faith, believers, adherents, or members, and may be less interested in monetary performance criteria. How far such values influence organizational behavior varies across nonprofit organizations, but the significant presence of values implies at the very least a more complex means–goal relationship between operational and ultimate objectives.

However, before we look more closely into questions of organizational structure and behavior, it is useful to review some of the basic facets of organizational theory. Organizational theory is among the most developed branches of the social sciences and is located at the intersection of sociology, economics, and management (Perrow 1986). In fact, the interest in organizations is as old as the social sciences themselves, and some of the central problems organizational theory addresses have very much remained the same since the early twentieth century, although the answers suggested have changed significantly as the field developed:

- *What is the relationship between organizational structure and task environment?* In other words, what is the best way to structure an organization, for what type of purpose, and for what type of tasks? Should the organization be centralized or decentralized, democratically run or with top-down decision-making? Should the organization be large or small, capital-intensive or labor-intensive? What kind of leadership is needed? What degree of participation or formality relative to a given task environment is needed?
- *How rational are organizations?* Organizations are tools for achieving specific missions and sets of objectives. For example, nonprofits might be set up to reduce child abuse, protect the environment, or promote music or the performing arts. Obviously, the organization should act in a rational manner to achieve set objectives, i.e. operate efficiently and effectively, and for the benefit of the mission primarily—and only secondarily for the benefit of the board, managers, or staff.
- *What shapes organizations and their evolution?* What makes some organizations succeed and others fail? Why are some organizations long-lived, and why do others become defunct after a relatively short period of time? Indeed, some of the longest-living organizations are in the nonprofit field, going back hundreds of years, but some of the frailest are in that sector as well. Some manage to evolve over time and adapt to changing environmental conditions, while others find it much harder to respond to changes, and react inadequately or remain inactive. Are organizations shaped by their environment and do they react to environmental conditions primarily, or is the relationship the other way around, where organizations forge their own future and destiny?

Of course, addressing these issues implies some agreement of what organizations are. However, there are many different conceptions, and "organization" is variously seen as:

The bureaucratic management model emphasizes the need for organizations to operate in a rational manner with specialization of labor, formal rules, and regulation, based on impersonality, a well-defined hierarchy, and a system of career advancement based on merit. The key factors are: stability of the task environment; the possibility of standardized procedures; and well-defined, hierarchically arranged job descriptions.

Theories of organization and management

The focus on bureaucratic efficiency was, of course, related to the expectations of owners and managers in terms of cost minimization, particularly in the field of production. The theory of scientific management developed by Frederick Winslow Taylor (1967) was one of the first attempts to use scientific methods to organize the workplace more efficiently, i.e. achieving the greatest possible output with the least input in a given time period. This led to the development of time–motion studies and similar approaches to optimizing organizational tasks. At the center of Taylorism is the direct link between output and pay and the assumption that workers would accept highly directive management as well as fractionated and routinized jobs in exchange for higher pay. Another assumption of Taylorism is based on acceptance theory, a notion introduced by Chester Barnard (1938). His administrative management model, which focuses on principles that can be used by managers to coordinate the internal activities of organizations, states that authority in organizations does not rest on managerial capability alone but primarily on the willingness of subordinates to accept orders.

The human relations model challenged both assumptions of Taylorism: first, the simplistic motivational model that reduced worker motivation to pay alone; and, second, the emphasis on hierarchy and authority relations between management and workers. Instead, human relations approaches include a broader set of motivations, in particular self-fulfillment, autonomy, and social needs. They introduced the importance of small group behavior and pointed to the critical match between formal and informal structures in organizations. What is more, they emphasized the difference between leadership and control, and suggested that adequate and accepted leadership is more beneficial to performance than top-down, impersonal control (see Perrow 1986).

The tension between Taylorism and the human relations school is well reflected in Douglas McGreogor's distinction between Theory X and Theory Y (1960):

- Theory X states that: most people dislike work and will try to avoid it; most people need to be coerced, controlled, directed to work toward organizational goals; most people want to be directed, shun responsibility, have little ambition, and seek security above all.
- Theory Y states that: people do not inherently dislike work; rewards are more important than punishment; people will exercise self-direction if given the chance and favor self-control over external control; people accept but seek responsibility; people value creativity and seek ways to express it.

In the 1970s, McGreogor's dichotomy expanded to include a Theory Z, which emerged from analyzing American and Japanese management models and the theories underlying their assumptions (Ouchi 1991). The American model is characterized by short-term employment, individual decision-making and responsibilities, explicit and formalized hierarchical control, high specialization, and segmented organizational cultures; by contrast, the Japanese model includes lifetime employment, consensual decision-making and shared responsibilities, implicit and informal control, less specialization, and holistic concerns. Ouchi (1991) proposed Theory Z, which can be reformulated to reflect the dictums of McGreogor:

- Theory Z states that: people seek long-term employment, consensual decision-making and individual responsibility; a combination of informal control with explicit and formalized evaluation criteria; moderately specialized job descriptions that allow for personal advancement; and a holistic concern for the organizational culture, including the well-being of employees and their families.

Two popular management styles are related to the Theory Z model of organization, and are worth mentioning here. Management by Objectives (MBO), developed by Peter Drucker (1954), is a process by which goals are set collectively for the organization as a whole and on the basis of thorough consultation and review involving all units and levels of hierarchy. These goals then form the basis for monitoring and evaluation.

In contrast to the goal emphasis of MBO, more recent approaches such as Total Quality Management (TQM) focus more on employee commitment and dedication rather than numerical performance criteria. Deming (2000) saw TQM as a quality control approach based on organization-wide commitments, the integration of quality improvement with organizational goals, and quality control efforts. The emphasis is on shared decision-making and responsibility.

Together, Taylorism and the human relations approach suggest a key insight of modern management theory (Perrow 1986): management approaches are ideologies that interpret, analyze, and legitimize the way organizations are set up and run. Indeed, the development of management approaches, which we will review in the next chapter, shows that they evolved from an emphasis on command-type structures that viewed organizations as machines in the sense of Weber's bureaucracy or Taylor's manufacturing plants, to the importance of informal groups in how organizations operate and the idea of organizations as some "quasi-family" in the human relations school. The notion that organizations are symbiotic systems that require commitment, participation, and common problem-solving are also based on strong ideological foundations about how we view organizations, and in particular how we judge people's motivations for performance and how we see the role of authority relations.

Organizations as rational and political institutions

Recognizing the intrinsic political nature of management and organizational design, theories moved away from the assumption of administrative rationality that underlies Weber's bureaucracy and Taylor's manufacturing plant, to the notion of limited or bounded rationality (Simon 1976). The concept puts emphasis on a greater understanding of

145

decision-making under incomplete information and uncertainty, and the trial and error behavior of management in problem-solving. Moreover, bounded rationality suggests that managers

- have inadequate information not only about the decision they reach but also about alternative options and their implications;
- face considerable time and cost constraints in decision-making; and
- have certain preset "frames" of reference that lead them to overlook some aspects while overemphasizing others.

Together, this suggests the image of more complex organizational behavior than under the rationality model, and notions such as "satisficing" and incremental approaches to management ("muddling through") challenged the concept of rational planning and optimization strategies:

- The *rational model* holds that managers engage in completely rational decision-making in the best interests of their organization, and reach optimal decisions with a wealth of full information available to them at the time.
- The *satisficing model* suggests that managers seek alternatives until they find one that appears satisfactory rather than continue searching for optimal decisions. Behind this model is the trade-off between increased search costs and the risk of not making a decision in time, on the one hand, and the risk of making a suboptimal decision, on the other.
- The *incremental approach* states that managers seek the smallest response possible to reduce a perceived problem to a tolerable level. The emphasis here is on short-term fixes rather longer-term goal attainment.

The response to organizations as rational constructions invited the view of organizations as political systems. This view is strongest in a perspective introduced by March and Olsen (1979), in which they describe organizations as organized anarchies and "garbage cans." They argue that conflicts over means and goals characterize the behavior of many organizations. Many managers and organizational subunits find it difficult to separate their own interests from that of the organization and therefore pursue self-interested strategies. March and Olsen suggest an image of organizations in which rationality plays only a minor role. They evoke not only the contingent nature of decision-making, but also the ambiguity of means–end relations and the confusion between problems and solutions. Some managers pick "goodies" from a garbage can (the organization) and discard their problems, which others then pick as their solutions to actual or perceived problems. The garbage can notion points to the scheming, seemingly chaotic behavior of organizations.

Related to but distinct from political systems and garbage can models is neo-institutional theory (Powell and DiMaggio 1991). It is called "institutional" because the theory focuses on the socially constructed, script-bound, embedded nature of mundane everyday behaviors as well as their importance. Neo-institutionalist theories have made significant inroads in a variety of disciplines, ranging from economics to political science and sociology (North

1990; Brinton and Nee 1998), and have also deeply influenced management and organizational thinking (Powell and DiMaggio 1991).

At the heart of neo-institutionalist thinking lies the belief that the rational actor model of organizations is insufficient and that organizational actions are formed and shaped by institutions; these institutions being the prevailing social rules, norms, and values that are taken for granted. Institutions constrain and also form individual and organizational behavior by limiting the range of available options that are perceived as legitimate. Legitimacy, understood as conformance with institutional expectations, thus becomes the central resource that organizations require for long-term survival.

In addition, since all organizations in a particular organizational field are subject to the same institutional expectations and constraints, they will tend to become homogeneous over time, a process called isomorphism. Powell and DiMaggio (1991) differentiate between three mechanisms of institutional isomorphic change:

- *Coercive isomorphism* appears as a reaction to direct or indirect pressure to abide by institutional expectations, and such pressures are typically exerted by organizations on which the pressured organization depends. For example, coercive pressures exerted by government and other funders help explain how nonprofits change from informal, voluntaristic, and amateuristic groups to increasingly bureaucratic and professionalized organizations through the coerced adoption of accounting, monitoring, performance, and certification requirements. Similarly, with the replacement of volunteers by service professionals, such as trained social workers, counselors, art historians, or educators, normative pressures effect change in the same direction (Sokolowski 2000).

- *Mimetic isomorphism* occurs in situations of technological or environmental uncertainty. Faced with uncertainty, organizations may mimic, or model themselves after, other organizations that are perceived as successful. For example, mimetic pressures help explain why nonprofits, facing considerable financial uncertainty, begin to utilize business techniques and profit-making activities. More broadly speaking, isomorphic trends are also largely responsible for the increased "borrowing" of American nonprofit management techniques, such as fund-raising, that has taken place in both Western Europe and Eastern and Central Europe over the past decade or so; as well as the modernization of nonprofit legal frameworks in Eastern and Central Europe after 1989.

- Finally, *normative isomorphism* derives from professional norms and standards that guide the work of professionals in organizations and thus shape organizational behavior. For example, the rules, regulations, and ethics of the social work profession contribute to similarities across social service and welfare agencies, irrespective of organizational form. The same holds for the medical profession, teachers, or airline pilots. In Mintzberg's terms (1979), professional bureaucracies are prime examples of normative isomorphism.

Neo-institutionalism is concerned with rational and non-rational actions, organizational–environmental relations, and taken-for-granted ideologies and behavioral patterns. Indeed, one of the key challenges neo-institutionalists address is the tension between economic models that strive for simplicity and emphasize rationality on the one hand, and sociological cognitive models that view organizations as more complex and multifaceted phenomena. They argue that the economic model of rational decision-making is just another, albeit important, one competing for the attention of managers who find themselves having to reconcile many conflicting demands, contradictory and incomplete information, and time pressures. For example, the new economics of organizations, pioneered by Williamson's theory of transaction costs (1975), sees organizations as a response to market failure. Organizations arise when the marginal cost of market transactions is higher than the marginal cost of organizing, and vice versa. For neo-institutionalists this argument becomes relevant for understanding organizational behavior once managers apply such abstract market-based thinking in their decision-making and view organizations as an alternative to markets.

Organizational environments and evolutionary perspectives

Several approaches address the relationship between organizational evolution and the organization's environment. One of the earliest examples is *contingency theory*, which views organizations as systems of interrelated parts, stresses the importance of environmental factors, and suggests that there is no one best way to manage. In contrast to *scientific management*, contingency theory argued that, rather than seeking universal principles that apply to all or most organizations, analysts should identify contingency principles that reflect the demands of particular types of task environments organizations work in. An example of contingency thinking would be the insight that bureaucracy is an organizational model that applies to stable task environments better than to volatile and uncertain conditions.

One of the most influential schools is *population ecology*, which models systems of organizations. Its key insight is that much change occurs as a result of variation in the birth and death rates of organizations, through selection rather than adaptation (Aldrich 1999). The notion of niches, resource dependencies, comparative advantages, and environmental carrying capacities are concepts to explain organizational development over time both at the individual and aggregate level. Recombination (use elements from different forms) and refunctionality (move into new niche, field) are important processes. Several concepts are important for understanding the approach of organizational population ecology.

Niches are relatively distinct combinations of resource sets that organizations use as input and which make them less prone to competition from others. Finding, defending, and optimizing niches on either the demand or the supply side become a key task of organizational survival and organizations that fail in these tasks are more prone to extinction over time. The term "niche" is a relative one, as the resources condition on the demand and supply side are relative to those of other organizations and potential competitors. For example, an art museum's niche refers to its revenue structure (endowment, giving, admissions fees), holdings (number of items and genres), visitor, membership and volunteer profile, its use by the artistic and art history community for research and teaching purposes, as well as the political and artistic support it enjoys among key stakeholders.

Next to *organizational niches*, there are *form niches*, and they consist of "the social, economic, and political conditions that can sustain the functioning of organizations that embody a particular form" (Hannan and Carrol 1995: 34). Nonprofit organizations would constitute one such form; the survival of nonprofits generally and irrespective of particular fields and organizational niches depends on the extent to which general form conditions can be maintained. For example, greater restrictions in the law of tax exemption could put large populations of nonprofit organizations at risk, as it would alter a basic condition of form maintenance. Likewise, making it easier for nonprofit saving and loan associations to operate like commercial banks triggered a migration of nonprofits into forprofit niches and created greater competition and far-reaching changes at the aggregate and the organizational level.

Related to the term niche is the notion of *environmental carrying capacity*, which refers to the number of organizations that can be supported by the social, economic, and political conditions, given available resources. To the extent that existing or newly founded organizations can draw on resources without competing against each other, the limits of the environment's carrying capacity have not been reached. However, once resources become scarcer, or some organizational forms become more efficient in resource use, the survival of other organizations will be put in question. For example, the significant growth of nonprofit organizations we reviewed in Chapter 4, would suggest that the carrying capacity described by social, economic, and political conditions has not been reached. However, as in some European countries, and in US states with severe budgetary problems such as California, welfare state and fiscal reforms will change some of the environmental conditions, and thereby also the carrying capacity of the social services and assistance fields.

Behind this reasoning is a basic insight of organizational population ecology, which sees organizational forms as being in more or less open competition with each other (Aldrich 1999). While policies define the rules of the game, over time mismatches develop between the potentials and constraints they impose on forms, and thereby either increase or decrease their competitive edge over others. Some of the underlying forces responsible for mismatches are related to the heterogeneity and trust theories discussed in Chapter 6: changes in the definition of goods and services, changes in information asymmetries, and policy changes more generally affect the environmental carrying capacity of given fields.

Over time, this dynamic leads to shifts in the composition of organizational fields in terms of form. Yet why do we find varying compositions across different fields? For example, why do nonprofit, forprofit, and public agencies exist in fields such as education, health care, social services, or the arts? The answer offered by organizational theory is threefold: first, for some periods, the carrying capacity of organizational fields may be such that different forms can survive, each operating with a comparative advantage that reduces direct competition; second, once conditions change, some organizations may be more favored in their survival than others and begin to expand, and others may succeed in establishing niches that allow them to continue to exist; third, new organizations may enter, being enticed by new opportunities and other considerations.

Given that virtually all fields in which nonprofit organizations operate have undergone major policy shifts over the last decades, it becomes clear that form diversity and different form composition are a function of environmental changes. Recent examples are welfare reform and health care reform in the US, which make it easier for forprofit organizations to enter into fields traditionally dominated by nonprofits. Examples outside the US can be

149

found in the housing market in Britain, the long-term social care field in Germany, and the Italian banking industry. In each of these cases, policy changes implied increased comparative advantages for some, and worsened conditions for other forms.

Yet where do forms come from? Organizational theory points to two basic processes that lead to the development of new forms, or speciation: recombination and refunctionality (Romanelli 1991). Recombination involves the introduction of new elements into an existing organizational form, for example, benchmarking, franchising, branding, and other corporate management tools in nonprofit organizations, or corporate responsibility programs in businesses. Refunctionality means the relocation of one form in a different context, e.g. the migration of forprofit providers into fields previously populated primarily by nonprofits, as in social services.

Next to population ecology, *resource-dependency approaches* recognize the contingent, open systems nature of organizations (Pfeffer and Salancik 1978). Resource-dependency theory argues that organizations face environmental constraints in the form of external control over resources the organization needs to ensure operational efficiency and continued survival.

Since few types of organizations are resource independent, they necessarily become interdependent with their environments. At the same time, external actors in control over critical resources will attempt to influence the organization and threaten managerial autonomy. Organizations will, however, not simply comply with external demands, but attempt to employ various strategies to manage dependencies and regain managerial freedom and autonomy. In the process, the organization influences and changes its environments as well. Pfeffer and Salancik (1978) suggest that among the strategies organizations employ are various types of inter-organizational linkages, including mergers, joint ventures, interlocking directorates, and the movement of executives within industries. This may either help reduce dependence on given critical resources or help obtain other resources that are in turn critical to the external actors trying to exercise control.

In the nonprofit context, the resource-dependency perspective is particularly useful in understanding the perpetual quest for a balanced mix of revenue sources. In both Western Europe and the US, the overly heavy reliance of some types of nonprofits on government financing has given rise to concerns about governmentalization, bureaucratization, and loss of autonomy, as well as goal deflection of nonprofits (Kramer 1981; Horch 1992; Smith and Lipsky 1993; Evers 1995; Anheier *et al.* 1997; O'Regan and Oster 2002). All of this can be understood as a failure of nonprofits to manage and neutralize dependency on government resources. It may also partially explain the current revived interest in fostering philanthropy and civic engagement in many countries (Anheier and Toepler 2002) as an attempt to regain resources with no "strings attached" that increase the managerial scope of action.

Developmental perspectives

Organizations develop not only in response to external forces inherent in the organizational environment; internal forces, too, shape organizations and their structures and cultures. Organizational theorists speak of life cycles and developmental stages through which organizations typically pass. Most of the stages organizational theorists have identified reflect the

Table 7.1 *Organizational life cycle*

	Birth stage	Youth stage	Midlife stage	Maturity stage
Bureaucracy	Non-bureaucratic	Pre-bureaucratic	Bureaucratic	Post-bureaucratic
Emphasis	Creativity, survival	Growth	Control, efficiency	Renewal
Structure	Informal, overlapping tasks	Formalization, specialization	Formal procedural control systems; centralization	Extensive financial controls; push toward decentralization
Management style	Entrepreneurial	Mission-driven	Accountability	Enabling, team approach
Transition requirements	Leadership crisis	Control crisis	Red tape crisis	Turn-around crisis

Table 7.2 *Organizational development and stages*

	Entrepreneurial stage	Collectivity stage	Control stage	Elaboration stage
Structure	Little	Informal	Centralization	Decentralization
Focus	Survival	Growth	Efficiency	Restructuring
Innovation	Invention	Enhancement	Implementation	Renewal
Planning	Little	Short-term	Long-range	Strategic
Commitment	Individual	Group	Complacency	Recommitment
Managers	Entrepreneurs	Entrepreneurs as managers	Managers as consolidators	Managers as strategists

experience of forprofit businesses, but they are to some extent also applicable to nonprofits, as shown in Tables 7.1 and 7.2.

At the founding stage of organizations, few formal procedures are in place; the culture and mode of operation is largely entrepreneurial and informal, with a premium on survival. Relations among staff are often trust-based, and leadership is based on creativity, even charisma. As the organization continues to grow and to implement a bureaucratic structure, formalization and standardization set in to improve efficiency and streamline administrative procedure. Staff relations become more contract-based, and mission statements rather than entrepreneurial vision guide the organization. Each of the four stages included in Table 7.1 points to typical crises that help the organization in its transitions from one stage to the next. Table 7.2 shows how the role of planning and management changes as the organization moves from an initial entrepreneurial state to a phase where managers take on the role of the founders and become consolidators and strategists.

ORGANIZATIONAL STRUCTURE AND BEHAVIOR

At the beginning of this chapter we mentioned that a key problem of organizing is the relationship between the organization and the nature of the task environment. In other words, what organizational model is best for what kind of task? Or, following contingency theory, what conditions suggest what kind of organizational structure? How formal or informal, centralized or decentralized, large or small should the organization be? To answer these questions, let us first look at what we mean by task environment a bit more closely.

The organizational task environment and uncertainty

The term "task environment" refers to the specific elements with which the organization interacts in the course of its operations. This includes first and foremost the nature of the product or service provided. Clearly, it will make a difference for organizational design if the organization is a manufacturer of consumables, or is a hospital, a church, or a disaster relief agency. Within the context of the product and service range, the task environment includes not only customers, clients, users, members, volunteers, staff, the board of trustees, suppliers, competitors and collaborators, supervising and government agencies, and professional associations, but also the levels of technology, information, communication, and logistics available to each. For one, each element can make different demands on the organizations and harbor varying expectations, yet the key point is that the various elements can introduce either uncertainty or stability in the organizational task environment—which the organization would have to reflect in its structure and operations. In Chapters 10 and 11 we see how the complexity of the task environment in which nonprofits operate relates to one of their signature characteristics: the presence of multiple stakeholders.

Environmental uncertainty refers to a situation where future circumstances affecting an organization cannot be accurately assessed and predicted. Obviously, the more uncertain the environment, the more effort management has to invest in monitoring, and the more likely are decisions to be short-term and tentative. The degree of uncertainty includes the following two major components (Duncan 1979):

- *Complexity* refers both to the number of elements in the organizational task environment and to their heterogeneity in terms of demands and expectations. If an organization has few task elements and all are fairly similar, such a homogeneous task environment would be less complex than a situation with many more elements that vary in their demands.
- *Dynamism* refers to the rate and predictability of change of the elements. If the elements change rarely or slowly and are relatively predictable, then the task environment is stable; however, if they change often, quickly, and in unpredictable ways, then the task environment is unstable or volatile.

Table 7.3 Environmental task environments and uncertainty

	Low complexity	High complexity
Low dynamism	Low uncertainty	Medium–low uncertainty
High dynamism	Medium–high uncertainty	High uncertainty

If we combine both dimensions, we arrive at four uncertainty scenarios, which are presented in Table 7.3.

- In low uncertainty scenarios, a small number of relatively homogeneous elements remain the same over an extended period of time. The funeral home industry, car registration, day care centers, and elementary schools are examples of such situations.
- Task environments with a large number of heterogeneous elements and low dynamism lead to medium–low uncertainty. The insurance industry, savings and loans associations, higher education, and culture and the arts are prominent examples.
- Moderately high uncertainty exists in cases where a small number of homogeneous elements change often and unpredictably, as with the fashion industry, catering, and many social and health care services.
- Large numbers of heterogeneous elements with high dynamism constitute high uncertainty task environments. Software- and internet-based companies are prime examples, as are disaster relief and humanitarian assistance programs.

From a structural perspective, organizations in low uncertainty environments are best organized as small and relatively bureaucratic: small, to maintain a relative degree of homogeneity, and bureaucratic, to enhance the efficiency of operations. By contrast, organizations in high uncertainty environments are best organized as entrepreneurial, with a minimum of bureaucracy and a premium on flexibility and innovation. Organizations operating under moderately low or moderately high uncertainty have the challenge of finding a balance between bureaucracy for efficiency's sake and flexibility to be able to cope with changing conditions.

While the complexity–dynamism dimensions tell us how bureaucratic or entrepreneurial an organization should be, Perrow (1986) goes one step further and introduces two additional aspects of the organizational task environment in discussing organizational design: the degree of coupling, and the complexity of interactions. His primary interest is in the degree of centralization (i.e. the extent to which decision-making authority resides at the organization's top level) and decentralization (i.e. the delegation of such authority to lower levels).

- *Loose vs. tight* coupling refers to how close to each other organizational units are arranged in terms of time, proximity, sequencing, etc. It addresses the degree of slack

153

Table 7.4 *Coupling and interactions of organizational design*

	Complex interactions	**Linear interactions**
Tight coupling	Incompatibility: tight coupling suggests centralization, and interaction complexity suggests decentralization	Centralization
Loose coupling	Decentralization	Centralization and decentralization possible

or flexibility in operations. For example, there is usually much flexibility in the way in which universities or research units are organized, but less so for continuous manufacturing, or railroad or airline companies.

- *Linear vs. complex* interaction refers to the extent to which interaction sequences in operations are well known, predictable, unambiguous, and recoverable among organizational units. For example, the way airline or train schedules interact is usually well known and predictable, but family counseling or drug treatment programs face greater challenges in these respects.

The key insight suggested by Table 7.4 is that the type of organizational structure in terms of centralization and decentralization depends on the relationship between coupling and interaction. What is more, some of the basic dilemmas of organizing are borne out in this table:

- *Loose coupling and complex interactions* are best accommodated by decentralized organizational structures, as decisions are best reached at lower levels where knowledge is greatest and organizational slack prevents "wrong" decisions from affecting the entire system. Social service providers, health care facilities, and research institutions are examples of such task environments.
- *Tight coupling and linear interactions* are best organized as centralized structures; since operations are well known in terms of interactions, and lower-level autonomy in decision-making could be detrimental to the system's stability, centralized bureaucracies are the preferred structure. Rail systems and continuous processing such as car manufacturing or assembly plants are cases in point.
- *Loose coupling and linear interactions* allow for either centralization or decentralization, and thereby invite political and cultural preferences to influence organizational structure. Universities are in this field, but so are many other nonprofit organizations in the fields of arts and culture, education, the environment, advocacy, philanthropy, housing and development, and religion.
- The combination of *tight coupling and complex interactions* suggests an incompatibility in organizational design. Tight coupling would require centralization of decision-making, while complexity would point to decentralized structures. Nuclear power plants are an example.

An important implication of the typology in Table 7.4 is that many voluntary organizations (though not all) would fall in the linear interaction/loose coupling combination. Because both centralization and decentralization are possible, it makes these nonprofits subject to the cultural and political preferences of boards or organizational elites more generally. In other words, by virtue of their task environment, many nonprofits can afford to operate with flexible and changing organizational structures.

Scale and scope

So far we have considered the relationship between task environment and organizational structure, and primarily the impact of uncertainty. A different perspective for understanding organizational structure is offered by economics, in particular the importance of cost considerations. Business historian Alfred Chandler (see Chandler and Takashi 1990) studied the development of the modern corporation and found two cost elements that are important for organizational design: economies of scale and economies of scope.

- *Economies of scale* refer to per unit cost reductions as output increases. This is the law of mass production and states that goods will be cheaper when produced in higher numbers, as fixed costs are shared across more output units.
- *Economies of scope* refer to overall cost reductions by combining the production or distribution of related products and services. Scope economies take advantage of synergies across products and markets, and thereby reduce combined total costs.

Chandler's main argument is that the development of the modern corporation in the nineteenth century saw first an expansion based on scale economies, both in terms of mass production and the emergence of large-scale bureaucracies. Beginning in the early twentieth century, corporations increasingly began to develop along scope economies and designed organizations to take advantage of synergies in the production and distribution of products. The chemical and pharmaceutical industries were among the first to develop along scale and scope economies, as did the automobile producers and consumer product firms. Retail firms such as department stores and supermarkets were soon to follow along the same lines.

Yet, as Table 7.5 shows, scale and scope economies apply to some product and distribution markets but not to others. Some products and services are highly specialized or have very limited demand so that neither scale nor scope economies are possible. Examples are the production of ancient musical instruments, specialized aircraft or yachts, or luxury goods shops. The size of organizations in such fields is typically small, and their organizational structure simple. In other fields, scale economies may be possible, while scope economies will be limited. Mining, agriculture, and the aircraft industry are cases in point: for example, it is typically only possible to grow one crop per field, and aircraft design is so highly specialized that scope economies via co-production of parts are limited. Other fields or product markets may allow for scope but have limited scale. The specialized tools industry is an example: tools and their parts can be modified and used in related products, thereby allowing for scope economies, but the very nature of the specialized tools market reduces scale economies.

155

Table 7.5 *Scale and scope economies and organizational size*

	Limited scope	**Scope**
Limited scale	Single production *Size: small*	Tool industry *Size: medium*
Scale	Agriculture, aircraft industry, mining *Size: medium*	Mass processing, retailing *Size: large*

Table 7.6 *Scale and scope economies for nonprofit organizations*

	Limited scope	**Scope**
Limited scale	Elementary school, kindergarten *Size: small*	Theater *Size: small to medium*
Scale	University *Size: medium to large*	Development NGO *Size: large*

Chandler's reasoning can be applied to nonprofit organizations (Table 7.6). Some nonprofits operate in fields or provide services that allow for scale and/or scope economies. For example, nonprofit theaters obviously have scale limitations due to capacity restrictions, but the stage itself as well as the production and marketing units can be put to multiple uses. The theater can be rented out to other companies, used for concerts or dance, the production unit can stage performances off-site, and the marketing department can serve other cultural institutions. As a result, theaters can grow into medium-sized organizations, with relatively complex structures.

Universities are an example of institutions with scale but limited scope potential. Clearly, adding degree programs, classes, and students increases the scale of operations, but, at the same time, possibilities for joint teaching or research between, let us say, the English, Economics, and Chemistry departments are few, and even within the Humanities, the Social Sciences, or the Natural Sciences, few cost-effective synergetic relationships emerge. As a result, universities are medium- to large-scale operations, sometimes for thousands of staff, with rather complex organizational structures.

Other nonprofits are in fields that allow neither for scale nor for scope economies, and are consequently smaller in size and simpler in organizational structure. Kindergartens and primary schools are good examples; their scale is limited by each school's catchment area (and commuting distance) and their scope limited by educational requirements and parental choices. For example, even though it would be possible to teach handicapped and non-handicapped children in the same classroom on some subjects, educational policies and parental values may rule out even small synergies in providing teaching.

Finally, there are nonprofits operating in fields that make both scale and scope economies possible. They tend to be the largest and most complex among nonprofits organizations, and they include religious institutions, health care organizations and social service providers, housing organizations, and international development and humanitarian assistance organizations. In each of these cases, it is possible to combine various product and service lines, and develop synergies across organizational units: religious services and social services for Catholic or Jewish charities; relief work and developmental assistance for organizations such as Oxfam, World Vision, or Save the Children; and housing and employment services combined with assisted living arrangements.

However, given the nature of personal social services and the localized demand for such services, larger nonprofits tend to develop into franchise systems, such as the YMCA or YWCA, but also as federations of service providers such as the Catholic Charities of Los Angeles. Franchise organizations are multi-site entities with semi-autonomous franchisees under one common umbrella organization or headquarters. They range from highly standardized organizational units ("chains"), offering identical product and service lines, to more loosely coordinated networks of organizations with greater individual autonomy.

With the possibility of scale and scope economies came increases in organizational size and managerial complexity, which in turn necessitated shifts in organizational structure. The organizational structure of many forprofits, public agencies, and nonprofits resembled that of the simple bureaucratic organization, with a president, a board, and a chief executive officer. Depending on its size, the organizational structure would include additional top, middle, and lower management positions (Figure 7.1a). The structure is based on functional criteria such as finance and accounting, service-provision, purchasing, and personnel, and follows the unit-of-command principle. The functional structure is commonly referred to as the *U-form*, or unitary form, as functions are grouped into one single unit at top-level management. The U-form allows for economies of scale.

The *M-form*, or multidivisional form, is a structure with functionally integrated hierarchies along not only product and service lines (Figure 7.1b), but also along geographic regions or user/customer groups. This form allows for combined economies of scale and scope, and the development of synergies across related services. In contrast to the unitary form, it devolves the organization into different units and allows for better information flows and the establishment of internal cost and revenue centers.

The U-form is best used for stable task environments, routine technology, and a relative interdependency within functions. Its strengths are: efficiency in resource use; in-depth expertise and centralized decision-making; and efficient coordination within functions. Disadvantages associated with the U-form include: poor coordination across functions; a backlog of decisions at the top; unilateral information and decision flows acting to discourage innovation; and information deficits among top management about actual performance at lower levels.

The M-form is better suited for unstable and uncertain task environments, specialized services and markets, changing technology and consumer preferences, and technical interdependence between functions. Its advantages include faster response to environmental changes, client and user focus, better coordination between functions, responsibility and performance more easily identified, and facilities for staff training across a range of tasks. Among the disadvantages are the obvious duplication of functions in each division, the higher overall administration costs, less control by top management, and the potential of neglecting overall goals.

157

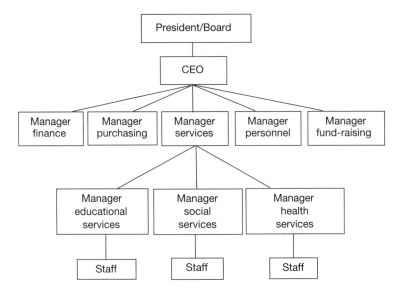

Figure 7.1 *(a) Functional structure—U-form*

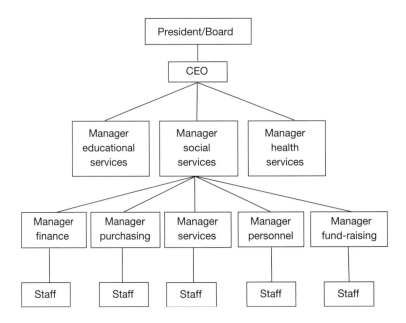

Figure 7.1 *(b) Divisional structure—M-form*

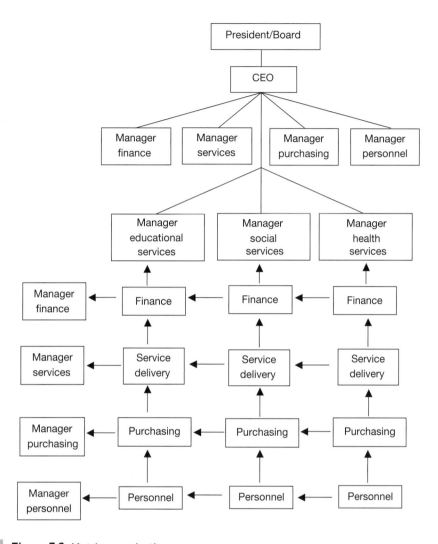

Figure 7.2 *Matrix organization*

Many hybrid forms exist that try to combine features of both the U-form and M-form by seeking better alignments of divisional and corporate goals, while keeping administrative and transaction costs to a minimum. The *matrix structure* is a prominent hybrid form in that it superimposes a horizontal set of divisional reporting relationships onto a functional, hierarchically arranged, organizational structure. It provides for simultaneous coordination across central functions and product/service lines, and, as Figure 7.2 shows, it aggregates information both horizontally and vertically. The matrix form is best applied in task environments that are highly uncertain and complex, and where information is time-sensitive. Its disadvantages are the high administrative and transaction costs, and potential loyalty issues that could lead to conflicts between division and corporation.

POWER, AUTHORITY, AND LEADERSHIP

The issues of power, authority, and leadership are among the most political and complex in any organization, but they appear even more demanding in nonprofits due to the important influence of values on organizational behavior, management style, and decision-making. Working for a supermarket, a computer factory, or a law firm requires little in terms of value commitment on behalf of managers or employees; working for a nonprofit, and indeed becoming a trustee, member, or volunteer, requires a closer examination of value alignment. This is particularly the case for nonprofits that are deeply based on, and guided by, religious, political, or cultural values. In such situations, questions of power, authority, and leadership are not only a matter of goal attainment and job performance but also a matter of personal commitment and expectations.

The importance of values in nonprofit organizations makes them intrinsically political institutions. Values do not exist in isolation but are imprinted in organizational cultures, enacted through day-to-day activities, and evoked on special occasions and during decision-making. The link between values, power, and politics is critical, and values form one of the bases of power. In Pfeffer's terms: "Power is a property of the system at rest; politics is the study of power in action"; politics are "those activities taken within organizations to acquire, develop and use power and other resources to obtain one's preferred outcome in a situation in which there is uncertainty due to dissensus about choices" (1981: 7).

Weber defined power as the probability that one actor within a social relationship will be in a position to carry out his own will despite resistance (1978). Sociologist Emerson (1962: 32) added an important corollary: "The power actor A has over actor B is the amount of resistance on the part of B which can be potentially overcome by A." Power means that one party changes behavior because of the preferences of another, although in most cases the exercise of power does not involve actual threats or force. In modern organizations, power is frequently codified, be it in labor or contract law, or staff rules and regulations.

Power and authority are closely related. The latter refers to the right to seek compliance. Authority is legitimate power and is defined in relation to the overall goals and objectives of the organization. For example, the supervisor of a social service agency can ask an employee or a volunteer to take on a particular case, provided it is within the realm of the relevant job description, but she may not ask them to run personal errands. Authority is limited power, and power specific to contractual and work-related circumstances.

More generally, there are several sources of power in organizations:

- *Referent power* is of particular importance in nonprofit organizations. It results from identification with, and commitment and dedication to, a particular organization, cause, or person. Given the value-based nature of many nonprofits, those representing the organization have referent power in addition to formal authority.
- *Legitimate power* stems from the location of a particular position in the organizational hierarchy and unit-of-command system and represents the authority vested in it.
- *Reward power* is the capacity to provide or withhold rewards from others, including promotions, pay rises, and bonuses, as well as recognition, feedback, greater autonomy, challenging projects, better office, etc.

■ *Coercive power* is the ability, vested in one's position, to sanction and punish others for failing to obey orders, meet commitments and contractual obligations, and for underperforming; coercive power includes the use of reprimands, demotions, exclusion from project, and employment termination. In membership organizations sanctions could imply expulsions, loss of voting rights, or fines.

■ *Information power* originates from access to, and control over, information that is critical to the organization's operations and future. In most organizations, including membership-based ones, informational elites emerge that control information flows and thereby organizational decision-making.

■ *Expert power* refers to the possession of expertise and knowledge valued by members of the organization. Professions such as physicians, nurses, lawyers, social workers, accountants, and teachers possess expert power, which affords them greater autonomy as well.

The six sources of power differ in the extent to which they are likely to bring about commitment, compliance, and resistance among subordinates, as Table 7.7 shows. Minimizing the use of coercive power and maximizing the use of other power bases are least likely to create resistance to leadership, and most likely to reinforce commitment and increase compliance. Relying more on referent and expert power is more likely to increase commitment, and use of legitimate power as well as information and reward power is likely to boost compliance.

Not only are power and authority closely related to each other, but so are both closely related to leadership. This last is the ability of one individual (or a board) to exercise influence on people's decisions and behaviors over and above what is required by authority relations and contractual or other obligations. Leadership is a process of influencing others to do what they would not do otherwise. Or, in the words of Tannenbaum *et al.*, "Leadership is a behavioral process in which one person attempts to influence other people's behavior toward the accomplishment of goals" (1961: 24). There are several types of leadership:

■ *Autocratic leadership* involves unilateral decisions, limited inclusion of employees or members in decision-making, dictating of work methods and performance criteria, and punitive feedback.

■ *Democratic leadership* is based on group involvement in decision-making where the group has a commonly shared mission, devolved power, and feedback based on helpful coaching.

■ *Laissez-faire leadership* is largely symbolic and implies that the group has far-reaching freedom in decision-making as long as it is in compliance with agreed-upon values and principles.

These first three types of leadership were suggested by psychologist Kurt Lewin ([1948], 1999) in the mid twentieth century and have been refined since by two concepts: initiating structure and consideration. Initiating structure refers to the degree to which leaders

161

Table 7.7 Sources of power and likely outcomes

Source of power use	Type of outcome		
	Increase commitment to organization	Increase compliance with requests	Create resistance to leader or organization
Referent	*Likely*, if in line with employee or member values	*Likely*, if in line with employee or member values	*Possible*, if it involves value contradictions and conflicts
Legitimate	*Possible*, if request is polite, very appropriate, and reflective of shared values	*Likely*, if seen as legitimate and necessary	*Possible*, if demands are seen as arrogant and improper, and not based on shared values
Reward	*Possible*, if used in subtle, personal way and evokes shared values	*Likely*, if used in fair, open, and personal way	*Possible*, if used in manipulative, scheming way
Coercive	*Very unlikely*	*Possible*, if used in non-punitive way and seen as necessary	*Likely*, if used in hostile and manipulative way
Information	*Possible*, if information is very convincing and reinforced by shared values	*Likely*, if request and information are reasonable	*Likely*, if used in secretive, manipulative ways
Expert	*Likely*, if request is persuasive and employees or members share same values and goals	*Possible*, if request is persuasive and not in violation of shared values	*Possible*, if request is less persuasive and potentially in violation of shared values

Source: Based on Yuki 1989: 44.

define the role of employees and members in terms of organizational mission and goal achievement. Initiating structure is about group inclusion and participation, and centers largely on task-related issues. Consideration is the degree to which a leader builds commitment and mutual trust among members, respects their opinions and inputs, and shows concerns for their personal lives and feelings. In this respect, leadership has a cognitive dimension that is about conceptualizing, guiding, planning, decision-making, and accomplishment; it also has an affective component that emphasizes emotional, social, and human relations, and, indeed, appeals to people's values but also to their frustrations and aspirations. The latter aspects are particularly relevant for charismatic leaders.

■ *Charismatic leadership* refers to the personal characteristics of leaders that inspire pride, faith, identification, dedication, and commitment and a willingness to follow directives and accept decisions.

Political leaders such as Nelson Mandela, religious leaders such as Pope John Paul II, or organizational leaders such as Lee Iaccoca (Chrysler Corporation) and Bernard Kouchner (Médecins sans Frontières) are positive examples of charismatic leadership, but the annals of history show many abuses of such leadership as well. Charismatic leadership is most useful in times of organizational uncertainty and transformation.

■ *Transformational leadership* involves the motivation of employees and members to perform normal expectations for meeting the organization's mission and for achieving organizational goals. It inspires staff and members to put aside personal self-interest for the common good of the organization and to have confidence in their ability to achieve the "extraordinary" challenges before them.

By contrast, charismatic leadership can be dysfunctional for "steady-state" organizations that perform in relatively stable task environments. In such circumstances, transactional leadership is more appropriate.

■ *Transactional leadership* is about maintaining an alignment between the organization's mission and goals on the one hand, and the motivation and interests of employees and members in achieving set objectives on the other.

As these last two leadership types suggest, there is a connection between organizational life cycle and leadership. Referring back to the stages of the organizational life cycle in Table 7.2, transformational leadership is appropriate during the entrepreneurial phase but also during the elaboration phase; transactional leadership applies to the collectivity and control stages. During these latter stages, leaders are more managers and less visionaries.

Nanus and Dobbs (1999) suggest that nonprofit leaders need to focus on four dimensions (see Figure 7.3):

■ internal organizational aspects, in particular the board, staff, volunteers, members, and users that the leader has to inspire, encourage, and unite behind a common mission;
■ external organizational aspects, in particular donors, policymakers, the media, and other constituencies whose support the leader needs for financial resources and legitimacy;
■ present operations such as organizational performance and service quality, demand, information flows, organizational conflicts and motivation, and community support; and
■ future possibilities, where the leader addresses questions of sustainability and potential threats and opportunities that may have important implications for the organization and its direction.

By combining these dimensions, Nanus and Dobbs (1999) arrive at a typology of nonprofit leadership roles (Figure 7.3), and suggest that effective leaders not only succeed in performing fairly well in all four, but also know when to focus on some more than others:

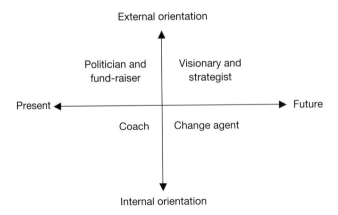

Figure 7.3 *Leadership roles in nonprofit organizations*

- focus on outside aspects and present operations requires leaders to generate resources from the environment (fund-raiser), and champion the organization's cause among crucial constituencies (politician);
- focus on present operations and the internal environment of the organization requires the leader to empower and inspire individuals and make it possible for them to realize their potential; in this scenario, the role of the leader is that of a coach;
- focus on the internal environment and future operations, however, sees the leader less as a coach but more as a change agent by changing its structure to fit better with the anticipated future task environment; and finally
- focus on external aspects and future operations requires leaders to act as both visionaries and strategists: visionaries, because they need to formulate a coherent vision of the organization that can be shared widely among core constituencies and provide legitimacy for change; strategists, because leaders have to identify and implement strategies that hold promise for achieving future objectives.

ALLIANCES, PARTNERSHIPS AND MERGERS

Alliances, partnerships, and mergers are part of a continuum that ranges from the coordination of activities to the full integration of two or more organizations into a new entity (Figure 7.4). While cooperation, partnership, and other forms of collective action have long been commonplace in the nonprofit sector, usually among organizations that share the same values, the topic of mergers and acquisitions is relatively new. Some argue that too many small nonprofit organizations exist that are organizationally weak, ineffective, and with little capacity to provide professional services. As a result, the total impact of the nonprofit sector, in terms of service provision, is less than it could be if larger and more effective organizations were in place. The counter-argument is that the very smallness of nonprofits allows them to be close to the communities they serve and remain sensitive to client needs. By turning into large-scale professional bureaucracies, they would lose this crucial advantage.

Yet between these two policy positions is a range of options that apply to the organizational level, and that are driven largely by economic considerations. Sometimes organizations lack the resources, financial or otherwise, needed to meet given objectives or needs. In such cases, they may seek out cooperative alliances to leverage available resources. Some of the "cooperation drivers" include:

- *Economies of scale* (i.e. increase of capacity to bring about unit cost reductions): for example, by adding capacity through the acquisition of an organization with similar service lines and programs, common costs can be shared, yielding a reduction in per unit costs.
- *Economies of scope* (i.e. combining program/service lines to reduce cost): this would be the case where two organizations have complementary programs, for example a convalescent home and a rehabilitation unit, and some form of cooperation and merger could bring about overall cost reductions.
- *Forward integration* (i.e. control of output markets) and *backward integration* (i.e. control of input markets) are two models closely related to scope economies. For example, a nonprofit music label seeking to control the distribution of its CDs and music tapes would be an example of forward integration, whereas a nonprofit food distribution network trying to produce its own food items would be an example of backward integration. Both forms of integration are powerful drivers aimed at cost reductions and greater control by cutting out intermediaries ("the middlemen"). Cooperatives are prime examples in this case.
- *Pooling of resources* (i.e. joint activities to reduce costs): such is frequently the case for advocacy functions, whereby organizations contribute to a program or organization to take on common tasks in the policy field. Collective action of this kind is facilitated by identifiable threats from outside the field; for example, government policies that would have negative impacts on the organizations involved.

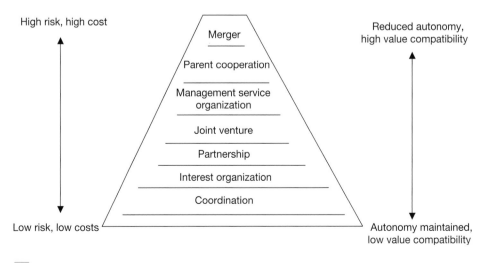

Figure 7.4 *The cooperation–merger continuum*

1 Coordination
(as need arises,
ad hoc and often informal)

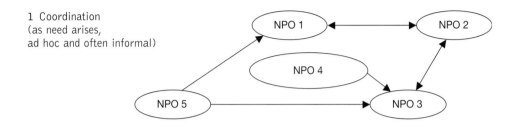

2 Interest organization
(pooling of resources to
represent and further
common interests)

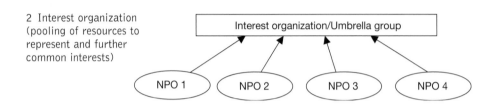

3 Partnership (for common program
activity and typically regulated by
contract e.g. business-to-business
relations)

4 Joint venture (simple form,
whereby parent organizations
remain in control, with the joint
venture run by a manager)

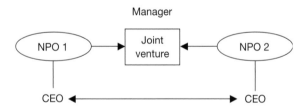

5 Joint venture (complex form,
whereby parent organizations
relinquish control, with the joint
venture run by a CEO)

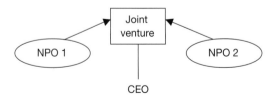

Figure 7.5 *Common organizational structures of cooperation and merger*

6 Service organization

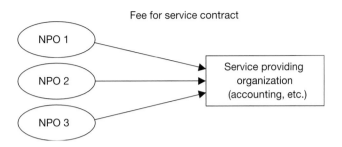

7 Parent corporation and franchise system

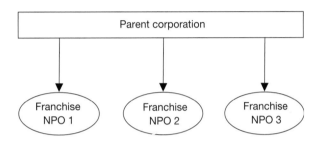

8 Merger

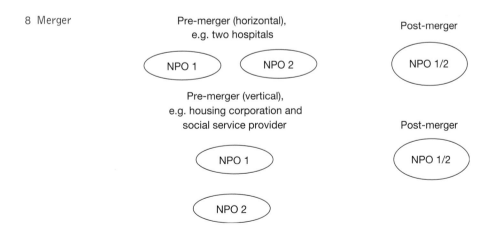

Figure 7.5 Continued

- *Leverage*, i.e. supplementary action to facilitate larger programs, is a common mode of cooperation for foundations and other philanthropic institutions. For example, by providing seed funding or topping off resources already in place, they seek to achieve greater impact.

In making decisions about the cooperation–merger continuum, organizations have to take into account four critical factors (see Austin 2000; Arsenault 1998):

- *costs*, which involve both actual costs of the cooperation–merger and estimated opportunity costs, i.e. the costs to the organizations for not cooperating/merging;
- *risks*, which refer to costs associated with failure of collective action and joined programs;
- *organizational autonomy*, which addresses operational, program, and strategic autonomy the organization will have as a result of the cooperation–merger; and
- *value compatibility*, which is particularly important in the nonprofit field, where many organizations are value-based and represent normative communities. For example, the religious and organizational cultures of Catholic and Buddhist day care centers may be too incompatible to invite cooperation beyond some basic coordination.

Figure 7.4 offers an overview of the cooperation–merger continuum, and Figure 7.5 shows some basic forms of common organizational structures.

CONCLUSION

The great organizational theorist Charles Perrow once wrote that we live in the age of organizations and that little of public life takes place in non-organizational settings. Fortunately, organizational theory offers us much insight into the operations of organizations, their structure, and their leadership. Against this background, the next chapter takes a closer look at the behavior, functions, and impact of nonprofit organizations.

REVIEW QUESTIONS

- How rational are organizations?
- What are some of the determinants of organizational structure?
- What is the relationship between values, power, and politics in organizations?
- When is leadership in organizations needed?

RECOMMENDED READING

Kanter, R. M. and Summers, D. S. (1987) "Doing Good While Doing Well. Dilemmas of Performance Measurement in Nonprofit Organizations and the Need for a Multiple Constituency Approach," in W. W. Powell (ed.), *The Nonprofit Sector: A Research Handbook,* New Haven, CT: Yale University Press.

Pfeffer, J. (1992) *Managing with Power: Politics and Influence in Organizations,* Boston, MA: Harvard Business School Press.

Powell, W. W. and DiMaggio., P. J. (eds.) (1991) *The New Institutionalism in Organizational Analysis,* Chicago, IL: University of Chicago Press.

Part III

Managing nonprofit organizations

Chapter 8

Nonprofit behavior and performance

This chapter looks at the behavior and performance of nonprofit organizations against the background of both nonprofit and organizational theory. The chapter also examines the functions and contributions of the voluntary or nonprofit sector in different fields, and explores if, and under what conditions, the sector performs distinct tasks. This includes a discussion of performance measurement models and approaches.

LEARNING OBJECTIVES

Against the background of the economic theory of nonprofit organizations and the organizational theory just presented, what can we say about the behavior and impact of this set of institutions? After considering this chapter, the reader should:

■ have a basic understanding of the organizational behavior of nonprofits;
■ know some of the major functions performed by nonprofit organizations;
■ be able to discuss whether institutional form matters for organizational behavior;
■ understand the difference between efficiency, effectiveness, and impact;
■ be familiar with some approaches of measuring nonprofit performance.

KEY TERMS

Some of the key terms introduced in this chapter are:

■ balanced scorecard
■ benchmarking
■ corporate dashboard
■ economy
■ effectiveness
■ efficiency

traditional human services, pursuit of economic opportunity, and promotion of human rights or expression.

Preliminary results from eleven of those countries (Salamon *et al.* 2000) indicated that nonprofit organizations did perform a distinctive role as service providers. While some nonprofits were found to be lower in cost and others to provide higher quality services than either government or business providers, the most commonly cited distinction was higher equity content. Furthermore, nonprofit organizations proved to be more innovative—therefore fulfilling the vanguard role—both in terms of the approaches they used and of the type of service they offered or clientele they reached.

Evidence that nonprofits perform a strong advocacy role was also significant. Indeed, nonprofit organizations were generally perceived as "credible advocates for larger community interests" (Salamon *et al.* 2000: 21). Notably, human service nonprofits appear to perform the advocacy role to the same degree as those directly engaged in promoting human rights and free expression. According to Salamon and his team (2000: 21): "Despite fears to the contrary, nonprofits appear to be combining a service delivery and advocacy role to a greater extent than many expect."

What appears to be the most distinguishing feature of nonprofit activity, according to these preliminary findings, is the linkage of roles: for example, service and advocacy, innovation and advocacy, etc.: "Even when they were delivering services that are quite similar to those provided by forprofit businesses or the state, therefore, nonprofits tended to provide them with a 'plus,' with some other activity" (Salamon *et al.* 2000: 23).

Despite the geographical breadth of this study, it is largely based on the qualitative judgments of nonprofit practitioners and experts, and is certainly more optimistic than some of the findings that look at nonprofit behavior using a quantitative, cross-form comparison (see below, pp. 184–7).

The results of the study profoundly demonstrate the importance of values behind the functions performed by nonprofit organizations (Salamon *et al.* 2000). James (1987) and Rose-Ackerman (1996) remind us that religious and otherwise ideologically motivated entrepreneurs are the most frequent founders of nonprofit organizations; and economists such as Steinberg (2003) and Weisbrod (1998a and 1998b) emphasize the importance of "sorting effects" that channel staff, volunteers, members, users, and clients to organizations that are closer to their own values and ideological dispositions, thereby reinforcing the value orientation of nonprofits. Some nonprofits state their values explicitly, as shown in Box 8.1.

MISSIONS AND VISIONS

The functions and values of nonprofit organizations find their expression in missions, or, more precisely, in mission statements. The mission is the principal purpose of the organization, and the very reason for its existence. Mission statements serve boundary functions, act to motivate staff, volunteers, and members, and help in evaluation and orientation. A good mission statement articulates:

- the organization's purpose and long-term goals;
- the needs that the organization fills;

BOX 8.1 VALUE STATEMENTS BY NONPROFIT ORGANIZATIONS

Independent Sector, a US umbrella and advocacy organization

- commitment beyond self;
- commitment beyond the law to the public good;
- respect for the value, dignity, and beliefs of individuals;
- responsible citizenship;
- openness, honesty, and accountability;
- prudent stewardship of resources;
- obedience to the rule of laws;
- embracing a wholeness that incorporates diversity;
- open, constructive response to change;
- appropriate risk-taking;
- honoring the roots of philanthropy and voluntary action while building for the future;
- excellence;
- collaboration and inclusiveness;
- commitment to social justice and to improving the quality of life in communities.

Goodwill Industries, a nonprofit helping the poor, disabled and unemployed

- respect for those we serve;
- service to the individual;
- assumption of responsibility by the individual (a hand-up, not a handout);
- quality service;
- thinking globally and acting locally;
- collaboration;
- the power of work;
- stewardship, financial responsibility, and efficient use of resources;
- autonomy of the member organization;
- best practices and innovation;
- diversity;
- heritage;
- volunteerism.

Catholic Charities of New York

Our belief that all people are made in the image and likeness of God requires both social service and social action to help empower people and to overcome injustices which prevent their full participation in the life of the community. To promote a just and compassionate society, Catholic Charities provides direct service to people who have been homeless, ex-offenders and the families of people in prison. Support is given to parishes and groups working to improve local neighborhoods.

177

Decision-making is top-down and hierarchical, and the controlling authority is vested in the owners or shareholders to whom the organization is also primarily accountable. Government agencies, by contrast, lack a clear bottom-line measure. Goals and mandates are both complex and ambiguous due to changing and at times conflicting political imperatives as well as interventions from outside interest groups. External accountability and the locus of control are split, with public agencies being ultimately accountable to the voters, while direct control is vested in elected officials, which serve as the electorate's proxies. The decision-making process is thus indirectly democratic (through the election of political officials), but internally and directly hierarchical. Ambiguity and conflicting accountability lead to rules-based formalized structures (Rainey and Bozeman 2000). Like public agencies, nonprofits also lack clear-cut bottom lines. Missions tend to be broad and vague, and members and stakeholders may join and support the organization for a diverse set of reasons leading to a complex and diffuse sets of goals. In contrast to public agencies though, nonprofits are primarily accountable to their members who vest operational control into the governing board (see below, p. 231). The proximity between membership as principal and the board as agent, however, is closer, decision-making procedures are directly democratic, and the organizational structure is informal.

Regarding participation, individual participation in the state is typically automatic (i.e. citizenship) and, given eligibility requirements, the same is also true for public sector agencies whether individuals choose to avail themselves of entitlements or not. In some types of public agencies, such as schools, prisons, or the military, participation is or can also be coercive. Participation in business firms is voluntary, although necessitated by economic needs. Participation in nonprofits is typically purely voluntary.

Choices concerning work participation can also be understood as a managerial sorting process (Weisbrod 1998b; Steinberg 1993) that depends on organizational objective functions and individual preferences, motivations, and perceived incentives. There are basically three types of incentives: material, solidary, and purposive (Clark and Wilson 1961; see also Etzioni 1975 for similar organizational typologies). Material incentives, such as tangible monetary rewards, dominate in business firms; whereas government agencies attract participants that respond more to purposive incentives, that is goal-related intangible rewards. Purposive incentives are also critically important for members and participants in nonprofit organizations (e.g. religious and political groups, human rights campaigns), in addition to the solidary incentives resulting from the act of association itself.

Lastly, organizations across the three sectors principally differ in the way they generate financial resources (see Chapter 9). Public agencies are predominantly financed in a coercive manner through the government's power to tax. Business firms employ commercial means of financing by way of charging market prices. Nonprofits, by contrast, ideally or typically rely on donative or philanthropic resources, including gifts and grants, dues, and public subsidies. Since donative financing is also subject to the free-rider problem, nonprofits face chronic resource insufficiency issues (see Chapter 6; Salamon 1995), which tend to restrict organizational size vis-à-vis public and business organizations.

While the ideal or typical comparison illustrates that there are similarities between nonprofits and both public agencies and business firms on a number of dimensions, these similarities cut across both sectors and thus prohibit a simple sorting of nonprofits into either public or business administration. Both apply partially, but neither fully; and nonprofits retain organizational characteristics that are specific to them. The implication for the development of management models, which we will review in Chapter 11, is therefore that nonprofit management is, at the minimum, characterized by greater stakeholder, goal, and structural complexity, resulting from push and pull between the state, market, and civil society and underlining the need for a multifaceted, organization-focused approach.

Does form matter?

Against the background of Table 8.1, the growing literature on the behavior of nonprofit organizations picks up predictions that follow from some of the basic theories we reviewed in Chapter 6, and focuses on one central question: does organizational form matter? In other words, does the nonprofit form make a difference? We will review three major studies that have examined this question from different perspectives and in different fields.

Child day care in Canada

Michael Krashinsky (1998) extends Hansmann's trust theory (see Chapter 6) to examine the relevance of the non-distribution constraint in Canada's child day care industry. He makes the assumption that managers in all institutional forms are profit seekers and that in the absence of effective enforcement mechanisms for the non-distribution constraint, the attributes of the nonprofit form disappear and resemble that of the forprofit firm. Krashinsky conducted a study of quality of day care by surveying the consultants employed by the Canadian provinces to inspect day care centers in order to ensure compliance with regulatory standards. He concluded: "The results on quality of auspice are striking . . . [T]he nonprofit centers provide on average a higher standard of care than the forprofit centers . . . In contrast, $\frac{1}{10}$ of the nonprofits fall below regulatory standards, compared with $\frac{1}{4}$ of the independent forprofits" (Krashinsky 1998: 117). In addition: "The spread of quality within each category of auspice is considerable, however, so that variation in quality within each auspice is more important than the differences in average quality of care among the auspices" (Krashinsky 1998: 117).

However, in a different survey he found that parents cannot judge day care services for their children accurately and that some were not able to differentiate between forprofit and non-profit. "If they could, of course, then, following Hansmann, there would hardly be a stronger argument for the existence of nonprofit centers in this sector" (Krashinsky 1998: 120).

So does auspice matter? According to Krashinsky, the answer is that it does in the case of the day care centers he examined but that using this finding for the formation of public policy is somewhat problematic. The results suggest that nonprofit day care centers do appear to offer somewhat higher quality than forprofit centers, but nonprofit centers can nonetheless be low quality, and forprofit centers can be high quality.

Krashinsky argues that there is reason to believe that the non-distribution constraint is indeed difficult to enforce when firms are small, as is the case for day care in Canada or homes for the elderly in countries like the UK. What is more, if governmental direct

Table 8.1 Ideal–typical comparison of nonprofits, government agencies, and businesses

	Business firm	Government agency	Member-serving nonprofit (association)	Public serving nonprofit (service provider)
Objective function	Profit maximization	Social welfare maximization	Member benefit maximization	Client group benefit maximization
Outputs	Private goods	Public/collective goods	Club goods	Collective and private goods
Distribution criteria	Exchange	Equity	Solidarity	Solidarity
External orientation	External, indiscriminate (customers)	External, indiscriminate (public, citizens)	Internal, discriminate (members)	External, discriminate (targeted client groups)
Goals	Specific, clear	Complex, ambiguous	Complex, diffuse	Complex, clear
Structure	Formal	Formal	Informal	Formal
Accountability and control	Owners/shareholders	Voters through elected officials	Members	Board
Decision-making	Hierarchical	Indirect: democratic Direct: hierarchical	Democratic	Hierarchical
Participants	Quasi-voluntary (economic needs)	Automatic/coercive	Voluntary	Voluntary/quasi-voluntary
Motivation	Material	Purposive	Solidary	Solidary/purposive
Resourcing	Commercial	Coercive (taxation)	Donative	Donative/commercial
Size	Large	Large	Small	Medium

Source: Based on Toepler and Anheier 2004.

subsidies (e.g. grants) and indirect subsidies (e.g. tax exemption) were provided only to nonprofit day care centers but not to forprofits, or if governments decided to bar forprofit centers from entering the day care market, there could be a significant risk that forprofit entrepreneurs would incorporate as nonprofits. Because enforcement mechanisms are lax, such policy-created nonprofit supply monopolies could lead to a situation where forprofit entrepreneurs infiltrated the nonprofit form. They would then operate what are called "forprofits in disguise," i.e. commercial entities under the cover of charitable organizations.

More generally, disguised profit-seeking behavior emerges in situations where disguised profit distribution is possible (James and Rose-Ackerman 1986: 50). Managers may, for example: decide to divert revenue to increase staff salaries and emoluments; do little to avoid x-inefficiencies such as empire-building among staff or pursuing displaced incentives; engage in shirking, i.e. avoiding work, duties, or responsibilities, especially if they are diffi-cult or unpleasant; or downgrade the quality of one service to support another, preferred, one. In other words, the non-distribution constraint alone may not be a perfect predictor of a nonprofit's organizational behavior.

Nursing homes and facilities for the mentally handicapped

In a series of studies, Weisbrod (1998a, b, c), too, explores the effects of institutional form on economic behavior. Does the non-distribution constraint reduce efficiency because managers have no incentive to enforce efficiency, because they cannot share in any profits? On the other hand, does it also motivate managers not to engage in socially inefficient activ-ities such as polluting the air or cheating consumers? Do profit maximizers supply to the highest bidder, while nonprofits supply to those most in need?

Weisbrod looks at behavioral differences between proprietary firms and two types of nonprofit organizations, church-related and non-church-related, in two industries, nursing homes and mentally handicapped facilities. Specifically, he examines: (1) opportunistic behavior by providers who are more knowledgeable than their consumers about the quality of service being provided; (2) consumer satisfaction with services, especially with those that are difficult to monitor; and (3) the use of waiting lists rather than prices to distribute outputs.

In one test, he takes the use of sedatives in nursing homes to examine if nonprofits or forprofits are more likely to take advantage of informational disparities. He finds that propri-etary homes used sedatives almost four times more than church-owned nonprofit homes. Taking other factors into consideration such as medical needs, this finding could suggest that proprietary homes use sedatives to control their patients because it is less costly than labor. In testing for differences in input utilization and consumer satisfaction, he found little difference across form; however, when looking at outputs, results revealed that nonprofit facilities are significantly and substantially more likely than proprietary facilities to have a waiting list. For nonprofit organizations, having a waiting list becomes a signal of reputa-tion, whereas for commercial firms it represents an opportunity to raise prices or expand capacity, or both. Thus, relative to forprofits, nonprofits appear less responsive to demand changes.

185

Health care providers

Schlesinger (1998) examined the organizational behavior of nonprofit and forprofit firms in a variety of circumstances, largely using US health care providers as the empirical test case. His research on the extent and nature of ownership-related differences brought up a number of important findings. One of these was that factors of the organizational environment have different effects on the behavior of nonprofit and forprofit organizations. More specifically, regulators such as governmental and industry supervisory and monitoring agencies, as well as community-based interest groups, show a larger influence on nonprofit than they do on forprofit behavior, and a greater compliance rate among nonprofits. Thus, combined with Weisbrod's findings, this suggests that nonprofits appear more sensitive to government requirements and community interests (i.e. being a good corporate citizen), but less responsive to increased demand (i.e. being an efficient provider of services demanded).

Schlesinger also finds that:

- In industries in which philanthropy plays virtually no role in the sense that donative income of nonprofits is insignificant and in which government assumes a major role in purchasing services provided by either nonprofit or forprofit firms, there will be little difference in performance between them.
- In markets in which proprietary behavior is the norm (for example, there has been substantial forprofit entry), behavior of nonprofits will become more like that of their forprofit counterparts. In markets in which nonprofit behavior remains the norm, the reverse is true.
- As competitive market pressures increase, professionals may use their power to keep the organization from deviating from its mission. As competition reduces the magnitude of ownership-related differences, the declines will be smallest in those dimensions of performance most favored by professionals and larger in others.
- What is more, the effects of professionalization can change the nature of competition altogether. Instead of competing for clients, the organization may compete for professionals who bring clients along with them. One example is physicians who bring with them a loyal patient roster; therefore hospitals compete for the physicians themselves instead of the clients. Thus, if professionals are a primary source for attracting clients, competition will increase ownership-related differences in dimensions that are most favored by professionals, but decrease them in dimensions that have less professional support.
- Because government regulators will be most concerned with issues of accountability, they will favor quantifiable measures of performance. In markets with greater regulatory influence, ownership-related differences will therefore be more closely associated with measurable non-pecuniary aspects of organizational behavior, such as the number of indigent clients the organization serves.
- Because philanthropists are motivated in part by self-aggrandizement, they will favor more concrete forms of organizational performance. For this reason, in markets where there is a more pronounced influence from community-based interests, the differences between nonprofit and forprofit behavior will emphasize readily observed features, such as new services, buildings, and the like.

■ Because government purchasing agents will be most concerned with assuring access for government-funded clients, the larger the influence that the purchasing agent has, the more similarities there will be in the behavior of nonprofits and forprofits in providing services used particularly by the clients of that agency. For example, health care agencies that rely heavily on government funding will become more alike, irrespective of their forprofit or nonprofit status.

In a case study of hospitals providing inpatient psychiatric services, Schlesinger (1998) looked more closely at some of the similarities and differences in nonprofit and forprofit behavior. When comparing the relative performance of nonprofit and forprofit hospitals in industries where the influence of both community groups and state regulators is high, nonprofit hospitals were more likely to treat state-financed patients, those with chronic conditions, and patients with no insurance at all. There were no discernible differences in the degree of innovation between nonprofit and forprofit hospitals. However, in environments with neither strong governmental monitoring nor watchdog groups, but with strong competition, nonprofit organizations seemed to shift their attention to the private sector and were no more inclined to address chronic illness or indigent care than their forprofit counterparts were. By contrast, in environments with low competition and limited influence by medical professionals, nonprofit hospitals differentiated themselves substantially by their treatment of the poor, were more innovative than forprofits, and were also more likely to establish contracts with the private sector.

Schlesinger (1998) concluded that the differences in legal ownership and its consequences related directly to the environment in which an organization operated and he reframed the question, "Does ownership matter?" as, "Under what conditions does ownership matter?" The answer will depend on the field or industry in question, but the work by Krashinsky, Weisbrod, and Schlesinger has provided some initial ideas about the factors involved: the degree of competition, professionalization, the funding mix, and the role of government and philanthropy.

Niche control

Galaskiewicz and Bielefeld (1998, 2001) use the term "niche control" to describe the extent to which performance and resource allocations are monitored and sanctioned by external agencies, be they government or watchdog groups. As Table 8.2 shows, they differentiate between two types of control, process control and output control, and two organizational forms, forprofit and nonprofit (although one could extend the analysis to include public agencies). While many nonprofits are exempt from strong process and output controls, some, for example, general hospitals, are not. Those that are in highly controlled niches find themselves competing on quality and price not only with other nonprofits, but also with forprofits and public agencies. In these niches or market segments, the behavior of forms will become more similar over time, whereas in niches with low controls, form differences will be more pronounced.

Galaskiewicz and Bielefeld explore how organizations react to controls by employing two arguments: the efficiency argument makes a case based on cost and revenue considerations;

187

Table 8.2 Niche control and form arguments

Process control	Output control	Organizational form		Form convergence, stability or divergence
		Forprofit argument	Nonprofit argument	
Strong	Strong	Efficiency	Efficiency	Convergence
	Weak	Efficiency	Legitimacy	Convergence and divergence simultaneously, but more divergence
Weak	Strong	Efficiency	Efficiency and legitimacy	Convergence and divergence simultaneously, but more convergence
	Weak	Neither, but in crisis: efficiency	Neither, but in crisis: legitimacy	Stability

Source: Based on Galaskiewicz and Bielefeld 2001: 24.

whereas the legitimacy argument rests on values, greater trustworthiness, and reputation. Specifically (see Table 8.2):

- *Strong process and output control*: nonprofits and forprofits compete against each other and become more similar (e.g. hospitals, savings and loan associations, and banks). Both emphasize efficiency, as legitimacy will have little resonance among users and consumers.
- *Strong process control and weak output control*: nonprofits will emphasize that they do "things the right way and for the common good," i.e. will be process-conforming and emphasize legitimacy, whereas forprofits will stress their efficiency of operations. Thus the two forms will employ different tactics. Nursing homes are a case in point.
- *Weak process control and strong output control*: both nonprofits and forprofits stress the efficiency of their operations, but nonprofits will also try to show that they are the more trustworthy and reliable provider by employing the legitimacy argument. Social services and day care centers illustrate this scenario.
- *Weak process and output control*: being left to themselves, and except in crisis situations, neither forprofits nor nonprofits need to employ strong arguments to maintain their respective niches. Advocacy and community groups, and religious institutions, are examples.

Coping with uncertainty

In Chapter 7 we stressed the importance of uncertainty for organizational behavior. What can we say about the reaction of nonprofit organizations to uncertainty? The following strategies have been observed (Galaskiewicz and Bielefeld 2001; Powell and Friedkin 1987; DiMaggio and Anheier 1990):

- Goal displacement is a process by which the original objective, while still being formally upheld, is replaced by new or secondary goals. For example, rather than working toward poverty alleviation, the organization may focus primarily on fundraising for its own survival and maintenance.

- Uncertainty often leads to a search for stability, either in terms of new niches to which the organization seeks to migrate, or in the form of copycat behavior, whereby the organization models itself after those organizations it perceives as successful. For example, nonprofits may copy the behavior of forprofits they regard as financially more successful.

- Stronger stakeholders crowd-out weaker or protected constituencies in organizations under distress, leading to new hegemonies and changes in the organization's balance of power among stakeholders. For example, financial managers rather than curators typically gain organizational power in efforts to save troubled art museums.

- In the face of cutbacks in government subsidies or drops in giving, some service providers redirect programs originally aimed at the poor to middle-income groups in order to lower costs and increase fee income.

- Some nonprofits drop controversial programs, and add more conventional ones in the hope of attracting donors and fitting better into governmental funding priorities; it is a "taming" effect that has been observed not only in controversial social service programs and health care (e.g. abortion), but also in the arts and culture, where theaters and orchestras choose standard repertoires with broader appeal rather than avant-garde tastes.

- Uncertainty also increases pressure toward professionalization, and invites more technocratic control of the organization—a process frequently related to the phase transitions of the organizational life cycle discussed in Chapter 7, e.g. the replacement of charismatic leadership by managers in an effort to consolidate operations.

Research has also identified the revenue structure as critical for avoiding the development of uncertainties in nonprofit organizations: as suggested by Galaskiewicz and Bielefeld (1998), and others, legitimacy is an important resource by which nonprofits maintain funding relations. Legitimacy is closely related to reputation, particularly in some nonprofit fields such as education, research, or arts and culture. Nonprofits prefer to stay with routinized funding mixes, and both private and public funders seek providers with a proven track record. This political economy, based on stability and reputation, can put newcomers and innovators at a disadvantage.

Resource-dependency theory implies that nonprofits relying on single-funder scenarios mirror the structure and behavior of their primary revenue source over time. In other words, nonprofit organizations that rely heavily on government funding will come to resemble the public agency over time, and nonprofits that rely on earned income will mimic the market firm. Good examples are the government-funded health care organizations discussed by Schlesinger (1998) above. According to this theory, both nonprofit and forprofit services are becoming more alike and will develop the characteristics of a public agency.

189

EVALUATION AND ORGANIZATIONAL PERFORMANCE MEASURES

Economic theory suggests, as we have seen in Chapter 6, that the nonprofit form is suitable for supply and demand situations where observing cost and revenue behavior, i.e. through the non-distribution constraint, is easier than monitoring actual performance in terms of service quality. Unlike forprofit firms in market situations, there are typically no information systems (such as, for example, prices) in place to signal both quality and quantity of delivery relative to demand; and unlike government agencies, nonprofits are not subject to an electoral process that periodically decides on performance. Thus, nonprofits easily face persistent uncertainties—not only about their revenue as suggested in the previous section—but also about their performance.

It is therefore not surprising, in particular in competitive funding environments, that nonprofit organizations seek evidence about their performance (Fine *et al.* 1998). They are also increasingly asked by funders and oversight agencies to supply such information at regular intervals or as part of grant stipulations. This is where evaluation comes in, and the various methods used represent different approaches to measuring performance aspects, such as efficiency, effectiveness, outcomes, and impact—terms we will define further below.

As Fine *et al.* (1998) suggest, most nonprofits engage in some form of evaluation, most commonly *program evaluation*. In essence, program evaluation examines the extent to which a program meets specified needs. It is a collection of methods for determining "whether a human service is needed and likely to be used, whether the service is sufficiently intensive to meet the unmet needs identified, whether the service is offered as planned, and whether the service actually does help people in need at a reasonable cost without unacceptable side effects" (Posavac and Carey, 1997: 2).

Evaluation models follow the logic of experimental design, but in reality it is often difficult, if not impossible, to establish separate experimental and control groups. In most cases, organizations use a model whereby the organization's performance and impact is measured for a specific time period, and then measured again at a later point in time, usually after a program intervention has taken place. Based on this simple model, there are numerous types of program evaluation, with *goal-based* evaluation among the most common.

Goal-based and, similarly, *outcomes-based* evaluations assess the extent to which programs are meeting predetermined goals or objectives. They typically include a comparison of pre-program needs and performance measures with current or post-program information. For example, a nonprofit after-school program would compare student test scores before and after certain changes in the curriculum, or nonprofits in the field of domestic violence would evaluate their goal achievement in prevention relative to a specified reduction in reported cases. The United Way of America (www.unitedway.org/outcomes/) offers an overview of goal-based and outcomes-based evaluation, including a program outcome model with examples of outcomes and outcome indicators for various programs.

Process-based evaluations, by contrast, are less about goal achievement and more about understanding how a program operates, how it produces the results it does. These evaluations are useful for long-term, ongoing programs that operate in volatile task environments,

190

or that appear to have developed inefficiencies over time. There are many different models of process evaluation, and, in the case of a service-providing nonprofit, they typically address questions such as:

- On what basis do employees decide that products or services are needed, and how would this differ from what customers or clients want?
- What skills, knowledge, and expertise are required of employees for delivering services at levels adequate to the needs profile?
- Are appropriate training facilities and programs in place for staff and volunteers?
- How do customers or clients typically hear about the organization, and how do they come into the programs offered?
- How do employees select which services to offer to the customer or client?
- What is the general process that customers or clients go through with the product or program?
- What do employees and customers or clients consider to be the strengths and weaknesses of the program?
- What do informed outsiders consider to be the strengths and weaknesses of the product or program?
- What typical complaints are heard about the program? Have they increased, and has their nature changed?
- What recommendations are there for improving the program and its performance?
- When and on what basis would the program and the services offered be no longer needed?

Clearly, evaluation requires the collection of systematic information about various aspects of organizational and program performance. While the actual kind of information may differ from case to case, there are a number of methods of data collection nonprofits can use. Each has advantages and disadvantages, and many organizations employ a combination of methods before, during, and after evaluations. Table 8.3 offers an overview of ways of collecting evaluation data.

A performance measures survey by Light (2002) found that 92 percent of executive directors of nonprofit organizations reported increased emphasis on outcome measures. The measurement and assessment of organizational performance and impact constitute a vast field of social science research, and a clutch of different tools and approaches has been suggested in the literature. Unfortunately, it is also a field that offers somewhat inconclusive advice to applied fields such as nonprofit organizations, in large measure due to the diversity of organizations and tasks involved.

For nonprofit organizations, evaluation is complicated by the absence of a fully tested and accepted repertoire of performance and assessment measures. Many available measures derive from public sector management and business applications. Nonetheless, recent years have seen significant developments in the field, in particular work carried out by Paton (1998a), Herman and Renz (1997), Osborne (1998), Murray (2000) and, particularly, Kendall and Knapp (2000).

191

Table 8.3 *Collecting information for evaluation purposes*

Method/When best used	Advantages	Disadvantages
Survey forms and checklists		
When expertise is in place; assumes good knowledge and understanding of evaluation purpose, program goals and operations	– confidentiality – inexpensive – non-threatening – analytic ease – involves many people	– developing valid questions – expensive and time-consuming – answers can be superficial – wording can bias – impersonal, "bureaucratic" – sampling can be problematic
Expert interviews		
When understanding of issues, processes, and outcomes is limited, and a need exists to learn more in-depth knowledge	– depth of information – develops relationship with experts – can be flexible	– time commitment – hard to analyze and compare – can be costly – interviewer can bias responses
Document review		
When program generated adequate and sufficient data on its performance and goal attainment while operating (client profiles, financial accounts, internal reports and reviews, memos, minutes, etc.)	– inexpensive once system in place – information over time – does not interrupt program and routines – few additional biases introduced	– takes time to set up – data may be incomplete – less flexible – data restricted to what already exists
Direct observation		
When it is possible to gather accurate information about how a program actually operates, particularly about processes	– views operations of a program as they are actually occurring – flexibility	– can be difficult to interpret seen behaviors – observer bias – influences those being observed
Focus groups		
When the discussion itself is important, and when topics and issues are not well understood but participants share common concerns; explores a topic in-depth	– quickly and reliably gets common impressions – can be efficient way to get much range and depth of information in short time – can convey key information about programs	– can be hard to analyze – needs good facilitator for safety and closure – composition important and can lead to biases
Case studies		
When it is possible to conduct comprehensive examination of specific case or program area with cross comparisons	– learning experience in program input, process, and results – useful means to portray program to outsiders	– expensive – issues of about how representative case is of program activity – depth rather than breadth of information

The key insights for the selection and use of performance measures from this and similar work are:

- Numbers are important "yardsticks" for planning and for measuring performance and goal attainment, but they are not an end in themselves, and they should not be taken out of context. Numbers need interpretation, and making them meaningful is a management task.
- Performance metrics have to be smart measures—and tied to bottom lines, and as most organizations are multifaceted and have multiple bottom lines, we need multiple performance measures.
- Measures should link the organization's mission with its activities to the greatest extent possible.
- Measures should be tested over at least one business year before implementing them fully.
- Comparing performance measures of even similar programs across different organizations can be misleading; many performance measures are organization and program specific.
- Most measures gain greater usefulness over time and with the availability of time series that track improvements.
- There is a risk that performance measures attract efforts to areas that are more easily measured, but less needy of resources.
- Performance measures can encourage "short-termism," and lead to a neglect of longer-term achievements.

Kendall and Knapp (2000: 114) follow the production of welfare framework (POW) that has been developed by the Personal Social Service Research Unit at the London School of Economics to assess the performance and impact of social service providers. With modifications, POW can be extended to apply to advocacy organizations and informal organizations as well. The main elements of the framework are:

- resource inputs (e.g. staff, volunteers, finance);
- costs associated with resource inputs, as indicated in budgets and similar accounts, including opportunity costs;
- non-resource inputs that are not priced (e.g. motivations, attitudes, and values of staff or volunteers);
- intermediate outputs (e.g. volumes of output, capacity provided, etc.); and
- final outcomes in terms of organizational goals and missions (welfare increase, quality of life, etc., including externalities associated with the organization's activities).

Figures 8.1 to 8.3 offer an overview of the basic approach taken by Kendall and Knapp (2000: 115–17) in measuring the impact of nonprofit organizations in the field of service provision. Figure 8.1 offers a conceptual framework on how the input–output–outcomes chain relates to crucial notions such as:

193

(a)

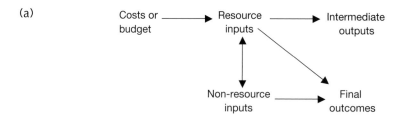

(b)

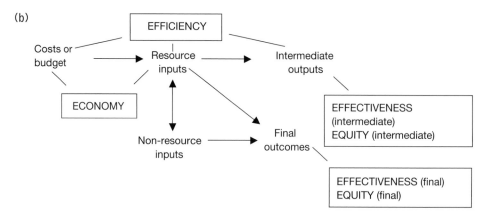

Figure 8.1 *Kendall's and Knapp's production of welfare model*

Source: Kendall and Knapp 2000: Figure 1, 115.

■ *economy*, i.e. the relationship between "costed" and "uncosted" resource inputs (resource savings);
■ *efficiency*, i.e. the economic cost relationship between inputs and intermediate outputs;
■ *effectiveness*, i.e. the relationship between inputs and organizational objectives; and
■ *equity*, i.e. the fairness and net welfare contribution achieved by the organization.

The POW framework suggests that nonprofits should aim for a broader approach to measuring organizational performance and impact, in such a way that indicators are available for inputs, outputs, and outcomes. Moreover, of critical importance are the relationships between the various measures, such as economy, efficiency, effectiveness, and equity.

Some of the major criteria and indicator sets used in the POW framework are presented in Figure 8.2. Figure 8.3 shows the relationship among the concepts in the case of a housing association providing low-cost housing to rural poor in developing countries. The POW framework makes use of economic measures such as expenditures and average costs but also non-economic ones such as participation and innovation.

Economy
- Resource inputs
- Expenditures
- Average costs

Effectiveness (service provision)
- Final outcomes
- Recipient satisfaction
- Output volume
- Output quality

Choice/pluralism
- Concentration
- Diversity

Efficiency
- Intermediate output efficiency
- Final outcome efficiency

Equity
- Redistributive policy consistency
- Service targeting
- Benefit–burden ratios
- Accessibility
- Procedural equity

Participation
- Membership/volunteers
- Attitudes and motivation

Advocacy
- Advocacy resource inputs
- Advocacy intermediate outputs

Innovation
- Reported innovations
- Barriers and opportunities

Figure 8.2 *Performance criteria and indicator sets*

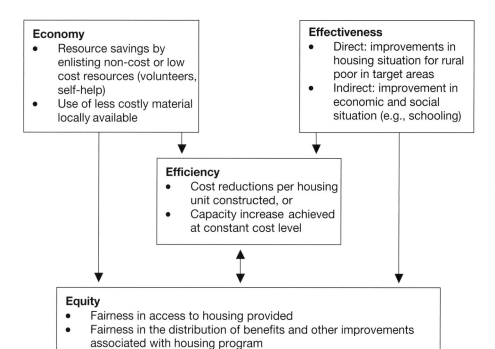

Economy
- Resource savings by enlisting non-cost or low cost resources (volunteers, self-help)
- Use of less costly material locally available

Effectiveness
- Direct: improvements in housing situation for rural poor in target areas
- Indirect: improvement in economic and social situation (e.g., schooling)

Efficiency
- Cost reductions per housing unit constructed, or
- Capacity increase achieved at constant cost level

Equity
- Fairness in access to housing provided
- Fairness in the distribution of benefits and other improvements associated with housing program

Figure 8.3 *Relations among evaluation criteria: low-cost housing provision*

195

3A Mental health services

- Number and percent of clients who score in a specified range on a Mental Health Outcomes Survey.
- Number and percent of clients whose caretakers rate them as healthy on a Mental Health Outcomes Survey.
- Number and percent of clients placed in less restrictive settings; number and percent of children returning to regular schools; number of hospitalizations during treatment.

3B Mental health/substance abuse education and treatment

- Number and percent of participants with increased knowledge of, or desired attitudes about, substance abuse.
- Number and percent of clients who are sober at 3/6/12 months after treatment.
- Number and percent of drug screening tests that are negative or show decreased amounts of substances at 3/6/12 months after program.

4 Homeless services

- Number and percent of clients who retained housing in which they were placed 3/6/12 months after leaving program.
- Number and percent of clients who were employed 3/6/12 months after leaving program.
- Number and percent of clients reducing the number of nights spent on the street by 50 percent.
- Number and percent of clients placed in a shelter or in housing.

5 Home repair programs

- Average annual energy savings of weatherization program clients.

6 Environmental programs

- Number of pounds of material recovered and recycled.
- Number of pounds of recyclable material diverted from landfills.
- Water clarity and quality measures.
- Number and percent of trees distributed for planting that were still alive one year later.

6A Environmental education programs

- Percent change in correct responses regarding knowledge of lake and pollutants from pre-test to post-test.
- Percent of citizens who throw various recyclables in the trash versus recycling them.
- Number and percent of participants who made one or more changes recommended for lawn care, began planting native plants, made changes related to specific practises (such as composting, fertilizing, weed-killing).

B   Reflecting service quality

1   Vocational rehabilitation and employment/job training programs

■ Number and percent of employers satisfied with program.

■ Number and percent of participants satisfied with specific aspects of program, including curriculum and instruction, results of training, readiness for employment, building conditions, lunchroom.

2   Youth services

■ Number and percent of participants rating overall program as helpful; helpfulness of information on colleges, financial aid, and college application processes; academic skills and SAT preparation; counseling; and helping parents.

■ Number and percent of parents of participants who were satisfied with the overall program.

3   Meals programs

■ Number and percent of participants satisfied with overall program.

■ Number and percent of participants satisfied with timely delivery of meals, adequacy of meals, promptness of responses to phone calls, delivery of services in a careful and caring manner, and availability of staff in emergencies.

■ Number and percent of clients who rated the meals as good, liked most of the foods, and reported that the meals arrived hot.

4   Health services

■ Number and percent of clients satisfied with services.

■ Number and percent of clients satisfied with overall quality of service, nurses, home health aides, convenience of visits, timely arrival of staff, information/explanations provided by staff and specific types of therapy/service.

■ Number and percent of families of Alzheimer's clients satisfied with overall program care and quality, staff responsiveness, activities, and specific types of care, such as skin care, personal hygiene, and compliance with medication/treatment.

4A   Mental health services

• Number and percent of clients satisfied with progress in treatment; staff attributes such as respectfulness, competence, and warmth; attitude of employees in facility; frequency of meetings; timely response to requests or questions; condition and convenience of facility; ease of getting referral to facility; cost of services.

• Number and percent of clients who started treatment within 10 days of intake.

4B   Mental health/substance abuse education and treatment

• Number and percent of participants rating program as aiding their recovery, supporting their building a balanced lifestyle, and providing a therapeutic structure.

5   Environmental programs

■ Number and percent of citizens satisfied with recycling program.

Source: Morley *et al.* 2001. © Independent Sector. Used with permission.

In addition to performance indicator banks, several approaches have been developed in recent years that help in the selection and adaptation of such measures, in particular the balanced scorecard, the corporate dashboard, and benchmarking. We will briefly present each in turn.

■ **The balanced scorecard** is a tool used to quantify, measure, and evaluate an organization's inputs, activities, outputs, and outcomes. Originally developed by Robert Kaplan and David Norton (2001) for the forprofit sector, it is based on the idea that traditional measures of performance, which track past behavior, may not measure activities that drive future performance. A balanced scorecard is a *results-oriented* approach to measuring organizational performance, with the assumption that "inputs of resources support activities that lead to service or policy outputs, which in turn produce the desired outcome" (Hudson 2003: 83).

Balanced scorecard indicators, then, consider performance over a range of dimensions and force managers to evaluate both the outcomes and the status of the organization producing them. There are four types of measures on a balanced scorecard: (1) *service users/ policy changes* measuring achievements of the organization's mission; (2) *internal processes* measuring planning and service delivery processes; (3) *learning and growth* measuring organizational capacity, evaluation, and learning; and (4) *financial* measuring of fund-raising, cost control, and productivity improvements. The balanced scorecard shifts the focus from programs and initiatives to the outcomes they are supposed to accomplish, and brings mission-related measures in contact with operational, learning, and financial aspects.

■ **Corporate dashboards** are a "snapshot" of key performance indicators and give an overview of the organization's progress. The idea behind corporate dashboards is that managers are normally overwhelmed with performance data and therefore need something that is quick and can be read, like a car dashboard, at a glance. Dashboards can be produced quarterly and given to board members and staff. Often viewed as an overview or "snapshot" of an organization's balanced scorecard, the corporate dashboard also incorporates the idea that a range of indicators is needed to get an accurate overview of performance.

As an example, the dashboard of Jewish Vocational Services (JVS) San Francisco contains only twelve of its 100 plus performance indicators, and is derived from its balanced scorecard (Hudson 2003). It is published quarterly and sent to all staff with comments from the CEO. The publication also coincides with board meetings for immediate feedback. Additionally, JVS has a volunteer performance measurement committee that meets three to four times a year to help analyze and refine the indicators. In conjunction with this, data from the performance system are used for staff evaluations and promotions.

■ **Benchmarking** is a management technique used to measure organizational performance. Benchmarking is a *comparison-oriented* approach as opposed to an *outcome-oriented* approach to performance measurement. The units of measurement used for comparison are usually productivity, quality, and value. Comparisons can be made between similar activities or units in different departments of the same organization, or across different firms in the same industry. Three techniques used in benchmarking are:

1   *best demonstrated practise* (BDP) is the comparison of performance between units within one organization. This way, superior techniques or greater efficiency can be isolated and identified;

2   *relative cost position* (RCP) is a detailed analysis of every element of the cost structure (i.e. supplies, labor, etc.) per dollar of sales, compared between two firms;

3   *best related practise* is similar to BDP but extends the comparison beyond a single firm to related firms.

Other techniques that complement the above three include: site visits to witness different management styles and procedures; systematic and formal collection of data to compare a range of performances; and the formation of "clubs" to exchange ideas. In the nonprofit field, benchmarking techniques are attractive because, according to Hudson (2003), organizations share a common philosophy of social justice and social service and therefore value collaboration in working toward a common good. This is in contrast to the business world where firms view each other as profit-maximizing competitors and therefore may not be willing to share best practises or techniques.

Benchmarking is also particularly important to nonprofit organizations because, due to their limited amount of resources, nonprofits must find innovative and efficient ways to provide services with the least costs. Benchmarking, then, "is an organizational learning process that bridges the gap between great ideas and great performance." However, Letts argues that benchmarking requires strong organizational leadership and, despite a culture of collaboration and shared goals, organizations must "be willing to risk exposing their organizations' strengths and weaknesses . . . to define their organizational learning needs . . . and present their case to funders and staff" (Letts *et al.* 1999, as quoted in Hudson 2003: 90).

CONCLUSION

In this chapter, we reviewed the organizational behavior of nonprofit organizations, and highlighted, among other aspects, the importance of values (religious, political, humanitarian, moral) as a distinct feature of many nonprofits, though not all. How far they influence organizational behavior varies, but the significant presence of values implies, at the very least, a more complex means–goal relationship between operational and ultimate objectives. Indeed, values can be enabling or restraining; protecting or stifling; leading or misleading; invigorating or distracting.

The presence of multiple stakeholders (trustees, staff, volunteers, members, users, clients, state agencies, etc.) combines with the value base of nonprofits to make them inherently political organizations. What is more, performance is often difficult to measure, although much progress has been made in recent years.

What does this entire scenario mean for the resources nonprofits need to accomplish their mission, and for the different funding sources they have? This is the topic of the next chapter.

REVIEW QUESTIONS

■ Why are mission statements needed?

■ What is the importance of values in nonprofit organizations?

■ Why is it difficult to measure the impact of nonprofit organizations?

REFERENCES AND RECOMMENDED READING

Flynn, P. and Hodgkinson, V. A. (eds.) (2001) *Measuring the Impact of the Nonprofit Sector*, New York: Kluwer Academic/Plenum.

Hudson, M. (2003) *Managing at the Leading Edge: New Challenges in Managing Nonprofit Organisations*, London: Directory of Social Change.

Letts, C. W., Ryan, W. P., and Grossman, A. (1999) *High Performance Nonprofit Organizations: Managing Upstream for Greater Impact*, New York: John Wiley & Sons.

Morley, E., Vinson, E., and Hatry, H. P. (2001) *Outcome Measurement in Nonprofit Organizations: Current Practises and Recommendations*, Washington, DC: Independent Sector.

Posavac, E. J. and Carey, R. G. (1997) *Program Evaluation: Methods and Case Studies*, Upper Saddle River, NJ: Prentice Hall.

Chapter 9

Resourcing nonprofit organizations

This chapter offers an overview of financial and human resources nonprofit organizations use for achieving their objectives. The chapter also reviews various revenue strategies for nonprofits, including fund-raising, and then presents an overview of human resources in the nonprofit sector, with emphasis on both paid employment and volunteering.

LEARNING OBJECTIVES

Like any other organization, nonprofits need resources in order to serve their mission and accomplish their objectives. How do nonprofits allocate and manage resources, and how do they differ from forprofits and public agencies in that regard? After considering this chapter, the reader should be able to:

■ identify the principal revenue sources for nonprofit organizations;
■ understand the various strategies available for mobilizing and allocating financial resources;
■ identify the paid and unpaid/volunteer work forms most relevant to nonprofit organizations.

KEY TERMS

Some of the key terms introduced or addressed in this chapter are:

■ commercialization
■ cross-subsidization
■ equilibrium wage rate
■ fund-raising
■ preferred vs. non-preferred goods
■ price discrimination
■ product bundeling
■ product portfolio map

- related and unrelated business income
- sheltered employment
- value–return matrix
- volunteering

INTRODUCTION

Broadly speaking, resources can be of three basic kinds: *monetary*, such as grants, donations, or revenue from sales and fees for services; *in-kind*, such as donated food; and *labor*, both paid and volunteer. Unlike forprofit firms, which rely on earned income primarily, and unlike public agencies, which are funded primarily through taxation, most nonprofits have a mix of different revenue streams. As we will see, nonprofits make use of various revenue sources—from grants and fees for services rendered to fund-raising and endowment building.

Following a discussion of financial revenue sources, this chapter then presents an overview of human resources in nonprofits, with a special emphasis on the particular challenges that arise from the value dimension inherent in many nonprofit organizations and the frequent presence of volunteers working alongside paid staff. The chapter reviews economic and sociological aspects of nonprofit sector employment and the different types of, and motivations for, volunteering. Please note that personnel management issues will be presented in Chapter 12.

REVENUE

Nonprofit organizations, forprofit firms, and public agencies alike all face a basic problem: how to get the resources to achieve the organization's mission and objectives? The revenue structure of nonprofit organizations is more complex than that of forprofits and public agencies, and nonprofits typically have a mix of different revenue sources that can be classified by:

- origin (public sector, market, organization, individual);
- kind (monetary or in-kind, e.g. time, goods, services);
- intent (transfers such as gifts and grants or exchanges of goods and services against money, and other transactions);
- formality (contract-based exchanges, recording transfers and transactions, informal donations);
- source (donations, user fees, sale of ancillary goods and services);
- restrictions (restricted or unrestricted funds).

The classification by origin or source, introduced already in Chapter 4, is the most commonly used one:

- *Public sector payments*, which include:
  - *grants and contracts*, i.e. direct contributions by the government to the organization in support of specific activities and programs;

- *statutory transfers*, i.e. contributions by the government, as mandated by law, to provide general support to an organization in carrying out its public programs; and
- *third-party payments*, i.e. indirect government payments reimbursing an organization for services rendered to individuals (e.g. health insurance, "vouchers," or payments for day care).

■ *Private giving*, which includes:

- *foundation giving*, including grants from grant-making foundations, operating foundations, and community foundations;
- *business or corporate donations*, which includes giving directly by businesses or giving by business or corporate foundations;
- *individual giving*, i.e. direct contributions by individuals and contributions through "federated fund-raising" campaigns.

■ *Private fees and charges ("program fees")*, which essentially include four types of business or commercial income:

- *fees for services*, i.e. charges that clients of an agency pay for the services that the agency provides (e.g. fees for day care or health care);
- *dues*, i.e. charges levied on the members of an organization as a condition of membership; they are not normally considered charges for particular services;
- *proceeds from sales of products*, which includes income from the sale of products or services, and income from forprofit subsidiaries;
- *investment income*, i.e. the income a nonprofit earns on its capital or its investments.

As will become clear in the next pages, complex interactions exist among the different sources, and increases in some may lead to reductions in others. For example, nonprofit organizations that seek to increase the share of fees for services and membership dues may experience a drop in donations if members regard the organization as less needy or worthy of voluntary contributions above the fees and dues already paid. Against the background of the economic and organizational theories presented in Chapters 6 and 7, there are four key issues for nonprofit revenue strategies:

■ How can nonprofits optimize revenue when they do not wish to maximize profit?
■ How can they set a price when no market prices exist?
■ How can resource dependencies be avoided?
■ How should they deal with negative interactions among revenue sources?

Nonprofits as multi-product organizations

Weisbrod (1998c) suggests that nonprofits are multi-product organizations that can produce three types of goods or services:

■ *A preferred collective good*, which is the organization's true output, and closely related to its mission: this good is difficult to sell in private markets because of the free-rider

Another reason for product diversification is to take advantage of scope economies and bundle products along shared cost items (see Chapter 7). By tapping into different revenue sources, and co-producing and co-distributing goods, nonprofits can capture efficiencies. For example, a college may offer undergraduate education as its core service, but run an extension program at weekends to reach out to the local adult population. Teaching staff, lecture halls, and registration facilities etc. are already available and can be used cost-effectively. Moreover, the undergraduate student pool and extension student pool do not compete with each other. As a result, the college may be able to cross-subsidize across service lines *and* achieve considerable scope economies.

A third reason for product diversification is the need to adjust programs and activities to the organizational mission. Demands for the organization's services can change, reduce the mission–activity fit, and make it necessary to seek programs that are more in line with the organizational purposes. For example, the YMCA has adjusted its range of services significantly over the decades, and evolved from a network of faith-based hostels to multi-service community organizations offering courses, sport facilities, cultural events, etc. In this sense, product diversification is a vehicle by which nonprofit organizations update their mission and mission–activity fit. Yet how are organizations to decide which programs to add and which ones to discontinue or reorganize?

Choosing viable programs: product portfolio map and value–return matrix

The *product portfolio* map (Figure 9.2) and the *value–return matrix* (Table 9.1) are two complementary ways that help management decide on program activities. The product portfolio map has two dimensions for each program (Oster 1995: 92–3):

■ *Contribution to organizational mission*: how much does a particular activity contribute to mission achievement and how close is the link to the core mission? The actual indicators are case-specific but would include qualitative measures such as clients served, number of members, participation rates, and also qualitative judgments by management, board members, clients, and outside experts.

■ *Contribution to economic viability*: how much does a particular activity or program contribute to revenue relative to its cost, and what past investments and future expenditures are involved? In measuring this dimension, the wealth of accounting information and financial indicators can be employed.

The primary purpose of portfolio maps is to help the organization find a balance between mission fit and economic viability across different programs and service lines. Activities in the upper right-hand corner of Figure 9.2 are the most attractive both from the mission perspective and in terms of economic viability. These would be the preferred public and private goods in Weisbrod's terms; they are also the most difficult ones to establish and to maintain, as they are likely to attract competitors. At the other extreme are programs that rank low in terms of mission fit and economic contributions. The organization should exit such programs. In other words, programs around non-preferred services should be added

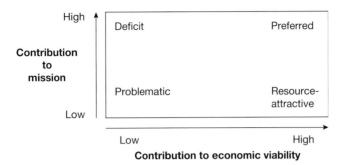

Figure 9.2 *Portfolio map*

or discontinued depending on their contributions to revenue and efficiency. Programs in the upper left-hand corner face budget problems, and their operations can only be maintained in the medium to long term, if counterbalanced by "resource-attracting programs" in the lower right-hand corner (Oster 1995: 93).

The value–return matrix in Table 9.1 offers a similar approach, based on two dimensions:

■ the social value the board attaches to the program; and
■ the financial return and resource effectiveness management can achieve with the activities the program entails.

It suggests that programs with high financial return and high social values for the organization's mission should be built upon and benefit from cross-subsidization and scope economies; and that programs with high financial returns and low mission values should be judged by their net contribution to other, preferred activities only. Programs with low financial returns and low mission values should be cut back, if not discontinued. Finally, for programs that rank high in terms of value but low when it comes to financial contribution, the organization may decide to lobby government for subsidies, apply to foundations for grants to increase revenue, approach corporations to underwrite some of the costs, or seek cooperation with other nonprofits in an effort to reduce costs.

Revenue options and allocation mechanisms

Nonprofits use a broad range of allocation mechanisms relative to market firms for supporting the production of preferred and non-preferred goods, but unlike forprofit firms, prices are not the primary allocation mechanism. Simply put, for nonprofits, those willing to pay a posted price can purchase the product or service; those unwilling or unable to pay the price, cannot. Of course, forprofits make use of different price models and mechanisms as well, from auctions to temporal price discrimination and sliding fee scales, but the key point is that nonprofits use various allocation mechanisms primarily to further their mission, whereas forprofits use them to increase revenue.

Beyond this basic difference, Steinberg and Weisbrod (1998: 66–7) ask if nonprofits differ in their use of specific allocation mechanisms from the behavior of forprofit firms,

- contrasting career structures; and
- different arrangements for bargaining, particularly in relation to pay, and the impact of unions.

They found some evidence to support the existence of a distinctive bundle of quality of work attributes in the nonprofit sector (having examined UK evidence at a number of levels, including economy-wide, relevant industries, and particular categories of relevant employees).

However, in general, empirical evidence as to whether pay and conditions systematically differ by sector is rare, particularly information that takes account of differences in organizational size, kind of industry or field, and the types of occupations and professions involved (see also Leete, forthcoming). This is partly because available labor statistics lack appropriate differentiation between certain forms of work and compensation (e.g. wages, fringe benefits) as far as the paid labor force is concerned. However, based on an analysis of the 1990 US Census, Leete (2000) suggests that wage differentials between the forprofit and the nonprofit sector are likely to persist. What is more, Emanuele and Simmons (2002) found that nonprofit organizations spend less on fringe benefits than business. They argue that employees of nonprofit firms are willing to accept both lower wages and lower fringe benefits because they elect to support the cause of the organization—a cause in which they believe—choosing to donate some of their time at levels below market rates relative to the skills they have.

Paid work

Typical forms

Typical work is usually defined as full-time work with an open-ended contract between employer and employee, regulated working hours, continuous wages or salary, and some kind of job protection. The term "permanent job" also applies to what is covered by typical work. Important features of typical forms of paid work in the nonprofit sector include:

- a certain level of wage or salary, linked to country-specific notions of a "living wage;"
- at least a minimum of social security associated with employment status; and
- some kind of fringe benefits additional to wages and salaries.

In contrast, most atypical forms of paid work and almost all forms of unpaid work lack one or more of these characteristics. However, there are significant differences across countries in the extent to which the standard version of typical work is found, applied, and enforced.

Atypical forms

Typical or regular work is also the starting point for the conception of work in the nonprofit sector. The cultural imprint of the "breadwinner" model that dominated the industrial workforce for many decades has left its mark in the nonprofit sector. In France, Germany, the Netherlands, and the Scandinavian countries, but less so in the US and the UK, the notion of regular work with high levels of job security as the standard was for a long time reinforced by the closeness of the nonprofit sector to the state, in particular in the health and social service fields. Nonetheless, over the last decade or two, there has been increasing awareness of the persistence and often growth of "atypical" or "non-standard" forms of work.

Atypical work is more easily defined by what it is not rather than by what it is; it covers numerous forms of work which deviate from the "classical" Western European and American "full employment" standard and from the "breadwinner" model of the post-World War II period. Atypical work includes temporary work, part-time work, job creation and related training schemes, second and multiple jobs, combining employment and self-employment, sheltered employment, "cash in hand," and other informal arrangements, including jobs on the borderline with the "black economy" with dubious or ambiguous legality, and numerous other forms. This heterogeneity makes generalizations difficult; and when it comes to atypical work in the nonprofit sector, which itself is a perfect example of a highly diverse and heterogeneous sector, generalizations are even more risky given the limited research that has been carried out on this topic to date.

However, "atypical" work forms are apparently becoming more and more widespread— not only in the nonprofit sector but also in the forprofit sector (Delsen 1995: 54). At the same time analysts such as Delsen (1995) suggest that the number of atypical work forms in the nonprofit sector seems to increase more rapidly and sharply than in other parts of the economy. One reason, as mentioned above, is the traditionally lower degree of unionization in nonprofit organizations (see Anheier and Seibel 2001, Chapter 4). Another reason is the greater share of newly created positions relative to the existing pool of jobs, as nonprofit organizations have grown disproportionately in recent years (Salamon *et al.* 1999a). These newly created jobs are less likely to be tied to long-established payment and social security schemes.

Some atypical work is concentrated overwhelmingly in or around the forprofit sector, including most informal and "black economy" jobs, and the bulk of casual, seasonal, temporary, agency, and seasonal work (Almond and Kendall 2000a and b). Prominent examples are migrant workers in agriculture, seasonal jobs in the retail industry, and also phenomena such as "temping" and "moonlighting." The most common forms of atypical work that seem to be disproportionately found in the nonprofit sector are part-time work, temporary work, self-employment, sheltered employment, and second and multiple jobs, which will be examined below (evidence is primarily from the US and the UK; see Almond and Kendall, 2000c and references therein). There is, of course, some overlap among these categories, as they involve variations in terms of time, control, and job security.

Part-time work

The concept of part-time work can be defined in different ways. It might involve all workers whose agreed normal working time lies on average below legal, collectively agreed, or customary norms. These norms vary across countries but in most cases the borderline lies

- Second, the definition provides a distinction between household work and volunteering. Household and family work is a form of unpaid work that relates to issues distinct from those concerning volunteers and should therefore be treated separately. Still there remain borderline cases such as services provided for relatives living close to the volunteer's own household.

- Third, according to the definition, other people have to benefit from the result of voluntary work. Hence it excludes sole consumptive activities such as certain forms of hobbies (e.g. wine tasting, walking). Since activities may contain consumptive aspects as well as productive ones the decisive factor usually is the "third person." If another person could carry out the respective activity, it is considered productive. For instance practising a musical instrument is not a voluntary service in terms of the definition, whereas playing in an orchestra can be regarded as a productive activity.

- Fourth, persons who are legally obliged to provide "voluntary" services—such as civil servants as part of their job description—are not considered volunteers, even if they do not receive adequate compensation.

Volunteering takes place in different forms across many fields and areas. The following exposition describes volunteer work in terms of various dimensions. Not surprisingly, the notions of what is volunteering and what is a volunteer vary across countries and are closely related to aspects of culture and history. Before turning to more economic aspects, it is useful to take a brief look at some of the sociological factors that shape the meaning, form, and pattern of volunteering. Certainly, the British and American concept of volunteering, the French *voluntariat*, the Italian *voluntariato*, the Swedish *frivillig verksamhet*, or the German *Ehrenamt*, have different histories, and carry different cultural and political connotations (see Anheier and Salamon, 1999).

In Australia or the UK, volunteering is closely related to the concept of a voluntary sector—a part of society seen as separate from both the business sector and from the statutory sector of government and public administration. This notion of voluntarism has its roots in Lockeian concepts of a self-organizing society outside the confines of the state. Civil society and voluntary action also resonate in the thinking of Scottish enlightenment philosophy, yet find their most eloquent expression in the work of Alexis de Tocqueville's *Democracy in America* ([1835] 1969). For de Tocqueville, voluntary action and voluntary association become cornerstones of a functioning democratic polity, in which a voluntary sector shields society from the tyranny of the majority. The link between voluntarism and democracy became deeply imprinted in American culture and the country's political self-understanding.

In other countries, however, the notion of volunteering is different in that it puts emphasis on communal service for the public good rather than social inclusion and democracy. The German term *Ehrenamt* (or honorary office) comes closest to this tradition. In the nineteenth century, the modernization of public administration and the development of an efficient, professional civil service within an autocratic state under the reformer Lorenz von Stein allocated a specific role to voluntarism. Voluntary office in the sense of trusteeship of associations and foundations became the domain of the growing urban middle class (Pankoke 1994; Anheier and Seibel 2001). A vast network of associations and foundations emerged in the middle and late nineteenth century, frequently involving paid staff, but run and managed by volunteers. However, unlike in the US, the German notion of voluntarism as a system of "honorary officers" took place in what was still basically an autocratic society where local and national democratic institutions remained underdeveloped. This trustee-ship aspect of voluntarism began to be seen separately from other voluntary service activities such as caring for the poor, visiting the sick, or assisting at school (these latter volunteer activities remained the domain of the church and, increasingly, also became part of the emerging workers' movement during the industrialization period).

At some levels, the distinction between voluntary and paid work is easier to make, and there is a clear difference in the status of volunteers as opposed to employees, even though the differences in atypical forms of work are increasingly becoming blurred. As a result, intermediate positions exist between totally unpaid work and work paid at labor market price. For example, as mentioned above, volunteers, in particular when serving on boards, are frequently reimbursed for related expenses, and some receive in-kind compensation. Similarly, larger nonprofit organizations in Germany provide benefits such as health and accident insurance to volunteers, and some charities cover the pension payments for those working as volunteers overseas.

Informal vs. formal volunteering

Volunteering can take place in highly formal types of organizations such as the Red Cross, with formal job descriptions for volunteers, but can also take place outside organizational settings. Informal volunteering is defined as giving a certain amount of time without working in or through a formal organization (Hodgkinson *et al.* 1996). Informal volunteering either takes place in smaller associations or groups without formally recognized roles for volunteers, or assumes the form of more infrequent and ad hoc participation on an "as needed" basis, for example, in the case of emergencies, or for special events such as community fairs and sports events. By contrast, formal volunteering occurs if a person contributes time to an organization, such as a hospital, welfare association, or school.

Type of work done

Regardless of the field in which voluntary work is carried out, there exists a wide range of different activities, such as raising money, committee work, personal care, and office work. Different patterns of volunteering pertain to individual countries and various types of organizations. Within organizations volunteering occurs on different levels of hierarchy. Volunteers can be found in leading positions, such as on the boards of nonprofit organizations, as well as in positions where they fulfill mainly operations activities, such as clerical tasks, cleaning facilities, greeting and looking after visitors, distributing leaflets, or helping with fund collection.

Corporate volunteering

Corporate volunteering is a specific form of work that predominantly occurs in the non-profit sector. In some countries, such as the US, it has become increasingly common that profit-oriented companies allow their personnel to work for other—mostly nonprofit—organizations within their paid working time. From the perspective of the person providing the work it is therefore not volunteer work, according to the applied definition. The nonprofit organizations on the other hand may consider the work as volunteering since they need not pay for it. Conceivably the work done by someone for the nonprofit organization might exceed the working time paid by the (profit) organization and therefore be partly volunteering.

Dimensions of volunteering and relative benefit

A continued problem in research on volunteering is the multidimensionality of the term, involving aspects of choice, remuneration, structure, and impact of the activity in question. Cnaan *et al.* (1996: 371) examined a wide range of definitions and forms of volunteering and used the classification provided in Table 9.3. These dimensions also involve different net costs to the volunteer, irrespective of the benefits contributed to particular groups or society at large. Cnaan *et al.* (1996: 374–6) suggest that the greater the net cost to the individual relative to the generalized benefit created through voluntary activities, the more altruistic volunteering becomes. Conversely, the less the net cost, and the more personal the benefits, the less the activity can be classified as volunteering and the more it resembles selfish, pecuniary action. For example, a highly paid manager working for an AIDS charity in her spare time would have higher net costs relative to the benefit generated than a college student doing community service as part of graduation requirements.

Motivational factors

Following Barker (1993: 28), we can identify three basic motivational factors to explain why people volunteer: altruistic, instrumental, and obligatory. He suggests a close connection

Table 9.3 Dimensions of volunteering

Dimension		Characteristics
Free choice	1	Free will
	2	Relatively un-coerced
	3	Obligation to volunteer
Remuneration	1	None at all
	2	None expected
	3	Expenses reimbursed
	4	Stipend/low pay
Structure	1	Formal
	2	Informal
Intended beneficiaries	1	Strangers
	2	Friends, relatives
	3	Oneself

Source: Anheier *et al.* 2003b: 20.

222

between the rise of instrumental motives and a change in volunteering toward greater output orientation. Specifically:

- *Altruistic motives* include notions of:
  - solidarity for the poor;
  - compassion for those in need;
  - identification with suffering people; and
  - hope and dignity to the disadvantaged.

- *Instrumental motives* are:
  - to gain new experience and new skills;
  - something worthwhile to do in spare time;
  - to meet people; and
  - personal satisfaction.

- Finally, *obligation motives* are:
  - moral, religious duty;
  - contribution to local community;
  - repayment of debt to society; and
  - political duty to bring about change.

Of course, these motivations rarely occur in isolation from each other. In reality, we find different combinations among them. The factor that bound these motivations in the past was frequently religion or, more specifically, religiosity. In fact, many studies (e.g. Wuthnow and Hodgkinson 1990; Sokolowski 1996) suggest that the degree of religiosity is one of the most important factors in explaining variations in volunteering both within countries and cross-nationally.[3] It is also a factor that seems to be declining in importance, particularly in Europe, Australia, and other parts of the developed world with pronounced secularization trends. In these countries, instrumental orientations seem to have gained in relative weight since the 1980s, while religious values and selfless motivations appear to have lost ground (Inglehart 1997). Moreover, as Barker (1993) suggests, younger cohorts in particular reveal more instrumental and less religious–moralistic attitudes toward volunteering compared to those over the age of fifty-five. Volunteering, it seems, is finding a new motivational basis, perhaps signaling a continuing shift in overall levels and types of voluntary activities over the next decade.

CONCLUSION

Nonprofit organizations are distinct from other organizational forms in that their revenue structure includes different income streams from various sources and also in that their human resources include both paid and unpaid staff. Managing and overseeing these resources and their allocation in furtherance of the organization's mission is the task of the organization's board and management—a topic to which we turn next.

REVIEW QUESTIONS

- What are some of the major revenue sources for nonprofit organizations?

- What are unrelated and related business income?

- What are some of the major allocation mechanisms for nonprofits and how do they differ in their use from forprofits?

- Why do people volunteer?

REFERENCES AND RECOMMENDED READING

Anheier, H., Hollerweger, E., Badelt, C., and Kendall, J. (2003a) "Work in the Nonprofit Sector: Forms, Patterns and Methodologies," Geneva: International Labour Office.

Gronbjerg, K. (1993) *Understanding Nonprofit Funding: Managing Revenues in Social Services and Community Development Organizations*, San Francisco, CA: Jossey-Bass.

Weisbrod, B. A. (ed.) (1998b) *To Profit or Not to Profit: The Commercial Transformation of the Nonprofit Sector*, Cambridge and New York: Cambridge University Press.

Chapter 10

Stakeholders, governance, and accountability

This chapter is in three parts. First, the chapter explores the role of stakeholders in nonprofit organizations, and the special requirements that arise for governance and accountability from the multiple constituencies. Against this background, the chapter considers the governance of nonprofit organizations, the role of the board, and the relationship between the board and management. And in the third part, we examine the different forms of accountability in the third sector.

LEARNING OBJECTIVES

This chapter explores the implications of nonprofit characteristics for the governance and accountability of private organizations for the public benefit. After reading this chapter, the reader should:

- be familiar with the notion of stakeholders and multiple constituencies;
- understand governance and the special challenges to nonprofit organizations;
- be able to understand the concept of accountability and its various forms;
- be able to make the link between governance, accountability, and management;
- understand the difference between normative models of governance and actual board behavior.

KEY TERMS

This chapter introduces several key management concepts (these will be important in the next chapter as well):

- accountability
- conflict of interest
- forms of accountability
- governance

- law of nonprofit complexity
- multiple constituencies
- principal–agent problem
- stakeholders
- transparency

INTRODUCTION

In Chapter 7, we looked at the special functions as well as structural and behavioral characteristics of nonprofit organizations. We return to some of these characteristics in this chapter, in particular the notions of mission, multiple constituencies, the value base of nonprofit organizations, and the complexity of establishing performance criteria.

Even though corporate governance is a relatively new topic in the management literature (Maw 1999: 808), it has been a major focus for nonprofit experts (Ostrower and Stone, forthcoming). In the corporate world, governance refers to the systems by which companies are directed and controlled, which, in large measure, refer to the relationship between board, management, staff, and shareholders, and others such as auditors or regulatory agencies. The most critical of these relationships is the triangle between shareholders, the board, and management. Ultimately, the dominant relationship is between shareholders (as the owners of the corporation) and the board, in the sense that the former entrust and empower the latter to operate on their behalf. Neither the dominant shareholder/ owner–board relationship nor the critical triangle exists in nonprofit organizations. What do we find instead? In contrast to businesses, which are ultimately about financial profit, nonprofit governance and management are ultimately about the organization's mission. Put simply, nonprofit organizations are mission-driven rather than profit-driven.

At the core of governance and accountability is what economists call the principal–agent problem. How can owners (i.e. the principals) ensure that managers (i.e. the agents) run the organization in a way and with the results that benefit the owners? In the business world, the owners/shareholders delegate the oversight authority to a board of directors. The board is then charged with the responsibility to make sure that management acts in accordance with the principal's goals and interest. In nonprofit organizations, by contrast, the situation is undetermined, and it is unclear who should be regarded or function as the owner. Members or trustees are not owners in the sense of shareholders, and while different parties could assume or usurp the role of principal, such a position would not rest on property rights (see Ben-Ner and van Hoomissen 1993; Oster 1995). The key to understanding the relationship between the special characteristics of nonprofit organizations and their governance and accountability requirements—and indeed, as we argue in the next chapter, nonprofit management generally—is to apply the principal–agent test and recognize the special importance of stakeholders rather than owners.

STAKEHOLDERS AND MULTIPLE BOTTOM LINES

Stakeholders are people or organizations that have a real, assumed, or imagined stake in the organization, its performance, and sustainability. Depending on the organization, stakeholders include members, trustees, employees, volunteers, clients or users, customers, funders, contractors, government, oversight agencies, community groups and watchdog organizations, etc. Figure 10.1 offers a stakeholder chart for a child day care center and an art museum to illustrate the complexity of stakeholder relations in nonprofit organizations.

This stakeholder complexity is a good avenue to approach the relationship between what in business firms is called the "bottom line" and the governance requirements of nonprofit organizations. The "bottom line" refers to the bottom line of a firm's profit and loss statement, but is more generally used as a reference to what really matters, or the heart of the matter. Clearly, the bottom line for a business is profit, even though other indicators such as market share or employee satisfaction are important as well. What could be the bottom line for nonprofit organizations, which, as seen in Chapters 6 and 8, operate under the non-distribution constraint?

One answer is found in conventional approaches to nonprofit governance and management: these seem to operate from the assumption that nonprofit organizations have no bottom line at all. Indeed, management expert Peter Drucker (1990) once suggested that, because of a missing bottom line, nonprofit organizations would be in *greater* need of management and good governance than forprofit organizations, where performance is often easier to measure and monitor. While this reasoning resonates with what we discussed in Chapters 8 and 9, there is a major difference: the governance and management challenge is not that nonprofit organizations have no bottom line at all, the problem is that they have several, and, some would say, "sometimes too many." A nonprofit organization has *several* bottom lines because no price mechanisms are in place to aggregate the interests of clients, staff, volunteers, and other stakeholders, and to match costs to profits, supply to demand, and goals to actual achievements.

In the forprofit world, we have market prices for goods and services linking sellers and buyers, wages linking employers and employees (collective bargaining), profits linking shareholders and management, and taxes linking the firm with the general public represented by government. Of course, there are many imperfections in the way such prices are established and brought to market. What is important to see is that at least in principle, all these prices and the financial information associated with them can coalesce into one "bottom line" of the profit and loss statement. Indeed, as Chapter 6 made clear, prices are the basic medium in transaction costs economics and the economic explanation for the existence of nonprofit organizations as a response to market failure (Williamson 1975).

Prices as a medium of information for internal and external activities may be lacking, incomplete, or set according to administrative cost considerations. Some may be proxy to market prices or may be influenced by value preferences. For these reasons, as we have seen in Chapter 8, performance indicators reach a high level of complexity and receive more attention from nonprofit managers and boards. What is more, in contrast to government, nonprofit managers do not typically have the legitimate authority to set terms and prices outside the narrow realms of their organization.

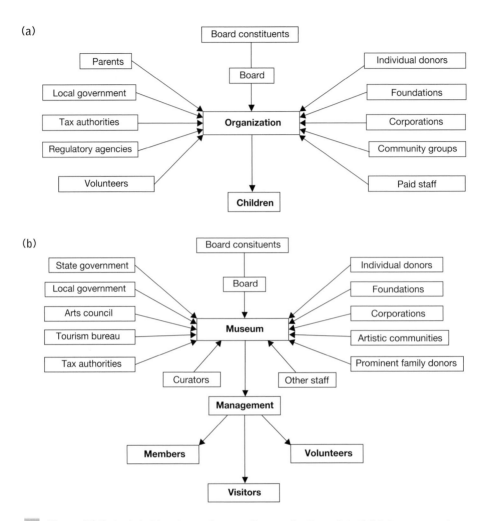

Figure 10.1 Stakeholder chart of nonprofit organizations. (a) Child day care center; (b) Art museum

The result is that several rationales, or bottom lines, operate in nonprofit organizations. Of course, not every nonprofit organization will have two, three, or more such bottom lines; the number will depend on the mission, objectives, task environment, number of significant stakeholders, and structure of the organization. Yet governance structures and management approaches need to be sensitive to the tendency of nonprofit organizations to have multiple bottom lines and recognize that it may be frequently difficult to judge which ones are more important than others. Such bottom lines are represented by:

■ The organization's *mission*, which not only gives the ambitions and long-term view, but is also subject to differing interpretations (see below, p. 247).

■ The *dual governance–management structure* of many nonprofit organizations, where operating procedures are the province of executive officers, and the overall governance is vested in the hands of boards; often the board emphasizes the mission of the organization—and not the financial bottom line primarily, as in the case of a shareholder board; by contrast, management focuses on operational aspects and financial matters in running the organization.

■ The frequent *importance of values* and deeply felt convictions held among board members, staff, clients and stakeholders; and related to this:

   – the complex *motivational structure* of staff, volunteers, and stakeholders, and the interplay between altruistic and egotistical goals;
   – the complex *organizational task environment* in which nonprofit organizations operate, with high degrees of uncertainty;
   – the different expectations and motivations held by core constituencies (e.g. the culture of local volunteer organizations versus the demands of the national unit managed by professional staff); and
   – the interests and needs of *clients and users* who may not be in a position to reveal their preferences (e.g. people with disabilities, children, and older people), or may not be able to pay prices that cover the cost of service delivery.

The multiplicity of performance indicators reflects multiple bottom lines and the interests different stakeholders will have in monitoring and emphasizing those performance aspects that are of greatest interest to them. Because these bottom lines are also close to the major political fault lines of nonprofit operations, we can easily see why the governance and management of nonprofit organizations becomes quite complex. We address this issue next.

THE "LAW OF NONPROFIT COMPLEXITY"

The missing profit motive and the prominence of substantive missions allows a great variety of preferences, motivations, and objectives to materialize in nonprofit organizations. As already noted, nonprofits operate in areas that are often "difficult": social services for people with disabilities, the socially excluded, and minorities; hospices and care facilities for frail older people; international humanitarian assistance; advocacy groups; and local community associations. Indeed, as we have seen in Chapter 6, the very existence of the nonprofit form is linked to the nature of services provided and the fields worked in. These areas are riddled with externalities, and operating in them involves trust and a concern for public goods. These and similar factors, as Hansmann (1996), Rose-Ackerman (1996), and others suggest, make business transactions more precarious, less efficient, and perhaps even inequitable.

In this context, the "law of nonprofit complexity" refers to the intricacy of governing and managing nonprofit organizations, and states that nonprofit organizations tend to be more complex than business firms of comparable size. In terms of its environment (managing diverse constituencies, stakeholders, and multiple revenue sources including donations and grants, fees and charges, and public sector payments such as subsidies, grants and contracts), and its internal components (board, staff, volunteers, members, clients, and users), any nonprofit organization of, for example, 50 employees and 100 volunteers would easily surpass the complexity of an equivalent forprofit firm of equal size.

Handy (1990) suggests that many voluntary organizations contain three distinct components: mutual support, service delivery, and campaigning. These components are weakly coupled and tend to develop their own dynamic and internal culture over time. In fact, we can take Handy's (1990) suggestion of a three-fold organization one step further and suggest that nonprofit organizations are frequently several organizations or organizational components in one. More generally, from a governance and management point of view, a nonprofit organization is a combination of different motivations, standards, challenges, and practises.

For example, a mid-sized nonprofit organization typically has the following components:

- a professional core of managers, including personnel officers, fund-raisers and accountants;
- a governing board of experts and community representatives;
- a client or user base and their representatives;
- a set of relations with foundations and other major donors;
- a set of contractual relations with different levels of government;
- a set of business contracts;
- a volunteer and membership component; and
- the actual service providers.

Each component part, while not wholly self-sufficient, puts forward claims on the organization, and develops its own "culture," routines, and procedures over time. Indeed, Kanter and Summers (1987: 164) suggest that the existence of multiple constituencies lies at the core of governance and management dilemmas in nonprofit organizations.

GOVERNANCE

The term governance comes from the world of business. Corporate governance is the system by which organizations are directed and controlled. The corporate governance structure specifies the distribution of rights and responsibilities among different participants in the corporation, such as the board, managers, shareholders, and other stakeholders, and spells out the rules and procedures for making decisions on corporate affairs. By doing this, it also provides the structure through which the company objectives are set and the means of attaining those objectives and monitoring performance.

Today, governance has taken on a meaning that takes it far beyond the confines of a single corporation and can be applied to entire societies. The Governance Working Group of the International Institute of Administrative Sciences issued a useful summary statement on this broader conception of governance:

- Governance refers to the process whereby elements in society wield power and authority, and influence and enact policies and decisions concerning public life and economic and social development.

230

■ Governance is a broader notion than government, whose principal elements include the constitution, legislature, executive, and judiciary. Governance involves interaction between these formal institutions and those of civil society.

■ Governance has no automatic normative connotation. However, typical criteria for assessing governance in a particular context might include the degree of legitimacy, representativeness, popular accountability, and efficiency with which public affairs are conducted.

Governance is different from management, which is primarily a staff function, although in many smaller and medium-sized organizations both functions overlap. It is useful to think of the board as the focal point of governance, and the chief executive officer as the focal point of management. For Hudson (1999: 42), the governance of nonprofit organizations is "about ensuring that the organization has a clear mission and strategy, but not necessarily about developing it. It is about ensuring that the organization is well managed, but not about managing it. It is about giving guidance on the overall allocation of resources but is less concerned with the precise numbers." Thus, governance involves the responsibility for the organization's performance and direction. Governance is primarily an organizational steering function and closely related to the notion of stewardship.

The board of trustees (or its equivalent) is the governing body of the nonprofit and the locus of the governance function. The board represents the organization to the outside world, in particular vis-à-vis legal authorities and the general public. In nonprofits, where no strict equivalents to "owners" exist, the board is entrusted with the organization, i.e. they are the trustees. The task of the board is to make sure that the organization carries out its agreed-upon mission "without the objective of making profit and with the promise not to distribute organizational assets to benefit individuals other than the clients the nonprofit was formed to serve. All nonprofits, even associations, have a binding legal commitment to this overall principle" (Bryce 2000: 31). Box 10.1 summarizes the basic responsibilities of nonprofit boards.

In essence, governance is about ensuring the fit between the organization's mission and its activities and performance. Kumar and Nunan (2002) examined the various functions and roles of boards, and the responsibilities that follow from them, and developed a useful classification, which is presented in modified form in Table 10.1. The table also shows how some key nonprofit umbrella and oversight agencies in the US (BoardSource) and the UK such as the National Council of Voluntary Organisations and the Charity Commission have operationalized the board functions and role.

Board members have a number of duties that vary by country and jurisdiction, but in the case of the US include the following (see Bryce 2000):

■ *due diligence*, i.e. an expectation that a board member exercises reasonable care and follows the business judgment rule when making decisions;

■ *duty against self-dealing*, i.e. an expectation that a board member discloses and scrutinizes potential and actual transactions between trustees and the organization;

■ *duty of loyalty*, i.e. an expectation that a board member remains faithful and loyal to the organization;

231

BOX 10.1 TEN BASIC RESPONSIBILITIES OF NONPROFIT BOARDS

1   Determine the organization's mission and purpose. It is the board's responsibility to create and review a statement of mission and purpose that articulates the organization's goals, means, and primary constituents served.

2   Select the chief executive. Boards must reach consensus on the chief executive's responsibilities and undertake a careful search to find the most qualified individual for the position.

3   Provide proper financial oversight. The board must assist in developing the annual budget and ensuring that proper financial controls are in place.

4   Ensure adequate resources. One of the board's foremost responsibilities is to provide adequate resources for the organization to fulfill its mission.

5   Ensure legal and ethical integrity and maintain accountability. The board is ultimately responsible for ensuring adherence to legal standards and ethical norms.

6   Ensure effective organizational planning. Boards must actively participate in an overall planning process and assist in implementing and monitoring the plan's goals.

7   Recruit and orient new board members and assess board performance. All boards have a responsibility to articulate prerequisites for candidates, orient new members, and periodically and comprehensively evaluate its own performance.

8   Enhance the organization's public standing. The board should clearly articulate the organization's mission, accomplishments, and goals to the public and garner support from the community.

9   Determine, monitor, and strengthen the organization's programs and services. The board's responsibility is to determine which programs are consistent with the organization's mission and to monitor their effectiveness.

10 Support the chief executive and assess his or her performance. The board should ensure that the chief executive has the moral and professional support he or she needs to further the goals of the organization.

Source: BoardSource. © BoardSource 2003. Used with permission. BoardSource, formerly the National Center for Nonprofit Boards, is the premier resource for practical information, tools, and training for board members and executive directors of nonprofit organizations worldwide. For more information, visit www.boardsource.org or call 800–883–6262. Text may not be reproduced without written permission.

Table 10.1 *Roles and characteristics of governance*

Role and core Commission characteristics	NCVO responsibilities of a trustee	BoardSource responsibilities of a trustee	Charity CC3a
Fiduciary responsibility/ Direction	Determine mission and purpose	Determine mission and purpose	
	Develop and agree long-term plan	Ensure effective planning	Take a long-term as well as a short-term view
	Develop and agree policies		
Steering/ Independence	Guard ethos and values	Ensure ethical integrity	Avoid conflict of interest and personal benefit
	Ensure adequate resources	Ensure adequate resources	Approve fund-raising campaigns
	Ensure assets are protected and managed	Manage resources effectively	Manage charities, affairs prudently
		Enhance public standing	
Process/ Leadership	Ensure activities are legal and constitutional	Ensure legal integrity	Act strictly constitutionally
	Ensure accountability legally and to stakeholders	Maintain accountability	
	Agree budget and monitor		
	Monitor organization's performance	Monitor organization's performance	
	Review board performance	Ensure board renewal	
	Establish human resources procedures	Select CEO	Give employment contracts and job descriptions
		Support and monitor CEO	
Process			Act together and in person and not delegate control

Source: Based on Kumar and Nunan 2002.

- *duty of obedience*, i.e. an expectation that a board member remains obedient to the central purposes of the organization and respects all laws and legal regulations;
- *fiduciary duty*, i.e. a responsibility of board members and the nonprofit board as a whole to ensure that the financial resources of the organization are sufficient and handled properly.

Research on board size, composition, and performance has generated some guidelines, as has the attention of policymakers and umbrella groups. Below is a list (adapted from BoardSource) about the range of activities board members are to undertake in discharging their duties:

INDIVIDUAL BOARD MEMBER RESPONSIBILITIES
- attend all board and committee meetings and functions, such as special events;
- be informed about the organization's mission, services, policies, and programs;
- review agenda and supporting materials prior to board and committee meetings;
- serve on committees or task forces and offer to take on special assignments;
- make a personal financial contribution to the organization;
- inform others about the organization;
- suggest possible nominees to the board who can make significant contributions to the work of the board and the organization;
- keep up-to-date on developments in the organization's field;
- follow conflict of interest and confidentiality policies;
- refrain from making special requests of the staff;
- assist the board in carrying out its fiduciary responsibilities, such as reviewing the organization's annual financial statements.

Conflict of interest

Conflict of interest situations arise whenever the personal or professional interests of a board member or a group of members are actually or potentially in contradiction to the best interests of the organization. Examples would be a board member proposing a relative or friend for a staff position, or suggesting contracting with a firm in which he or she has financial interest. While such actions may benefit the organization and indeed find board approval, they still indicate a potential conflict of interest for the individual board member in discharging his or her duties, and can, consequently, make the organization vulnerable to legal challenges and public misunderstanding.

The distinction between the wider understanding of conflict of interest ("if it looks like a conflict of interest, it most likely is one, and should be avoided") and the legal definition is critical. In most countries, the legal definition of conflict of interest is very specific and covers a limited set of circumstances. However, most conflicts of interest are in a gray area where ethical considerations, stewardship, and public perception may be more relevant than legal aspects. Indeed, loss of public confidence in the organization resulting from conflict of interest situations, and a damaged reputation among key stakeholders, can be more damaging than the possibility of legal sanctions.

BOX 10.2 CONFLICT OF INTEREST POLICY

1   Full disclosure

Board members and staff members in decision-making roles should make known their connections with groups doing business with the organization. This information should be provided annually.

2   Board member abstention from discussion and voting

Board members who have an actual or potential conflict of interest should not participate in discussions or vote on matters affecting transactions between the organization and the other group.

3   Staff member abstention from decision-making

Staff members who have an actual or potential conflict should not be substantively involved in decision-making affecting such transactions.

Source: www.boardsource.org.

In Chapter 6, we discussed the centrality of trust, and the importance of public confidence in nonprofit organizations. To safeguard this trust against the potentially harmful impact arising from conflicts of interest, nonprofits seek to avoid the appearance of impropriety, and adopt specific policies (Box 10.2). Such policies typically include (BoardSource website):

- limitations on business transactions with board members and the requirement that board members disclose potential conflicts;
- disclosure of conflicts when they occur so that board members who are voting on a decision are aware that another member's interests are being affected;
- requesting board members to withdraw from decisions involving any potential conflict;
- establishing procedures (competitive bids, asking external agencies to carry out contracting, etc.) to ensure fair value in transactions.

Normative and analytic approaches

Middleton (1987) and others have questioned the rationality assumption that underlies the common perception of board behavior. Murray calls the normative approach the view that the board has the final authority on governance decisions, and that, in turn, the board is accountable to the organization's stakeholders, for which it acts as trustee. In other words, the board is both legally and morally the agency to see to the organization's mission and performance. Normative approaches are modeled on the classic principles of rational strategic planning.

■ public accountability to the public at large as well as representative organizations and regulatory agencies; this includes submission of IRS Form 990 (or equivalents), publication of annual reports, if required, or voluntary measures such as website and other activities to keep the public informed about the organization's mission and programs.

Leat (1988) differentiates between three analytic types of accountability: explanatory, responsive, and accountability with sanctions.

■ *Explanatory accountability* means that one party explains and gives an account of actions to another party, either verbally or by filing more formal, written statements. For example, watchdogs and voluntary oversight bodies in the field of environmental protection may request reports from businesses or government organizations, but they may have no statutory right to this information, nor can they express formal sanctions. However, they may use public pressure to enforce compliance.
■ *Responsive accountability* implies that management and the board are to take into account the views of those to whom they are directly and indirectly accountable, even though there may be no legal obligation to do so, and no formal sanctions in place. An example would be a foundation in the process of strategic planning and deciding to change its grant-making priorities. To ensure responsive accountability, the board may engage in board-based stakeholder consultations that involve different perspectives and diverse interests. Responsive accountability addresses the organization's public responsibility to take private action for the public good.
■ *Accountability with sanctions* refers to the formal, legal aspect of accountability. It is accountability to those stakeholders that have formal sanctions in place, legal or otherwise. This is, for example, the requirement for most US 501(c)(3) nonprofit organizations to file tax returns with the IRS, or for English charities to submit reports to the Charity Commission, or for German voluntary associations to clear their tax status with the local tax authorities. Yet formal accountability also includes accountability to funders such as foundations and local governments and their potential sanction to withhold or even withdraw funding.

Kumar (1996) suggests several accountability forms in addition to those identified by Leat (1988), each capturing a specific facet of the wider obligations nonprofit organizations may have to diverse stakeholder groups:

■ *Management accountability* (rather than board accountability) refers to the obligations of management in terms of fiscal accountability to parties involved in financial transactions; legal accountability in complying with statutory provisions and regulations; program accountability in ensuring the effectiveness in meeting stated objectives; and process accountability in achieving and, reporting on, stated efficiency levels.
■ *Internal accountability* refers to obligations within the organization, such as between management and the board, whereas external accountability addresses the reporting

> ## BOX 10.3 TEN ASPECTS OF ACCOUNTABILITY
>
> 1 Public information/disclosure, including annual reports, 990s, Internet postings, messages conveyed to the public, audits, etc.
>
> 2 Legal and regulatory compliance and requirements.
>
> 3 Governance, meaning board oversight and fiduciary responsibilities.
>
> 4 Peer accountability, including field reviews, self-regulation, distribution of best practices.
>
> 5 Organizational effectiveness regarding accountability.
>
> 6 Fund-raising ethics and integrity.
>
> 7 Responsiveness to constituencies, including donors, donees, and paid and volunteer staff.
>
> 8 Integrity of the organization's mission, meaning the ways in which an organization works for the good of the public.
>
> 9 Avoidance or resolution of conflicts of interest.
>
> 10 Stewardship of public resources, including funds and volunteer time.
>
> Source: www.independentsector.org/programs/leadership/accountability_forums.html.

requirements to parties that are either supervisory bodies or other external stakeholders linked to the organization.

■ *Approval accountability* is a special version of external accountability, and refers to the way in which nonprofits "seek to project themselves to the outside world" (Kumar 1996: 243). This kind of accountability is closely related to seeking and maintaining legitimacy not only among key stakeholders but also within the public at large. It is a generalized cultural capital on which the organizations could draw if need be. It also refers to the sense that nonprofits, in return for tax and other privileges, are accountable to the public at large.

Note that accountability is different from transparency. The latter refers to the provision of, and access to, information about the behavior of an organization's board, managers, employees, volunteers, and members. Transparent organizations provide information directly and in a form that is accessible and understandable to key stakeholders as well as the general public. Box 10.3 summarizes key aspects of accountability of nonprofit organizations.

CONCLUSION

Demands for better governance and greater accountability have increased significantly in recent years, following in part the increased importance of the nonprofit sector in many

239

countries. At the same time, scandals have rocked the business world, government, and the nonprofit sector, and undermined public trust in many institutions. Prominent examples include the Enron debacle of 2002, the mutual funds scandal, and highly publicized corrupt practises in government, be it at the local level or the federal government. Yet the nonprofit sector is not immune to wrongdoing: the United Way of America scandal of 1995, the failure of New Era Philanthropy in the same year, questions about the use of funds raised by the American Red Cross in the aftermath of the September 11 attacks on New York City and the Pentagon in 2001, and other incidents, have all brought nonprofit governance and accountability closer to the public eye in the US and other countries.

It is important to keep in mind one of the paradoxes of modern society: it is not so much the case that nonprofit organizations, businesses, and government have become more prone to accountability and governance failures than in the past. It is more likely that the opposite is true; and even if it is difficult to provide convincing evidence of this, one can assume that today's governments, businesses, and nonprofits are somewhat more reliable and trustworthy than they were 100, 50, or 25 years ago. What has changed more than the actual organizational behavior, is the public expectation that favors control over institutions, rather than relying on confidence in them. Power (1999) uses the term "audit society" to describe a general political and cultural element of modern society: all major institutions are subject to more or less regular oversight regimes and public accountability requirements. The nonprofit sector, having become more important and more visible than in the past, is now also more within the compass of the audit society and its cultural code of public suspicion.

REVIEW QUESTIONS

- Why is governance of nonprofit organizations different from that of businesses and public agencies?

- What are some of the basic forms of accountability?

- What could be some of the tensions between the board and the CEO?

- What is the relationship between governance, accountability, and transparency?

RECOMMENDED READING AND SOURCES

A good resource on accountability issues and the US nonprofit sector:
www.independentsector.org/issues/accountability/standards.html

Ethics statement by Association on Nonprofit Executives:
www.anetn.org/ethics/

Good website to see accountability in "action" in the field of education:
www.nea.org/accountability/accountability.html

On transparency specifically:
  www.learnwell.org/eth14.shtml

Other useful resources include:
  www.boardsource.org
  www.ncvo-vol.org.uk

Other sources for information on governance and accountability:
  Center for Creative Leadership
  Council of Better Business Bureaus
  Council on Foundations
  Evangelical Council for Financial Accountability
  The Foundation Center
  InterAction
  National Center for Family Philanthropy
  National Charities Information Bureau
  National Committee for Responsive Philanthropy
  National Council of Nonprofit Associations
  Nonprofit Sector Research Fund
  National Society of Fund Raising Executives

Chapter 11

Management I: models

The chapter reviews the background to nonprofit management and introduces a normative–analytical management approach based on the notion that nonprofits are multiple stakeholder organizations.

LEARNING OBJECTIVES

What is so special about managing nonprofit organizations? How can we approach the management of private institutions for public benefit? What does the presence of multiple stakeholders mean for managing one of these institutions? After reading this chapter, the reader should:

- be familiar with the basics of nonprofit management;
- understand the differences between nonprofit management and public sector as well as business management;
- be able to make the connection between multiple stakeholders and the special challenges of nonprofit management.

KEY TERMS

This chapter introduces several key management concepts and dilemmas:

- hierarchy vs. network
- management
- new public management
- outer-directedness vs. inner-directedness
- palace vs. tent
- technocratic culture vs. social culture

INTRODUCTION

Since the 1990s, the need for management knowledge, skills, and training in the nonprofit sector has increased. The proliferation of nonprofit management programs in the US, the UK, Canada, Germany, and many other countries is a good indication of this greater need. To a large extent, this increase is due to significant changes in the institutional environments in which nonprofits operate and the greater policy recognition they receive. At the same time, no specific, generic nonprofit management approach has emerged, and the literature continues to debate whether nonprofit management is a variation of business management or of public sector management, or if, indeed, a new managerial discipline of nonprofit management is needed.

Accordingly, nonprofit management thinking has been subject to various ideas and concepts emanating either from the business world or from public administration. In this chapter we explore these issues, and look at nonprofit management in relation to other management approaches.

Let us look first at new public management (NPM), an approach that developed in response to what was regarded as inefficient and ineffective government bureaucracies (Ferlie 1996; Kettl 2000; Reichard 2001) and one which has, since the early 1990s, changed the way public administration operates. Specifically, Hood (1995) identifies seven underlying doctrines of NPM:

1   reorganization of the public sector into corporate units organized along product or service lines—in essence the shift from the unitary, functional form to the multidivisional form described in Chapter 7;
2   more contract-based competitive provision, with internal markets and term contracts—the introduction of "managed markets" with the public agencies as funders and contract managers, and private forprofit and nonprofit providers as contractors;
3   stress on private sector styles of management practise, including more flexible hiring and firing, greater use of marketing, and improved budget policies;
4   more stress on discipline and frugality in resource use, including a better cost and revenue accounting;
5   more emphasis on visible hands-on top management, fewer middle management levels, and increased span of control for executive management;
6   greater use of explicit, formal standards and performance measures; and
7   greater emphasis on output rather than input controls.

These NPM principles have to be seen in the wider context of two factors: first, the degree of distinctiveness from the private sector in the sense that public management is based on equity considerations, and primarily about managing public and semi-public goods that carry the potential of market failures; and second, the need for rules separating political and managerial decision-making to establish and maintain some "buffer" between the world of politics on the one hand, and service provision on the other. These context conditions are similar for nonprofit organizations, however, with the major difference that the nonprofits are much less guided by equity considerations and much more guided

243

by values. In any case, NPM brought to nonprofit management, among other things, concerns about outcomes versus outputs, efficiency versus effectiveness, as well as account-ability and performance measurement.

While new public management has influenced nonprofit management in contracting, organizational structure, and governance, business administration contributed *inter alia* to an increased consumer orientation (Drucker 1990), marketing management concepts (Kotler and Andreasen 1991), and most recently a focus on social entrepreneurship (Borzaga and Santuari 1998; Borzaga and Defourny 2001; Dees *et al.* 2001).

On the one hand, these various concepts and pressures have led to a number of competing ideas and fashions of nonprofit management (Light 2000). On the other, they have so far prevented the development of generally accepted, comprehensive management models that are distinctly different from those of business and public administration, and that go substan-tially beyond the discussion of typical nonprofit management tasks and issues. Given this background, the question arises as to why the evolution of a specific nonprofit management science is necessary or desirable in the first place. To the extent that nonprofits are no more than an extension of government, public administration and management concepts would be sufficient to address management challenges. To the extent that nonprofits are no more than "forprofits in disguise" (Weisbrod 1988), traditional business administration might well suffice.

Yet could there be a third option? Could it be that some aspects of nonprofit manage-ment are rather close to business management, while others call for models from public administration, including new public management? Importantly, could it also be that other aspects yet are *specific* to the nonprofit form? If nonprofit organizations perform a set of special functions that set them apart from both government and the business sector, as we have seen in Chapter 8, and if a number of structural differences exist across the three sectors, would such a situation not require distinct approaches to managing nonprofits? Before proceeding to answer these questions, however, it is useful to review some basic management concepts.

WHAT IS MANAGEMENT?

Management is the process of planning, organizing, directing, and controlling activities to accomplish the stated organizational objectives of organizations and their members. Management is different from governance, as we have seen in Chapter 10, although there is some overlap between both functions. Management makes an organizational mission operational, and works toward achieving its objectives. There are several core management activities:

- planning (i.e. engaging in long-term strategic planning, making decisions affecting major divisions, functions, and operations);
- controlling (i.e. allocation of human, financial, and material resources);
- monitoring (i.e. developing, measuring, and applying performance measures);
- supervising (i.e. overseeing the work of subordinates);

244

- coordinating (i.e. coordinating with other managers and staff outside direct area of control);
- marketing (i.e. "selling" the product/service to customers; watching field, "market");
- external relations with stakeholders, other organizations, government agencies, etc.;
- consulting with peers and other professionals.

For Magretta (2002), management involves three critical points. First, the chief responsibility of management is "value creation" in relation to the organization's stated mission. For example, if the mission is to help the homeless to gain paid employment, then all management activities are to contribute to the stated objectives around that mission, i.e. "create value" for the organization in fighting homelessness. In this sense, management is all about how that mission is to be accomplished within the guidelines established by the board.

Second, even within the guidelines established by the board, management involves making critical, clear, and consistent choices. This means weighing trade-offs and establishing boundaries. It is as much about what to do well as it is about what not to do at all.

Third, the design of organizations and their management styles is contingent upon mission, strategy, and task environment (see Chapter 7). No management model fits all circumstances equally well, and like organizational structure, management approaches are context- and task-specific.

Against this background, it is useful to recall the notion from Chapter 10 that nonprofit organizations consist of multiple components and complex, internal federations or coalitions among stakeholders. The structure of nonprofit organizations may require a multi-faceted, flexible approach to management and not the use of singular, ready-made models carried over from the business world or from public management. This is the true challenge nonprofit management theory and practise face: how to manage organizations that have multiple bottom lines and are therefore intrinsically complex. In the next section, we turn to this task.

TOWARD A COMPREHENSIVE NONPROFIT MANAGEMENT APPROACH

While forprofit and public management approaches offer important insights into how to manage nonprofit organizations, they still fail to provide a more contextual and comprehensive approach. Models are needed to more fully account for the fact that nonprofit organizations are multitudes of different organizational components. Fortunately, the management concept suggested by Gomez and Zimmermann (1993) offers a useful step toward the development of management models that are more fully in tune with the realities of nonprofit organizations. Among the key facets of their approach applied to the nonprofit field are:

- A *holistic conception* of the organization that emphasizes the relationship between it and its environment, the diversity of orientations within and outside it, and the complexity of demands put upon it. A holistic view of organizations is particularly needed in the nonprofit field, where they are frequently part of larger public–private systems of service delivery. In such systems where multiple bottom lines are in operation, information available to management is frequently incomplete, dated, and distorted.

■ A *normative dimension* of management that includes not only economic aspects, but also the importance of values and the impact of politics, as exemplified by the value guardian and advocacy roles of nonprofits (see Chapter 8). Thus, in addition to management under uncertainty that is the result of incomplete information, we are dealing with organizations that involve different perceptions and projections of reality as well as different assessments and implications for different constituencies. The normative dimension of nonprofit organizations has been emphasized by a number of researchers (Herman and Renz 1997; Paton 1998b), and this suggests that it may be wrong to approach nonprofit management as if value and normative orientations would not matter.

■ A *strategic–developmental dimension* that sees organizations as an evolving system encountering problems and opportunities that frequently involve fundamental dilemmas for management. This dimension views nonprofit organizations as entities that change over time as they deal with the opportunities and constraints confronting them as part of a larger political economy (Grønbjerg 1993).

■ An *operative dimension* that deals with the everyday functioning of the organization, such as administration and accounting, personnel and service delivery. This is indeed the part that has been the focus of conventional nonprofit management (e.g. Herman 1994; Oster 1995).

Thus, organizations are seen as economic and political systems that have normative and strategic as well as operative dimensions. As nonprofit organizations evolve, their basic structural features reflect choices on how to combine, integrate, or control the various component parts. In other words, if we understand organizations as systems with various component parts, we can begin to analyze central organizational dimensions as a series of choices made (or not made) by management or the governing body over time. This is the key to nonprofit management.

From organizational theory in Chapter 7, we learned of the close relationship that exists between key characteristics of task environments and organizational structure. For some tasks, a centralized, hierarchical approach works best for both efficiency and effectiveness, while for other task environments, an organizational structure made up of decentralized and flexible units seems best suited (Perrow 1986). In the case of nonprofit organizations, we find a complex picture: some parts of the organizational task environment are best centralized, such as controlling or fund-raising; other parts of the organizational task environment could be either centralized or decentralized, depending on managerial preferences or the prevailing organizational culture; yet other parts, typically those involving greater uncertainty and ambiguity, are best organized in a decentralized way. In other words, nonprofit organizations are subject to both centralizing and decentralizing tendencies. For example, environmental organizations are often caught between the centralizing tendencies of a national federation that emphasizes the need to "speak with one voice" in policy debates, and the decentralizing efforts of local groups that focus on local needs and demands.

The key point is that the multiple bottom lines present in nonprofit organizations demand different management models and styles. Thus, various management models are possible, and indeed needed, in nonprofit organizations. What is more, the different stakeholders and constituencies associated with specific bottom lines are likely to favor, even push for, "their" way of running the organization. The image we gain from this description is that of organizations whose management is subject to the "push and pull" of their various component parts. How could the various push and pull factors in nonprofit organizations be identified, and what overall framework would allow us to put them in the context of each other and the requirements of the organizational task environment?

An analytic–normative model of nonprofit organizations

Against the background laid out above, the model of nonprofit organizations as conglomerates of multiple organizations or component parts represents one possible analytical framework that can be used to understand the various dimensions, dilemmas, and structures involved in nonprofit management. Such a model involves several crucial dimensions:

- performance–time axes that address the permanence and objectives of the organizations;
- task–formalization axes that deal with the task environment and organizational culture;
- structure–hierarchy axes that relate to aspects of organizational design; and
- orientation–identity axes that address the relation between the organization and its environment.

Palace vs. tent

The performance–time axes lead to a critical first dimension between "palace" and "tent." A *palace organization* values predictability over improvisation, dwells on constraints rather than opportunities, borrows solutions rather than inventing them, defends past actions rather than devising new ones, favors accounting over goal flexibility, searches for "final" solutions, and discourages contradictions and experiments (Hedberg *et al.* 1976; Weick 1977). For example, many of the larger nonprofit service providers, think-tanks and foundations have become more palace-like in their organization. By contrast, a *tent organization* (Hedberg *et al.* 1976; Starbuck and Dutton 1973; Mintzberg, 1983) places emphasis on creativity, immediacy, and initiative, rather than authority, clarity, and decisiveness; the organization emphasizes neither harmony nor durability of solutions and asks, "Why be more consistent than the world around us?" Civic action groups and citizen initiatives, self-help groups among people with disabilities, and local nonprofit theaters are frequently tent-like organizations.

Few nonprofit organizations are either "pure" tent or "pure" palace. Instead, nonprofit organizations are frequently both. Behind this tent–palace duality is the notion that some of the multiple components of nonprofit organizations tend to be more *tent-like*, while others are more *palace-like*. For example, administration tasks tend to favor palace-like

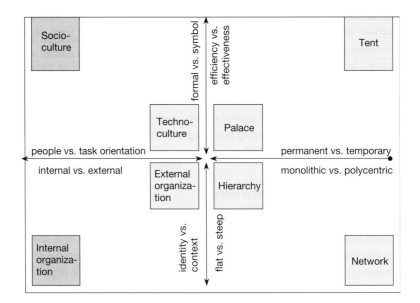

Figure 11.2 *Dimensions of organizational structure*
Source: Based on Gomez and Zimmerman 1993.

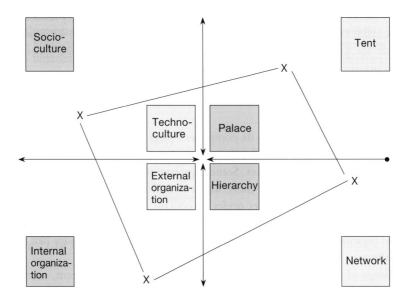

Figure 11.3 *Positioning of management styles and structure*

and our own resources and capabilities?" (Figure 11.3). In this sense, we can easily see that nonprofit management becomes more than just cost-cutting, the exercise of financial control, and formal accountability, and, generally, more than just the sum of its component tasks. Management becomes concerned with more than just one or two of the numerous bottom lines nonprofit organizations have. In other words, management becomes not the controlling but the creative, enabling arm of nonprofit organizations.

Dimensions and structural elements of organizations

Drucker questions[1]

The notion that nonprofit organizations are entities made up of multiple components and with multiple stakeholders fits well with the approach suggested by Peter Drucker, who suggests that nonprofit institutions need a healthy atmosphere for dissent if they wish to foster innovation and commitment (1990). Since many organizational decisions are important to some if not most stakeholders, they are likely to be controversial. At the same time, however, the organizational culture of nonprofit organizations encourages conflict avoidance rather than engagement. Value commitments and dedication to public benefit make it more likely that members, volunteers, staff, and board will not seek constructive disagreements, precisely *because* everybody is committed to a good cause.

Drucker suggests that five simple questions can help nonprofit organizations in seeking the constructive engagement needed for key stakeholders. They are also useful for helping locate stakeholders in the "organizational space" shown in Figure 11.3. The questions are:

1   **What is our mission?**

   ■   What is the current mission?
   ■   What are our challenges?
   ■   What are our opportunities?
   ■   Does the mission need to be revisited?

2   **Who are our customers (members/clients/users)?**

   ■   Who are our primary and supporting customers?
   ■   How will our customers change?

3   **What do our customers value?**

   ■   What do we believe our primary and supporting customers value?
   ■   What knowledge do we need to gain from our customers?
   ■   How will we participate in gaining this knowledge?

4   **What are our results?**

   ■   How do we define results?
   ■   Are we successful?

- How should we define results?
- What must we strengthen or abandon?

5 **What is our plan?**
- Should the mission be changed?
- What are our goals?

As Drucker and his associates suggest (1990), the questions are straightforward—and deceptively simple. Yet by going through the self-assessment of answering these questions, and by giving voice to each key stakeholder, nonprofit organizations will be in a better position to match mission, structure, and organizational cultures.

CONCLUSION

Multiplicity is the signature of nonprofit organizations. The challenge for management, then, is to develop models that identify these components, their cultures, goals, and operating procedures in an effort to establish some coherence and identity between mission, activities, and outcomes. What are the implications of this discussion in the context of current developments? A full account of implications that follow from the approach suggested here is beyond the scope of this chapter. Nonetheless, two theoretical and management-related implications are apparent:

Avoiding inertia and inefficiency

Meyer and Zucker (1989) have commented on the persistence of nonprofit organizations despite low performance. This view, echoed by Seibel (1996), diagnoses the longevity of nonprofits as a case of permanent failure rather than success. They suggest that because of their complicated governance structure and minimal influences from markets and the electorate to check on performance, nonprofits can easily be maneuvered into a state of hidden failure. In the context of the management model suggested here, we can easily understand why and how this can happen. Different organizational components may be unknowingly locked into a stalemate, unable to change matters without giving up their own position. Truly successful nonprofit organizations require proactive management models, not management by exception. Because performance signals from markets and electorates are incomplete, if not totally missing, proactive management frequently has to position and locate the organization—particularly at critical stages of organizational development (see Chapter 7).

Form rigidities

Not all nonprofits must necessarily remain nonprofits. The notion of nonprofit organizations as multiple organizations contains the possibility that some components may acquire a more businesslike or market-driven character over time. If this component (for example, service delivery, marketing, fund-raising) becomes dominant, management must consider if the nonprofit form is still appropriate given prevailing demand and supply conditions. This is the case in the US health care field, where many hospitals and clinics are migrating to the for-profit sector, having lost their distinct multiplicity and having become simpler organizations in the process. Likewise, organizations may decide to protect their core mission from commercial pressures and find a form and structure suitable for that purpose.

REVIEW QUESTIONS

- What are some of the main challenges of nonprofit management?
- What does a normative approach to nonprofit management mean?
- How do the five Drucker questions relate to the notion that nonprofit organizations have multiple stakeholders?

REFERENCES AND RECOMMENDED READING

Drucker, P. F. (1998) *The Drucker Foundation Self-Assessment Tool: Participant Workbook*, San Francisco, CA: Jossey-Bass.

Magretta, J. (2002) *What Management Is: How it Works and Why it's Everyone's Business*, New York: The Free Press.

Ott, J. S. (ed.) (2001) *The Nature of the Nonprofit Sector*, Boulder, CO: Westview Press.

Chapter 12

Management II:
tools and special topics

This chapter reviews a number of basic management tools and issues that reflect the normative–analytical management approach introduced in Chapter 11. More specifically, the chapter looks at human resource management and strategic management, presents a number of planning techniques appropriate for nonprofits, and concludes with a brief overview of financial management, business plans, and marketing.

LEARNING OBJECTIVES

Having reviewed management models and presented the case for a normative management approach in the previous chapter, this chapter is concerned with more specific tools and planning techniques that are appropriate and useful for nonprofit organizations. After reading this chapter, the reader should:

- be familiar with basic aspects of human resource management;
- have an understanding of strategic planning and management planning tools;
- be familiar with the basic financial relationships in nonprofit organizations;
- understand the notion and purpose of a business plan.

KEY TERMS

Some of the key terms introduced in this chapter are:

- alignment model
- balance sheet
- break-even analysis
- budget (line-item, performance, zero-based, program)
- business plan
- cash flow statement

- Delphi method
- human resource management
- income and expense statement
- issue-based planning
- marketing
- PEST analysis
- scenario planning
- stakeholder survey
- strategic management
- strategic planning
- SWOT analysis

INTRODUCTION

Management is about creating value in accordance with the organization's mission. Among the various management functions we reviewed in Chapter 11, several stand out particularly, and are critical for current performance and long-term sustainability: human resource management, strategic management, and financial management. We present each in turn.

HUMAN RESOURCE MANAGEMENT

In this section, we take a brief look at some of aspects of personnel management in nonprofit organizations. Human resource management includes all the activities related to the recruitment, hiring, training, promotion, retention, separation, and support of staff and volunteers. As mentioned in Chapter 9, nonprofit organizations tend to be labor-intensive rather than capital-intensive. Because of this characteristic, multiple stakeholder influence, and the complex nature of goods and services produced, human resource management increases in importance.

Nonprofits compete for workers with forprofits and public agencies using three types of incentives: wages, benefits, and non-wage aspects. Nonprofits tend to do less well on the first two and better on the third. Nonprofit employment involves "sorting" processes among potential applicants based on value preferences, in a labor market based less on wage considerations alone. What is more, many nonprofits have flat hierarchies and offer fewer opportunities for advancement within the organization; hence, changing employer as a way of "moving up" is frequent, resulting in high job mobility.

Research (see Leete, forthcoming) suggests that nonprofit wage differentials persist even when controlled for job and worker differences. In this respect, nonprofit staff may explicitly or implicitly donate part of their wages to the organizational mission. At the same time, incentive contracts are rare among nonprofit managers (in business firms they are used to reduce principal–agent problems) as they may clash with the values of the organization. Principal–agent problems arise when agents (managers) have incentives *not* to follow the directives of the principals (board members).

While the flat hierarchies found predominantly in nonprofit organizations encourage relatively high job turnover as noted above, they also offer an incentive by increasing individual employee control, thereby setting up a wage–autonomy trade-off. In other words, people may decide to work for nonprofits because they value autonomy more than wage maximization. This is especially likely in fields and organizations in which professionals (e.g. social workers, teachers, curators, etc.) can exert a strong influence. As such, nonprofits are the prototype of professional bureaucracies (Mintzberg 1979), as opposed to conventional bureaucracy where less autonomy rests with individual professionals (see Chapter 7).

The wage–autonomy relation puts emphasis on coordinating and collateral relationships. This makes human resource management in nonprofits more complex than in firms that rely on line and supervisory relationships:

■ A *main line-managerial* relationship involves assigning duties and responsibility, appraising performance and ability, and forwarding staff development. It implies authority to join in selection of staff, to prescribe work in as much detail as may be required, and to initiate promotion, transfer, or dismissal.

■ A *supervisory* relationship involves inducting, giving technical instruction, assigning tasks, checking performance, and helping with problems. Unlike a managerial relationship it does not imply authority to reallocate duties, or to initiate promotion, transfer, or dismissal.

■ A *coordinating* relationship involves preparing and issuing detailed plans and programs to forward agreed objectives, keeping informed of actual progress, and attempting to overcome obstacles and setbacks. It implies authority to obtain information on progress and to decide what should be done in situations of uncertainty. It does not imply authority to set new directions, to override sustained disagreements, or to appraise personal performance or ability.

■ A *collateral* relationship implies mutual dependence without any authority of one over the other. Sustained disagreements can be resolved only by reference to higher authority, where one exists.

Much of human resource management is concerned with motivation. Locke's theory (1991) suggests that staff and volunteers are motivated when they:

■ have clear and challenging goals to achieve;
■ are involved in setting the goals themselves; and
■ are provided with feedback on progress en route to agreed-upon goals.

By contrast, few challenges, little involvement, and little feedback may lead to passivity, dependence, and a sense of "psychological failure."

Hackman's and Oldham's job satisfaction theory (1975) offers a complementary set of insights into personnel management. It suggests that a number of basic job dimensions are closely related to job satisfaction and high performance:

- *skill variety*—jobs require a variety of skills and abilities;
- *task identity*—the degree to which the job requires the completion of a whole and identifiable piece of work;
- *task significance*—the degree to which the job has substantial and perceived impact on the lives of people;
- *autonomy*—the degree to which the job gives freedom, independence, and discretion in scheduling work and in determining how it will be carried out;
- *feedback*—the degree to which the worker gets information about the effectiveness (and not only efficiency) of performance.

These theories could be applicable to the management of volunteer resources as well. However, volunteers require a rather different treatment since the wage incentive is missing. As discussed in Chapter 9, Barker (1993: 28) identifies three basic motivational factors why people volunteer: altruistic, instrumental, and obligatory. People volunteer both to help an organization and to gain experience. Volunteers are attracted to organizations with compelling missions that craft their volunteer opportunities so as to both utilize existing talents of volunteers and to add to those talents. Matching volunteer interests and talents to organizational needs is an important management task. Indeed, managing and training volunteers is a way of attracting and retaining them. At the same time, and in contrast to paid staff, volunteer motivation is primarily non-monetary and cannot be managed along incentives lines but more on the grounds of commitment to the cause and long-term career benefits. This implies that strategies for managing employees and volunteers are typically different, and management has to try to avoid tensions between personnel management based on commitment and those based on monetary incentives.

This task, however, is complicated by the mixed motivational structure of many paid staff. Often, employees—like volunteers—are also stakeholders and identify with the vision and mission of the organization and the values it represents. What is more, the variety of work forms, e.g. part-time, temporary, etc. reviewed in Chapter 9, add to the complexity of human resource management in nonprofit organizations.

STRATEGIC MANAGEMENT[1]

Strategic management is the process by which organizations develop and determine their long-term vision, direction, programs, and performance. Strategic planning involves various techniques and tools to ensure careful formulation, effective and efficient implementation, and evaluation. Strategic management integrates organizational functions and units into a more cohesive, broader strategy. In most cases, it involves the ability to steer the organization as a whole through strategic change under conditions of complexity and uncertainty. Specifically, strategic management:

- encompasses the whole organization (mission, goals, structure, revenue, stakeholders);
- is outward-looking, and examines the organization in the context of the larger field or environment for developing strategies for action based on a broader understanding of the organization's position;

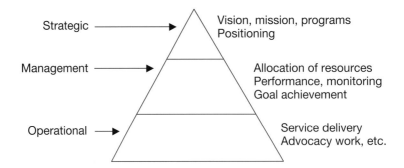

Strategic ⟶ Vision, mission, programs
Positioning

Management ⟶ Allocation of resources
Performance, monitoring
Goal achievement

Operational ⟶ Service delivery
Advocacy work, etc.

Figure 12.1 *Management levels*

■ is forward-looking, tries to anticipate the likely conditions in the external environment in the medium to long term, and seeks to identify the major changes that will have to be made to the organization if it is to pursue its mission effectively in the future.

In essence, strategic management is different from everyday management and standard operations (Figure 12.1). The need for strategic management arises from social change: most organizations operate in environments that are changing at a different pace, for sometimes unknown reasons and with uncertain outcomes. This creates a need to understand these changes and their implications for the benefit of the organization's mission, operations, and accomplishments. In the business sector, strategic management is used primarily to improve a firm's medium- to long-term profitability; by contrast, in the nonprofit sector, strategic management is used for (re)formulating a mission and objectives, and for achieving them more effectively and efficiently.

Strategic management involves self-examination and reflection, which require the organization to look backward as well as forward and to formulate post hoc as well as ad hoc rationalizations of objectives, programs, and activities. For Mintzberg (1979) and others, the process of strategic management is as important as the outcome. It typically involves nine steps, suggested in Box 12.1.

Strategic management is about how an organization relates to actual and anticipated change. In this sense, strategic management implies a theory of agency that is either implicitly or explicitly part of the board's or the management's self-understanding. Hasenfeld (1992: 25) suggests four major action models by which organizations relate to or address change:

■ *proactive action*: the organization actively scans its environment in an attempt to anticipate environmental change;
■ *adaptive action*: the organization becomes aware of environmental change and makes incremental changes to cope with it;
■ *reactive action*: the organization is hit by the implications of unforeseen changes, is perhaps thrown into crisis, and changes in response; attempts to manipulate the environment may follow;

BOX 12.1 STEPS OF STRATEGIC MANAGEMENT

Step 1: Getting started and participation
- Formulate a clear mandate and purpose; set feasible goals as well as a realistic time-frame; state agreed-upon outcomes and expectations.
- Involve all major stakeholders; designate focal points in relevant departments and units; involve "champions" to the extent possible.

Step 2: Develop or review the mission of the organization
- Examine if the organization's vision and mission are still adequate.
- Identify what part of the vision and the mission needs to change and why.

Step 3: Internal scan
- Review the fit between vision, mission, objectives, and organizational structure.
- Examine available human resources and the skill levels and motivations of paid staff and volunteers.
- Examine financial aspects such as assets, liabilities, and projections on costs and revenue.
- Review programs and program alternatives.

Step 4: Environmental and future scan
- Examine organization in context of wider conditions and changes (see PEST analysis — politics, economy, society, technology).
- Conduct stakeholder surveys.
- Conduct organizational field analysis.

Step 5: Analysis
- Combine insights and results from steps 1–4 in an overall assessment; apply SWOT analysis (strengths, weaknesses, opportunities and threats).

Step 6: Identifying strategic issues
- Focus on fundamental policy issues that are relevant to the organization's mission, effectiveness and efficiency, client/user/member profile, stakeholders, financial health, governance and management structure, and organizational design.
- Set priorities and concentrate on these.

Step 7: Strategic development
- For each priority, develop appropriate strategies and actions.

Step 8: Implementation plan
- Formulate time-frame.
- Set goals and specific deliverables.
- Identify and designate focal points for implementation.

Step 9: Further review

- organizational units, programs, activities, and stakeholders to be involved and addressed;
- objectives of scenario sessions and key issues to be explored;
- definition and deadline for deliverables.

Building scenarios involves a number of steps such as, for example: a brainstorming session to explore different "drivers of change" (funding shifts, technological and socioeconomic factors, etc.); explore the possible impact each driver might have; estimate the likelihood of events, i.e. establish what is very likely to happen, and should therefore be included in all scenarios, and what is less likely; and, finally, identify and focus on critical uncertainties, i.e. drivers whose impact and force may be unknown or difficult to fathom. In a second step, the participants should: explore the interrelationships between the drivers; how mutually exclusive and exhaustive possible scenarios are; whether each scenario constitutes a different version of the future; and develop engaging and succinct descriptions of each scenario.

In a series of workshops or meetings, participants can then explore the range of options around each scenario, and also how to translate these into a strategic plan. In the long term, scenario planning will help chart the course of the organization and, through learning processes, contribute to organizational knowledge and expertise. In the short term, scenario planning can serve as an effective early warning system for the organization by gauging levels of preparedness for contingent events.

Tools for strategic management

The various models suggested above refer to a number of specific planning tools. The purpose of such tools is to help in the gathering, analysis, and interpretation of information. They can be used separately or together, and are usually employed at the early stages of the strategic planning process.

PEST analysis

PEST analysis forces the organization to examine its internal and external environment and search for relevant political, economic, social, and technological factors:

- *Political* factors include aspects of the wider policy and regulatory environment in which the organization operates but also the role of key stakeholders:

  - How stable is the overall political environment?
  - Are new laws proposed that will influence how the organization operates (e.g. fiscal aspects, labor law, welfare reform)?
  - Are budget policies shifting, and if so, to what effect?
  - What is on the political agenda of supervisory agencies, umbrella groups, and professional and business associations in the field?
  - What are actual and potential political cleavages on the board?
  - Are there other internal political issues and developments?

- *Economic* factors refer to the long-term prospects for the economy as a whole, as well as in the field where the organization operates, and include a host of issues such as interest rates, unemployment, income levels as well as demand- and supply-side aspects from changing needs for services and expected foundation pay-outs, to the degree of competition and cost developments.
- *Socio-cultural* factors include socio-demographic changes such as population growth and migration patterns, gender issues as well as value and attitudinal changes that might affect the organization.
- *Technological* factors, finally, refer to technological developments and innovations in the broad sense. Will they affect the organization by creating new needs, changing its mode of operation, and creating shifts in costs and revenue? How will technological advances change communication patterns within the organization, and among stakeholders?

Stakeholder surveys

Stakeholder surveys can be used to allow an organization to gather and analyze different opinions and assessments from a range of perspectives. Such surveys typically include all the major organizational stakeholders (board members, staff, volunteers, members, users, funders, etc.) but can also include representatives of other nonprofits, government, and the business community that might be relevant in the context of a particular planning context.

Complementing data on organizational performance with data from stakeholder surveys is particularly important in complex planning processes. Information obtained from the stakeholder survey carries substantive and methodological challenges that need to be taken into account. This includes concerns about the social desirability of answers, the response rate, as well as the potential effect of reinforcing rather than challenging existing "myths" about the organization. Therefore, to correct for biases introduced by subjective opinions and selection effects, it is useful to combine the results of the stakeholder survey with financial and other indicators.

The Delphi method is one prominent way of carrying out stakeholder surveys of perceived impact. A "Delphi" is a method for structuring a group communication process. The aim is to address a complex problem and to reach, if possible, some form of consensus or to establish some demarcation around an area of dissent. In most cases, the result would be to reach an agreed-upon diagnosis and plan of action for the organization. The Delphi method documents the basis and extent of the consensus or dissent achieved and shows the process by which it was established over dissenting opinions, if any. There are many different versions of the Delphi method, but it typically involves several steps:

- *Selection of Delphi participants*. The selection of Delphi participants has to follow certain guidelines, which are largely dictated by the issue and planning problem at hand. Some issues or problems require broad selection criteria in an effort to include all the major stakeholders, while others focus on particular expertise and experience. Clearly, the composition of participants has a significant impact on Delphi results. Depending on the purpose, the selection process can emphasize the likelihood of

265

Table 12.1 *Example of SWOT analysis for hypothetical nonprofit*

Strengths	Threats
■ Mission clarity	■ Additional resources hard to get
■ Good mission–organization fit	■ High competition
■ Programmatic strengths	■ Community not interested
■ Staff (highly skilled, motivated)	■ New policies not in our favor
■ Location is good	■ Other organizations are ahead of us
■ Size of organization is right	■ Government suspicious
■ Revenue structure sufficient	■ Funders attracted elsewhere
■ Asset base solid	■ Possible conflicts on board
■ Participation and community links good	■ Outreach difficulties

Weaknesses	Opportunities
■ Some program weaknesses	■ New policies in our favor
■ Recent staff problems (skills, motivation)	■ Diversification possible
■ Stakeholder conflicts	■ New board members can be brought in
■ Inexperience	■ Volunteer potential significant
■ Board weak, not engaged	■ Other organizations want to collaborate
■ Outreach limited	■ Government support growing
■ Track-record mixed	■ Business community wants to help
	■ International contacts

THREATS

- What are the obstacles that are most likely to emerge?
- Are there old and new competitors that could pose a threat?
- Are supply and demand changes taking place that could threaten the organization?
- What technological changes could pose a threat?
- Are there debt or cash flow problems?
- Could changes in policy affect the organization negatively?

FINANCIAL MANAGEMENT

Nonprofits, like all other organizations, have to manage their finances and put in place a system that keeps track of financial aspects. Financial management is needed for governance and accountability reasons: management has to report to the board on the organization's financial status, and the board reports to the fiscal authorities by filing tax returns, to funders by submitting project reports, or to the general public by publishing an annual report. In the US, many nonprofit organizations required to submit Form 990 to the Internal Revenue Service have to file this annual tax declaration after the end of each fiscal year. In the UK, charities submit annual statements to the Charity Commission, and German nonprofits to the local tax office.

In addition to its use for external and internal accountability, financial management is needed as a management tool in planning and decision-making as well as for monitoring performance and everyday operations. Indeed, strategic planning, performance, and finance are closely related: in particular for larger nonprofits, where they are part of larger information management system that includes, in addition to financial aspects, information on mission accomplishments, efficiency and effectiveness, personnel (paid staff, volunteers), and member-, client-, and user-related data.

Basic financial relationships

Financial reporting standards and fiscal requirements for nonprofit organizations vary by country as well as by state and local laws. They are also different depending on the size and purpose of the organization, the field in which it operates, and its revenue sources. For example, in the US, nonprofits with less than $25,000 of annual turnover are not required to submit Form 900 to the IRS, foundations have greater fiscal reporting requirements than 501(c)(3) organizations, and the latter greater requirements than religious congregations. Organizations operating in the health care or education field have stricter and more complex reporting requirements (to sometimes multiple supervisory agencies) than nonprofits in the field of culture. Organizations receiving government grants tend to have more complex and time-consuming financial reporting requirements than do organizations relying primarily on individual contributions or grants.

There are two basic kinds of bookkeeping: small organizations in particular simply record when a cash transaction takes place, either as expenditure or as revenue. In contrast to this "cash accounting" method, the "accrual" method factors in future obligations and sets "accounts payable" apart from "accounts receivable," which together offer a more realistic view of the organization's overall financial situation. However, the financial system of a nonprofit organization includes more than expenditures and revenue: there are assets, loans, investments, depreciation, and many other kinds of flows that affect its financial situation and are, therefore, of interest to the board and management.

Indeed, it is useful to think of the finances of a nonprofit organization as a more or less continuous flow of internal and external transactions and transfers. Sophisticated accounting and computer programs are able to keep track of these flows and analyze them for a variety

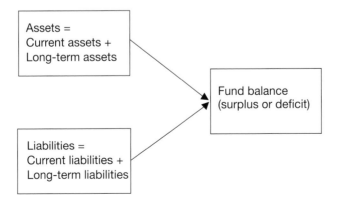

Figure 12.2 *The balance sheet*

Budgets

Budgets are different from balance sheets and cash flow statements. They are comprehensive financial work plans covering a specific project or program over a specified period. Budgets are instruments for showing:

■ planning considerations—setting goals, priorities, and strategies, and the coordination of them; a budget will put plans into an expenditure framework and identify what activities can take place and at what level;

■ political influences—a budget can show competing scenarios and hence be used to influence policy; a budget can help expose underlying assumptions and their implications;

■ social and economic considerations—granting and denying privileges, changing cost items and funding levels, affecting the growth and capacity of an organization, and the community it serves;

■ legal considerations—monetary expression of entitlements and fiscal responsibilities such as government payments; they are also tools for accountability and transparency.

There are many different types of budgets or budget approaches, but they share several common line items:

■ Staff- or employee-related costs:

  – *direct*: salaries, wages, overtime, bonuses, and payroll taxes;
  – *benefits*: termination, pension, allowances, medical and accident insurance, and life assurance;
  – *other*: recruitment, relocation, legal, training, etc.

■ Non-staff items:

  – materials and supplies;
  – transportation and travel;
  – communication;
  – bank fees, bookkeeping, and payroll services;
  – insurance and legal;
  – rent;
  – utilities;
  – maintenance and repairs;
  – dues.

A very common type of budget for nonprofit organizations is the *line-item budget*. The primary objective of line-item budgets is to account for expenditures, very much along the items listed above. Line-item budgets are used for financial and fiscal reporting, for accountability purposes, and, from a managerial perspective, for calculating input units (for example, of staff hours or materials used). By contrast, *performance budgets* are used less for reporting purposes. Their primary use is for estimating the minimum inputs needed to achieve a desired standard of output. Thus in addition to input items, a performance budget requires specified output units. The emphasis in a performance budget is on efficiency such as input/output ratios and other performance measures.

Both line-item and performance budgeting are incremental in the sense that the organization makes use of past cost behavior to estimate future cost behavior. In a sense, the last year's budget becomes the blueprint for next year's budget. Such path-dependent budgeting can create cost increases, as some items are not explicitly examined. To counteract such tendencies, some agencies use *zero-based budgets*, which require that all line-items be reviewed and approved every year, with no assumptions made as to the increments of previous base budgets.

Program budgeting takes a different starting point, and begins by listing the organization's core programs based on their mission relevance. Each program is then budgeted separately, either using line-item or performance budgets, even if they share common inputs and cost centers. This assumes no scope economies among programs, as the intent is to estimate the "stand-alone" costs of each program separately, and the cost advantages that can be achieved by joint production, i.e. running multiple programs in support of the organization's mission. In a second step, then, these cost links and commonalities are estimated and used to build a cross-program budget.

Break-even analysis

Nonprofits have a variety of cost types (see Box 12.2), and when developing a budget, it is important to understand the cost and revenue structure of the proposed project or program organizations. Break-even analysis is a popular planning tool for exploring the financial viability of proposed activities. The break-even point is defined as that level of activity where total revenues equal total expenditures. At that level, the nonprofit will neither realize a surplus nor incur an operating loss.

Conducting a break-even analysis is relatively simple, and requires that the organization estimates fixed and variable costs for the time period in question, and calculates a price for each unit produced. Thus, the break-even revenue would be:

(number of units × unit price) = (fixed costs + variable costs)

Example: sale price is $2 per unit; variable costs are $1 per unit; fixed costs are $3,000.

And the break-even number of units:

fixed costs/unit contribution margin,

with the unit contribution margin (UCM) (what the sale of one unit contributes to cost coverage):

UCM = selling price – variable costs.

In the above example: $3,000/($2 – $1) = 3,000. In other words, 3,000 units must be sold at $2 per unit in order to just cover costs.

BOX 12.3 DEFINING PROBLEMS

Causality

- individual causation versus systematic (former stresses choice and culpability; the latter stresses impersonal and unavoidable forces)
- intentional vs. accidental causes
- causes due to character of values
- complex causal systems vs. simple causal agents

Severity

- distinguishes between the acknowledged existence of a problem (e.g. recession) and how serious it is
- severity — usually measured against some backdrop or context, such as trend lines (getting better or worse), specific populations (big problem only for group x), or what is considered normal or deviant

Incidence

- who is affected generally?
- what subgroups are affected and why?
- what patterns of incidence are most important?

Novelty

- is the issue or problem new?
- is it unexpected?

Proximity

- how close does the problem hit home?
- depends on how home is defined, e.g. children valued for any group's survival so anything affecting children negatively is bad

Crisis

- largely a rhetorical device to signal urgency

Problem populations

- problem definition can also define people who are potential targets of policy interventions
- deserving vs. undeserving of help
- definitions that emphasize capacities vs. dependency

Instrumental vs. expressive orientation

- difference between focusing on ends (the instrumental intent to solve the problem) and the means (degree to which what you do expresses an important symbol or value, e.g. refusing to negotiate with terrorists even if hostages harmed)

Solutions

- solutions sometimes precede problem and help to shape it, e.g. commitment to vouchers as policy instrument to deal with range of problems
- are solutions available — can something be done to solve a problem, or merely take action for its own sake?

Source: Based on Rochefort and Cobb 1994.

Key elements covered in business plans are:

■ vision, mission, and values guiding the organization;
■ organizational description (size, activities, units, etc.);
■ needs assessment, "market" analysis;
■ services provided, at what quality and quantity;
■ operations (how services will be delivered and why);
■ marketing and outreach plan;
■ governance, list of board members;
■ management approach and personnel policies;
■ financial analysis: funds available and needed, projected costs and income; and
■ assessment and program evaluation; performance indicators.

The business model for nonprofits typically involves a theory of change, i.e. how it proposes to address a social need or a cultural, political, or economic problem or set of problems. In other words, the business plan spells out why the organization's mission and purpose are relevant, and why and how the organization proposes to pursue them. Defining "the problem" is the first step in developing such a theory of change. Rochefort and Cobb (1994) offer a useful checklist of key elements in defining a problem (Box 12.3).

Marketing

Marketing has assumed greater relevance for nonprofit organizations and now involves a range of activities such as the marketing of services provided, cause-related marketing, image marketing, and branding. As part of a business plan, marketing analysis has become a seemingly indispensable tool for looking at how the organization intends to approach its customers, members, users, or the public at large. According to Kotler and Andreason (1991), marketing is the analysis, implementation, and control of exchange relationships between the organization and its external as well as internal stakeholders. Since nonprofit organizations are multiple stakeholder entities, nonprofit marketing must be sensitive to different audiences and adjust its communication patterns and other approaches accordingly.

The term "marketing mix" is used to refer to the range of approaches, techniques, and tools organizations use to reach their customers, users, or audience. Marketing researchers use the so-called "four Ps," which organizations employ to support and reinforce their competitive position. The four Ps stand for:

■ product (quality, features, options, style, branding, warranties, etc.);
■ price (list price, discounts, allowances, payment and credit terms, etc.);
■ place (channels, coverage, locations, inventory, etc.); and
■ promotion (advertising, publicity, public relations).

Of course, the notion of the marketing mix was developed against the background of the business firm, and needs to be adapted to fit the needs of nonprofit organizations and the specific target audience they seek to reach.

277

REVIEW QUESTIONS

■   What makes human resource management in nonprofit organizations different?

■   Why do nonprofit organizations engage in strategic planning?

■   What are some of the basic financial relationships in nonprofit organizations?

RECOMMENDED READING

Bryce, H. J. (2000) *Financial and Strategic Management for Nonprofit Organizations*, San Francisco, CA: Jossey-Bass.

Futter, V. (2002) *Nonprofit Governance and Management*, Chicago, IL: American Bar Association.

Oster, S. (1995) *Strategic Management for Nonprofit Organizations*, New York and Oxford: Oxford University Press.

Part IV

Policy and special topics

> ## BOX 13.1 SOME BASIC FACTS OF STATE–NONPROFIT RELATIONS
>
> 1. The evolution of the nonprofit and voluntary sector in many countries defies theories that imply that the expansion of government "crowds out" the voluntary organizations.
>
> 2. The continued expansion of the nonprofit sector is closely related to government funding.
>
> 3. Cross-nationally, the government is the principal source of funding for social service agencies, and the second most important overall. In the US, the share of governmental funding for social services is 37 percent.
>
> 4. Third-party payment schemes constitute a typical pattern in the US and other countries (UK, France, Germany, Netherlands, etc.) and involve the distinction between finance and provider roles.

process of altering and stopping programs. Even though there are also disadvantages involved (e.g. difficulty to maintain equal standards, loss of public control and accountability, monitoring costs), both government and nonprofits have incentives to cooperate.

The theory that nonprofit organizations and governments are adversaries is supported by public goods arguments and social movement theory: if demand is heterogeneous, minority views are not well reflected in public policy; hence self-organization of minority preferences will rise against majoritarian government. Moreover, organized minorities are more effective in pressing government (social movements, demonstration projects, think-tanks); however, if nonprofits advocate minority positions, the government may in turn try to defend the majority perspective, leading to potential political conflict.

Young (2000) has suggested a triangular model of nonprofit–government relations (Figure 13.1), and argues that, to varying degrees, all three types of relations are present at any one time, but that some assume more importance during some periods than in others. For example, in the US, the relationship between civil rights groups and some state governments were adversarial in the 1950s and 1960s but changed to a more complementary role later on in the context of welfare provision and education policies.

Using the UK as an example, we see that nonprofit–government relations were:

- *Supplementary*: nonprofits provided voluntary services not covered by the welfare state: lifeboats, counseling, and other voluntary services in response to government cutbacks in the 1980s (public goods argument—minority tastes).
- *Complementary*: contracts and partnerships between government and nonprofit agencies were formed in response to new public management and outsourcing (transaction costs argument—greater efficiency).
- *Adversarial*: nonprofits included groups advocating the rights of needy people left unserved and under-served by state (public goods argument—policy preference of majoritarian government).

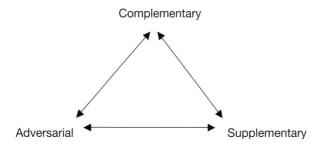

Figure 13.1 *Nonprofit–government relations*

Najam's Four Cs model (2000) offers a more detailed view of nonprofit–government relations by examining the extent to which their respective organizational goals and means overlap (see Table 13.1):

- *Cooperative*: If the goals and means are similar, then government and nonprofit organizations develop a cooperative relationship. Najam offers the cooperation between the Canadian government and the International Campaign to Ban Landmines as an example.
- *Complementary*: If the goals are similar but the means are dissimilar, then a complementary relationship between government and nonprofit organizations emerges. For example, many nonprofits in the field of social service provision and community health care complement basic government services.
- *Co-optive*: If the goals are dissimilar and means are similar, then government tries to build a co-optive relationship with nonprofit organizations. An example would be the humanitarian assistance funds channeled to local grassroots organizations in African countries for programs that are similar to governmental ones. In such situations, government may try to co-opt grassroots organizations and nonprofits to further its own goals.
- *Confrontational*: If the goals and means are both dissimilar, then government and the nonprofit sector are in a confrontational relationship. Examples include the activities of Greenpeace to pressure governments on environmental issues, an advocacy group demanding better welfare services for the urban poor, or the anti-globalization groups demonstrating against the World Trade Organization.

Social movement approaches depart from the traditional dualist models of government–nonprofit relations. The latter assume that government and nonprofits form two distinct sectors, while social movement theory argues that the two sectors are deeply intertwined. Social movements are loosely structured informal groups with no legal status that over time become more institutionalized and may eventually incorporate into legal entities, for example, possibly becoming 501(c)(3) organizations. Social movements begin first with private concerns and private action; as momentum builds, the movement may evolve into formal organizations and incorporate hundreds or thousands of individuals and organizations;

285

Table 13.1 *Four Cs model of government–nonprofit relations*

		Goals	
		Similar	Dissimilar
Means	Similar	Cooperation	Co-optation
	Dissimilar	Complementarity	Confrontation

Source: Najam 2000. © John Wiley & Sons Inc. Used with permission.

ultimately, successful social movements may influence government policy by translating private concerns into public issues.

Examples of successful social movements include the women's movement, the civil rights movement, and the environmental movement, which each spawned hundreds of formal legal entities, such as advocacy organizations (i.e. NAACP, NOW, Greenpeace, etc.), as well as direct service organizations, such as domestic violence shelters, rape crisis centers, or nonprofit nature reserves. In short, social movements are the impetus for the creation of nonprofits, from advocacy organizations that directly lobby the government and influence public policy, to service organizations that provide counseling and assistance. Social movements provide the organizational and political mechanism for translating private concerns into public issues. This translation process makes social movement perspectives critical for understanding not only the government–nonprofit relationship, but also policy change more generally.

In this sense, a social movement perspective adds to the models presented by Young and Najam above (pp. 284–6). Social movements, as private action to change government policy, have a deliberately conflictual relationship with government. What is more, successful social movements have the potential to change government policy and thus create a legal and regulatory environment in which nonprofit organizations can grow and flourish, leading to more collaborative or neutral relations. Since social movements involve political activity and political associations, social movements also have the potential for an ongoing politicization of nonprofit–government relations.

The government–nonprofit relationship, then, as viewed through a social movement perspective, can be described as a cycle: private actions are translated into public concerns via formal legal entities, which evolved from the initial social movement; these formal legal entities also influence government policy and government responds either by directly addressing the issue, or a more popular response is to fund nonprofits that in turn address these public concerns. As a consequence, nonprofit organizations must adjust their behavior and programs to reflect public policy and government priorities.

INSTRUMENTS OF GOVERNMENT FINANCING OF NONPROFIT ACTIVITY

In supporting nonprofit organizations financially, government can make use of several instruments and use a variety of channels, some of which we have already encountered in Chapters 4, 5 and 9. Among them are:

286

Grants, contracts, and third-party payments

The history of direct grants and contracts from government to nonprofits underwent significant changes in the decades following World War II, and is closely related to the history of welfare provision in the US. In the 1950s, subsidies to nonprofit organizations were relatively small, accountability requirements were minimal, and nonprofits had wide discretion on whom to serve. However, as public funding of nonprofits increased in the 1960s and states such as Massachusetts began contracting-out many state functions to nonprofits, oversight, regulation, and accountability became more important. Contracts thus began to have more stringent accountability and standard operating procedures attached to them.

These arrangements generally take the form of purchase-of-services contracts, where government entities buy services from nonprofit contracting agencies. Programs that rely on contracting often require contractors to be nonprofit entities. Such contracts are characterized by relatively short funding cycles where the government funder enjoys varying degrees of control over admission criteria, service delivery, and discharge decisions for clients of the contracted services. Smith and Lipsky (1993) refer to this partnership configuration as a contracting regime, in which public and private agencies are involved in a mutually dependent but not equal relationship. They suggest that these contractual arrangements typically subordinate nonprofit agencies to a hegemonic state that often serves as more of a sponsor than a partner to contracting nonprofits (Smith and Lipsky 1993: 44–5).

Government dealt with the nonprofit service provider directly until the 1980s when a wave of managed care models added additional layers of bureaucracy between the government and nonprofit service providers. Managed care for such services as foster services, mental health, and general health added players such as "third-party agencies" and "subcontractors." Managed care complicated the relationship between government and nonprofits, and there were trade-offs between accountability and efficiency.

Governments also finance nonprofits through third-party payments—an umbrella term for an assortment of revenue sources collected from individuals and organizations. Payments under this heading also include vouchers and other subsidies from the government, which are earmarked in some way for the services or product the nonprofit provides. Examples include rent payments from homeless shelter residents, reimbursements from public and private health insurance programs, direct payments from clients, and income from technical assistance programs. Also included are Medicaid reimbursements and subsidies such as Section 8.[1]

Tax credits, deductions, and preferential treatment

Governments finance nonprofits through tax credits or deductions for individuals or forprofit corporations, thus giving incentives for individuals to support the nonprofit sector, although these benefits are not restricted to nonprofits. Two examples are the child care and dependant tax credits and the low-income housing tax credit. Nonprofits can also use tax-exempt bonds to finance capital improvement projects. Moreover, some government regulations and procedures give preference to nonprofits in some social service fields, for example, housing and humanitarian assistance, which reduces the range of competitors.

EXTENT OF THE PUBLIC–PRIVATE PARTNERSHIP

The mutual dependence between the public and private sectors was established in large part during the Great Society days of the 1960s and 1970s, a period during which much of the sector's growth occurred. Nonprofit organizations received over 50 percent of federal social service expenditures in 1989, compared with almost nothing in 1960 (Lipsky and Smith 1989–90). "In a sense, government became the principal philanthropist of the nonprofit sector, significantly boosting nonprofit revenues in a wide variety of fields and freeing the sector of its total dependence on the far less-reliable base of private charitable support" (Salamon 1999: 168). While government contributions to nonprofit organizations vary within and among public service industries, government funding remains the second most important source of income for the sector, coming behind fee income. As noted earlier, overall government support accounts for 36 percent of nonprofit organizations' income (Salamon 1999).

Some small organizations rely on government funds for their entire budgets (Lipsky and Smith 1989–90). In fact, public money is so important to the ongoing financial stability of many nonprofit social service agencies that nonprofit coalitions, advocacy groups, and "affinity groups" now exist whose partial or sole mission is to lobby the government for increased government spending for a variety of their social and economic welfare causes, from youth services to care for the elderly (Oliver 1999).

While government support of the nonprofit sector continues to grow—albeit at a slower pace and mostly in the health care industry—recent policy trends have begun to alter the long-standing public–private partnership arrangement. Beginning with the presidency of Ronald Reagan in 1980, the federal government has pursued an ongoing campaign to both "reduce big government" and "reinvent government," which are catch phrases for retrenching social program spending and streamlining government bureaucracy.

In keeping with this dual agenda, devolution of responsibility for a wide variety of health and welfare issues has simultaneously changed the structure and reduced the level of government funding for nonprofit activities across the board. Since the 1980s, fifty-seven federal grant categories have been consolidated into nine block grants that carry lighter funding for state programs (Coble 1999). Also, as part of this process, funding structures for social service agencies have shifted from the reimbursement plans of conventional contracting to performance contracts that emphasize efficiency and capacity (Behn and Kant 1999; Ryan 1999).

With this new focus on accountability and performance came a new-found recognition of qualities that forprofit firms could bring to the service provision table. Throughout the past decade, public funders at all levels of government began relaxing their historical resistance to contracting with forprofit organizations to manage and deliver social welfare services. The consequences of this trend for the nonprofit sector are an increasing level of competition for government contracts and the encroachment of forprofit firms in social service industries that had traditionally been nonprofit domains. As government spending shrinks and competition from forprofit providers increases, nonprofit organizations must find alternative funding sources. Increasingly, the nonprofit sector has come to rely more heavily on commercial income, which accounted for over half of the sector's revenue growth from 1977 to 1996 (Salamon 1999: 70–1).

Consequences of public sector support[2]

According to the nonprofit literature, the consequences arising from the mutual dependence of the public and private sector are two-fold. One set of consequences involves nonprofit sector changes—potential and actual—due to reliance on public funds in general. For example, some scholars argue that fundamental differences in priorities between the public and private sectors create myriad opportunities for conflict, the underlying assumption being that nonprofits will tend to adjust their behaviors to satisfy the agendas of their public funders. To the extent government agendas differ from those of the nonprofit organizations seeking funding, nonprofits are at risk of having to stray from their intended missions to attract and keep public funding. In fact, Lipsky and Smith caution:

> Government contracting may alter nonprofit agencies' approaches to services and clients, even if their goals are entirely compatible with those of government. In essence, they may be forced to conform to standards imposed by contracting policy at the expense of their homegrown notions of what constitutes effective service delivery.
>
> (1989–90: 638)

In particular, nonprofit scholars worry that nonprofit organizations will become too bureau-cratized, over-professionalized, and politicized as a result of governmental influence. Nonprofits might also lose their autonomy and flexibility regarding a number of organizational goals and succumb to "vendorism," where the organizational mission is distorted in the pursuit for government support (Salamon 1995).

Competition leads to commercialization

We have already looked at commercialization pressures in Chapter 9. It is worth revisiting this issue in the context of public–private partnerships and the impact of forprofit encroachment into nonprofit fields of operation and the accompanying emphasis on efficiency and capacity within government contracting. To both compete and compensate for shrinking federal dollars, nonprofit firms are becoming increasingly commercialized with moves into sales and investment. The extent of this commercialism within the nonprofit sector varies considerably by industry (see Weisbrod 1998b, Table 1.2: 17). Nonetheless, nonprofits in a variety of industries are now engaged in selling theme license plates, opening health clubs and off-site museum stores, leasing mailing lists, sponsoring conferences, publishing journals, loaning their logos, licensing and patenting discoveries, among many other fee-generating income strategies (Weisbrod 1998a, b; Young 1983).

In addition to commercial outputs, nonprofits are commercializing in terms of the labor market as well. As Ayres-Williams writes:

> The sector can now afford to be an employer of choice. Gone is the image of do-gooders working inefficiently and at pittance wages for the sheer pleasure of helping others. The reality of operating with multimillion dollar budgets has led most nonprofits to adopt a more focused business approach.
>
> (1998: 110)

289

With commercial activity representing the largest proportion of income growth for nonprofits across the board, the question remains whether and to what extent nonprofit commercialism affects both public–private partnerships and the character of the nonprofit sector as a whole.

As nonprofits increasingly embark on commercial activities and as government funders place more weight on performance and capacity measures in contracting relationships, the argument that nonprofit organizations are the most effective mechanisms for managing and delivering public goods is called into question. The prevailing concern is that the nonprofit response to increasing competition will be to adopt more businesslike management strategies that compromise the social benefits nonprofit organizations contribute in a variety of industries. The health care field, for example, has seen dramatic growth in commercialization, mergers, and conversions to forprofit status among nonprofit hospitals and other nonprofit health care organizations. The aftermath of these transformations provides an opportunity to evaluate the continuing role of the nonprofit sector in health care provision.

Still worthy of special treatment?

Some scholars now speculate about the justification of continued preferential treatment of nonprofit organizations from the government. Again from the health care field, Bloche (1998) argues that the "putative social advantages" of the nonprofit form over forprofit ownership status in health care financing are uncertain and do not compensate for the costs of government protection. He claims that nonprofit health care facilities are no more likely to provide free care to the poor than forprofits and vary in their production of other social benefits, such as research and health care promotion. Therefore, according to Bloche, these uncertain social benefits do not sufficiently mitigate direct and indirect economic costs to the government to warrant continued protection of health care-based nonprofit organizations. This perspective contends that the government should pull even further away from the nonprofit sector and allow a more free market approach to social service delivery.

Other scholars find that nonprofit organizations do still behave in traditionally beneficial ways, justifying continued government support of the nonprofit form. Ryan (1999) argues that nonprofits generally spend surplus on mission-related activities, promote civic virtues, and act as advocates for the publics they serve. Weisbrod writes that these other findings of "differential organization behavior suggest, but do not necessarily prove, that when financial constraints allow, nonprofits do behave in a fundamentally different manner from forprofit organizations" (1998b: 12). This argument maintains that these behavioral differences between nonprofit and forprofit organizations should give the nonprofit form a comparative advantage in the competition for public funds.

Ryan (1999) cautions that the community benefits nonprofits do offer are threatened by forprofit encroachment. When competition drives prices down, nonprofits are likely to be left with less surplus revenue to spend on mission-related activities. In addition, competition with forprofits for government contracts may divide the client pools. Forprofits will be likely to seek those clients who are easiest to serve, leaving harder, more expensive cases to nonprofit providers. This perspective suggests that continued or even increased government support of the nonprofit sector is crucial to preserve the collective benefits that nonprofit organizations provide.

Another perspective on government support of nonprofits holds more to the notion that the public–nonprofit relationship has been and should remain mutually dependent. Melnick *et al.* (1999), for example, suggest that changing organizational behavior within the nonprofit sector actually warrants closer attention to the sector in terms of regulation. They argue that nonprofit organizations respond to regulatory pressures better than forprofit firms. So by retaining their close relationships with the nonprofit sector, government funders are still in a good position to control the output of collective goods from the nonprofit sector (Lipsky and Smith 1989–90). This leverage may be especially apparent within periods of constricted government spending where there is increased competition for less funding.

Schlesinger *et al.* (1996) extend this argument by suggesting a regulatory division of labor within the government for the nonprofit sector. They maintain that the Internal Revenue Service should define the parameters of the potential community benefit of the nonprofit sector and define these benefits broadly enough to capture all possible dimensions of nonprofit contributions. According to their scheme, other policymakers should then be left to prioritize these benefits because they may be more aware and better informed of trade-offs among competing goals for public action and who might well be more responsive to contemporary public concerns particularly in the healthcare and social services fields (1996: 738). This perspective recognizes the political nature of service provision and government contracting, arguing that the government needs to do more than provide funding to assure that collective goods provision meets demand.

NEW RELATIONSHIPS?

There is not much doubt about whether or not nonprofits can survive in this new competitive climate because nonprofit commercial activities tend to be innovative and profitable. In fact, nonprofit responses to external pressures from the forprofit sector increasingly involve some degree of coordination and collaboration among the public, nonprofit, and forprofit sectors. The danger surrounding this issue, however, is that nonprofit organizations might succumb to "institutional cusp pressures" and become more forprofit-like as boundaries between the nonprofit sector and the forprofit sector continue to blur.

Government funds still play an important role in the financial stability of nonprofit organizations across industries, but this role has changed to accommodate forprofit entrance into traditionally nonprofit service areas and the resulting collaboration between sectors. More and more, public money becomes a linchpin for nonprofit partnerships with forprofit entities. Nonprofit organizations increasingly find that they must team up with forprofit firms to compete for larger, consolidated funding streams. This trend is partially the result of push factors from the government. Social spending retrenchment, emphasis on accountability in contracting relationships, devolution of social welfare responsibility to states and local governments, and the dismantling of many New Deal/Great Society welfare programs have disrupted long-standing partnerships between government agencies and nonprofit social service providers.

For example, in the late 1990s, the YWCA of Greater Milwaukee faced a 40 percent revenue reduction as the Wisconsin legislature consolidated existing social service programs to develop an aggressive welfare reform package. On their own, YWCA did not have the resources to make a competitive bid for the new $40 million welfare-to-work contract. Their response was to seek out a partnership with two forprofit firms to build the scale and managerial capacity to win the contract. The newly formed YW Works soon provided almost every service that welfare recipients needed in finding a job (Ryan 1999).

Other cases of nonprofit partnerships with forprofit firms demonstrate how public money can help give nonprofit organizations leverage with local businesses, inspiring a variety of collaborative efforts in service delivery. For example, seven states have developed trust funds for affordable housing, ranging from $10 million to $50 million. These funds are awarded to local community developers to build and manage low- and moderate-income housing. Nonprofit housing coalitions in various states have been able to use the local infusion of trust fund money to leverage additional revenue from local realtors and homebuilders in the form of real estate transfer fees (Ryan 1999).

New partnership example: microfinance

The US credit industry offers another example of how new welfare policy initiatives, government funds, and regulation create an environment that fosters public partnerships with nonprofit and forprofit organizations in a variety of combinations. In the process of dismantling several public assistance programs, lawmakers have adopted "hand up, not hand out" rallying slogans in support of new programs that promote self-sufficiency. Some of the most politically popular self-sufficiency-type initiatives are microfinance programs. Borrowed from similar initiatives implemented throughout the developing world, these programs are designed to provide credit and financial training to low-income entrepreneurs and homebuyers (Edgecomb *et al.* 1996). Various forprofit and nonprofit microfinance institutions receive public funds for lending to targeted low-income individuals for their credit needs and to groups for specific projects, such as affordable housing development, neighborhood renewal projects, and commercial revitalization projects.

Lawmakers have an interest in providing funds for such initiatives so they can fulfill social welfare objectives that begin to compensate for retrenchment of other public assistance programs. However, in keeping with the trend of reducing government, they do not want to administer these lending programs. They rely heavily on forprofit and nonprofit partnerships to develop and manage these initiatives. In turn, forprofits, particularly banks, have an interest in participating in these microfinance initiatives to boost their public image, meet certain regulatory demands for local investment, and tap federal funding streams. Nonprofit organizations also have an interest in taking advantage of these federal dollars so they can continue to provide investment capital in their service areas in spite of cuts in other federal programs. Because nonprofit microlending programs are rarely self-sufficient, however, they often need to coordinate with local banks and businesses for additional funding, technical assistance provision, and client referrals. Nonprofit lenders also maintain relationships with local banks so they may refer clients back to the banks when the clients' needs grow beyond microfinance lending caps.

292

Through these microfinance initiatives, millions of federal dollars filter from the US Department of Housing and Urban Development (HUD) and the Small Business Administration (SBA) down through various structures of local governments, forprofits, and nonprofit organizations to individual borrowers. These sectors partner up in various ways to disburse these funds and pool financial and technical resources. For example, the SBA and HUD Program for Investments in Microentrepreneurs (PRIME) funnels federal dollars to private forprofit venture capital and other investment companies for investment in local small business initiatives. These investment coalitions often coordinate with local banks for additional funds and technical expertise and with nonprofit agencies for their existing network access to the targeted areas and populations and for their service expertise.

New kind of mutual dependency?

A simultaneous and important trend in public–private sector relationships is the government's reversal of its historically hostile stance toward forprofit firms. Forprofit firms have been bidding for and getting government contracts to manage social welfare programs since 1996 in the wake of massive welfare reform initiatives. While the move of forprofit firms into this traditionally nonprofit turf was initially dismissed as "poverty profiteering," forprofit firms are now managing dozens of new multi-million dollar welfare-to-work programs nationwide (Ryan 1999). Outsourcing to forprofit firms has been an answer to the government's desire to off-load the management responsibilities of large-scale social welfare programs. Driving the increasing reliance on forprofit firms is the assumption that forprofits are more experienced at managing complex systems than nonprofit organizations. Not only do forprofit firms generally have better management information systems, but they also have more collateral to guard against contract failure than most nonprofits. So, forprofit firms are the logical outsourcing choice for lawmakers intent on reducing governmental bureaucracy.

Instead of shutting nonprofit service providers out of the market, though, forprofit encroachment has actually inspired a new kind of mutual dependency between forprofit firms and nonprofit organizations. In this new scheme, the government contracts out with forprofit firms for the management of social programs, and the forprofits then contract with nonprofit organizations for service provision. Forprofit firms may have the technical expertise and organizational capacity to manage large-scale delivery systems, but they often lack local access and specialized service provision expertise. As a result, forprofit firms come to rely on nonprofit organizations to help them fulfill their contracts at the provision end of the delivery system. In effect, forprofits become the middleman entity between government purchasers and nonprofit providers.

A new role for the state?

Importantly, the different forms of government–nonprofit relations imply different roles for the state. Schuppert's (2003) four types of state orientations and actions in relation to the public good in modern societies are very useful in this respect. Each of the four types involves a different role for the nonprofit sector and points to different scenarios:

different facilities, or referring clients with religious interests to congregations. Whether the Charitable Choice provision will have any impact on the strategies of FBOs already working with government will certainly be a subject of future research and debate.

OTHER EXPERIENCES

United Kingdom

In Chapter 2, we already sketched some of the main characteristics of the long and complex history of the voluntary sector in the UK, with a focus on England. This history involved major shifts in voluntary sector–government relationships. As Lewis (1999) shows, from the late nineteenth century to the 1990s, that relationship went through several distinct phases that represent quite radical turns and reversals.

Under the Victorian model of the late nineteenth century, the government's role was to "provide a framework of rules and guidelines designed to enable society very largely to run itself" (Harris 1990, as quoted in Lewis 1999: 258). It advocated a small government, with the life of society expressed through voluntary associations and local community rather than through state. In the early part of the twentieth century, the policy understanding was that state and voluntary agencies addressed similar needs, but had different principles or goals in Najam's terminology (Table 13.1). Government was about power and politics, and voluntary associations about charity as a moral duty and a principle of social participation. The influential reformers at that time, Sidney and Beatrice Webb, introduced the notion that government and the voluntary sector formed "parallel bars."

With social and economic problems on the rise, and further amplified by the experiences of two World Wars, the early to mid twentieth century saw the development of a welfare model with the establishment of various national social programs (the elderly, health) with universal coverage. The state became the primary agent for solving social problems; consequently tax-based and employment-related finance mechanisms became more important, and government began to support charities through grants and contracts. The relationship between government and the voluntary sector changed from "parallel bars" to a system whereby private charities became the "extension ladder" of state efforts.

The system was challenged in the 1970s and 1980s by what became know as new public management (Hood 1995; see also Chapter 11). The welfare state consensus that dominated British politics for much of the post-war period was replaced by market-oriented approaches that emphasized efficiency criteria in service provision. Contracting regimes and quasi-markets took the place of governmental grants and subvention schemes. The voluntary sector became an *alternative* to state provision rather than its extension. The relationship changed from "extension ladder" to something closer to third-party government arrangements in the US.

A major difference between the US and the UK is, of course, the greater decentralization of the American federal system. In the UK, the closer institutional proximity of a highly centralized government, the Charity Commission, and the representative bodies of the voluntary sector (e.g. National Council of Voluntary Organizations) facilitated a profound policy dialogue. At the core of the policy debate was the relationship between government

BOX 13.2 THE LABOUR GOVERNMENT'S COMPACT WITH THE VOLUNTARY SECTOR, 1998

Principles

- Independent and diverse voluntary and community sector is fundamental to the well-being of society
- In the development and delivery of public policy and services, the government and the sector have distinct but complementary roles
- There is added value in working in partnership towards common aims and objectives
- The government and nonprofit sector have different forms of accountability but common values of commitment to integrity, objectivity, openness, honesty, and leadership

Government's undertakings

- To recognize and support the voluntary sector's independence
- On funding inter alia common, transparent arrangements for agreeing and evaluating objectives . . . the use of long-term . . . funding to assist . . . stability
- To consult the sector on issues that are likely to affect it
- To promote mutually affective working relations
- To review the operation of the Compact annually

Voluntary sector's undertakings

- To maintain high standards of governance and accountability
- To respect the law
- To ensure users and other stakeholders are consulted in presenting a case to government and developing management of activities
- To promote mutually affective working relations
- To review the operation of the Compact annually

Source: Based on Home Office 1998.

and the voluntary sector in an age of welfare reform, with greater emphasis being placed on individual responsibility and social entrepreneurship.

Throughout the 1990s, a series of reports was issued on these topics, culminating in what became known as the Deakin Report (Deakin 1996). This report advocated an explicit policy statement or concordat between government and the voluntary sector. The statement was signed in 1998 as a Compact (see Box 13.2) to become the platform for future policy developments involving government–voluntary sector relations. While the Compact has received much praise, it was also met with some criticism. Observers such as Bennington (2000) and Dahrendorf (2001) fear that the governmental embrace could challenge the independence and legitimacy of the sector and lead to enhanced expectations of what nonprofits can do.

Germany

In contrast to the UK situation, nonprofit–government relations in Germany are based on the principle of subsidiarity (Chapter 2). In essence, subsidiarity means that the state takes on only the functions that the private sector cannot meet, and that larger units, such as the central government, concern themselves only with tasks that are beyond the capabilities of smaller units, such as regional and local government, but also private units such as the congregation or the family (Anheier and Seibel 2001). Subsidiarity combines elements of decentralization and privatization of public functions—a combination that makes it such an attractive option in current policy debates in Europe and elsewhere.

Subsidiarity, as we have seen in Chapter 2, is not an age-old principle that has been operating for centuries, although it fits well into the German tradition of decentralization and local self-governance. It emerged from the long-standing conflict between state and church, particularly Catholicism. In economic terms, however, subsidiarity appears as a fairly new engine underlying nonprofit sector growth in Germany, having achieved its full impact from the 1970s onward. The subsidiarity principle is primarily found in the fields of social services and health care. Because the same large networks of nonprofit organizations, i.e. the free welfare organizations (Caritas, *Diakonie*, Parity Association, Red Cross, Workers' Welfare, Jewish Welfare), are involved in both health care and social service provision, the dividing line between these two fields is somewhat fluid in the German context.

In the German case, the welfare associations became the embodiment of the principle of subsidiarity, particularly the Protestant and Catholic associations that form the largest of the six networks. Their role became deeply imprinted in the relevant social welfare legislation. Until the mid 1990s, this translated more or less into a situation whereby the six welfare associations, and not just any voluntary or nonprofit organizations in general, found themselves in a rather privileged position. The public sector should respect the autonomy and presence of the free welfare associations, and support them in achieving their objectives. For example, article 10 of the Social Assistance Act states:

> The public bodies shall support the free welfare associations appropriately in their activities in the field of social assistance . . . If assistance is ensured by the free welfare associations, the public bodies shall refrain from implementing their own measures.

The principle of subsidiarity meant that public welfare programs were often implemented through the network of the free welfare associations, which then grew and expanded accordingly. The principle of subsidiarity has provided the political and economic bedrock for the German nonprofit sector. It spelled out a specific form of partnership between the state and parts of the nonprofit sector. Where this partnership developed, as it did in the field of social services, the nonprofit sector grew substantially, and where it did not develop, as in the field of education, the growth of the sector was less pronounced.

298

CONCLUSION

Cooperation between government and the nonprofit sector has a long history. In the US, the relationship is deeply rooted in the country's ideological and cultural make-up. Over time, however, this system of third-party government has been neither stable nor comprehensive in its coverage. Pushed along by major policy initiatives that periodically seemingly revolutionized the substance and practise of government–nonprofit relations, public–private partnerships remained a flexible and open system, unaffected by standardization that any more comprehensive policies would bring about. In the UK, the development from parallel bars to extension ladders, and from there to alternative systems and the Compact, signals a relationship that has changed in major ways over the last century. In Germany, the principle of subsidiarity is perhaps the clearest expression of an explicit public–private partnership.

Many theories of the nonprofit sector argue that public collaboration with nonprofit agencies also represents a division of labor in the provision of collective goods, coordinating the relative strengths and weaknesses of each sector. These theories describe the relationship between government and the nonprofit sector as complementary and symbiotic. The third-party government theory (Salamon 1995), for example, conceives of the nonprofit sector as the preferred mechanism for the provision of public goods. From this perspective, solving new and expanding social and economic problems is most appropriately and effectively accomplished on a voluntary bottom-up basis (Lipsky and Smith 1989–90). Government is the secondary institution that steps in when the voluntary sector "fails." Reliance on the nonprofit sector for performance of various government functions, in turn, allows the US government to promote general welfare without expanding its administrative apparatus (Salamon 1995).

The public goods theory, on the other hand, flips the logic of the third-party government theory. From this perspective, the government, whose responsibility it is to produce public goods, fails to provide goods and services that meet the needs of the entire population, particularly in heterogeneous societies with a diversity of needs. The nonprofit sector exists to satisfy demands for collective products and services left unfulfilled by the government (Weisbrod 1988). While the different logic of the third-party government theory and of the public goods theory make different assumptions about how government and nonprofits come to be mutually dependent, both see such coordination as optimal within modern industrialized economies.

The assumption among many scholars of the nonprofit sector is that nonprofit organizations offer the state a flexible, localized way to respond to emerging or entrenched social and economic problems. These organizations are more able than government bureaucracies to be both responsive to shifting public needs and to establish long-term service relationships with clients. Government agencies can rely on existing, often community-based, organizations to manage and deliver specialized goods and services that would be costly for them to establish and maintain. In doing so, the government also shifts the financial and political risks of collective good provision to the nonprofit sector. In turn, nonprofits receive reliable streams of funding and clients, tax exemption, and preferential regulatory treatment from public sources.

REVIEW QUESTIONS

■ What accounts for the complexity of the relationship between government and the nonprofit sector?

■ What are some of the consequences of public–private partnerships?

■ How does the US experience of public–private partnerships differ from that in other countries?

REFERENCES AND RECOMMENDED READING

Ascoli, U. and Ranci, C. (eds.) (2002) *Dilemmas of the Welfare Mix: The New Structure of Welfare in an Era of Privatization*, New York: Kluwer Academic/Plenum.

Boris, E. and Steuerle, C. E. (eds.) (1999) *Nonprofits and Government: Collaboration and Conflict*, Washington, DC: Urban Institute Press.

Smith, S. R. and Lipsky, M. (1993) *Nonprofits for Hire: The Welfare State in the Age of Contracting*, Cambridge, MA: Harvard University Press.

Chapter 14

Foundations

This chapter first looks at the history of foundations and how the modern foundation evolved over the centuries, with a particular emphasis on the evolution of the grant-making and the operating foundation. The chapter then presents different types of foundations, and surveys their sizes, activities and developments over time, in both the US and other countries. The chapter also introduces theoretical perspectives on the role of foundations in modern society, and concludes with a brief overview of current developments in the field of philanthropy.

LEARNING OBJECTIVES

We have already briefly looked at foundations in Chapter 3, and encountered them in other chapters as well. Foundations are among the most interesting institutions of modern societies: as private institutions for public benefit and beholden to neither market expectations nor the democratic process, but in command of their own assets, they enjoy significant independence. After considering this chapter, the reader should:

■ have a basic understanding of foundations, their historical developments, and forms;
■ know some of the major contours of the foundation field;
■ understand the theories that address the role of foundations in modern society;
■ be familiar with some of the challenges facing foundations;
■ have a sense of recent developments in the field of philanthropy.

KEY TERMS

Some of the key terms introduced in this chapter are:

■ community foundation
■ corporate foundation
■ donor-advised funds

In no other civilization have such instruments been utilized so widely as in the US. It may even be said that the foundation had become the ascendant American device for disposing of large accumulations of surplus wealth.

It becomes clear that the rise of the American foundation in the early part of the twentieth century highlights their financial, redistributive function as well as their potential for triggering social change in addressing social problems. However, the service delivery function that was one of the major *raisons d'être* of the European foundations was much less pronounced. In the past, Americans have shown a high propensity to transfer excess wealth to private foundations serving public purposes; moreover, against the backdrop of low government social spending and a rudimentary social welfare system, foundations in the US occupy a more prominent role in public life than in other countries. In addition, the international presence of the Ford, Gates, and Rockefeller Foundations, among others, has further emphasized this particular variant of "American Exceptionalism" (see Chapter 2) not only in the US, but also in many parts of the world.

DEFINITIONS AND PREVAILING TYPES

In its most basic form, the foundation is based on the transfer of property from a donor to an independent institution whose obligation it is to use such property, and any proceeds derived from it, for a specified purpose or purposes over an often-undetermined period of time. Since this process involves the transfer of property rights, most countries provide a regulatory framework that usually also holds some measure of definition. During the 1950s, Andrews (1956: 11) proposed a definition that was later adopted by the New York-based Foundation Center, a clearing house for information on US foundations. According to this definition, a foundation is:

> a nongovernmental, nonprofit organization with its own funds (usually from a single source, either an individual, a family, or a corporation) and program managed by its own trustees and directors, established to maintain or aid educational, social, charitable, religious, or other activities serving the common welfare, primarily by making grants to other nonprofit organizations.
>
> (Renz 1997: 111 see Renz, various years)

Under common law, foundations typically take the form of a *trust*, which is, legally speaking, not an organization but a relationship between property and trustees. Most common law countries, including the UK and Australia, use this rudimentary legal definition, and leave the actual development of foundation law to case law. An exception to this is the US, which, in 1969, established a precise, though negative, definition: foundations are tax-exempt organizations under section 501(c)(3) of the International Revenue Code that are neither public charities nor otherwise exempted organizations. This basically means that under American tax law, foundations are those charitable organizations that receive most of their resources from one source and are as such considered to be donor-controlled.

304

By contrast, in civil law countries such as Germany, Austria, and the Netherlands, the essence of a foundation, as a legal personality, is its endowment, which is the fundamental difference to the other major type of nonprofit organization, the member-based voluntary association. In most civil law countries, however, legal definitions of foundations are usually very broad. In the German and Austrian cases, for instance, the Civil Code falls short of an explicit definition, but mentions three necessary characteristics. Foundations need to have: (i) one or more specific purposes; (ii) an asset base commensurate with the need for the actual pursuit of the purpose(s); and (iii) some kind of organizational structure for carrying out activities. The Dutch legal definition is equally broad, stating that foundations are organizations without members with the purpose of realizing objectives specified in their charters by using property allocated to such objectives (see van der Ploeg 1999).

Anheier (2001a) proposed a modification of the structural-operational definition (see Chapter 3; Salamon and Anheier 1997c) used for nonprofit organizations. Accordingly, a foundation is:

- *An asset-based entity, financial or otherwise:* the foundation must rest on an original deed, typically a charter that gives the entity both intent of purpose and relative permanence as an organization.
- *A private entity:* foundations are institutionally separate from government, and are "nongovernmental" in the sense of being structurally separate from public agencies. Therefore, foundations do not exercise governmental authority and are outside direct majoritarian control.
- *A self-governing entity:* foundations are equipped to control their own activities. Some private foundations are tightly controlled either by governmental agencies or corporations and function as parts of these other institutions, even though they are structurally separate.
- *A non-profit-distributing entity:* foundations are not to return profits generated by either use of assets or commercial activities to their owners, family members, trustees, or directors as income. In this sense, commercial goals neither principally nor primarily guide foundations.
- *An entity for a public purpose:* foundations should do more than serve the needs of a narrowly-defined social group or category, such as members of a family, or a closed circle of beneficiaries. Foundations are private assets that serve a public purpose.

The term foundation covers a rich variety of different forms. Behind this complexity, however, are nonetheless only a few basic types:

- *Grant-making foundations,* i.e. endowed organizations that primarily engage in grant-making for specified purposes. They range from multi-billion dollar endowments such as Ford, Rockefeller, Carnegie, or Kellogg to very small family foundations. Other examples include the Annenberg Foundation in the US, the Leverhulme Trust in the UK, the Volkswagen Stiftung in Germany, the Bernard van Leer Foundation in the Netherlands, and the Carlsbergfondet in Denmark.

Grant-making foundations are usually regarded as the prototype of the modern foundation, which, as we argued above, is largely a reflection of the US experience and its post-war dominance in the field of philanthropy (Toepler 1999). Whereas in the US, over 90 percent of the existing 60,000 foundations are grant-making, the majority of foundations in Europe are either operating (see below, p. 314), or pursue their objectives by combining grant-making activities with the running of their own institutions, programs and projects.

■ *Operating foundations,* i.e. foundations that primarily operate their own programs and projects. Examples include the Russell Sage Foundation in New York (social science research), the Institut Pasteur in France (chemistry), the Pescatore Foundation in Luxembourg (which runs a home for senior citizens), and the Calouste Gulbenkian Foundation in Portugal (the arts).

Historically, of course, foundations were operating institutions primarily, e.g. hospitals, orphanages, schools, and universities, although many did distribute money (alms-giving) and contributions in kind (food or wood, for example). The sharp distinction between grant-making and operating foundations emerged much later historically, and is largely a product of the nineteenth and early twentieth centuries for both the US and Europe (Karl and Katz 1987; Bulmer 1999).

■ *Corporate foundations* come in several subtypes. The most prominent type is the company-related or company-sponsored foundation. Corporate foundations vary in the extent to which they maintain close links to the parent corporations in terms of governance and management. Examples include the IBM Foundation (computers), the Cartier Foundation in France (luxury accessories), the Fundación BBVA in Spain (banking), the Agnelli Foundation in Italy (cars), or the Wallenberg Foundation in Sweden (diversified holding).

■ *Community foundations,* i.e. grant-making organizations that pool revenue and assets from a variety of sources (individual, corporate, and public) for specified communal purposes. Cleveland, Ohio, is the birthplace of the modern community foundation, and they exist today in over 100 US cities as well as in countries such as the UK, Germany, and Australia.

■ *Government-sponsored or government-created foundations,* i.e. foundations that fit the structural–operational definition but are either created by public charter or enjoy high degrees of public sector support for either endowment or operating expenditures. Examples include the Inter-American Foundation and the Asia Foundation in the US, the Federal Environmental Foundation in Germany, the Fondation de France, the Government Petroleum Fund in Norway, or the public foundations in Turkey.

Of course, other forms exist, and many foundations are mixed types, i.e. engage in grant-making, initiate their own projects, and operate their own institutions. Examples include the Getty Trust in Los Angeles and the Robert Bosch Stiftung in Germany. In most cases, however, one area of fund disbursement or use dominates. What, then, can we say about the size and scope of foundation activities?

306

SIZE AND SCOPE

A brief look at US foundations in Figure 14.1 shows a consistent rise in the number of foundations after a period of relative stagnation for much of the late 1970s and early 1980s. The chart illustrates that more than half of all existing foundations in 2001 were created in the previous two decades, a finding that has also been shown in other countries such as Germany. The changes in assets have been even more pronounced, suggesting that foundations have not only become more numerous but also richer in endowment (Figure 14.2). Much of the increase in assets, represented in constant dollars in Figure 14.3, took place in the late 1990s, in particular the years 1996 to 1999.

Stock market losses and the impact of the September 11 terrorist attacks (2001), with resulting uncertainties about economic performance and political stability, meant a decline in foundation assets in 2001 and 2002—the first decreases reported since 1981. Foundation assets of $477 billion in 2001 were almost 4 percent lower than the year before. Only six of the top fifty US foundations reported asset increases above 10 percent, whereas twenty-nine posted double-figure losses in percentage terms. Accordingly, grants paid declined by nearly $220 million in 2002 to just over $30 billion (Foundation Center 2003). Even with these losses, asset values, and grant dollars paid out by US foundations remain at much higher levels than a decade earlier.

Nearly nine in ten US foundations are grant-making, and 6.3 percent are operating foundations (Figure 14.4a). Community foundations make up only a relatively small segment of US foundations (1 percent), as do corporate foundations with 3.5 percent. However, in terms of assets, community foundations are relatively larger, commanding 6.4 percent of total assets (Figure 14.4b). Over time, the composition of the US foundation sector has not changed much, although community foundations and corporate foundations have become relatively more numerous.

The most prominent grant-making fields are education, health, human services, and arts and culture, which together account for nearly three-quarters of the $17 billion in total grants spent in 2001 (Figure 14.5). Other significant fields are public affairs (11 percent) and environment and animal welfare (6 percent). Among the major funding fields, health increased by over 100 percent in total grant amounts between 1998 and 2001, education by almost 90 percent, environment by 93 percent, human services by 59 percent, and arts and culture by around 42 percent (Foundation Center, 2003).

A COMPARATIVE PROFILE OF FOUNDATIONS

There is great variation among countries in the number of foundations (see Table 14.1), ranging from a high of more than 60,000 in the US, 20,000–30,000 in Sweden, around 14,000 in Denmark, 13,500 in Japan, approximately 11,000 in Switzerland, 6,000 in Spain, and 3,000 in Italy, to lows of 600 in Austria, 533 in Estonia, 400–600 in Portugal (excluding foundations registered under canonical law), 500–700 in Greece, and 112 in Ireland. In some countries, such as the Netherlands, there is no clear estimate of the total number of foundations. The data suggest that there are around 80,000–90,000 foundations in Europe as a whole (including Greece and Turkey), or an average of around 4,500 per country.

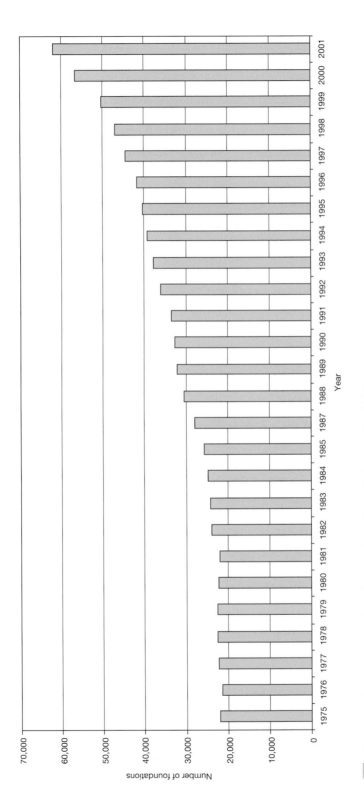

Figure 14.1 *Figure 14.1 Growth in number of foundations, 1975–2001*

Source: Based on the Foundation Center, *Foundation Yearbook* 2003.

Notes: Years are approximate; reporting years varied. The search set includes all private and community foundations in the US. Only grant-making operating foundations are included. Data for 1986 unavailable.

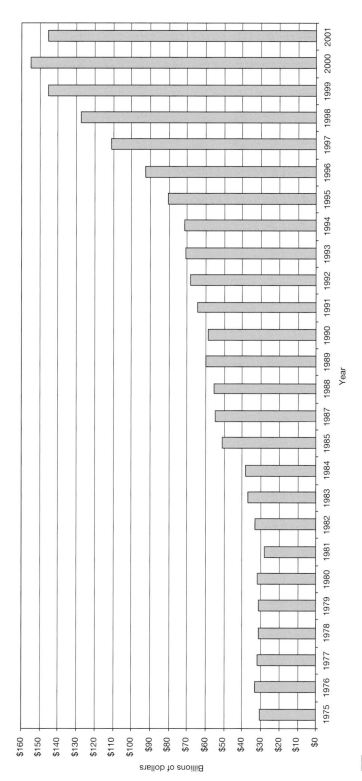

Figure 14.2 *Change in foundation assets adjusted for inflation, 1975–2001*

Source: Based on Foundation Center 2003.

Notes: Years are approximate; reporting years varied. Dollars in billions. Constant 1975 dollars based on annual average Consumer Price Index, all urban consumers. See US Census Bureau (2001), *Statistical Abstract of the United States, 2002*, Washington DC (122nd edition). Data for 1986 unavailable.

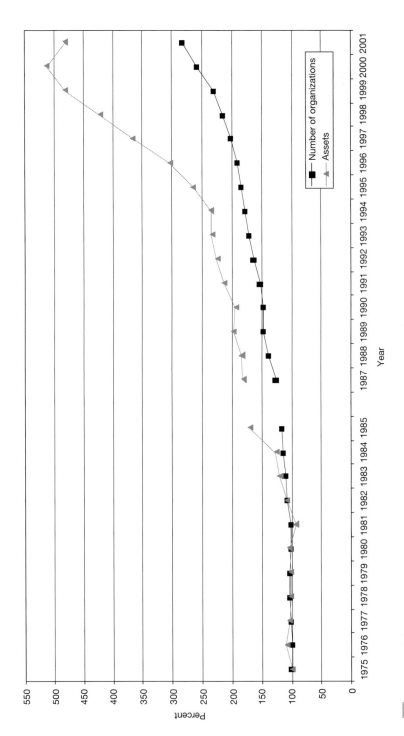

Figure 14.3 *Index of number of foundations and assets (1975 = 100%)*

Source: Based on Foundation Center 2003.

Notes: Years are approximate; reporting years varied. Dollars in billions. Constant 1975 dollars based on annual average Consumer Price Index, all urban consumers. See US Census Bureau (2001), *Statistical Abstract of the United States, 2002*, Washington DC (122nd edition). The search set includes all active private and community foundations in the US. Only grant-making operating foundations are included. Data for 1986 unavailable.

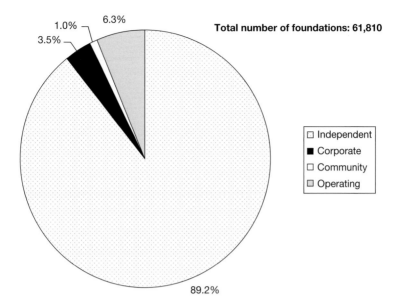

Figure 14.4 *(a) Percentage of foundations by type, 2001 (national level)*
Source: Based on Foundation Center 2003.

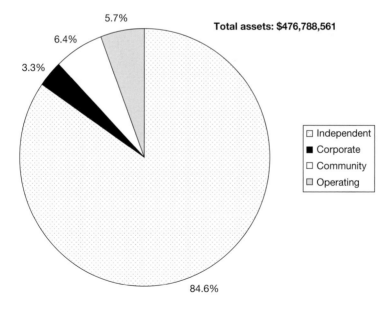

Figure 14.4 *(b) Assets by foundation type, 2001 (national level)*
Source: Based on Foundation Center 2003.
Note: Dollars in thousands. Due to rounding, figures may not add up.

311

Total dollar value of grants: $16,763,304,000

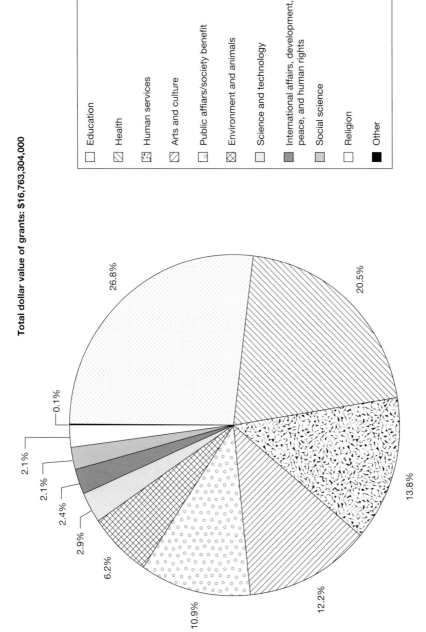

Education

Health

Human services

Arts and culture

Public affairs/society benefit

Environment and animals

Science and technology

International affairs, development,
peace, and human rights

Social science

Religion

Other

26.8%

0.1%

2.1%

2.1%

2.4%

2.9%

6.2%

10.9%

12.2%

13.8%

20.5%

Figure 14.5 *Distribution of foundation grants by subject categories, c.2001.*

Source: Based on the Foundation Center, *Foundation Giving Trends* 2003.

Note: Based on grants of $10,000 or more awarded by a national sample of 1,007 larger US foundations (including 800 of the 1,000 largest ranked by total giving). For community foundations, only discretionary grants are included. Grants to individuals are not included in the file.

Figures for the countries of Central and Eastern Europe tended to fluctuate in the 1990s due to changes and reforms to the laws governing foundations. In the Czech Republic, for example, 5,238 foundations were listed in 1997 whereas this number had fallen to 969 in 1999, a year after the new foundation law came into effect.

Types of foundation

As also shown in Table 14.1, the economic weight of operating institutions, programs, and projects tends to be more important than actual grant-making activities among European foundations. For example, in Spain foundations employ approximately 64,332 full-time staff, which accounts for 13.5 percent of all employment in the country's nonprofit sector. Estimates of employment in German grant-making foundations in 1995 ranged between 3,000 and 5,000 employees, whereas operating foundations employed over 90,000. The majority of German foundations, however, employ no staff at all: nine out of ten foundations are run and managed by volunteers only. In Scandinavia, similar results can be found: only a few of Denmark's 14,000 foundations have paid employment at all, and only eight of the over 2,500 Finnish foundations have more than ten full-time staff. Similarly, in Italy, over 85 percent of foundations have fewer than ten employees, while less than 1 percent of foundations employ more than 250 people. In Poland, foundations employ more than 13,000 people, although full-time employees can be found only in one in three foundations. In 2000, fewer than 10 percent of private and public foundations in Hungary had full-time employees, making foundations particularly dependent on part-time employees and volunteers. Operating foundations typically run service-providing organizations such as hospitals, homes for the elderly, and hospices as well as museums, schools, and research institutes.

Asset size

Asset estimates are the most difficult data to obtain on foundations, especially cross-nationally, given the influence of different valuation measures and techniques. Irrespective of these difficulties, available estimates reveal significant cross-national variations. For example, the assets held by the twenty largest Japanese foundations amount to 443,000 million yen, whereas the twenty largest US foundations are, with the equivalent of 12,000,000 million yen, about twenty-eight times larger. The assets of German foundations are €354 per head; the figure is higher for foundations in the UK (€536), and over €1,000 for foundations in Italy,[2] Sweden, and Switzerland.[3] Perhaps not surprisingly, the highest per head assets are reported for Liechtenstein, with a figure that exceeds €12,000 because of offshore foundation assets. Portugal represents a rather unusual case whereby assets are concentrated in the largest foundations. Indeed, the Gulbenkian Foundation has ten times as many assets as the next largest foundation, while the majority of foundations are set up with a capital of less than €100,000 (Anheier and Daly 2004). In Belgium, the Ministry for Justice estimates that the assets of foundations vary between €3,000 and €40 million. Estimates from Norway suggest that a typically large foundation will have assets of €12–16 million, but less than 5 percent, or 30–50, foundations belong to this category (Anheier and Daly

Table 14.1 Number and types of foundations in selected countries

Country	Number	Relative share of grant-making foundations	Relative share of operating foundations	Mixed type
Austria	600			Majority
Belgium	310	Few		Majority
Britain	~8,800	Great majority		
Canada	1,353	Great majority		Very few
Denmark	~14,000			
Estonia	533			
Finland	2,522	50%	30%	20%
France	404		Majority	
Germany	9,000–10,000	~50%	~25%	~25%
Greece	~500–700	Few	Majority	Few
Ireland	112	27%	70%	3%
Italy	~3,000	15%	39%	43%
Japan	13,553	Not known		
Liechtenstein	~600		Majority	
Luxembourg	143		Majority	
Netherlands	~1,000	Majority		
Norway	2,989			Majority
Portugal	~400–600		Majority	
Spain	~6,000	5%	95%	
Sweden	~20,000–30,000			
Switzerland	~11,000	5%	Majority	
Turkey	9,326			Majority
US	61,810	Majority	6.3%	

Source: Anheier 2001a; Anheier and Daly 2004; Foundation Center 2003.

Note: ~ = approximately

2004). In Austria, the total assets of all charitable foundations are estimated to be €7–7.1 million.

Foundation sectors can be grouped into three classes: small, medium, and large, with the middle group further divided into subcategories. Given the data situation, it is not possible to construct a strict and consistent ranking of countries in terms of foundation sector size. Yet, taken together, the various size indicators suggest three groups or clusters, though even such an admittedly crude classification involves some qualitative judgments. The relative size of the foundation sectors of European countries and the US can be classified as follows:

- countries with a small foundation sector: Austria, Belgium, France, Greece, Ireland, Luxembourg, and countries of Central and Eastern Europe;
- countries with a medium-to-small foundation sector: Portugal, Spain, and Turkey;
- countries with a medium-to-large foundation sector: Denmark, Finland, Germany, the Netherlands, Norway, Japan, Canada, and the UK;
- countries with a large foundation sector: the US, Italy, Liechtenstein, Sweden, and Switzerland.

Foundation areas of activity

Two fields clearly dominate the profile of foundation activity in Europe: education and research, with an average of 30 percent of foundation activity overall, and social services (25 percent). Together, both fields account for over one-half of foundation activities measured. In fact, education and research and social services are the main categories of foundation activity in eight of fifteen countries covered in a study conducted by Anheier and Daly (2004). Adding health care, with an average of 17 percent of foundation activity, pushes the total share up to 71 percent. In other words, two-thirds of foundations operate in just three fields, the same fields that also dominate the nonprofit sector at large (Salamon et al. 1999a and b).

The field of arts and culture accounts for the next largest share of foundation activities. It is the most important area of activity of foundations in Spain, with 44 percent of all foundations involved in this field, and is relatively prominent in Finland, Germany, Italy, Portugal, and Switzerland. Some countries show clear concentrations in one field in particular: this is the case for health care foundations in France, housing foundations in Ireland, international activities in the Netherlands, and cultural foundations in Spain. Such concentrations are the result of specific historical developments, e.g. urgent demand for affordable housing in early twentieth-century Ireland, or institutional effects, such as the prominence of large health care research foundations in France, e.g. Institut Pasteur and Institut Curie (Archambault, Boumendil, and Tsyboula 1999).

Growth patterns of foundations

Foundations are largely a product of the period following World War II, with a veritable foundation "boom" seeming to have set in from the late 1980s. More foundations were created in the 1980s and 1990s than in the three preceding decades, and more of the foundations existing in the early 2000s were established after 1950 than prior to that date. However, this growth is not evenly spread across countries.

- *High-growth countries*, such as the US, Italy, Spain, Turkey, and Portugal. From 1980 onward, the US experienced one of its most sustained expansions in the growth in the number of foundations as well as the amount of assets held. In Europe, with the exception of Turkey, high-growth countries are those in which foundation law underwent a major reform: in Italy, Law 218/1990 (or Amato law), in Spain, the Foundation Act, 1994, and in Portugal, Law 460/1977, with the proven effect that foundations increased sharply in number. In Portugal, where 56 percent of all foundations were established after 1980, and Spain, where over 90 percent of cultural foundations and 70 percent of educational foundations were founded in the same period, the rapid growth could also be a delayed effect of democratization in the 1970s, when both countries shed their autocratic regimes. The high growth is also a reflection of the rapid economic development of the countries of Europe's south, in particular Portugal, Spain, and Turkey (see Baloglu 1996).

■ *Medium-growth countries,* such as Finland, Germany, Greece, Switzerland, and the UK. In Finland, for example, the economic boom of the 1990s was marked with the registration of 663 new foundations. (However, in 2001 alone some 200 foundations related to savings banks were dissolved due to crises in the financial sector.) With the exception of Greece, these are countries with already sizable foundation sectors, and recent growth rates of 20–30 percent per decade add to a relatively high base. Finland, Germany, Switzerland, and the UK are high-income countries with stable political systems. We can assume that the foundation boom of recent years is in large measure a function of political stability and economic prosperity, amplified by a more self-confident middle class. Greece has a small foundation sector, and the expansion is probably the result of increased economic prosperity and greater political stability. The 1990s in particular witnessed a period of substantial activity in the establishment of foundations, which can be attributed to factors such as the stabilization of the Greek economy, a growing immigrant population, and preparations for the Olympic Games (Anheier and Daly 2004).

■ Some countries in Central and Eastern Europe enjoyed moderate growth in the late 1990s. The Czech Republic saw an €7 million increase in endowment size between 1999 and 2002. In Poland, the number of foundations increased from 288 in 1989 to 6,065 in 2000. The problem with such high growth figures, however, is that many of these foundations may be inactive, and not foundations according to the definition suggested above.

■ *Low-growth countries,* such as Austria, Belgium, and France. All three of these countries have relatively small foundation sectors to begin with. Japanese foundations grew significantly between 1980 and the early 1990s, but they have largely stagnated since, because of difficult economic conditions. At the same time, however, the regulatory environment has become more encouraging for foundations in Japan generally. However, the same cannot be said for countries such as France. The relatively few foundations in France are, on average, older, with one half pre-dating the post-war period, and with fewer foundations being established during the expansion period that began in the 1980s. Similarly, growth rates have changed little in Austria and Belgium over the last four decades, even though a slight upward trend is discernible. In Austria, the 1994 Private Foundations Act encouraged some public welfare organizations to adopt the form of the foundation, which is perceived as more flexible and less bureaucratic. However, this law has also attracted criticism and controversy as a useful tool for capital markets as it does not stipulate that a foundation must have a public purpose. The reasons for the slow growth in some countries are largely legal and procedural. For example, the establishment of foundations in France or Belgium is highly regulated and complicated, providing relatively few incentives for potential founders.

THE FUNCTIONS OF FOUNDATIONS

Against the backdrop of the empirical information presented above, what can we suggest about the role and functions of foundations in modern society? Common assumptions have long ascribed to foundations a number of special roles that transcend their limited function as financial intermediaries of the nonprofit sector. Accordingly, in addition to the functions associated with the nonprofit form generally (see Chapter 8), the literature often suggests that foundations are uniquely qualified to enable innovation, take social risks, and serve as philanthropic venture capital—more generally suggesting that they "have a special mandate to enter fields of controversy, where the explosive nature of the issues would make suspect the findings of less independent organizations and where needed financing from other sources might prove difficult" (Andrews 1956: 19).

The argument that foundations have these special competencies rests on the assumption that foundations, unlike other institutions, are largely free from direct external control, as they are not accountable to voters, members, consumers, shareholders, or other stakeholders. Typically self-supported by endowment income, foundations and their trustees are usually bound only by the donor's will, as laid down in the charter, of course, within the constraints of the overall legal and regulatory framework. This potential of endowed grantmaking foundations has long been recognized and also somewhat glorified. The 1949 report of a program and policy study committee of the Ford Foundation, for instance, noted that the "freedom from entanglements, pressures, restrictive legislation, and private interest endows a foundation with an inherent freedom of action possessed by few other organizations" (quoted in Andrews 1956: 21).

However, the foundation literature testifies to the difficulty of using private funds to the greatest public benefit possible. The absence of market and political correctives also implies that no stakeholders are present to monitor whether foundations meet these functions fully. Unfortunately, however, little systematic research has been carried out on this topic. Nonetheless we can suggest a few answers on the extent to which foundations perform their role or functions. Leat (1999) describes an exploratory study of British grant-making trusts, which yielded three more or less distinct types of "grant-making cultures." According to this study, foundations may act as "gift-givers," "investors," or "collaborative entrepreneurs," progressing from passive, uninvolved funders to proactive social entrepreneurs that set their own tasks and work quite closely with their grantees to accomplish them. A similar distinction is made by Beyer (1999) who differentiates between an "administrative" and an "entrepreneurial" way of foundation management.

Arguably, the adoption of any of these distinct styles or cultures will influence foundation performance with regard to the functions commonly ascribed to these organizations. More specifically, the entrepreneurial style, i.e. foundations that use creative powers to discover social needs (Beyer 1999) or identify a voluntary organization to work with to create what they want (Leat 1999), appears to be closely related to the innovation, venture capital, or risk capital function. By contrast, the pursuit of innovative new concepts and ventures, and the taking of risks in doing so, may hardly be expected from passive "gift-givers," whose gifts are gifts and success and failure are not really at issue (Leat 1999), or from "administrators," where the management function is reduced to the bureaucratic execution and control of projects (Beyer 1999).

317

These findings seem to imply that the special functions of foundations are most pronounced when they adopt an entrepreneurial approach, and that their contributions are limited when foundations approach their goal achievement more passively (Anheier and Leat, 2002). This further suggests that normative prescriptions are geared toward a more active approach to foundation management, involving longer-term relations with grantee organizations, rather than short-term project support (Letts *et al.* 1997), and stronger emphasis on evaluation (Council on Foundations 1993).

However, such prescriptions are not without problems, as proactive, entrepreneurial foundation management requires a high degree of expertise that many foundations tend to lack (see Leat 1999; Anheier and Leat 2002). Expertise as well as close working relationships with grantees or the development of self-designed and executed programs and projects also requires a higher level of human resources and concomitant administrative expenses. This, in turn, poses a public accountability problem, making foundations vulnerable to criticisms concerning "self-absorption" (i.e. diverting too much of their resources to administration rather than maximizing their pay-outs) and inflexibility due to bureaucratization (Frumkin 1997).

Perhaps more significantly, the majority of foundations might simply not control sufficient resources to pursue a strategy of philanthropic entrepreneurialism. In 1996, only 12.2 percent of US foundations surveyed with less than $5 million in assets reported having paid staff. Moreover, small foundations with assets up to $10 million controlled only 15.5 percent of total foundation assets, while accounting for 94 percent of all foundations. Similar financial concentrations of the foundation sector are evident elsewhere in the world (see Leat 1999; Strachwitz and Toepler 1996), indicating that the majority of foundations are limited in their ability to adopt proactive strategies seeking out innovative, high-impact funding ventures. Indeed, with regard to the British study, Leat (1999) concludes that by far the most common culture of grant-making among the foundations studied was that of the gift-giver.

This implies foremost that the "venture capital paradigm" might apply to only a small number of well-endowed, professional foundations and cannot reasonably be generalized across the whole foundation field. So what then would be the potential role of small foundations? To a large extent, their role would be to serve special constituencies and interests that would be under-served by tax-based public sector funds, or outside the scope of forprofit operations. Taken together, the sheer number of smaller foundations would contribute to pluralism in funding and provision, and expand the institutional choice available in a given society.

This thinking resonates with the other functions or roles that have been suggested in the literature (Prewitt 1999; Anheier and Toepler 1999a and b; Anheier 2001a; Anheier and Leat 2002). While some overlap exists among them, they lead to different implications for foundation impact and policy.

■   *Complementarity*: The first function is that of complementarity, whereby foundations serve otherwise undersupplied groups under conditions of demand heterogeneity and public budget constraints.

- *Substitution*: this role expects foundations to take on functions otherwise or previously supplied by the state. In this role, foundations substitute for state action, and foundations become providers of public and quasi-public goods.
- *Redistribution*: foundations are also supposed to engage in, and promote, redistribution of primarily economic resources from higher to lower income groups.
- *Innovation*: promoting innovation in social perceptions, values, relationships, and ways of doing things has long been a role ascribed to foundations.
- *Social and policy change*: this role entails promoting structural change and a more just society, fostering recognition of new needs, and empowering the socially excluded.
- *Preservation of traditions and cultures*: by contrast, foundations are also hypothesized to oppose change, preserving past lessons and achievements that are likely to be swamped by larger social, cultural, and economic forces.
- *Promotion of pluralism*: foundations are expected to promote experimentation and diversity in general, protect dissenters/civil liberties against the state, and challenge others in social, economic, cultural, and environmental policy.

In Chapter 8, we also encountered another function: efficiency (Prewitt 1999). This function suggests that foundations allocate philanthropic funds more efficiently than markets and government agencies could. By implication, cost-to-benefit ratios for foundations would be expected to be higher than for government allocations based on tax revenue, and business allocations based on investment income and profit.

Of course, these roles assume different meanings in specific policy contexts. The neo-liberal argument is that foundations exist to provide an alternative to the state. The reasoning is clear: exclusively state provision of the wide range of welfare, educational, and cultural services would violate the neo-liberal ideological precept of limited government (Prewitt 1999: 2). In the same vein, but somewhat differently, Strachwitz (quoted in Anheier and Toepler 1999b: 4) finds that "for the state, foundations tend to be vehicles for semi-privatizing certain tasks that are not as easily or as efficiently accomplished within the bounds of state administration." Along similar lines, it has been suggested that foundations reclaim societal space for a functioning civil society from what conservative observers, such as Olasky (1992), regard as an "overextended welfare state" (Anheier and Toepler 1999b: 5). Foundations can also adopt a longer-term perspective than is possible for governments driven by electoral timetables and political expediency (Odendahl 1990; Prewitt 1999; Anheier and Toepler 1999a; Anheier 2001a).

Different types of foundations may exist as solutions to somewhat different problems. So, for example, corporate foundations may be seen as a way of defusing criticism of "tainted money" by managing corporate donations more openly and systematically. Community foundations present themselves as local devices for avoiding big government, reducing the tax burden, humanizing global capitalism, and, crucially, maintaining, or even strengthening, local control (Covington 1994; Bertelsmann Foundation 1999).

Two important points are worth highlighting here. First, explanations of the existence of foundations are intimately intertwined with assumptions about and attitudes toward the role of the state. Second, none of the explanations addresses the question why foundations

319

For many of these "new philanthropists," philanthropy is an investment, not charity, designed to create social wealth. It is considered advantageous from the point of view of both good business and good citizenship, not to mention the tax advantages that can be realized with the appropriate strategies. However, one problem that seems to prevail is that the new philanthropists are results-oriented; they want to see the impact and the results of their giving immediately. This is often in direct conflict with the realities of the nonprofit sector and the systemic problems that exist in cultures and communities as well as historical information about the development of social movements. None of these were created overnight and, therefore, they cannot be changed overnight. In spite of this, there seems to be some indication that aspects of the new "bottom-line thinking" are proving to be a valuable addition to the nonprofit sector's operations because it creates a new way of thinking and operating that, in the long term, could be a value-added commodity.

Strategic philanthropy

Strategic philanthropy refers both to the working philosophy and the program strategies of a foundation. It originates from an entrepreneurial view of foundation activities that focuses on strategy, key competencies, and striving for effective contributions to social change. According to the International Network of Strategic Philanthropy (www.insp.efc. be), it involves:

- a vision of the desirable society of the future,
- a distinct value orientation in [the foundations'] activities,
- a concept of social change to the effect of greater social justice rather than mere grant-making to address social problems,
- the conviction that foundations serve as laboratories to develop model solutions, new ways of thinking, and new understanding for resolving societal problems,
- the awareness that innovative models and approaches should include both blueprints and a focus on practical implementation and applicability,
- a concern for the effectiveness of their philanthropic endeavors,
- a proactive approach, be it in their own activities, be it in partnering or grant-making,
- an awareness for capacity building and organizational learning among grantees/partners,
- a public policy orientation driven by the potential of taking project results to scale on policy levels,
- the insight that philanthropy provides for investment in the production of public goods, preferably aiming at innovations or increased effectiveness.

New philanthropic institutions

There is a variety of new vehicles for giving that are enabling and empowering these new philanthropists:

- *Donor-advised funds* offer philanthropists an attractive alternative to establishing and operating their own foundations. Such funds, typically held at investment banks or community foundations, are increasingly popular because they allow individuals to direct their own giving, and bring a growing number of individuals of moderate wealth into philanthropy.
- Similarly, *interest/identity funds* are increasingly common and target specific donor interests rather than serving a broad geographic community. Donors use them to support specific causes and particular interests.
- *e-Philanthropy* relates primarily to the tool of fund-raising and fund-distribution, i.e. the internet. Potential donors either search grantee/applicant websites or solicit proposals. Upon evaluating and selecting grantees, the e-philanthropist would then make a contribution to causes in line with the fund's objectives.

Developments in other countries

The growth of foundations and similar philanthropic intermediaries, or "foundation-like organizations," appears to be at least as dramatic in developing and transition countries as in the US and Europe. Of course, philanthropic foundations vary in form, meaning, and operations from one country or region to another. Indeed, the foundations at work today in developing countries and transition economies are different in a number of critical aspects. In the first place, very few are founded by wealthy families or individuals, although a good number are founded and funded by corporations or groups of corporations. Furthermore, very few have endowments that are large enough to support both their administration and grant-making programs, and many have no significant endowment at all. As a result, most rely on diverse funding from public and private sources, both domestic and international.

In this way, it is the lack of resources rather than their availability that spurs foundations and "foundation-like organizations" in developing and transition countries to take risks and to innovate themselves (Anheier and Winder 2004). They have little choice but to be strategic and entrepreneurial in programming and in mobilizing resources within their own philanthropic cultures. But unlike independent foundations in the US and Europe, most foundations in poorer and transition countries have no "inherent freedom of action." Instead they must respond to many stakeholders—donors, community members, political leaders, and, in many cases, leaders of the broader nonprofit sector. The successful ones, however, turn this requirement into a resource rather than a hindrance, drawing on these ties to influence policy, mobilize additional resources, raise awareness of under-recognized issues, etc.

CONCLUSION

The creation of foundations depends on two crucial factors: the availability of financial capital and other forms of assets, such as real estate, and the willingness of individuals or organizations to dedicate such funds to a separate entity, i.e. a foundation, and its dedicated purpose. As the examples from developing countries and transition economies just reviewed suggest, assets might well be small initially, and can be built up over time. Even in developed countries, the time factor in the emergence of a significant philanthropic community is critical: the current foundation boom in the US largely represents a supply phenomenon, whereby financial assets created during the burst of growth in the stock market of the 1980s and 1990s were transformed into foundation capital by a greater number of people than in the past, indicating a revival of philanthropic and dynastic values in American society. In the same way, the growth in the number of foundations observed in Germany could be explained by the unparalleled wealth that has been amassed in there since World War II, and the "retirement" of the generation of entrepreneurs and industrialists who helped create this wealth since the 1950s (Anheier and Topeler 1999a).

Thus, we can assume that variations in the creation of foundations over time depend not only on the demand for the functions they serve, but also on the extent to which the economy generates, or otherwise makes available, assets that can be transformed into foundations—and the degree of philanthropic entrepreneurship in society.

Writing in a European context, Strachwitz (1999) observes that foundations frequently confront an ambiguous public image: they are seen as exotic institutions by some, and as bulwarks of conservatism by others; or as playgrounds for the rich, and self-less expressions for humanitarian concerns. This picture is by no means unique to Europe: in *The Big Foundations*, Waldemar Nielsen (1972: 3), writing about the US, says: "foundations, like giraffes, could not possibly exist, but they do." As quasi-aristocratic institutions, they flourish on the privileges of a formally egalitarian yet socially as well as economically highly unequal society; they represent the fruits of capitalistic economic activity; and they are organized for the pursuit of public objectives, which is seemingly contrary to the notion of selfish economic interest.

Seen from this perspective, foundations are not only rare, they are also unlikely institutions or "strange creatures in the great jungle of American democracy," to quote Nielsen (1972: 3). With foundations becoming increasingly more common, it seems that the "golden age" of foundations neither began nor ended when the "big foundations" were established by Rockefeller and Ford. Within little more than two decades, foundations in many countries have passed from a period of relative decline through to a phase of unprecedented growth. Thus, foundations in many countries—not only in the US—represent essentially a late twentieth-century phenomenon destined to grow and expand in the twenty-first century.

REVIEW QUESTIONS

■ What are some of the major types of foundations?

■ What functions do foundations serve?

■ What sets foundations apart from other nonprofit organizations?

REFERENCES AND RECOMMENDED READING

Anheier, H. K. and Leat, D. (2005) *Creative Philanthropy*, London: Routledge.

Anheier, H. K. and Toepler, S. (eds.) (1999a) *Private Funds, Public Purpose: Philanthropic Foundations in International Perspective*, New York: Kluwer Acedemic/Plenum.

Schlueter, A., Then, V., and Walkenhorst, P. (eds.) (2001) *Foundations in Europe: Society, Management and Law*, London: Directory of Social Change.

Chapter 15

International issues and globalization

The chapter examines the internationalization of the nonprofit sector in the context of globalization and explores some of the reasons for the significant expansion of cross-border activities. Next the chapter focuses on the management of international nongovernmental organizations and other types of nonprofits that operate across borders. The chapter also covers the implications of globalization and cross-border activities in the fields of service delivery, humanitarian assistance, and advocacy.

LEARNING OBJECTIVES

Like other aspects of economy and society, the nonprofit sector is becoming more international and part of the globalization process. Even though most nonprofits are and remain local, regional, and national in orientation, the international components of nonprofit activities are expanding. After considering this chapter, the reader should:

- have an understanding of the scale of cross-border activities;
- be familiar with the reasons for the internationalization of nonprofit organizations;
- be aware of the management implications of international nonprofit operations.

KEY TERMS

Some of the key terms introduced or discussed in this chapter are:

- global civil society
- international NGO (INGO)
- international philanthropy
- transnational advocacy networks

INTRODUCTION

As we have seen in Chapter 4, the last few decades have witnessed the expansion of nonprofit sectors at and to levels unknown in the past, accounting for about 6 percent of total employment in OECD countries (Salamon *et al.* 1999a). While most remain domestic organizations, the scope of the nonprofit sector is increasingly international, and some larger nonprofits have grown into veritable global actors (Anheier *et al.* 2001a; Clark and Themudo 2004; Lewis 2001; Lindenberg and Bryant 2001). Oxfam, Save the Children, Amnesty International, Friends of the Earth, the Red Cross, and Greenpeace have become "brand names" among international nongovernmental organizations that operate in two or more countries with significant budgets, political influence, and responsibility. Indeed, by the late 1990s, the ten largest development and relief INGOs alone had combined expenditures of over $3 billion, which represented about half of the official US aid budget (Lindenberg and Dobel 1999).

The internationalization of the nonprofit sector is not a recent phenomenon (Anheier and Cunningham 1994). Of course, the Catholic Church and Islam have long had transnational aspirations and maintained far-reaching operations for centuries. The modern, internationally active NGO emerged from anti-slavery societies, most notably the British and Foreign Anti-Slavery Society in 1839, and from the International Committee of the Red Cross (ICRC), founded by Henri Dunant in 1864 after his experiences in the Battle of Solferino. By 1874, there were 32 INGOs (Chatfield 1997), which increased to 804 by 1950 (Tew 1963), although with significant fluctuations between 1914 and the end of World War II.

What seems new, however, is the sheer scale and scope that international and supranational institutions and organizations of many kinds have achieved in recent years. In this chapter we describe the growing internationalization of the nonprofit sector and explore some of its causes. What are the key drivers behind this internationalization process and its growing momentum? What are the management and policy implications of internationalization, and what are likely future developments?

DIMENSIONS OF THE INTERNATIONALIZATION OF THE NONPROFIT SECTOR

Since no comprehensive data are available on the internationalization of the nonprofit sector, we begin our analysis by presenting three related facets of globalization and philanthropy: the scale and revenue of international activities of the nonprofit sector in the US and selected countries; the rise of international nongovernmental organizations and the emergence of what has been called global civil society (Anheier *et al.* 2001a; Kaldor 2003); and the growth of international philanthropy.

The scale and revenue structure of nonprofit international activities

The Johns Hopkins Comparative Nonprofit Sector Project (Anheier and Salamon, forthcoming; Anheier and List 2000; Salamon *et al.* 2003) attempted to measure basic economic

Table 15.1 Size of international nonprofit sector activities in the UK, the US, Japan, Germany, and France, 1995

	Employment and volunteers		
	Full-time equivalent employment	Percent of total nonprofit sector employment	Volunteers in full-time equivalent jobs
UK	53,726	3.6	7,298
US	123,253	1.7	45,026
Japan	7,693	0.3	37,785
Germany	9,950	0.7	28,510
France	17,403	1.8	30,986

Sources: Based on Salamon et al. 1999b; Anheier and List 2000.

indicators of the size of nonprofit organizations engaging in international activities, including exchange and friendship programs, development assistance, disaster and relief, and human rights advocacy, in a broad cross-section of countries. These data allow us to fathom at least some aspects of the scale of international nonprofit activities, albeit from a country-based perspective. For the twenty-eight countries for which such data are available, INGOs amount to 1–2 percent of total nonprofit sector employment, or 134,000 full-time equivalent jobs. They also attract a larger number of volunteers, who represent another 154,000 jobs on a full-time basis. In the US, estimates suggest that over 4 million people volunteer for international causes, which would equal about 45,000 full-time jobs, or close to a third the number of FTE paid employees in the field (Table 15.1).

For some countries, it is possible to examine growth over the 1990s. Between 1990 and 1995, employment in French INGOs grew by 8 percent (Archambault et al. 1999b: 89), over 10 percent in Germany (Priller et al. 1999b: 115), and over 30 percent in the UK (Kendall 2003). Even though the data are limited, the resulting pattern is in line with some of the other evidence we present below: international nonprofit activities have expanded significantly, and while they continue to represent a small portion of national nonprofit sectors, their share has nonetheless increased.

In terms of revenue structure, the internationally oriented nonprofits, as measured by the Johns Hopkins team (Salamon et al. 2003), receive 29 percent of their income through fees and charges, including membership dues, 35 percent from both national and international governmental organizations in the form of grants and reimbursements, and 36 percent through individual, foundation, and corporate donations. With volunteer input factored in as monetary equivalent, the donation component increases to 58 percent of total "revenue," which makes the international nonprofit field the most voluntaristic and donative part of the nonprofit sector after religious congregations (73 percent), just ahead of civic and advocacy (56 percent) and environmental groups (56 percent), and far more than is the case for domestic service-providing nonprofits.

As Figure 15.1 suggests, the revenue structure of "international activities" in all five countries differs significantly from that for the nonprofit sector as a whole. Most of the difference is due to a more pronounced share of private giving combined with a reduced portion of income from private fees and payments: whereas the voluntary sector in the UK receives, as a whole, 44 percent of its revenue in the form of private fees and payments, the corresponding share is only 27 percent for international activities. At the same time, the importance of private giving more than triples to 33 percent. We find even more dramatic reversals in the importance of commercial income and giving in the case of the US, France, and Germany. Even in Japan, where private donations make up 3 percent of the sector's revenue as a whole, giving amounts to 27 percent for international activities. By contrast, the share of government payments changes much less. These findings suggest that the revenue structure of international voluntary sector activities is characterized to a significant extent by private giving.

The rise of international nongovernmental organizations[1]

Governmental and multilateral funds channeled through NGOs for development and relief activities have increased significantly since the 1970s, with many NGOs having become large-scale organizations (Table 15.2). In the 1970s, aid channeled through NGOs as a share of all aid flows from OECD countries to developing countries was 11 percent. Since then the INGO share has doubled, with most of the gain in the 1990s, a period which coincides with the significant expansion of INGO operations more generally.

The change in the economic weight and political importance of INGOs is highlighted even further when we look at the composition of total aid flows, using estimates compiled by Clark (2003: 130). In the 1980s, INGOs increasingly became an additional circuit of official development and humanitarian assistance flows, with the share of such resources in total INGO revenues jumping from 44 percent to 55 percent between 1980 and 1988. However, the 1990s saw a remarkable reversal: official aid flows declined overall, both directly (bilateral and multilateral) and indirectly via INGOs. In 1990 dollars, official grants to INGOs fell from $2.4 billion in 1988 to $1.7 billion in 1999. By contrast, private donations, including individual, foundation, and corporate contributions, more than doubled from $4.5 billion to $10.7 billion. These figures underscore the significant expansion of INGOs in the changing development field of the 1990s, and the major private mobilization effort they represent.

Dispersal

The growth of INGOs and their organizational presence is, of course, not equally spread across the world. Not surprisingly, Europe and North America show the greatest number of INGOs and higher membership densities compared with other regions of the world (Anheier and Katz 2003). And even though, as we will show below (p. 337), cities in Europe and the US still serve as the INGO capitals of the world, a long-term diffusion process has reduced the concentration of INGOs to the effect that they are now more evenly distributed around the world than ever before.

Table 15.2 *INGOs and INGO networks*

NGO-network	Turnover or related monetary figure in US$	Operating in number of countries	Other size indicators, information
Association of Protestant Development Agencies in Europe	$470 million combined (Clark 2003: 135)	n/a	In liaison with World Council of Churches
CARE (USA)	From 2002 annual report: revenues $428 million including agricultural commodities and non-cash, non-food in kind; program expenses $392 million including cash expenses for programs and agricultural commodities and non-food in kind	Over 60 countries	CARE US is one of 11 member organizations with about 10,000 staff members
International Cooperation for Development and Solidarity	$951 million combined (Clark 2003: 136)	Four continents: Latin America, Africa, Asia-Pacific, and Southeast Asia	Association of 14 Catholic development and relief NGOs
International Federation of Red Cross and Red Crescent Societies	From 2000 annual report: income $335 million; expenditure $337 million	178	115 million volunteers
Médecins sans Frontières	$304 million (Clark 2003: 135)	80	Volunteer centers in 18 countries with thousands of members

Organization			
Oxfam International	117	From 2001 annual report: $349 million in revenues, $303 in expenditure	In 2000, worked with 3,000 local organizations in over 100 countries; in 2000 their "Face-to-Face" campaign recruited 70,000 volunteers in 5 countries
Plan International	45	From 2001 annual report: $303 million in revenue; and $301 in expenditures	6,700 staff members; supports 1.3 million children in 45 countries; over 930,000 sponsors or members, 60,000 volunteers
Save the Children (USA)	45	From 2002 annual report: $202 million in revenue and support; with about $200 million in expenditure	85,000 sponsors in 2002 supporting more than 500,000 children
World Vision	96	From 2002 annual report: raised $732 in contributions, total of $1.032 billion if non-monetary contributions included; expenditures $1.032 billion for programs and also non-monetary aid	18,000 staff members (2002)
World Wildlife Fund USA	50	$350 million (Clark 2003: 135)	5 million members worldwide

Source: Based on annual reports from agencies listed above and Clark 2003: 134.

Figure 15.2 shows the growth in INGO membership for different world regions. As is to be expected, INGO memberships increased in all regions, but more in some than in others. The highest expansion rates are in Central and Eastern Europe, followed by Central Asia, and then by East Asia and the Pacific. The growth in Central and Eastern Europe is clearly linked to the fall of state socialism and the introduction of freedom of association, whereas the growth in Asia is explained by economic expansion and democratic reform in many countries of the region. Figure 15.3 adds a different dimension and shows the INGO membership growth in relation to economic development. Growth rates throughout the 1990s were higher in middle-income countries (East Asia, Central and Eastern Europe, parts of Latin America) than in the high-income countries of Western Europe, the Pacific, and North America. What is more, the expansion rate of INGOs in low-income countries is higher than that for richer parts of the world.

Together, these data indicate that the growth of the organizational infrastructure of global civil society does not involve concentration but rather dispersion, and points to inclusion rather than exclusion. In organizational terms, global civil society today is less a Western-based phenomenon than in the past, and the significant growth rates of recent years contributed to its expansion outside North America and the European Union. In the terms of David Held *et al.* (1999), the organizational infrastructure of INGOs has attained wider reach (extensity) and higher density (intensity), a finding also supported by Anheier and Katz (2003).

To illustrate the process of dispersion, it is useful to review some basic patterns of INGO location over time, and to go back briefly to the beginnings of modern INGO development. In 1906, only two of the 169 INGOs had their headquarters outside Europe; by 1938, 36 of the total of 705 INGOs existing at that time were located outside Europe. By 1950, with a significant increase of US-based INGOs, and with the establishment of the United Nations,

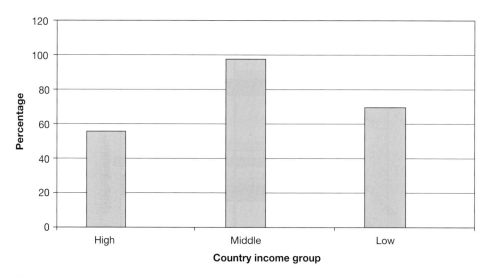

Figure 15.3 Growth in INGO membership, by country income group, 1990–2000

Source: Based on data provided by the Union of International Associations.

124 of the 804 existing INGOs were based outside Europe. With the independence movements leading to decolonization and the generally favorable economic climate of the 1950s and early 1960s, the number of INGOs increased to 1,768, of which 83 percent were located in Europe, 10 percent in the US, and 1–2 percent each in Asia, South America, Central America, Africa, the Middle East, and Australia (Tew 1963).

By 2001, much of this concentration gave way to a more decentralized pattern around an emerging bipolar structure of INGOs with two centers: Western Europe and North America. Europe still accounts for the majority of INGO headquarters, followed by the US, but other regions such as Asia and Africa have gained ground. Nonetheless, among the ten countries hosting the greatest number of intercontinental organization headquarters in 2001, eight are European countries (the UK, France, Switzerland, Belgium, Netherlands, Germany, Italy, and Austria), and the other two are the US and Canada. In terms of cities, we find that, by 2001, the traditional role of Paris (729), London (807), Brussels (1,392), Geneva (272), and New York (390) has not been diminished in absolute terms. They are, however, less dominant in relative terms: more than ten other cities on four continents have over one hundred INGO headquarters and another thirty-five on five continents over fifty INGO headquarters.

Organizational links

The infrastructure of global civil society in terms of INGOs not only became broader in geographical coverage, it also became much more dense and interconnected throughout the 1990s. In 2001, the Union of International Associations reported over 90,000 such links among NGOs, and 38,000 between INGOs and international governmental organizations. The average number of links jumped from an average of 6.7 in 1990 to 14.1 in 2000—an increase of 110 percent. In terms of an organization's participation in founding or creating an INGO, mutual and joint memberships, and joint activities, substantial increases took place after the 1980s, indicating that INGOs have not only become more interconnected among themselves but also to international institutions such as the United Nations and the World Bank.

Composition

Next to scale and connectedness, field of activity or purpose is another important dimension in describing the infrastructure of global civil society. When looking at the purpose or field in which INGOs operate (Figure 15.4), we find that among the INGOs based on data provided by the *Union of International Associations*, two fields dominate in terms of numbers: NGOs based in economic development and economic interest associations (26.1 percent), and knowledge-based NGOs in the area of research and science (20.5 percent). At first, the pronounced presence of these activities and purposes among INGOs seems a surprise, yet it is in these fields that the needs for some form of international cooperation, exchange of information, recognition, standard-setting, and other discourse have been long felt. There are thousands of scholarly associations and learned societies that span the entire range of academic disciplines and fields of human learning. Similarly, there is a rich tradition of

337

business and professional organizations reaching across national borders, from international chambers of commerce and consumer associations to professional groups in the field of law, accounting, trade, engineering, transport, civil service, or health care.

Indeed, the earliest available tabulation of INGOs by purpose lists 639 organizations in 1924, with nearly half in either economic interest associations (172), or learned societies and research organizations (238) (Otlet 1924). Only fifty-five organizations fell into the category "political," twenty-five in religion, and fourteen in arts and culture. In other words, the political, humanitarian, moral, or religious value component to INGOs is a more recent phenomenon. Although some of the oldest humanitarian organizations date back to the nineteenth century, e.g. the Red Cross or the Anti-Slavery Society, their widespread and prominent presence at a transnational level is a product of the latter part of the twentieth century.

As Figure 15.4 also shows, value-based INGOs in the areas of law, policy, and advocacy (12.6 percent), politics (5.2 percent), and religion (5.2 percent), today make up the second largest activity component, with a total of 23 percent of all INGOs. This is followed by a service provision cluster, in which social services, health, and education together account for 21 percent of INGO purposes. Smaller fields such as culture and the arts (6.6 percent), the environment (2.9 percent), and defense and security make up the balance.

Yet next to a greater emphasis on values, the changes in the composition of purposes that took place in the 1990s brought a long-standing, yet often overlooked, function of INGOs to the forefront: service delivery has become a visible and important part of INGO activity. Indeed, the number of organizations with social services as a main purpose grew by 79 percent between 1990 and 2000, those with health services by 50 percent, and those with education by 24 percent.

The data show that INGOs have expanded significantly since 1990, both in terms of scale and connectedness. We also saw that the relative focus of these organizations, taken together, shifted more toward value-based activities and service provision. Overall, the expansion of INGOs and the value–activity shift imply both quantitative and qualitative changes. Shedding some light on these changes will be the task in the next section, once we have taken a brief look at international philanthropy.

International philanthropy

Philanthropy is perhaps the least internationalized component of the nonprofit sector; at the same time, foundations are among its most visible components internationally. Large foundations such as the Ford Foundation and the Rockefeller Foundation, the network of Soros Foundations in Central and Eastern Europe, and now Central Asia, the Robert Bosch and Bertelsmann Stiftungen in Germany, and the Rowntree Foundation in the UK enjoy high cross-national recognition. Prominent examples of philanthropic gifts for international causes are the Bill and Melinda Gates Foundation's program to develop vaccines for malaria and the HIV/AIDS virus; the John D. and Catherine T. MacArthur Foundation's grant-making program in environmental protection and natural resource management; and the Ford Foundation's support of human rights.

At the same time, the relative share of US foundation grants to US-based organizations engaged in international affairs, development, and peace remained steady for much of the

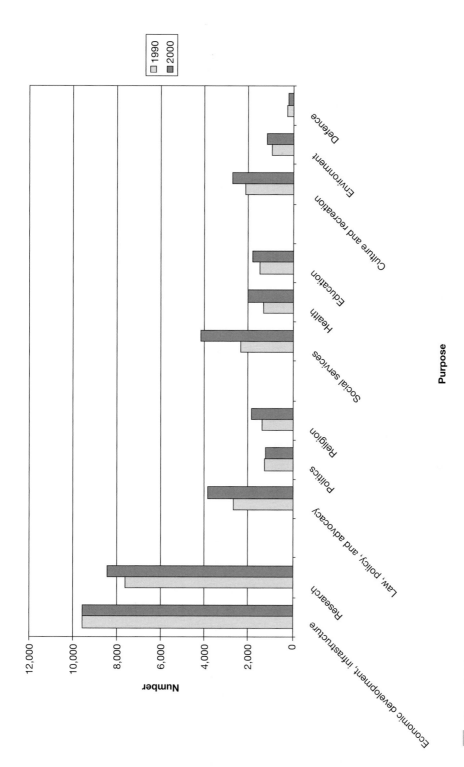

Figure 15.4 *INGOs by purpose, 1990–2000*

Source: Based on data provided by the Union of International Associations.

1990s, at 3–4 percent of total grant dollars awarded. By 2000, that share had slipped to 2.8 percent, although the number of grants grew by 12 percent and the amounts awarded by 20 percent, from $350 million to $414 million. In other words, while funding of international affairs grew in the 1990s in absolute terms, it declined in relative terms somewhat, being overshadowed by the growth in other funding areas (Foundation Center 2002).

However, the picture for cross-border giving by foundations, i.e. grants made to organizations outside the US, is different. According to the Foundation Center (2003), US private foundations, including corporate foundations, made about $2.5 billion in grants to organizations in other countries in 2001, up from $1.5 billion in the early 1990s. Whereas in 1982, around 5 percent of all grant dollars went abroad, that share increased to 16 percent twenty years later. As shown in Figure 15.5a, of these grant dollars, 12 percent went to the UK alone and 13 percent to the rest of Western Europe, making Western European organizations the largest recipients of overseas grants made by US foundations. In terms of purpose (Figure 15.5b), international development was the primary target (18 percent of all foundation grant dollars given abroad), followed closely by health (15 percent).

Information on transnational philanthropy in other countries is much more limited. Europe, Sweden, the UK, Germany, the Netherlands, and Italy have larger foundations that engage in grant-making abroad. However, as in the US, most foundations remain domestic actors, being constrained by their deed and held back by the higher transaction costs of operating across borders.

FACTORS FAVORING INTERNATIONALIZATION[2]

Perhaps the most popular explanation for the recent growth of INGOs is their increase in popularity with donors. Ideological changes such as the "new public management" in the public sector and the rise of the "new policy agenda," in the international aid system, which combines neo-liberal market privatization with democratic governance (Edwards and Hulme 1995), have put nonprofit organizations and NGOs at the forefront of policy implementation (Lewis 2001).

Clarke (1998) argues that, since the 1980s, the political environment favored NGOs as agents of development. Conservatives, neo-liberals, and radicals all saw NGOs as a solution to problems with the state. Conservatives saw NGOs as private agents that are more efficient, more flexible, and more innovative than state agencies. Delivering development aid through NGOs was therefore a way to reduce the state apparatus and bring about more efficiency. Neo-liberals, on the other hand, saw NGOs as providing a necessary balance to state power. NGOs bring about greater pluralism and democratization of the development process. Finally, radicals saw NGOs as bottom-up initiatives capable of promoting social change and addressing inequalities of power. NGOs became therefore the favorite child, some would even argue the "magic bullet" (Edwards and Hulme 1995) of development policy.

The last two decades have witnessed various high-profile humanitarian emergencies that received worldwide media attention and public support. Prominent examples are the famine in Ethiopia in the mid 1980s, which led to the "Live Aid" phenomenon, the complex

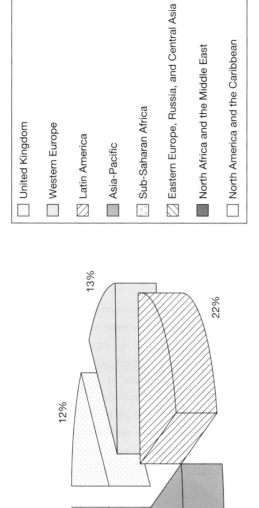

Figure 15.5a *US foundation grant dollars given abroad, by country, 2001*

Source: Based on the Foundation Center 2002: 52–4.

United Kingdom

Western Europe

Latin America

Asia-Pacific

Sub-Saharan Africa

Eastern Europe, Russia, and Central Asia

North Africa and the Middle East

North America and the Caribbean

monitoring, and evaluation, which previously consumed significant travel, phone, fax, and other costs.

Technology has also facilitated the emergence of newer organizational forms in the nonprofit sector: i.e. "dot causes" (Clark and Themudo 2004). For example, dot causes such as Attac are social networks that mobilize support for particular policy campaigns primarily (but not necessarily exclusively) through a website. They fit Keck's and Sikkink's (1998: 2) definition of transnational advocacy networks as "actors working internationally on an issue, who are bound together by shared values, a common discourse, and dense exchanges of information and services." Some of the earliest examples were the Free Burma campaign network, starting in 1995, followed by networks waging campaigns against Shell in Ogoniland, Nigeria, and against McDonalds, i.e. McSpotlight (O'Neill 1999).

The development of a "world culture" or "world society" is a generally less discussed but important supply-side driver contributing to the internationalization of the nonprofit sector (Meyer et al. 1997). World-society researchers argue that a world culture of institutions such as citizenship, human rights, science and technology, socioeconomic development, education, religion, and management has emerged that penetrates virtually all human endeavor (Meyer et al. 1997). This increasingly global social organization of rationalized modernity has its logic and purposes built into almost all nation-states, which, bound by international treaties to remain domestic actors, "spin off" NGOs as agents of international contact in addition to the transnational corporation. NGOs are one way in which countries open up to globalization.

Berger (1997) suggests that attitudes toward globalization are a reflection of four conflicting cultures that themselves are closely allied to specific institutions: the *Davos Culture* is the global culture, lifestyle, career patterns, and expectations of the international business community; the *Faculty Club* is the intellectual response to globalization, largely on a reform course by trying to "tame" and "humanize" the process, and is the realm of many INGOs; *MacWorld* refers to the spread of consumerism and Americanization of popular culture; and *Religious Revival* describes the efforts of largely Protestant and Islamic groups at proselytizing and gaining greater influence. The value systems around these cultures are on a collision course as they make very different claims on the nature of globalization, with INGOs emerging as one institutional vehicle to advance their particular causes, in particular for the *Faculty Club* and *Religious Revival* camps.

Kaldor et al. (2003b) develop a different, though complementary approach and identify political/value positions on globalization. These positions are held by actors such as NGO leaders as well as political parties, governments, business executives, and individuals. They argue that there are very few out-and-out supporters of globalization (i.e. groups or individuals who favor all forms of global connectedness such as trade, money, people, law, and politics); at the same time, there are very few total rejectionists. Rather, the dominant responses to globalization are mixed. Specifically, "regressive globalizers" are individuals, groups, and governments who favor globalization on their own terms and when it is in their particular interest. Reformers or "redistributive globalizers" are groups, individuals, governments, and multilateral institutions that, like Berger's "Faculty Club," favor "civilizing" or "humanizing" globalization.

344

INGO development trajectory

Pulling these factors together, as summarized in Table 15.3, the development of INGOs since the 1970s has shown a remarkably consistent trajectory. Specifically, we suggest that:

■ The growth and expansion of INGOs seems closely associated with a major shift in cultural and social values that took hold in most developed market economies in the 1970s. This shift saw a change in emphasis from material security to concerns about democracy, participation, and meaning, and it involved, among other things, a movement toward cosmopolitan values such as tolerance and respect for human rights (see Inglehart 1997).

■ These values facilitated the cross-national spread of social movements around common issues that escaped conventional party politics, particularly in Europe and Latin America, and led to a broad-based mobilization in social movements, with the women's, peace, democracy, and environmental movements as the best examples of an increasingly international "movement industry" (Diani and McAdam 2003; McAdam et al. 2001).

■ The 1990s brought political openings and a broad-based mobilization of unprecedented size and scale (Kaldor 2003), which coincided with the reappraisal of the role of the state in most developed countries and growing disillusionment with state-led multilateralism in the Third World among counter-elites (Edwards 1999).

■ In addition to this broadened political space, favorable economic conditions throughout the 1990s, combined with the vastly reduced costs of communication and greater ease of organizing, facilitated the institutional expansion of global civil society in organizational terms (Anheier and Themodo 2002; Clark 2003).

By 2002, the changed geopolitical environment and the economic downturn challenged both the (by now) relatively large number of INGOs and the broad value base of cosmopolitanism in many countries across the world, in particular among the middle classes and elites. As a result, new organizational forms and ways of organizing and communicating have gained in importance, with social forums and internet-based mobilization as prominent examples.

Implications for management

Since the industrial revolution of the eighteenth and nineteenth centuries, organizational history has seen three major epochal developments that cut across the constraints of existing forms. The first, identified by Max Weber (1924; see Perrow 1986), was the full development of the modern bureaucracy, a major innovation that made the nation-state and the industrial corporation possible. With a premium on stability, predictability, responsibility, and the long term, bureaucracies were efficient tools of administration and production. State agencies, industrial giants, and even charities and religious organizations, became bureaucratic organizations. The second major organizational innovation of the industrial era involved, according to Chandler and Takashi (1990), the fundamental shift from

Relational forms try to balance centralization and decentralization imperatives empha-sizing the autonomy of internal components. Relational forms are somewhat "fluid" organizations that are particularly suited for highly variable organizational environments. Without central coordination, decisions are made at the local levels with a minimum of costs for consultation and negotiation. Adaptability is maximized when undertaken by small independent units rather than large bureaucratic organizations. By implication, the lack of coordination reduces opportunities for scale economies, for example by way of standard-ization and bulk purchasing.

More critical, however, is the way that extreme decentralization leads to difficulties in sharing development costs, as well as brand and knowledge management, i.e. activities that require some form of collective action and common identity. In other words, while the network form has many advantages, it also invites free-riding. Thus, this form constrains identity formation, collective action, and perhaps the legitimacy of the organization to speak with one voice.

On balance, and on largely economic grounds, the global organizational environment for INGOs can be said to favor the network form with decentralized and autonomous units. There is some empirical evidence to support this claim. Using data from the Union of International Associations, Smith et al. (1997) looked into the organizational forms of INGOs. They found that between 1973 and 1993 the number of coalitions increased from 25 to 40 percent of the total number of INGOs. These observations were made against an overall rise in the organizations observed from 183 (in 1973) to 477 (in 1993) demon-strating that coalitions rose in absolute and relative terms.

Organizational dynamics

Most INGOs, perhaps one hundred years ago, would have been basically membership and non-membership organizations modeled after the Weberian model of bureaucracy. They included scholarly associations, the International Chamber of Commerce, the Red Cross Federation, and various political party alliances such as Socialist International. Non-membership organizations such as the Catholic Church, too, were outgrowing their late medieval past and developing into formal bureaucracies at local, national, and international levels, resembling the modern state administration. Some organizations, such as some national Red Cross societies or the Salvation Army, incorporated distinctive military elements in their organizational design and structure.

INGOs, with observer status at the UN from the 1950s onward, were rather conven-tional bureaucracies, too, and largely indistinguishable in their structure from national organizations, and perhaps even state agencies. Yet, as suggested above, the growth of INGOs into more global organizations has brought new challenges and opportunities that push them away from the model of nineteenth-century bureaucracies to experiment with multidivisional and network forms. INGOs such as Amnesty International and Action Aid are in an ongoing process of reorganization in order to capitalize on the new opportunities and respond to the new environmental challenges. These reorganizations are search pro-cedures for innovations in organizational forms that are more suitable for the complex task environment of a globalizing world than are bureaucracies and multidivisional forms, or variations thereof.

Form diversity

Organization theory (Hannan and Freeman 1977; Aldrich 1999) suggests that organizational forms will be *as diverse as the environment that supports them*, and that organizations are more sustainable if they adapt to environmental conditions. This symmetry between environment and form is more difficult to achieve when organizations face not one, but multiple, complex environments, as is the case for INGOs with activities across the globe:

- *Funding sources*: INGOs raise funds from a wide variety of donors (e.g. sympathizers, foundations, and bilateral and multilateral agencies) and other sources (sales, fees, and charges) that will be spread across different countries. This typically involves a geographical separation of contributors and beneficiaries (Edwards and Hulme 1995; Hansmann 1996).
- *Staff, members, and volunteers*: INGOs typically hire staff from a number of different countries, and recruit members and volunteers from a sometimes even larger number of countries and regions. For example, of Care International's 10,000 employees, 9,000 are nationals of the countries in which they work (www.care-international.org). UIA requires "universal membership organizations" to be present in at least sixty different countries and territories.
- *Diversity of missions*: from the preservation of wetlands to the promotion of micro-credit, from working with recycling in the North to supplying humanitarian assistance in conflict areas, INGOs are concerned with a multiplicity of issues and missions. Depending on local conditions, within the same organization different parts of the mission may be emphasized at the expense of others. For example, developing country parts of environmental INGOs will pay greater attention to development aspects of environmental protection than their developed country counterparts (Clark 2001; Princen and Finger 1994).
- *Local interpretations of global mission*: working in very diverse cultural environments, INGOs must address the question of different local interpretations of their mission. The Jubilee 2000 campaign to reduce Third World debt was perceived differently by members in developed countries from members in developing countries. Similarly the importance of class, caste, or gender relations will vary in different cultures, with immense implications for management.
- *Need to be locally responsive, to conform to national regulations, and to be globally relevant*: INGOs work with very different beneficiaries who have different views of a "good society" and require very different tasks and management models. The local–national–global link requires skillful handling of needs, resources, and expectations. Being able to link the local with the global is essential for the effectiveness of NGOs in general (Edwards *et al.* 1999) as well as for global INGOs.

349

has argued that US civil law practises have spread to other parts of the world (e.g. Central and Eastern Europe), helped by donor encouragement of regulatory frameworks favorable to civil society.

Tied to the development of a world culture are normative pressures for isomorphism derived from the growth of an international professional elite. Members of this elite study in similar environments and share similar views about the world. Many INGOs are run by members of this elite, who try to shape their organizations into similar, sanctioned organizational forms. Indeed, in conditions of high uncertainty associated with global complexity, organizations tend to mimic and imitate organizations that they perceive to be successful (see Powell and DiMaggio 1991).

Another powerful set of coercive isomorphic tendencies derives from the global funding environment. INGOs' resource dependency on a limited set of funders increases the possibility of external influence on organizational form (see Pfeffer and Salancik 1978). There are indications that competition for scarce funding is intensifying for global civil society (Foreman 1999; Lindenberg and Dobel 1999). At the core of the greater competition for resources is the fact that, in some fields, such as development and humanitarian relief, the growth of INGOs seems to have surpassed the expansion of resources available to them, either from private (donations and dues) or public (government grants and contracts) sources. Of course, competition need not necessarily lead to isomorphism, as donors can and often do encourage innovation and diversity. However, there has been a general trend for donors to emphasize bureaucratization (Edwards and Hulme 1995) and efficiency over diversity and innovation (Salm 1999). Competition brings with it calls for reduction of administrative costs, greater professionalization, and flexibility. Moreover, as governmental and private funding (foundations) operate in national jurisdictions, they "impose" reporting requirements in accordance with national regulations, which are thereby seemingly "exported" to the global level.

Pressures for isomorphism come not only from competition, but also from increased collaboration both among INGOs and also between INGOs and public or private agencies. The need to create conditions for mutual understanding and language has forced many INGOs to adapt to other organizational forms with which they collaborate. As such isomorphism also applies across sectors. Some authors have expressed fears that some INGOs (nonprofits and NGOs) are becoming increasingly like state agencies and form a quasi-state sector allied with official donor agencies in complex public–private partnerships (e.g. Edwards and Hulme 1995). Others fear that INGOs are becoming more like businesses as high competition for foundation and government grants drives them to exploit alternative sources such as related and unrelated business income to support their mission.

Going global

Dealing with globalization is the single most important concern for all types of multinational enterprises, including INGOs (Micklethwait and Wooldridge 1996). The degree of globalization experienced by an organization varies with respect to: (1) the proportion of activities undertaken that are international (as compared to national) measured by the income of foreign affiliates to domestic income; and (2) the number of countries in which the organization either conducts activities or obtains resources and revenue. At low levels of "globalization," an INGO develops an awareness of international issues. Some of its activities are concerned with scanning and monitoring the international environment for threats and opportunities (e.g. funding). As internationalization increases further, the organization establishes increasingly formal relations with organizations in other countries. It may even join a formal international coalition/network or enter into partnership agreements with foreign organizations. At the highest levels of globalization it becomes a global organization either by creating franchises or by setting up federations.

What is the impact of changes in the level of globalization on organizational form? When developing into transnational organizations, most INGOs tend to adopt a multilevel structure that involves local, national, and international components. As mentioned above, multinational NGOs work in different cultural, political, and economic settings, often with very different problems and organizational tasks. Environmental variations across local chapters and national societies are high, which suggests that a decentralized mode is best suited for achieving results locally. Decisions should be made at levels where expertise and knowledge are greatest—which may not necessarily be at the central level at all.

In situations where tasks and resources vary across geographically dispersed organizations, a federal model or federation is the best. In this model, the main purpose of the central body is two-fold: first, to maintain diversity and expertise at appropriate levels; and second, to coordinate between units and to take on collective action vis-à-vis third parties. This is typically done along a division of labor between local and non-local tasks.

At the global level, the organizational form is determined by the need for affiliate self-determination, economies of scale, resource acquisition, protection of global brand, pressures for global accountability, scale of impact, and technology (Lindenberg and Dobel 1999). Unitary or corporate models facilitate coordination and help maintain a single clear brand identity. On the other hand weakly coordinated networks maximize organizational autonomy and adaptation to local conditions.

Impact of organizational forms

The dynamics of the organizational infrastructure explored above have important implications for global civil society and its impact on society in general. Here we explore the implications for organizational efficiency and survival, democratization, North–South tensions, and an increasing presence in cyberspace.

Organizational efficiency and survival

Global complexity tends to breed new forms and leads to hybridization. As INGOs adapt to this complexity they take on a variety of forms to increase overall fit between environment and mission. By finding the right level for decision-making and mobilizing resources to areas of need, global INGOs increase their effectiveness. So they increase their impact on social change in terms of, for example, alleviating poverty, promoting human rights, and environmental conservation. The more effective their organizational form is, the greater the social impact.

353

and efficiency, promote democratization (electronic voting), and provide more voice opportunities to Southern groups to participate in global decision-making. But virtualization can also promote a reduction in decision-making transparency. And the digital divide can aggravate the North–South power rift. These opportunities and challenges pose critical questions for traditional INGOs that are increasingly using internet technology, as well as for virtual organizations such as dot-causes (Clark and Themudo 2004).

CONCLUDING COMMENTS

Underlying the discussion of organizational forms in global civil society is the realization that *being global is different*. Being global is more than an increase in scale of national work. It is *qualitatively* different from being national. Global governance and management require more than simply adding national governance systems together. Global NGOs need to balance global and national missions. Yet accountability still rests mainly at the national level because of the nature of membership or support as well as INGO regulation.

Two of the most important differences between the global and national levels are the absence of a state or regulatory agency and cross-national cultural variations. These factors reduce the impact of coercive and normative pressures for isomorphism that are more clearly present at national levels. At the same time, the high cost of operating globally on limited budgets combined with a strong competitive environment encourages mimetic isomorphism as INGOs seek to imitate successful organizations.

The combination of less pronounced coercive and normative isomorphism with a stronger mimetic isomorphism appears to encourage INGOs to be more like businesses (multinational enterprises) and less like the state (for which there is no global model). There is some support for this hypothesis. Over a decade ago, Korten (1990) argued that many NGOs were simply "public sector contractors" behaving like bureaucratic businesses that work for government. More recently, Edwards (2004) claimed that there is a trend among NGOs everywhere to internalize market values and dilute the links to a social base. *The Economist* (January 29, 2000: 25–8) made a similar observation: membership NGOs are perceived as "existing to promote issues deemed important by their members. [However] as they get larger, NGOs are also looking more and more like businesses." Clearly, this trend, if true, will have wide ranging implications for global civil society.

Donors play an important role in this trend and in the tension between diversity and isomorphism, which is critical for the adaptability, survival, and efficiency of INGOs. In terms of isomorphism, donors can evaluate INGOs on their efficiency and promote the adoption of best practises. In terms of diversity and innovation, donors can evaluate the innovativeness of different funding proposals, and provide "seed" funding for pilot projects. Donors can also create more flexible systems, so that a greater variety of organizations can approach them—not only the large bureaucratic ones with an extensive track record. Unfortunately, it appears that, so far, donors have put too much emphasis on promoting cost-effectiveness from organizations and less on innovation. At least within development INGOs, this donor tendency has promoted strong isomorphism in terms of organizational structure (e.g. federation), objectives (e.g. donor fads), and work (e.g. the project format, logical framework evaluation). This isomorphism can increase efficiency and impact, but it can also signal wide co-option and vulnerability to changes in environmental conditions that can ultimately put the survival of the sector at risk.

Being global is different from being national in that there are a lot fewer models indicating how to work globally. INGOs must resist the pressures to become more like business or more like the state. Their ability to do so will rest partly on their ability to attract more funding with few strings attached (see Edwards and Hulme 1996; Smillie 1995), but will also rest on their ability to seek innovative forms that break away from constraints inherent in the traditional forms or forms of other sectors. They must also be able to practise what they preach and seek greater internal democracy and equality in North–South relations. They must experiment with different possibilities of governance, accountability, decision-making, and resource generation and distribution. Donors can help INGOs in their search for effectiveness and innovation, but it is ultimately up to INGOs to ensure it.

We have described some of these innovations and some of the generalized solutions to organizational form problems (isomorphism). Whatever the future contours of INGOs in thirty or fifty years time will be, they are likely to be as different from conventional NGOs today as the industrial giants of the twentieth century are from present transnational network organizations. Future INGOs will also most likely be as different as the European Union is from the League of Nations. These are stark contrasts, admittedly, but nonetheless there are indications that epochal transformations are beginning to take hold. They are likely to lead to an innovation push in the way global civil society is organized, bringing about new ways and means that go well beyond currently existing INGOs.

The internationalization of the nonprofit sector has not been homogeneous across the different regions of the world. Access to cheaper technology and travel, knowledge of English, and openness of domestic political structure vary dramatically between countries. Similarly, access to wealthy private givers and government donors differs. As a consequence the opportunities for internationalization vary dramatically between countries. In this internationalization, "NGOs are all equal but some are more equal than others." The North has internationalized a lot more than the South (see Anheier and Themudo 2002), and this has implications for global civil society and for global governance in general.

We also argue that global civil society is likely to enter a new phase of restructuring in coming to terms with a changed and uncertain geopolitical situation. This process will involve both different outcomes for major policy positions and actors, and innovations such as social forums, new kinds of alliances and coalitions, and increased use of internet-based forms of communicating and organizing. Indeed, the contrast between the 1990s and the 2000s is striking: the 1990s represented a period of growth and consolidation, demonstrated by the rapid expansion of INGOs. At the beginning of the twenty-first century, by contrast, we are witnessing a renewed mobilization of people and movements, and a renewed emphasis on self-organization and activism. In the 1990s, the predominant political force behind globalization was a coalition between supporters and reformers, in transnational corporations, as well as in governments and intergovernmental organizations, and in INGOs. The Davos World Economic Forum represented an annual expression of this coalition. It was the combination of supporters and reformers that pressed for the globalization of the rule of law and of technology, as well as of the economy, although there was disagreement on the globalization of society and culture. This combination, mainly associated with the

357

INTRODUCTION

In this chapter we move from macro-level perspectives to more specific policy-oriented issues. We will re-examine the factors affecting the supply and demand conditions for the emergence and sustainability of the nonprofit organization. Next, the chapter discusses a number of critical policy issues such as the devolution of the welfare state, the social capital debate and the dual role of nonprofit organizations as service providers and vehicles of community-building. In a closing section, the chapter returns to the broader, long-term issues and explores different scenarios for future nonprofit development. In so doing, the chapter draws on material presented in the previous sections of this book, and in particular the history of the nonprofit sector, theories and organizational analysis, and government–nonprofit relations.

SUPPLY AND DEMAND FACTORS REVISITED[1]

We begin by revisiting the critical supply and demand conditions responsible for the emergence of different types of organization, as presented in Chapter 6, and ask: *what are the broader circumstances that affect these conditions, and thus organizational choice and sector shifts over time?* It is beyond the scope of this chapter to provide a full answer, and indeed, economic theories are still struggling with this question (Ben-Ner and Gui 1993). What we can do, however, is to suggest a number of initial avenues that might be usefully explored in this context. Several aspects of the economic, social, and political order of the twentieth and early twenty-first centuries have been, and are, affecting supply and demand conditions, and therefore sectoral shifts. These include the massive growth in scope and complexity of economic activity; the effects of the World Wars, the Depression, and political upheavals; the prolonged prosperity in many OECD countries after World War II; fundamental technological changes; and changing demographic trends.

Massive growth

Throughout the twentieth century and into the twenty-first century, organizations—forprofit firms, employee-owned firms, government agencies, and nonprofit organizations—have become more numerous, and generally larger and more complex. This growth, however, did not affect all sectors equally, or at the same time. On the contrary, characteristic of growth patterns over the last century has been the disproportionate expansion of one sector, which was then followed by expansions in others, often in an upward "push and pull" fashion. For example, the emergence of the multidivisional form in the first half of the twentieth century created organizations of hitherto unprecedented proportions: capitalizing on both economies of scale and scope, industrial giants emerged that soon became the central nodes in production and distribution networks spanning national and international economies (Chandler and Takashi 1990). With much delay, the multidivisional form took root in the nonprofit sector as well, as we have seen in Chapters 7 and 15.

The massive expansion of the forprofit firm created immense regulatory and social welfare demands, which led to an expansion of government, particularly in response to the

Depression of the 1930s. The public sector, expanding both in scale and in scope, took on new responsibilities, first as part of the New Deal era and the emerging war economy, later as part of welfare state legislation. Frequently, greater governmental responsibilities implied more opportunities for nonprofit organizations, particularly in the fields of social services, education, and health. As we have seen in Chapter 13, in particular, government turned to private providers to implement social services and other programs it found either less efficient or less politically opportune to deliver itself (Salamon 1995).

Institutional effects of the World Wars and the Depression

Wars and economic depression had a profound impact on long-term institutional development. The greater role of government in Europe, the US, and Japan was facilitated by both the two World Wars and the Depression of the 1930s. The origins of the modern military–industrial complex, accounting for significant shares of GDP during the Cold War, reach back to the early twentieth century; social security legislation in countries as different as the US, France, and Germany are closely related to the demands and the aftermath of war economies.

Without the demands for a social security system that war widows put on the US legislature (Skocpol 1992) and without the labor shortage created by the draft and the war economy, the health care system in the US would very likely have taken a very different path. Similarly, without the GI Bill (legislation that provided for free higher education for war veterans after World War II), America's educational system would probably look very different today, with a significantly smaller presence of public institutions. Similarly, with the regaining of Alsace and Lorraine in 1919, the centralized French state was forced to extend the "German" social security system to the rest of the country in an effort to diffuse the impact of different legal and social welfare systems on national unity (Archambault 1996).

Finally, the German example shows how the bankrupt and discredited system of centralized public service provision during the Nazi era gave way, after 1945, to a preference for private, nonprofit organizations in the fields of social services, health, and, to some extent, education. Over time, state provision regained ground, particularly in education, but the principle of subsidiarity, which attaches a priority to private rather than public service delivery, has its true contemporary roots in the years between 1945 and 1967, when the modern welfare state first developed (Anheier and Seibel 2001).

Thus the economic demands imposed by war and depression could not be satisfied by forprofit firms through the mechanism of the market, and gave rise to provision by government organizations. When the ability of governments to provide the myriad of services was taxed, they had to turn some of their responsibilities over to other types of organization. Because of the nature of these services, nonprofit organizations rather than forprofit firms were formed or expanded to fill in the gap between demand and supply.

Central and Eastern European countries are a case in point. After World War II, these countries were left behind the Iron Curtain and what remained of their nonprofit sectors was co-opted or replaced by the communist governments coming to power, or went underground. With the end of the Cold War and the re-democratization of most countries in the social services, with the social security systems to be similarly affected in the foreseeable future. These trends have almost universally increased demand for services that are generally provided by the nonprofit or government sectors.

Second, with falling birth rates—in some countries below replacement rate—and increasing life expectancy, the baby boomer cohorts will find themselves in growing disproportion to the sizes of younger cohorts, thereby putting additional strain on existing social security, health, and welfare systems. In turn, this will create demand for all sorts of providers, and lead to probable shifts in the sectoral structure of economies.

While the impact of the baby boom cohorts has and continues to influence many demand parameters, a third factor has had an at least equally profound impact: this is the increased labor force participation of women. Women make up the majority of employees in most service industries, have led to shifts in the gender composition of most other fields as well, and have led to a reduction in the importance of production of various services within households. The subsequent demands for child care, family, and related services have generated opportunities for forprofit, nonprofit, cooperative, and government providers alike.

Finally, nearly all developed market economies have experienced, mostly since the 1960s, migration of people from other countries. The reasons for and consequences of this are manifold, but in the present context it is worth noting that one probable effect has been the lowering of social solidarity at the national level in many countries, where support for social safety nets, redistribution of income, and many forms of collective action have declined, reducing the demand for government services. At the same time, increased heterogeneity in many communities has had the effect of reducing the potential for collective action at the local level, often limiting the potential for supply of organizational forms other than forprofit firms.

Of course, individually, these factors may mean very little and seem to pose as many questions as they answer; but when taken together and put in the legal, political, and cultural context of particular countries against the background of the basic supply and demand conditions introduced above, they emerge as useful tools to help us understand sectoral shifts over time.

Sectoral shifts

We have argued that, in the course of the last century, sectoral shifts and the organizational choices they reflect have occurred in economic settings that are generally characterized by expansion and greater complexity, the prolonged effects of periods of war and depression, the long period of prosperity since about 1950, technological advancement, and demographic changes. We can describe the interplay between these factors and the basic conditions of supply and demand as "push and pull" influences. In some instances, we observe a push toward market solutions; in other cases, we see a pull toward non-market solutions.

However, the extent to which these pull and push tendencies in sectoral shifts can materialize depends on a number of factors, and the interactions among them. Past choices often influence present options, and the path-dependency of sector development is a product of the interaction between the basic supply and demand conditions. These interactions are shaped by long-term developments like demographic tendencies and ways of organizing that are frequently supported by powerful cultural patterns and political preferences. How these factors and tendencies play out, and if they exert influences that expand or reduce the size and opportunities for specific sectors, is the topic in this section.

The legal system

A country's legal and regulatory system can play an enabling as well as a restrictive role with respect to the extent to which different types of organization are affected by changes in the factors outlined above. Many aspects of the legal and regulatory system have had profound impacts on sectoral shares and shifts over time. The following examples suggest the importance of the system for the varying boundaries of sectors over time and across countries:

■ entry restrictions for forprofit firms in particular markets (e.g. the blood industry);
■ barriers to entry for nonprofit organizations (e.g. the high capitalization requirements for Japanese foundations);
■ discrimination against forprofit firms (e.g. the disadvantageous position of forprofit providers in some social services in Germany);
■ restrictions on the nonprofit sector (e.g. laws that severely complicate the ownership of real estate by voluntary associations in France);
■ favorable tax laws for nonprofit organizations (now in place in most developed market economies);
■ the absence of suitable legal incorporation forms that support the fundamental role of particular types of organization (such as for private nonprofit organizations in China).

More generally, effective systems of market control by government reduce the potential ill effects of information asymmetries for consumers and open up opportunities for organizational forms. For example, Hansmann (1990) reports how the regulation of the US banking industry in the late nineteenth and early twentieth centuries decreased the default rate for forprofit banks, and increased their trustworthiness. As a result, they began to crowd-out nonprofit providers and today nonprofit organizations play a marginal role in the US banking industry. In Europe, cooperation between municipal and county governments on the one hand, and local savings banks and occupational groups on the other, reduced the degree of "moral hazard" in the financial industry. Thus the enabling and restrictive aspects of legal and regulatory environments have a significant impact on the sectoral composition of entire economies as well as fields of activity.

The cultural system

While cultural aspects are, of course, important in many ways, their precise impact on sectoral shifts is difficult to capture, particularly cross-nationally. There are, however, two aspects of culture that are directly relevant for our purposes. The first is the degree of ethnic, linguistic, and religious heterogeneity of a country's population, and the extent to which this heterogeneity is transformed into effective demand and effective supply.

365

corporations as well. Thus, as we have seen in Chapter 13, the US government works closely with the nonprofit sector to address a variety of social problems. Whereas common notions of the welfare state assume that welfare provision corresponds to the size of the public social service apparatus (Quadagno 1990), the American version of the welfare state consists of a public sector that makes policy, generates tax revenue, and hires private nonprofit agencies to manage and deliver goods and services.

Europe: searching for a Third Way?

In contrast to both neo-liberal policy approaches and traditional social-democratic policies, Third Way thinking pays the greatest and most systematic attention to the nonprofit or voluntary sector. The Third Way rose to prominence in the mid to late 1990s, with a succession of influential speeches, pamphlets and books (see Blair 1998; Giddens 1998; The White House 1999; Blair and Schroeder 1999), and political successes in the UK, Germany, France, Italy, and the Netherlands. While some of these successes were cut short when conservative politicians came to power (France, Italy, the Netherlands) and despite much criticism (see review by Giddens 2000), the influence of the Third Way continues, in large measure because it is the only major ideological challenger of neo-liberal policies.

At the same time, it is difficult to identify what the Third Way is, in particular its ideological core. In many ways, it is still an emerging political vision to modernize "old-style social democracy" that rested on solidarity and state-led welfare, and seeks to develop a comprehensive framework for a renewal of both state and society to counteract neo-liberal policies that are regarded as socially blind, simplistic, and unsustainable. The Third Way calls for decentralized forms of government based on transparency, efficient administration, more opportunities for direct democracy, and an environmentally friendly economy. The role of the state changes from welfare provider to risk manager and enabler—a fundamental redefinition of the social democratic welfare state, and one that is complemented by a change in the notion of citizenship that stresses individual rights and responsibilities alike (Mulgan 2000).

The Third Way foresees a reorganization of the state that requires a renewal and activation of civil society, social participation, the encouragement of social entrepreneurship, and new approaches to public–private partnerships in the provision of public goods and services. Specifically, the framework involves: a renewal of political institutions to encourage greater citizen participation; a new relationship between government and civil society that involves an engaged government as well as a vibrant set of voluntary associations of many kinds; a wider role for business organizations as socially and environmentally responsible institutions; and a structural reform of the welfare state away from "entitlement" toward risk management (Giddens 1998, 2000).

Clearly, the Third Way and the nonprofit sector are close to each other as far as policies are concerned, especially in the areas of civil society and welfare reform. In Tony Blair's words, a "key challenge of progressive politics is to use the state as an enabling force, protecting effective communities and voluntary associations and encouraging their growth to tackle new needs, in partnership if appropriate" (Blair 1998: 4). Mulgan (2000: 18) is explicit in spelling out the principles that guide Third Way policies toward the voluntary or nonprofit sector:

> First, a good society is founded on a balance between the interests of business, government and the voluntary sector. Second, institutions of the nonprofit sector are insulated from the immediate pressures of the market and electoral democracy and are, therefore, not only able to identify and anticipate needs, but also to act as guardians of much longer-term value. Third, institutions of the nonprofit sector can play a crucial role in fostering habits of responsibility and cultures of co-operation, self-control and self-expression.

As introduced in Chapter 13, the Compact is the clearest policy addressing the relationship between government and nonprofit sector in Third Way policies (Home Office 1998). It is a common platform, which rests on four principles:

- an independent voluntary sector with its own agenda is good for society;
- government and the voluntary sector have complementary roles in delivering social services;
- there is added value in public–private partnership; and
- government and the voluntary sector have different forms of accountability but similar values and commitments to public benefit.

How does the policy program envisioned by the Third Way line up with nonprofit sector realities and changes in developed market economies? As we will see, the answer to this question is at first perplexing. In essence, the various policy developments across Europe expect nonprofit sector organizations to be efficient providers of services in the fields of health care, social services, humanitarian assistance, education and culture, *and* agents of civic renewal by forming the infrastructure of a bourgeoning civil society. The fact that Third Way and neo-liberal approaches alike harbor such expectations basically suggests that the growing economic and political role of the nonprofit sector is somewhat independent of "new politics" and part of more fundamental changes taking place in post-industrial societies.

Balancing goals

In developed and developing countries alike, the nonprofit–government partnership, based on interdependence, is now seen much more broadly and in the context of privatization and "market-building." The rise of quasi-markets and public–private partnerships under the heading of "new public management" stresses the role of nonprofits as providers of services, typically as contractors of services paid for, at least in part, by government (Ferlie 1996; McLaughlin *et al.* 2002). As a broad label, new public management includes several related aspects that draw in the nonprofit sector specifically:

- from "third-party government" (Salamon 1995), where nonprofits serve as either extension agents or partners of governments in service delivery, to a mixed economy

369

of social care and welfare that includes businesses and public agencies next to nonprofit providers (Knapp *et al.* 2001); and

■ from simple contracts and subsidies to "constructed markets" (Le Grand 1999), particularly in health care and social services, with a premium on managed competition; for example, long-term care insurance in Germany and services for the frail elderly in Britain are based on competition among alternative providers through competitive bidding for service contracts.

With the rise of new public management, particularly in the US and Europe, the emphasis on nonprofits as service providers and instruments of privatization casts nonprofit organizations essentially in a neo-liberal role. Examples are: Germany's efforts to modernize its subsidiarity policy by introducing competitive bidding into social service contracting (Anheier and Seibel 2001); New Labour's Compact in the UK (Mulgan 2000; Plowden 2001; see also Chapter 13); or France's unemployment policy of "insertion" (Archambault 1996).

The key point here is that nonprofits are no longer seen as a "poor cousin" of the state, or as some outmoded organizational form, as conventional welfare state literature would have it (see Quadagno 1990; Esping-Anderson 1990). On the contrary, they have become instruments of welfare state reform guided by the simple equation: "less government = less bureaucracy = more flexibility = greater efficiency" (see Kettl 2000). New public management has changed the established role of nonprofit organizations as providers of services, addressing special demands for quasi-public goods to complement state provision (see Weisbrod 1988) increasingly to that of an equal partner (or competitor) along with other organizational forms.

Under what conditions can NGOs serve both goals, i.e. being a service provider in fields that are becoming "big growth industries'" increasingly populated by corporations (health, education, social services, and environment), *and* being a bedrock of civil society and engine for the formation of social capital, trust relations, social inclusion, etc.? What can we say about the future trajectories of the nonprofit sector in the countries of North America and Europe?

The capacity of nonprofits to combine a value-orientation with managerial rationality has become a major theme in the literature (see Moore 2000), and the general tenor seems to suggest that it is indeed very difficult to combine both missions equally successfully. What is more, authors such as Frumkin (2002) and Frumkin and Andre-Clark (2000) see a differentiation in the nonprofit sector between value-based nonprofits and commercial, managerialist service providers.

As we pointed out in Chapter 6, the nonprofit sector faces a wide range of demands for its services and activities from a variety of different stakeholders. Importantly, governments are "downsizing" and are in a process of "off-loading" some of their traditional tasks to private nonprofit institutions and commercial providers. In an era of budget cutting, lean management, and privatization efforts, the nonprofit sector is confronted with great challenges and opportunities. Will the nonprofit sector be able to meet these challenges, and should it seize all opportunities created by a retreating state? While accounts differ on the extent to which they diagnose a zero-sum relationship between state and nonprofit sector (see Salamon 1995), they are generally doubtful as to the sector's ability to compensate for public provision beyond a certain level (Steuerle and Hodgkinson 1999).

Differentiation

Ultimately, we need to re-examine the relationship of the four great institutional complexes of households/families, businesses, government, and associations/foundations to the public good and collective well-being in present and future societies. There are core government functions such as defense, the rule of law, and basic infrastructure. There are also pure private goods that are best handled by markets. In between these extremes, however, is a vast array of goods and services that are either quasi-public or quasi-private, and that is where most of the current disagreement about the meaning and culture of collective goods takes place (see Barr 1998). Importantly, new organizational forms emerge primarily in the contested terrain, and it is also here, we suggest, that most of the growth of the nonprofit sector has occurred. It is important to keep in mind that in these contested fields of activity, two or, typically, three organizational forms are possible, and that the nonprofit form is only one of several possibilities.

In the future we are likely to see greater differentiation in the nonprofit sector. Some organizations will move closer to market firms, or relocate altogether. Other organizations, already increasingly close to governments, e.g. NGOs in international development finance, will become more agency-like over time and resemble public bureaucracies. Some will remain nonprofit organizations in the conventional sense. Yet we suggest that, above and beyond the differentiation within the nonprofit sector, similar differentiation processes are also taking place in the public and the forprofit sectors, bringing more fundamental forces into play.

Behind this reasoning is an insight for organizational theory, which sees organizational forms in more or less open competition with each other. While policies define the rules of the game, over time, mismatches develop between the potentials and constraints they impose on forms, and thereby either increase or decrease one's competitive edge over others. Some of the underlying forces responsible for mismatches are related to the heterogeneity and trust theories described in Chapter 6, e.g. changes in the definition of goods and services, and changes in information asymmetries, among others.

This dynamic leads to shifts in the composition of organizational fields such as health care, social services, or arts and culture: the role and share of organizational forms (nonprofit, forprofit, public) will vary and change over time. Yet where do forms come from? Organizational theory points to two basic processes that lead to the development of new forms, or speciation: *recombination* and *refunctionality* (Aldrich 1999). As stated in Chapter 7, recombination involves the introduction of new elements into an existing organizational form. We suggest that the two processes of recombination and refunctionality are, and have been, happening at greater rates in recent years.

As we discussed above, the shift toward a service economy is a major driver behind these processes, which are reinforced by demographic developments. Political and ideological changes have played a significant role as well. Specifically, political frameworks and resulting legislation often decide how existing demand is channeled to the nonprofit sector. Indeed, the highest growth rates for the nonprofit sector are in those countries with policies that put in place some sort of working partnership between government and nonprofit organizations. Examples are the principle of subsidiarity in Germany, the system of *verzuilling* in the Netherlands, the concept of third-party government in the US, and, increasingly, the Compact in the UK. In essence, such a partnership means that nonprofit organizations deliver services with the help of government funds, and typically as part of complex contract schemes.

Nonetheless, there is a deeper ideological reason for the growth of the nonprofit sector: the changing role of the state itself. Even though some European countries see themselves in a different ideological tradition, the political currents of both neo-liberalism and Third Way approaches imply a reallocation of responsibilities between state and society. The state, no longer so sure about its role, and without the vision that characterized the social reforms of the 1960s and 1970s, proclaims the active citizen—a citizen who assumes new and old freedoms and responsibilities in the sense of classical liberal republicanism.

As the political and institutional consensus of the late industrial society is breaking up, an economic, political, and social space opens up for the nonprofit sector. Here we find traditional nonprofit and voluntary organizations but also new forms of work and organizations. Examples are the commercial nonprofits in the US, the new mutualism in Britain, the new cooperative movement in Italy, and the search for new legal ownership structures to combine charitable and forprofit activities—all these are indications for fundamental shifts occurring in our societies. In other words, the growth of the nonprofit sector is more than a quantitative phenomenon: it is a qualitative change as well.

SOCIAL CAPITAL AND CIVIL SOCIETY

Yet while their economic function, particularly in terms of service provision, has been a common, though often overlooked, feature of nonprofits in most developed countries, an emphasis on nonprofits as civil society institutions is new, and reflects profound changes in the wider political environment. The political discourse about the nonprofit sector has expanded from the welfare state paradigm that long characterized the field to include what we call pronounced neo-Tocquevillian elements, that, again, figure not only in Third Way approaches but also among neo-conservative perspectives. In the 2000 presidential election in the US and in the 2002 parliamentary elections in the UK, the major political parties—be they Democrats or Republicans, Labour or Tory—favored a greater role for nonprofit voluntary associations, including faith-based communities, in local social policy.

In contrast to the basically quasi-market role nonprofits assume under new public management, the neo-Tocquevillian approach emphasizes their social integrative and participatory function as well as their indirect contributions toward community-building. Nonprofit institutions are linked to the perspective of a "strong and vibrant civil society characterized by a social infrastructure of dense networks of face-to-face relationships that cross-cut existing social cleavages" (Edwards *et al.* 2001: 17).

According to neo-Tocquevillian thinking, nonprofit organizations create as well as facilitate a sense of trust and social inclusion that is seen as essential for the functioning of modern societies (e.g. Putnam 2000; Anheier and Kendall 2002; Halpern 1999; Offe and Fuchs 2002). As indicated in Chapter 3, the link between nonprofits and social trust was first suggested in the 1993 book *Making Democracy Work* by Putnam *et al.*; they showed that dense networks of voluntary associations were the main explanation for northern Italy's economic progress over the country's southern parts. As we showed subsequently in Chapter 4, the genius of Putnam (2000) was to link de Tocqueville's nineteenth-century description of a largely self-organizing, participatory local society to issues of social fragmentation and isolation facing American and other modern societies today.

However, the focus on the role of the nonprofit sector in generating social capital comes at a time of growing evidence of decreasing trust levels in the US, in particular among the marginalized groups of society: the less educated, some ethnic minorities, and the elderly (Wuthnow 2002). For mainstream America, trust and participation levels have remained more or less constant. For Wuthnow, the challenge is to find ways and means by which marginalized groups can generate the social capital that allows them to build bridges to society at large.

Skocpol (2002) goes one step further and suggests that the US is moving toward a society where "ordinary citizens are less and less likely to be mobilized into parties and civic groups; instead, the wealthier among them are repeatedly asked to write checks" (p. 134). Indeed, Skocpol argues that the classic America of balanced civic life and broad participation that we described in Chapter 2 is coming to an end. This unique pattern of state–society relations included mass public education and opportunities for social mobility, democracy, and a multi-layered democratic government that "deliberately and indirectly encouraged federated voluntary associations" (Skocpol 2002: 135). This allowed for a highly participatory society, in which markets and government expanded without subsuming civil society. For the future, Skocpol sees the emergence of a civic order that is based less on membership in traditional voluntary associations than on the work of professional nonprofit organizations that are more corporate than associative in nature.

However, the work of Putnam, Wuthnow, Skocpol, and others suggests a very profound lesson: creating social capital seems more demanding today than in the past, and new institutions might be needed to integrate the more marginal groups suffering erosion in social capital, and the better-off segments of society, who are replacing traditional forms of social capital with professional ways of organizing. This will certainly challenge the long-standing function of voluntary associations of providing cohesion for members with similar interests and serving as a mechanism for inclusion among different segments and groups of the community.

THE CONTINUED IMPORTANCE OF INSTITUTIONAL PATTERNS

Let us take a closer look at the political and institutional context in which these developments are taking place. Anheier and Seibel (2001) compare the US with the German experience and identify critical differences in the embeddedness and role of the nonprofit sector historically. These differences continue to reflect an individual mobility and a general mistrust of central state power so that, in the US, voluntarism and associational life evolved as a compromise between individualism and collective responsibility (see Lipset 1996). Greatly simplified for purposes of comparison, this Tocquevillian pattern evolved into the system of third-party government and a patchy welfare state. However, the German development and resulting state–society relations are strikingly different. Three different principles emerged separately in the complex course of the last two centuries of German

recent years is a more-or-less conscious but highly centralized government attempt to enlist the voluntary sector in social service delivery while reducing public sector provision. One result of this policy is the emergence of competitive contract schemes and engineered quasi-markets, which will lead to an expansion of the UK nonprofit sector via larger flows of both public sector funds and commercial income. As a result, the US and UK nonprofit sectors may become even more alike in the future.

The situation in social democratic countries is very different. A broad public consensus continues to support state provision of basic health care, social services, and education. The role of nonprofit organizations in service provision, while likely to increase, will happen at the margins, and typically in close cooperation with government, leading to the emergence of public–private partnerships and innovative organizational models to reduce the burden of the welfare state. These expansions into service delivery, however, are likely to push the sector away from public sector funding, encouraging nonprofit organizations to seek commercial forms of income. For example, any significant expansion in other parts of the Swedish nonprofit sector seems unlikely. With the great majority of all Swedes already members of some of the country's very numerous associations, and with a revenue structure that relies on fee income, Swedish civil society is more likely to *restructure* rather than expand in its organizational underpinning. Specifically, the country is undergoing a significant secularization trend that is likely to lead to a reduction of church-related organizations, and an expansion of cultural and recreational activities.

One would be tempted to summarize the current policy situation in corporatist countries with the French adage, "*le plus ça change, le plus ça reste la même*" ("The more things change, the more they stay the same"). The French government is channeling massive sums of public sector funds to the nonprofit sector to help reduce youth unemployment, while keeping some of the same restrictive laws in place that make it difficult for nonprofit organizations to operate more independently of government finances. In Germany, too, the nonprofit sector continues to be a close tool of government policies, not only in the area of unemployment policies but also more generally in the process of unification. It is only a slight overstatement to conclude that the German government is trying to build the East German nonprofit sector with the help of public funds. Yet given increased strains on public budgets, unification will most likely result in greater flexibility in how the subsidiarity principle is applied. In policy terms, these developments are shifting the focus of subsidiarity away from the provider of the service and more toward the concerns of the individual as a consumer, thereby introducing market elements in an otherwise still rigid corporatist system. There are now first moves in this direction, and it likely that the German nonprofit sector will rely more on private fees and charges in the future. In contrast, growth in volunteering and private giving will remain modest. Like in France, however, current tax laws prevent nonprofit organizations from utilizing their full potential in raising private funds (Zimmer and Priller 2003).

Finally, in statist countries such as Japan the first signs of change in the government's posture toward the nonprofit sector may be appearing. Today, the Japanese government speaks more favorably about the role nonprofit organizations can play in policy formulations. The state grudgingly acknowledges the nonprofit sector's abilities in addressing emerging issues that confront Japan, such as the influx of foreign labor, an aging society,

376

and environmental problems. In general, if the state shares a common interest with a particular nonprofit, it will provide financial support, but also exert great control over the organization. By contrast, if the state does not share common interests with a nonprofit, the nonprofit may be ignored, denied nonprofit legal status, not considered for grants or subsidies, or not given favorable tax treatment. Overall, however, Japan's nonprofit policies have not changed much, and any changes have been incremental and not a fundamental shift. Though nonprofits are now considered more mainstream than ever before, the state still regards them as subsidiaries of the state. As subsidiaries, nonprofits are subject to extensive and burdensome bureaucratic oversight. In sum, unless major reforms take place, Japan's nonprofit sector will continue to exist and grow under close state auspices, with little change in the overall structure and dimensions of the sector.

CONCLUDING REFLECTIONS

The numerous government policy initiatives currently under way and being considered in the US and elsewhere are therefore suggestive of a more fundamental policy shift whose ultimate objective may, however, not be clear: what kind of "society" and what kind of "community" do the current US administration, New Labour, etc. want? What kind of relationship between the nonprofit sector and government (at various levels) do governments and civic leaders have in mind? What is the role of "business" and corporate social responsibility in that regard? How do these ideas differ from those of other political parties? How do international issues figure in this context, if at all? In the US social policy context, transnational issues and globalization rarely figure; in the UK policy debate, "Europe is the dog that did not bark," according to Plowden (2001).

But at national levels in North America, Europe, and Japan, a puzzling aspect of current policy debate about welfare and governmental reform, civic renewal, and community-building is the absence of a wider vision of what kind of future society we have in mind when we discuss the role of the nonprofit sector. What kind of society did the Clinton and Bush administrations have in mind with their emphasis on faith-based communities as part of welfare reform? What future British society does New Labour envision when it links devolution with a greater reliance on the voluntary sector? Or what future German society does the governing coalition of Social Democrats and Greens have in mind as a blueprint when they discuss the renewal of civic engagement and the introduction of competitive bidding in social care markets at the same time?

In the absence of such a debate, or explicit policy blueprints, we suggest the following scenarios as markers to chart the deeper policy visions that government, opposition, and nonprofit sector representatives may have in the future:

■ *New public management scenario*: nonprofits are seen as a set of well-organized, corporate entities that take on tasks and functions previously part of the state administration, but now delivered through competitive bidding processes and contractual arrangements, trying to maximize the competitive advantages of nonprofit providers in complex social markets under state tutelage.

377

Appendices

1 300 Other recreation and social clubs

- **Recreation and social clubs**
  provision of recreational facilities and services to individuals and communities;
  includes playground associations, country clubs, men's and women's clubs, touring
  clubs, and leisure clubs.
- **Service clubs**
  membership organizations providing services to members and local communities, for
  example: Lions, Zonta International, Rotary Club, and Kiwanis.

GROUP 2: EDUCATION AND RESEARCH

Organizations and activities administering, providing, promoting, conducting, supporting,
and servicing education and research.

2 100 Primary and secondary education

- **Elementary, primary, and secondary education**
  education at elementary, primary, and secondary levels: includes pre-school
  organizations other than day care.

2 200 Higher education

- **Higher education (university level)**
  higher learning, providing academic degrees; includes universities, business
  management schools, law schools, and medical schools.

2 300 Other education

- **Vocational/technical schools**
  technical and vocational training specifically geared toward gaining employment;
  includes trade schools; paralegal training, and secretarial schools.
- **Adult/continuing education**
  institutions engaged in providing education and training in addition to the formal
  educational system; includes schools of continuing studies, correspondence schools,
  night schools, and sponsored literacy and reading programs.

2 400 Research

- **Medical research**
  research in the medical field; includes research on specific diseases, disorders, or
  medical disciplines.
- **Science and technology**
  research in the physical and life sciences, engineering, and technology.

■ **Social sciences, policy studies**
research and analysis in the social sciences and policy area.

GROUP 3: HEALTH

Organizations that engage in health-related activities, providing health care (both general and specialized services), administration of health care services, and health support services.

3 100 Hospitals and rehabilitation

■ **Hospitals**
primarily inpatient medical care and treatment.
■ **Rehabilitation**
inpatient health care and rehabilitative therapy to individuals suffering from physical impairments due to injury, genetic defect, or disease, and requiring extensive physiotherapy or similar forms of care.

3 200 Nursing homes

■ **Nursing homes**
inpatient convalescent care and residential care as well as primary health care services; includes homes for the frail elderly and nursing homes for the severely handicapped.

3 300 Mental health and crisis intervention

■ **Psychiatric hospitals**
inpatient care and treatment for the mentally ill.
■ **Mental health treatment**
outpatient treatment for mentally ill patients; includes community mental health centers and half-way homes.
■ **Crisis intervention**
outpatient services and counsel in acute mental health situations; includes suicide prevention and support to victims of assault and abuse.

3 400 Other health services

■ **Public health and wellness education**
public health promoting and health education; includes sanitation screening for potential health hazards, first aid training and services and family planning services.
■ **Health treatment, primarily outpatient**
organizations that provide primarily outpatient health services—e.g. health clinics and vaccination centers.
■ **Rehabilitative medical services**
outpatient therapeutic care; includes nature cure centers, yoga clinics, and physical therapy centers.

385

GROUP 6: DEVELOPMENT AND HOUSING

Organizations promoting programs and providing services to help improve communities and the economic and social well-being of society.

6 100 Economic, social and community development

- **Community and neighborhood organizations**
  organizations working toward improving the quality of life within communities or neighborhoods—e.g. squatters' associations, local development organizations, poor people's cooperatives.
- **Economic development**
  programs and services to improve economic infrastructure and capacity; includes building of infrastructure such as roads, and financial services such as credit and savings associations, entrepreneurial programs, technical and managerial consulting, and rural development assistance.
- **Social development**
  organizations working toward improving the institutional infrastructure, the capacity to alleviate social problems, and the general public well-being.

6 200 Housing

- **Housing associations**
  development, construction, management, leasing, financing, and rehabilitation of housing.
- **Housing assistance**
  organizations providing housing search, legal services, and related assistance.

6 300 Employment and training

- **Job training programs**
  organizations providing and supporting apprenticeship programs, internships, on-the-job training, and other training programs.
- **Vocational counseling and guidance**
  vocational training and guidance, career counseling, testing, and related services.
- **Vocational rehabilitation and sheltered workshops**
  organizations that promote self-sufficiency and income generation through job training and employment.

GROUP 7: LAW, ADVOCACY, AND POLITICS

Organizations and groups that work to protect and promote civil and other rights, or advocate the social and political interests of general or special constituencies, offer legal services, and promote public safety.

7 100 Civic and advocacy organizations

- **Advocacy organizations**
  organizations that protect the rights and promote the interests of specific groups of
  people—e.g. the physically handicapped, the elderly, children, and women.
- **Civil rights associations**
  organizations that work to protect or preserve individual civil liberties and human
  rights.
- **Ethnic associations**
  organizations that promote the interests of, or provide services to, members
  belonging to a specific ethnic heritage.
- **Civic associations**
  programs and services to encourage and spread civic mindedness.

7 200 Law and legal services

- **Legal services**
  legal services, advice, and assistance in dispute resolution and court-related matters.
- **Crime prevention and public safety**
  crime prevention to promote safety and precautionary measures among citizens.
- **Rehabilitation of offenders**
  programs and services to reintegrate offenders; includes half-way houses, probation
  and parole programs, and prison alternatives.
- **Victim support**
  services, counsel, and advice to victims of crime.
- **Consumer protection associations**
  protection of consumer rights, and the improvement of product control and quality.

7 300 Political organizations

- **Political parties and organizations**
  activities and services to support the placing of particular candidates into political
  office; includes dissemination of information, public relations, and political fund-
  raising.

GROUP 8: PHILANTHROPIC INTERMEDIARIES AND VOLUNTARISM PROMOTION

Philanthropic organizations and organizations promoting charity and charitable activities.

8 100 Philanthropic intermediaries and voluntarism promotion

- **Grant-making foundations**
  private foundations; including corporate foundations, community foundations, and
  independent public law foundations.

Appendix 2

Exercises and discussion material

1 SAMPLE STUDY QUESTIONS FOR CHAPTERS 1–7 AND 13–16

1 "In theory the state is accountable via the democratic political process, and private firms are accountable to owners and customers via the market. However, there is a view that nonprofit organizations are accountable neither through elections, nor through the market, leading to a structural accountability gap." Critically examine this statement.

2 Drawing on the appropriate literature, in particular resource-dependency theory, discuss to what extent nonprofit organizations are dependent on their environment.

3 Why does government contract out services to nonprofit organizations. How has purchase-of-service contracting affected the nonprofit sector?

4 Drawing on organizational change literature, discuss both internal and external factors that contribute to organizational transformation. Illustrate your answer through a case study.

5 "It is neither feasible not desirable to have a one-size-fits-all definition of the nonprofit sector." Using examples, discuss this statement.

6 "Increased financial reliance on fees and charges are changing the basic nature of the nonprofit sector, thereby undermining its autonomy." What are the arguments for and against this proposition? What lessons can be learned from other countries in this regard?

7 Describe the main elements of the "social origins" approach to explaining international variation in the scope and scale of the nonprofit sector. What are the main strengths and weaknesses of this approach?

8 "The behavior and impact of voluntary organizations in complex social care and service markets defies evaluation, or any form of systematic performance measurement." Do you agree with this assertion? Why, or why not?

9 Why is the nonprofit sector more involved in public policy today than in previous eras? What are the major positive and negative aspects of this development?

10 Under what conditions are nonprofit organizations likely to cooperate in specific projects, seek alliances, create joint ventures, or merge? Use examples in presenting the conditions for each of the four outcomes.

11 If nonprofit organizations are a reflection of trust-related problems inherent in the goods or services being provided, as Hansmann argues, what are the implications of reductions of such trust problems? Specifically address how such reductions will affect: (a) the need for trustworthiness; and (b) the composition of organizational fields over time.

12 What is third-party government, and how does it relate to the interdependence theory?

13 What is the difference between social capital, civil society, and the nonprofit sector?

14 What are some of the drivers of the internationalization of the nonprofit sector?

15 What are likely policy scenarios for the nonprofit sector in the fields of: (a) welfare services; (b) the environment; and (c) arts and culture? (The environment field has not received much attention in this book, though the topic would certainly lead to an interesting discussion. How about international development assistance as a substitute? Or religious congregations?)

2 ASSIGNMENTS AND CASE STUDIES FOR CHAPTERS 8 TO 12

Assignment: Mission and vision

Submit a one-page discussion of the mission statement of a nonprofit organization of your choice, addressing the question: "Does mission matter?" In answering this question, you should address three topics:

1 Is the mission specific enough in giving guidance for the actual objectives and activities of the organization?

2 What is the relationship between mission and organizational design (business model)?

3 How would you improve the mission statement, and why?

Attach a copy of the mission statement to your report.

Assignment: Stakeholder analysis

Using a nonprofit organization of your choice, draft a two-page stakeholder analysis, following these steps:

1 Looking at the mission statement and the organization's structure and operations, list the various stakeholders and their specific "stake," and identify their degree of influence on the organization.

2 Selecting the three most influential stakeholders, describe their relations among each other, and the conflict potential about the organization's mission.

3 Looking at the organizational governance structure (to the extent to which you can understand it from the material you have), are there particular stakeholders that have little or no voice? Is this a problem, and, if so, how would you fix it?

Case study 1: When missions collide

Mission statements of the "People for the American Way"

2003 VERSION

In times of hardship, in times of crises, societies throughout history have experienced wrenching dislocations in their fundamental values and beliefs . . . . We are alarmed that some of the current voices of stridency and division may replace those of reason and unity. If these voices continue unchallenged, the results will be predictable: a rise in "demonology" and hostility, a breakdown in community and social spirit, a deterioration of free and open dialogue, and the temptation to grasp at simplistic solutions for complex problems.

PEOPLE FOR THE AMERICAN WAY was established to address these matters. Our purpose is to meet the challenges of discord and fragmentation with an affirmation of "the American Way." By this, we mean pluralism, individuality, freedom of thought, expression and religion, a sense of community, and tolerance and compassion for others. People for the American Way will reach out to all Americans and affirm that in our society, the individual still matters; that there is reason to believe in the future—not to despair of it—and that we must strengthen the common cords that connect us as humans and citizens.

The long-term agenda of PEOPLE FOR THE AMERICAN WAY is broad. It includes reducing social tension and polarizations, encouraging community participation, fostering understanding among different segments of our society, and increasing the level and quality of public dialogue. As an educational institution, we shall communicate with the American people through printed materials, radio, television, public lectures and discussions.

We will gather information, analyze it, and distribute our findings to the public in a manner that provides for full and fair exposition on the issues. Our highest purpose is to nurture a national climate that encourages and enhances the human spirit rather than one which divides people into hostile camps.

By educating the American people and raising their level of understanding about the basic tenets by which our society is sustained, PEOPLE FOR THE AMERICAN WAY will fulfill its mission.

1985 VERSION

In times of hardship, in times of crises, societies throughout history have experienced wrenching dislocations in their fundamental values and beliefs. The decades of the 1980s and 1990s will be troubled times—some predict the most turbulent since the 1930s—and we are alarmed that some current voices of stridency and division may replace those of reason and unity. If these voices continue unchallenged, the results will be predictable; an increase in tension among races, classes, and religions, a rise in "demonology" and hostility, a breakdown in community and social spirit, a deterioration of free and open dialogue, and the temptation to grasp at simplistic solutions for complex problems.

PEOPLE FOR THE AMERICAN WAY was established to address these matters. Our purpose is to meet the challenges of discord and fragmentation with an affirmation of "the American Way." By this we mean pluralism, individuality, freedom of thought, expression, and religion, a sense of community, and tolerance and compassion for others. We stand for values and principles, not for single issues, chosen candidates, or partisan causes.

PEOPLE FOR THE AMERICAN WAY will reach out to all Americans and affirm that in our society, the individual still matters; that there is reason to believe in the future—not to despair of it—and we must strengthen the common cords that connect us as humans and as citizens.

The long agenda of PEOPLE FOR THE AMERICAN WAY is broad. It includes reducing social tension and polarization, encouraging community participation, fostering understanding among different segments of our society, and increasing the level and quality of public dialogue.

Yet, we cannot address everything at once. So, we are confronting first what we believe to be the greatest immediate threat to our pluralistic society: the growing power of the Religious New Right.

This new movement—as documented by the statements of some leaders of the Religious New Right—would impose on the public debate a rigid and absolutist set of positions on what is and is not "Christian," implying that there is only one Christian position on any given political issue. We support the right of the religious community to speak out on social and political issues. However, religious leaders overwhelmingly contend—and we also believe—that "it is arrogant and destructive to assert that one set of political questions is Christian, and endorsed by God, and that all others are un-Christian."*

As an education institution, we shall communicate with the American people through printed materials, radio, television, public lectures, and discussions. We will gather information, analyze it, and distribute our findings to the public in a manner that provides for full and fair exposition of the issues.

Our highest purpose is to nurture a national climate that encourages and enhances the human spirit rather than one that divides people into hostile camps. By educating the American people and raising their level of understanding about the basic tenets by which our society is sustained, PEOPLE FOR THE AMERICAN WAY will fulfill its mission.

Task

Compare the 1985 and 2003 statements.

1   What is the biggest difference?
2   Why do you think the mission statement was changed?
3   What do you see as the strengths and weaknesses of the 2003 mission statement?
4   How would you change it?

Case study 2: Government dependence

Children's Theater Company

You are a founding board member of the Children's Theater Company (CTC) and have volunteered for the organization for over fifteen years in helping with productions,

---

* Statement of the Washington Inter-religious Staff Council.

promotion and fund-raising. The mission statement has not been changed since twelve parents from different Westside neighborhoods founded CTC to compensate what they saw as a serious deficit in arts curricula at local schools:

> to bring an appreciation of the performing arts, in particular the classical Greek and English stage, to the children of Los Angeles, and thereby improve their cultural repertoires, quality of education and life chances.

Normally, CTC has twenty-five children aged between 12 and 16 enrolled in theater classes, and stages two productions per year, typically a Greek tragedy in the fall and a "lighter" Shakespearean comedy in the spring. CTC owns a small "warehouse-like structure" in West LA that has been transformed into a theater over the years, consuming countless hours of volunteer time. CTC's budget is supported through membership dues and donations that make up about 40 percent of its total annual budget of $50,000; the balance has been made up by a grant from the City of Los Angeles. Funding has been stable for the last ten years.

In a letter, the City informs you that they are no longer in a position to continue financial support unless CTC expands its artistic repertoires and includes a broader range of theatrical traditions that would be of greater interest to LA's diverse communities.

At the next board meeting you argue for this change in your organization's mission; other board members however are opposed and see it as a dilution and unnecessary distraction from what unites CTC behind a common goal and passion.

Facing this dilemma, develop arguments for and against changing the CTC's mission, and the implications involved.

Case study 3: Board behavior

Who is overreacting?*

National Center for Nonprofit Boards

Edited by Kenneth G. Koziol

Todd Stoddard's familiar footsteps sounded slightly different this morning as he rounded the corner of the new activities center and headed for his office.

"How was the meeting?" asked Linda, his administrative assistant.

"Lousy," said Todd. "Terrible."

"What happened?"

"For starters, he wants to meet with me every Tuesday at seven in the morning. Says he wants to see this place start running like a business."

---

* This case first appeared in *Board Member,* published by the National Center for Nonprofit Boards (now BoardSource).

"Oh!"

"If that's not bad enough, he says he's got someone in mind to take over Jill's job in fund-raising when she leaves."

"It looks like things are going to be different from now on," Linda said.

"I'm not finished yet: he said he thought his predecessor was too distant from day-to-day activities."

Linda was silent.

"I need time to think," Todd said, closing his office door behind him.

Speaking to no one in particular, Linda said: "It looks like the new board chair isn't wasting any time—elected on Friday and stirring the pot on Monday."

Todd Stoddard, 38-year-old up-and-coming administrator, has been executive director of the medium-sized, Midwestern youth center for three years. It is Todd's first job as CEO—and precisely the right launching pad that will put him in a position to land the top job at a major national youth services organization in the future. That has been Todd's career plan from the beginning—ever since getting his MBA on top of his under-graduate and Master's in social work. His tenure here has earned him high marks, espe-cially nationally—number of youngsters served is up, fund-raising up, operating budget in the black though not lush, and new programs galore. Todd is the imaginative creative type, doing that part of the job hands-on. He even shoots baskets with the kids sometimes. He likes to delegate the financial and administrative nitty-gritty to others.

Linda noticed one of the buttons on her telephone light up. Todd was on the phone. Linda knew he was either calling his wife—or Paul, his long-time mentor, colleague, and personal friend who is now CEO of one of the top foundations.

"Paul, it's Todd. How are you?"

"Great. What's up?" asked Paul.

"I need help."

"Sure, buddy, shoot."

"Last Friday I got a new board chair. And he met with me today—Monday."

"Uh-oh, red flags," interrupted Paul.

Todd continued: "My former chair retired. She was the person who hired me. She was great. She let me alone, supported me when I needed it, stayed away, ran pretty good meetings, asked pretty good questions, but let me run the shop."

"What about the new guy?"

"He's CEO of the power company . . . early 50s . . . elected to the board two years ago. I was all for it . . . he' s a heavyweight in the community, especially with some of the younger folks, good for fund-raising. He's a member of a couple of corporate boards. He's a go-getter."

"What happened during your meeting?"

"It started out okay, but then several things came up that really disturb me. First, he wants to meet with me every week and go over budgets, statistics, fund-raising progress, lots of administrative stuff.

"Then he told me he's got a good candidate for our fund-raising job—our top person just got raided away from me.

"Finally, he confided to me—in a kind of conspiratorial tone—that he thought the previous board chair was too lax, didn't pay enough attention. He said to me: 'I think we should run this place more like a business.'

"All of these things are clues I don't like. I think I'm going to have a problem. I think this guy sees me as the fair-haired boy of the old chair. What should I do, Paul?"

In answering this question, try to identify and "map" the possible relationships of the various stakeholders that might be involved here, and try to understand their "reading" of the situation and possible scenarios. So put yourself in the position of Paul, Todd, board members, clients, funders, etc.

Case study 4: Board behavior

Looking at a gift horse*

Corporate attorney Cynthia Woodside, volunteer chair of the twenty-two-member board of directors of the River Junction Historic Preservation Association, dialed the telephone number of her closest board confidante, assured that she would receive frank advice.

"Susan, I hope you received your agenda book in today's mail? I want to talk with you about it," Cynthia Woodside said.

"No, I didn't," came the reply.

"Well, I need to talk out my problem anyway. Do you have time to talk now?"

"Of course. What's the problem?"

"It's agenda item #—a grant proposal for $900,000 that Richard says is a sure thing to be funded."

Richard Smith-Trent, the association's 29-year-old highly regarded chief executive, came from a neighboring community foundation and was recruited by Cynthia Woodside herself—largely on the strength of his fast-track fund-raising credentials.

"You mean to say you have a problem with Richard getting us a $900,000 grant—and after only six months on the job? I'd say that's pretty good. I'd say that's why we hired him. What's wrong with you, Cynthia, and what's the grant for?"

"That's my problem. The grant is to restore those last two Victorian houses at the foot of Light Street right at the river and to use them for low income housing."

"Wonderful," said Susan. "We've been wanting to get funding to restore those houses for years now.

"No, it's not wonderful," replied Cynthia Woodside. "The money is coming from a consortium of foundations that are investing in affordable housing for low-income families throughout the country. The grant doesn't even mention anything about historic preservation and those foundations don't care about it."

"So?"

"Susan, we're in the business of historic preservation. We're not in the business of low-income housing. May I remind you that our name is River Junction Historic Preservation Association?"

* From: BoardSource 1828 L Street NW Suite 900, Washington DC 20036–5114, www.boardsource.org.

"It's $900,000, isn't it?"

"That doesn't matter. May I next read to you from our mission statement: to preserve the heritage of historic downtown at the junction of the two rivers by preserving its historic structures, particularly the barge dock, the grain elevator, the railroad siding, the warehouses and other commercial establishments, and the nearby Victorian homes."

Susan paused for a moment. "I think I see now what you're getting at."

"As chair of this organization I and all board members—you included—are responsible to see that we hew the line to our goals and objectives. I've seen too many organizations get deflected from their mission by accepting money to do something that is peripheral. That is one of the worst mistakes an organization can make."

"But if we don't accept this grant, Cynthia, you'll be branded as a right-wing conservative against low-income housing. And what kind of an organization will Richard think he's gotten himself involved with?"

"I know, I know. That's why I wanted to talk this out with you. I recognize that it could sound like I am against low-income housing, which of course I am not. It also could seem that I am fighting Richard—which I am not. But he may see it in another light."

"I suppose you want my advice, don't you?" asked Susan.

What advice would you give Cynthia Woodside?

In answering this question, try to identify and "map" the possible relationships among the various stakeholders that might be involved here, and try to understand their "reading" of the situation and possible scenarios. So put yourself in the position of Cynthia, Susan, Richard, other board members, local media, funders, people seeking housing, etc.

Case study 5: Board composition

Your organization: You are entrusted by a wealthy donor to set up a nonprofit with a $250 million endowment to deliver after-school SAT tutoring sessions to disadvantaged high school students from LA County and to help them with college applications.

Your task: To set up a ten-member founding board and to appoint the chair. What kind of board members would you look for? What would be their characteristics? What about the chair?

- Consider factors such as: gender, age, ethnicity, experience, expertise, reputation, legitimacy, field or sector represented, but also the needs of the board and the organization.
- List the ten "types" and make a case for the overall composition. What are the strengths and weaknesses you anticipate?
- What kind of CEO would you be looking for in terms of background and qualifications?

3   SAMPLE FINAL PAPER

The final paper is a 2,500-word paper on a topic of your choice relating to any the aspects covered in class or that come within the compass of the study of nonprofit theory, management and policy. The actual choice of topic should be cleared with the instructor, but you are encouraged to be innovative and intellectually provocative. The emphasis of the final paper should be on creativity and on applying the concepts, approaches, and evidence learned to a relevant topic. Possible topics can be literature-based or, preferably, involve a case study.

The paper should have four component parts:

1   A clear statement of purpose, and a succinct summary of the central argument and key findings (about 250 words)
2   Main body of the text, with a brief introduction of background, context, and methods if necessary, and the presentation of empirical evidence in support of items detailed in the first part of the paper (1,500—1,750 words)
3   Assessment and implications for theory, management, or policy (250–500 words)
4   Conclusion (250 words).

You are to consult the literature, and find at least five articles or chapters not listed in either the course syllabus or course handouts.

Notes

CHAPTER 2: HISTORICAL BACKGROUND

1   See Lyons (2001) for a summary treatment of Australia's nonprofit sector.

CHAPTER 3: CONCEPTS

1   It should not be thought, however, that Europe proposes a single model of the social economy; see, for example, Archambault (1996).
2   See, for example, Hansmann (1996); Ben-Ner and Gui (1993); Weisbrod (1988); Salamon and Anheier (1998b).
3   The United Nations (1993) distinguishes six institutional sectors: the Non-financial Corporations Sector, the Financial Corporations Sector, the General Government Sector, the Households Sector, the Nonprofit Institutions Serving Households Sector, and the Rest of the World.
4   According to the SNA-1993, "prices are economically significant when they have a significant influence on the amounts the producers are willing to supply and on the amounts purchasers wish to buy" (United Nations 1993, para. 6.45). The European System of Accounts transposes this notion in operational terms: a price is economically significant as from the moment when the sales cover more than 50 percent of the production costs.

CHAPTER 4: DIMENSIONS I. OVERVIEW

1   Note that the 50,000 funding intermediaries largely refer to the number of foundations that existed in the mid 1990s; as of 2003, the number of foundations is over 60,000 (see Chapter 14).
2   "The target population for the employee component is all employees working in the selected workplaces who receive a Customs Canada and Revenue Agency T-4 Supplementary form. If a person receives a T-4 slip from two different workplaces, then the person will be counted as two employees on the WES frame." For more information on Statistic Canada's Workplace and Employee Survey (WES) please visit: www.statcan.ca/english/sdds/2615.htm.
3   Figures are from the National Survey of Giving, Volunteering and Participating (NSGVP). The report can be downloaded at www.givingandvolunteering.ca.
4   This section draws in part on Salamon and Anheier (1999) with data updated from Salamon et al. (2003).
5   The EVS (see Halman 2001) covers the following countries: Britain, France, Germany, Austria, Italy, Spain, the Netherlands, Belgium, Denmark, Sweden, Iceland, Northern Ireland,

Ireland, Estonia, Latvia, Lithuania, Poland, Czech Republic, Slovakia, Hungary, Romania, Bulgaria, Croatia, Greece, Russia, Malta, Luxembourg, Slovenia, Ukraine, Belarus, and the US. The countries where the positive relationship between trust and memberships in voluntary associations either does not exist or is weak are: Romania, Russia, Ukraine, and Belarus.

6   This includes memberships in health and social welfare associations, religious/church organizations, education, arts, music, or cultural associations, trade unions and professional associations, local community groups and social clubs, environmental and human rights groups, youth clubs, women's groups, political parties, peace groups, sports and recreational clubs, among others.

7   Measured by the following question: "Generally speaking, would you say that most people can be trusted or that you need to be very careful when dealing with people?"

8   World Values Survey (2000). US Survey, conducted by Gallup for Virginia Hodgkinson, Helmut K. Anheier, and Ronald Ingehart.

9   See also Putnam's analysis of trust in the US (2000: 139).

10 The information presented here with regard to social capital comes from *The Social Capital Community Benchmark Survey*, a project coordinated by the Saguaro Seminar at Harvard University. The project, conducted in 2000, included a separate survey of Los Angeles County and over forty-one other US cities and regions, in addition to a national sample. This allows us to compare Los Angeles data to national results and also to compare different cities within the county. We will start with a Los Angeles–National comparison of social capital, and then compare social capital and nonprofit organizations in two cities in the Los Angeles metropolis: Sherman Oaks, a middle-class city in the San Fernando Valley; and Lynwood, a lower-class city in South Los Angeles.

11 It is, however, somewhat weaker for African Americans, who show relatively high affiliation rates combined with somewhat lower trust levels. African Americans are also the group most likely to have reported experiencing racial discrimination.

CHAPTER 5: DIMENSIONS II. SPECIFIC FIELDS

1   We will revisit some of these distinctions in Chapter 6 on the social origins theory. Roemer included a fourth, the socialist system, based on the model of the former Soviet Union, a category that now seems less relevant.

2   Also includes legal services.

3   The number given for nonprofit social service establishments in Figure 5.1 is higher than the number in Figure 4.6 (approximately 66,500 human service organizations), which is based on organizations rather than establishments. One organization can have multiple establishments.

4   The equivalent data for education given in Figure 4.6 report 1996 data and are slightly below the 18 percent reported here for 1997.

5   See Figure 4.6 and estimates in Wyszomirski (2002: 188).

6   The shares reported by Wyszomirski differ from the shares reported for 1996 in Figure 4.7, particularly in terms of government sources, due to reductions in funding for the National Endowment for the Arts and the National Endowment for the Humanities after 1995 (Wyszomirski 2002: 189).

7   Note that data in Figure 4.7 differ from Sokolowski's and Salamon's estimates because the former do not include "political organizations," which account for the bulk (about 80 percent) of "civic" association revenues.

CHAPTER 6: THEORETICAL APPROACHES

1   This section draws in part on Salamon and Anheier (1998b).

CHAPTER 8: NONPROFIT BEHAVIOR AND PERFORMANCE

1   This section draws in part from Toepler and Anheier (2004).

CHAPTER 9: RESOURCING NONPROFIT ORGANIZATIONS

1   Figures for the US are for 1996; figures for the UK and cross-nationally are for 1995.
2   This section draws in part on Anheier *et al.* (2003a).
3   In population surveys, religiosity is typically measured by the frequency of religious attendance in church, synagogue, mosque, etc. This is a better predictor of volunteering than religious affiliation or denomination, i.e. Catholic, Protestant, Jewish, Islam, etc.

CHAPTER 11: MANAGEMENT I. MODELS

1   *The Drucker Foundation Self-Assessment Tool: Participant Workbook*, a publication of the Drucker Foundation and Jossey-Bass, Inc.

CHAPTER 12: MANAGEMENT II. TOOLS AND SPECIAL TOPICS

1   Strategic management and strategic planning are used synonymously.

CHAPTER 13: STATE–NONPROFIT RELATIONS

1   Established by the US Housing and Community Development Act of 1974 and formalized as the Section 8 Housing Choice Voucher Program in 1998, this is a federal program for low-income families to afford housing in the private market. Vouchers subsidize rent for low-income families, thereby allowing families to live in "fair market rent" neighborhoods or "middle income" neighborhoods rather than public housing.
2   This section and the following one draw in part on Moulton and Anheier (2000).

CHAPTER 14: FOUNDATIONS

1   Large investment banks or community foundations hold donor-advised funds usually; the donor or a donor-appointed committee recommends eligible recipients and grantees. In the case of donor-designated funds, the donor specifies that the fund's income and assets be used for the benefit of one or more designated grantees.
2   The high amount of assets per head for Italian foundations is a function of the privatization of the banking sector in Italy (Law 218/1990, or Amato law). Most public savings banks were previously quasi-public, "nationalized" nonprofit organizations, and became stock corporations as a result of the 1990 reforms (see Barbetta 1999). The shares in the privatized banks became the endowment for the new "foundations of banking origin," which, not surprisingly, have significant assets of between €50,000 million and €75,000 million combined.
3   In Switzerland estimates of foundations' assets are CHF30 billion (€19 billion), with payouts equivalent to 2 percent of the federal government's budget (Anheier and Daly 2004).

CHAPTER 15: INTERNATIONAL ISSUES AND GLOBALIZATION

1 This section draws in part on Anheier *et al.* (2001a) and Kaldor *et al.* (2003b).
2 The balance of this chapter draws on Anheier and Themudo (2002).
3 We use the term "federation" as originally understood by Handy (1989) as organizations based on the principle of subsidiarity whereby power ultimately rests with the local units rather than the coordinating center. As such it includes both "federations" and "confederations" in Lindenberg's and Dobel's (1999) and Clark's (2001) typologies.

CHAPTER 16: POLICY ISSUES AND DEVELOPMENTS

1 This section draws in part on Anheier and Ben-Ner (1997).

Bibliography

Abramson, A. J. and Spann, J. (eds.) (1998) *Foundations: Exploring their Unique Roles and Impacts in Society*, Washington, DC: Aspen Institute.

Abramson, A. J., Salamon, L. M., and Steuerle, E. (1999) "The Nonprofit Sector and the Federal Budget: Recent History and Future Directions," in E. Boris and E. Steuerle (eds.) *Nonprofits and Government: Collaboration and Conflict*, Washington, DC: Urban Institute Press.

Accion International, home page, www.accion.org/programs/main.asp.

Aldrich, H. (1999) *Organizations Evolving*, Thousand Oaks, CA and London: Sage.

Almond, S. and Kendall, J. (2000a) "Taking the Employees' Perspective Seriously: An Initial United Kingdom Cross-Sectoral Comparison," *Non-profit and Voluntary Sector Quarterly* 29(2): 205–31.

—— (2000b) "Low Pay in the United Kingdom: The Case for a Three Sector Comparative Approach," *Annals of Public and Co-operative Economics* 72(1): 45–76.

—— (2000c) "Paid Employment in the Self-Defined Voluntary Sector in the late 1990s: An Initial Description of Patterns and Trends," Working Paper No. 7, London: Centre for Civil Society, London School of Economics.

Amenta, E. and Carruther, B. G. (1988) "The Formative Years of U.S. Social Spending Policies: Theories of the Welfare State and the American States During the Great Depression," *American Sociological Review* 53(5): 661–78.

Amnesty International, home page, www.amnesty.org.

Andrews, F. E. (1956) *Philanthropic Foundations*, New York: Russell Sage Foundation.

Anheier, H. K. (2002) "The Third Sector in Europe: Five Theses," Working Paper, London: Centre for Civil Society, London School of Economics and Political Science.

—— (2001a) "Foundations in Europe: A Comparative Perspective," in A. Schlüter, V. Then, and P. Walkenhorst (eds.) *Foundations in Europe*, London: Directory of Social Change.

—— (ed.) (2001b) *Organisational Theory and the Nonprofit Form*, CCS Report #2, London: London School of Economics.

—— (ed.) (2000a) *Third Way—Third Sector: Proceedings of a Policy Symposium Organised by the LSE Centre for Civil Society*, London: Centre for Civil Society, London School of Economics.

—— (2000b) *Managing Nonprofit Organisations: Towards a New Approach*, Working Paper No. 1, London: Centre for Civil Society, London School of Economics. Available online: www.lse.ac.uk/Depts/ccs/pdf/cswp1.pdf.

—— (1998) "Das Stiftungswesen in Zahlen: Eine sozial-ökonomische Strukturebeschreibung deutscher Stiftungen," in Bertelsmann Foundation (ed.) *Handbuch Stiftungen*, Wiesbaden: Gabler.

Anheier, H. K. and Ben-Ner, A. (eds.) (2003) *The Study of the Nonprofit Enterprise: Theories and Approaches*, New York: Kluwer Academic/Plenum.

—— (1997) "The Shifting Boundaries: Long-term Changes in the Size of the Forprofit, Nonprofit, Cooperative and Government Sectors," *Annals of Public and Cooperative Economics* 68(3): 335–54.

Anheier, H. K. and Cunningham, K. (1994) "Internationalization of the Nonprofit Sector," in R. D. Herman & Associates (eds.) *The Jossey-Bass Handbook of Nonprofit Leadership and Management*, San Francisco, CA: Jossey-Bass.

Anheier, H. K. and Daly, S. (2004) *The Roles and Visions of Foundations in Europe*, Project Report, London: Centre for Civil Society, London School of Economics.

Anheier, H. K. and Katz, H. (2003) "Mapping Global Civil Society," in M. Kaldor, H. K. Anheier, and M. Glasius (eds.) *Global Civil Society 2003*, Oxford: Oxford University Press.

Anheier, H. K. and Kendall, J. (2002) "Interpersonal Trust and Voluntary Associations: Examining Three Approaches," *British Journal of Sociology* 53(3): 343–62.

—— (2001) *Third Sector Policy at the Crossroads: An International Nonprofit Analysis*, London: Routledge.

Anheier, H. K. and Leat, D. (2002) *From Charity to Creativity: Philanthropic Foundations in the 21st Century*, London: COMEDIA in association with the Joseph Rowntree Reform Trust.

—— (2005) *Creative Philanthropy*, London: Routledge.

Anheier, H. K. and List, R. (2000) *Cross-border Philanthropy: An Exploratory Study of International Giving in the United Kingdom, United States, Germany and Japan*, West Malling: Charities Aid Foundation and London: Centre for Civil Society, London School of Economics.

Anheier, H. K. and Mertens, S. (2003) "International and European Perspectives on the Nonprofit Sector: Data, Theory and Statistics," in Organization for Economic Co-operation and Development (OECD) *The Non-profit Sector in a Changing Economy*, Paris: OECD.

Anheier, H. K. and Salamon, L. M. (forthcoming) "The Nonprofit Sector in Comparative Perspective," in W. W. Powell and R. S. Steinberg (eds.) *The Nonprofit Sector: A Research Handbook* (2nd edn), New Haven, CT: Yale University Press.

—— (1999) "Volunteering in Cross-National Perspective: Initial Comparisons," *Law and Contemporary Problems* 62(4): 43–66.

—— (1998a) "Introduction: The Nonprofit Sector in the Developing World," in H. K Anheier and L. M. Salamon (eds.) *The Nonprofit Sector in the Developing World, The Johns Hopkins Nonprofit Series*, Manchester: Manchester University Press.

—— (eds.) (1998b) *The Nonprofit Sector in the Developing World, The Johns Hopkins Nonprofit Series*, Manchester: Manchester University Press.

—— (1998c) "Nonprofit Institutions and the 1993 System of National Accounts," Working Paper No. 25, Baltimore, MD: Johns Hopkins Comparative Nonprofit Sector Project.

—— (1998d) "Nonprofit Institutions and the Household Sector," in United Nations Statistics Division (ed.) *The Household Sector*, New York: United Nations.

Anheier, H. K. and Seibel, W. (2001) *The Nonprofit Sector in Germany: Between State, Economy, and Society*, New York: Palgrave.

—— (1998) "The Nonprofit Sector and the Transformation of Eastern Europe: A Comparative Analysis," in W. W. Powell and E. Clemens (eds.) *Public Goods and Private Action*, New Haven, CT: Yale University Press.

—— (eds.) (1990) *The Third Sector: Comparative Studies of Nonprofit Organizations*, Berlin and New York: DeGruyter.

Anheier, H. K. and Themudo, N. (2002) "Organisational Forms of Global Civil Society: Implications of Going Global," in M. Glasius, M. Kaldor, and H. K. Anheier (eds.) *Global Civil Society 2002*, Oxford: Oxford University Press.

Anheier, H. K. and Toepler, S. (2002) "Bürgerschaftliches Engagement in Europa: Überblick und gesellschaftspolitische Einordnung," *Aus Politik und Zeitgeschichte* 9: 31–8.

—— (eds.) (1999a) *Private Funds and Public Purpose, Philanthropic Foundations in International Perspectives*, New York: Kluwer Academic/Plenum.

—— (1999b) "Philanthropic Foundations: An International Perspective," in H. K. Anheier and S. Toepler (eds.) *Private Funds, Public Purpose: Philanthropic Foundations in International Perspective*, New York: Kluwer Academic/Plenum.

—— (1999c) "Commerce and the Muse: Are Art Museums Becoming Commercial?," in B. Weisbrod (ed.) *To Profit or Not to Profit: The Commercial Transformation of the Nonprofit Sector*, New York: Cambridge University Press.

Anheier, H. K. and Winder, D. (eds.) (2004) *Innovations in Strategic Philanthropy — Lessons from Africa, Asia, Central and Eastern Europe, and Latin America*, Gutersloh: International Network for Strategic Philanthropy, Bertelsmann Foundation.

Anheier, H. K., Glasius, M., and Kaldor, M. (eds.) (2001) *Global Civil Society 2001*, New York and Oxford: Oxford University Press.

Anheier, H. K., Priller, E., and Zimmer, A. (2001b) "Civil Society in Transition: East Germany Ten Years after Unification," *East European Politics and Society* 15(1): 139–56.

Anheier, H. K., Toepler, S., and Sokolowski, W. (1997) "The Implications of Government Funding for Nonprofit Organizations: Three Propositions," *International Journal of Public Sector Management* 10(3): 190–213.

Anheier, H. K., Hollerweger, E., Badelt, C., and Kendall, J. (2003a) *Work in the Nonprofit Sector: Forms, Patterns and Methodologies*, Geneva: International Labour Office.

Anheier, H. K., Katz, H., Mosley, J., and Hasenfeld, Y. (2003b) *Positioning for the Future: The Nonprofit and Community Sector in Greater Los Angeles*, Los Angeles, CA: UCLA School of Public Policy and Social Research.

Archambault, E. (1996) *The Nonprofit Sector in France*, Manchester: Manchester University Press.

Archambault, E., Boumendil, J., and Tsyboula, S. (1999a) "Foundations in France," in H. K. Anheier and S. Toepler (eds.) *Private Funds, Public Purpose: Philanthropic Foundations in International Perspective*, New York: Kluwer Academic/Plenum.

Archambault, E., Gariazzo, M., Anheier, H. K., and Salamon, L. M. (1999b) "From Jacobin Tradition to Decentralization," in L. M. Salamon, H. K. Anheier, R. List, S. Toepler, S. W. Sokolowski, and Associates (eds.) *Global Civil Society Demensions of the Nonprofit Sector*, Baltimore, MD: Johns Hopkins Center for Civil Society Studies.

Arendt, H. (1963) *On Revolution*, New York: Macmillan.

—— (1968) *The Origins of Totalitarianism*, New York: Harcourt Brace Jovanovitch.

Arias Foundation For Peace and Human Progress (1992) *The State of Philanthropy in Central America*, San Jose, Costa Rica: Arias Foundation.

Arnove, R. (ed.) (1980) *Philanthropy and Cultural Imperialism: The Foundations at Home and Abroad*, Boston, MA: GK Hall and Co.

Arrow, K. J. (1963) "Uncertainty and the Welfare Economics of Medical Care," *The American Economic Review* 53: 941–73.

Arsenault, J. (1998) *Forging Nonprofit Alliances: A Comprehensive Guide to Enhancing Your Mission Through Joint Ventures and Partnerships, Management Service Organizations, Parent Corporations, Mergers*, San Francisco, CA: Jossey-Bass.

Ascoli, U. and Ranci, C. (eds.) (2002) *Dilemmas of the Welfare Mix: The New Structure of Welfare in an Era of Privatization*, New York: Kluwer Academic/Plenum.

Atingdui, L., Anheier, H. K., Larelya, E., and Sokolowski, W. (1998) "The Nonprofit Sector in Ghana," in H. K. Anheier and L. M. Salamon (eds.) *The Nonprofit Sector in the Developing World*, Manchester: Manchester University Press.

Austin, J. (2000) *The Collaboration Challenge: How Nonprofits and Businesses Succeed through Strategic Alliances*, San Francisco, CA: Jossey-Bass.

Australian Association of Philanthropy (1993) *The Australian Directory of Philanthropy*, Port Melbourne: Australian Association.

Ayres-Williams, R. (1998) "Changing the face of nonprofits," *Black Enterprise* 28(10): 110–14.

Badelt, C. (2003) "Entrepreneurship in Nonprofit Organizations: Its Role in Theory and in the Real World Nonprofit Sector," in H. K. Anheier and A. Ben-Ner (eds.) *The Study of the Nonprofit Enterprise Theories and Approaches*, New York: Kluwer Academic/Plenum.

—— (1999) "Ehrenamtliche Arbeit im Non-profit Sektor," in C. Badelt (ed.) *Handbuch der Non-profit Organisationen*, Strukturen und Management, Stuttgart: Schäffer-Poeschl.

—— (1997) "Der Nonprofit Sektor in Österreich," in C. Badelt (ed.) *Handbuch der Nonprofit Organisationen*, Stuttgart: Poeschl.

Baloglu, Z. (ed.) (1996) *The Foundations of Turkey*, Istanbul: TÜSEV.

Barbetta, G. P. (1999) "Foundations in Italy," in H. K. Anheier and S. Toepler (eds.) *Private Funds, Public Purpose: Philanthropic Foundations in International Perspective*, New York: Kluwer Academic/Plenum.

—— (1997) "The Nonprofit Sector in Italy," in H. K. Anheier and L. M. Salamon (eds.) *The Johns Hopkins Nonprofit Series*, Manchester: Manchester University Press.

Barker, D. G. (1993) "Values and Volunteering," in J. D. Smith (ed.) *Volunteering in Europe*, London: Voluntary Action Research, Second Series, No. 2: 10–31.

Barnard, C. I. (1938) *The Functions of the Executive*, Cambridge, MA: Harvard University Press.

Barr, N. (1998) *The Economics of the Welfare State*, Oxford: Oxford University Press.

Barsh, R. L. (1993) "Measuring Human Rights: Problems of Methodology and Purpose," *Human Rights Quarterly* 15(1): 87–121.

Bauer, R. and Betzelt, S. (1999) *NETS: New Employment Opportunities in the Third Sector, Final Country Report Germany*. Available online: www.lunaria.org/tertium/ricerca/conclusi/nets/germany_final.pdf (accessed January 15, 2001).

Beaudry, T. L. (2002) "Paradox in the Voluntary Sector: Expanding Democracy While Band-aiding Realities," Masters Dissertation, University of Regina, Canada.

Beck, U. (2000) "The Postnational Society and its Enemies," Public Lecture, London School of Economics and Political Science, February 24.

—— (1992) *Risk Society: Towards a New Modernity*, London: Sage.

Bediako, G. and Vanek, J. (1998) Trial International Classification of Activities for Time-use Statistics, New York: United Nations Statistic Division. Available online: www.un.org/Depts/unsd/timeuse/icatus/expnote_1.pdf (accessed February 20, 2001).

Beer, S. (1984) "The Viable Systems Model, Its Provenance, Development, Methdology, and Pathology," *Journal of Operational Research Science* 25(1).

Behn, R. D. and Kant, P. A. (1999) "Strategies for Avoiding the Pitfalls of Performance Contracting," *Public Productivity & Management Review* 22(4): 470–89.

Beise, M. (1998) "Politische Stiftungen," in Bertelsmann Stiftung (ed.) *Handbuch Stiftungen*, Gabler: Wiesbaden.

Bellah, R. N. (1985) *Habits of the Heart*, Berkeley, CA: University of California Press.

Ben-Ner, A. and Gui, B. (eds.) (1993) *The Non-profit Sector in the Mixed Economy*, Ann Arbor, MI: University of Michigan Press.

Ben-Ner, A. and Van Hoomissen, T. (1993) "Nonprofit Organizations in the Mixed Economy: A Demand and Supply Analysis," in A. Ben-Ner and B. Gui (eds.) *The Nonprofit Sector in the Mixed Economy*, Ann Arbor, MI: University of Michigan Press.

—— (1991) "Nonprofit Organizations in the Mixed Economy: A Demand and Supply Analysis," *Annals of Public and Cooperative Economics* 62(4): 519–50.

Bennington, J. (2000) "Governing the Inter-relationships Between State, Market and Civil Society," in H. K. Anheier (ed.) *Third Way—Third Sector*, Proceedings of a Policy Symposium organized by the LSE Centre for Civil Society (June 7, 1999), Report No. 1, London: Centre for Civil Society, London School of Economics and Political Science.

Berger, P. L. (1997) "Four Faces of Global Culture," *The National Interest* 23(7).

Berry, J. M. (1999) *The New Liberalism: The Rising Power of Citizen Groups*, Washington, DC: The Brookings Institution.

Bertelsmann Foundation (ed.) (2000) *Handbuch Bürgerstiftungen*, Gutersloh: Bertelsmann Foundation.

—— (1999) *The Future of Foundations in an Open Society*, Gütersloh: Bertelsmann Foundation.

Beyer, H. (1999) "Toward an Entrepreneurial Approach to Foundation Management," in H. K. Anheier and S. Toepler (eds.) *Private Funds, Public Purpose Philanthropic Foundations in International Perspective,* New York: Kluwer Academic/Plenum.

Biermann, B., Cannon, L., and Klainberg, D. (1992) *A Survey of Endowed Grantmaking Development Foundations in Africa, Asia, Eastern Europe, Latin America, and the Caribbean*, New York: Synergos Institute (mimeo).

Billis, D. (1989) "A Theory of the Voluntary Sector: Implications for Policy and Practice," Working Paper No. 5, London: Centre for Voluntary Organisations, London School of Economics.

Blair, T. (1998) "The Third Way: New Politics for a New Century," Fabian Pamphlet 588, London: Fabian Society.

Blair, T. and Schroeder, G. (1999) *Europe: The Third Way—die Neue Mitte*, London: Labour Party and SPD.

Bloche, M. G. (1998) "Should Government Intervene to Protect Nonprofits?," *Health Affairs* 17(5): 7–25.

BoardSource, home page, www.boardsource.org/.

Boli, J. (1999) "Conclusion," in J. Boli and G. Thomas (eds.) *Constructing World Culture: International Nongovernmental Organizations Since 1875*, Stanford, CA: Stanford University Press.

Boli, J. and Thomas, G. M. (1997) "World Culture in the World Polity: A Century of International Non-governmental Organization," *American Sociological Review* 62(2): 171–90.

Bolman, L. G. and Deal, T. E. (1991) *Reframing Organizations*, San Francisco, CA: Jossey-Bass.

Boris, E. T. (1987) "Creation and Growth: A Survey of Private Foundations," in T. Odendahl (ed.) *America's Wealthy and the Future of Foundations*, New York: Foundation Center.

Boris, E. T. and Krehely, J. (2002) "Civic Participation and Advocacy," in L. M. Salamon (ed.) *The State of Nonprofit America*, Washington, DC: The Brookings Institution.

Boris, E. T. and Steuerle, C. E. (eds.) (1999) *Nonprofits and Government: Collaboration and Conflict*, Washington, DC: Urban Institute Press.

Boris, E. T. and Wolpert, J. (2001) "The Role of Philanthropic Foundations: Lessons from America's Experience With Private Foundations," in H. K. Anheier and J. Kendall (eds.) *Third Sector Policy at the Crossroads: An International Nonprofit Analysis*, London: Routledge.

Borzaga, C. and Defourny, J. (eds.) (2001) *The Emergence of Social Enterprise*, London: Routledge.

Borzaga, C. and Santuari, A. (eds.) (1998) *Social Enterprises and New Employment in Europe*, Trento: Regione Autonoma Trentino-Alto Adige.

Bothwell, R. O. (2001) "Trends in Self-Regulation and Transparency of Nonprofits in the US," *The International Journal of Not-for-Profit Law* 2(3).

Boulding, K. E. (1962) "Notes on a Theory of Philanthropy," in F. G. Dickinson (ed.) *Philanthropy and Public Policy*, Washington, DC: National Bureau of Economic Research.

Bourdieu, P. (1986) "The Forms of Capital," in J. G. Richardson (ed.) *Handbook of Theory and Research for the Sociology of Education*, New York: Greenwood.

—— (1984) *Distinction: A Social Critique of the Judgement of Taste*, London: Routledge.

Breiteneicher, C. K. and Marble, M. G. (2001) "Strategic Programme Management," in A. Schluter, V. Then, and P. Walkenhorst (eds.), *Foundations in Europe, Society, Management and Law*, London: Directory of Social Change.

Bremner, R. H. (1956) "Scientific Philanthropy, 1873–1893," *Social Service Review* 30: 168–73.

411

Brilliant, E. L. (2000) *Private Charity and Public Inquiry: A History of the Filer and Peterson Commissions*, Bloomington, IN: Indiana University Press.

Brinton, M. and Nee, V. (eds.) (1998) *The New Institutionalism in Sociology*, New York: Russell Sage Foundation.

Brown, C. (2000) "Cosmopolitanism, World Citizenship, and Global Civil Society," *Critical Review of International Social and Political Philosophy* 3: 7–26.

Brown, G. (2000) *Goodman Lecture 2000*, London: National Council of Voluntary Organisations.

Brown, K., Kenny, S., Turner, B., with Prince, J. (2000) *Rhetorics of Welfare Uncertainty, Choice and Voluntary Associations*, Basingstoke: Macmillan.

Brown, L. D. and Tandon, R. (1994) *Institutional Development for Strengthening Civil Society*, Institute for Development Research (IDR) Report, 11(9).

Bruce, I. and Leat, D. (1993) *Management for Tomorrow*, London: VOLPROF, City University Business School.

Brummer, E. (ed.) (1996) *Statistiken zum Deutschen Stiftungswesen*, München: Maecenata.

Bryce, H. J. (2000) *Financial and Strategic Management for Nonprofit Organizations*, San Francisco, CA: Jossey-Bass.

Bühlmann, J. and Schmid, B. (1999) *Unbezahlt—aber trotzdem Arbeit. Zeitaufwand für Haus- und Familienarbeit, Ehrenamt, Freiwilligenarbeit und Nachbarschaftshilfe*, Neuchâtel, Switzerland: Bundesamt für Statistik.

Bulmer, M. (1999) "The History of Foundations in the United Kingdom and the United States: Philanthropic Foundations in Industrial Society," in H. K. Anheier and S. Toepler (eds.) *Private Funds and Public Purpose, Philanthropic Foundations in International perspectives*, New York: Kluwer Academic/Plenum.

Bundesministerium für Familie, Senioren, Frauen und Jugend (2000) *Ehrenamtliches und bürger-schaftliches Engagement in unserer Gesellschaft*, Berlin: Bundesministerium.

Burger, A. and Dekker, P. (eds.) (2001) *Noch Markt, Noch Staat. De Nederlandse Non-Profitsector in Vergelijkend Perspectief*, Den Haag: Sociaal en Cultureel Planbureau.

Burger, A., Dekker, P., van der Ploeg, T., and van Veen, W. (1997) *Defining the Nonprofit Sector: The Netherlands*, Working Papers of the Johns Hopkins Comparative Nonprofit Sector Project, No. 23, Baltimore, MD: Johns Hopkins Institute for Policy Studies.

Burger, A., Dekker, P., Toepler, S., Anheier, H. K., and Salamon, L. (1999) "Netherlands," in L. M. Salamon, H. K. Anheier, R. List, S. Toepler, S. W. Sokolowski, and Associates (eds.) *Global Civil Society Dimensions of the Nonprofit Sector*, Baltimore, MD: Johns Hopkins Center for Civil Society Studies.

Burke, E. (1904) *Selected Works*, Oxford: Clarendon Press.

Burkeman, S. (1999) *An Unsatisfactory Company? The 1999 Allen Lane Lecture*, London: The Allen Lane Foundation.

Burlingame, D. (2001) "Corporate Philanthropy's Future," in H. K. Anheier and J. Kendall (eds.) *Third Sector Policy at the Crossroads: An International Nonprofit Analysis*, London: Routledge.

Burt, R. S. (2000) "The Network Structure of Social Capital," in R. I. Sutton and B. M. Staw (eds.) *Research in Organizational Behaviour*, Greenwich, CT: JAI Press.

—— (1992) *Structural Holes: The Social Structure of Competition*, Cambridge, MA: Harvard University Press.

Cabinet Office (2002) *Private Action, Public Benefit: A Review of Charities and the Wider Not-for-profit Sector*, London: HM Government Strategy Unit Report, September.

Cadge, W. and Wuthnow, R. (forthcoming) "Religion and the Nonprofit Sector," in W. Powell and R. Steinberg (eds.) *The Nonprofit Sector: A Research Handbook* (2nd edn), New Haven, CT and London: Yale University Press.

CAF (1993) *Individual Giving and Volunteering in Britain: Who Gives What and Why?*, Tonbridge: CAF (6th and 7th editions).

412

—— (1987) *The Charitable Behaviour of the British People: A National Survey of Patterns and Attitudes to Charitable Giving Conducted by Abacus Research*, London: CAF and Abacus Research.

Cain, L. and Meritt Jr., D. (1999) "Zoos and Aquariums," in B. A. Weisbrod (ed.) *To Profit or Not to Profit: The Commercial Transformation of the Nonprofit Sector*, New York: Cambridge University Press.

Calhoun, C. (1997) "The Public Good as a Social and Cultural Product," in W. W. Powell and E. Clemens (eds.) *Private Action and the Public Good*, New Haven, CT: Yale University Press.

Canadian Center for Philanthropy (1991) *Canadian Directory to Foundations*, Toronto: Canadian Center.

Cardoso, F. H. (1979) "On the Characterization of Authoritarian Regimes in Latin America," in D. Collier (ed.) *The New Authoritarianism in Latin America*, Princeton, NJ: Princeton University Press.

Care International, Brussels, home page, www.care-international.org.

Carlson, N. (2000) "But Is It Smart Money? Nonprofits Question the Value of Venture Philanthropy," *Responsive Philanthropy* (Spring): 11–14.

Carrington, D. (2002) *The Investor Approach: A Way Forward for the Community Fund?*, London: Community Fund.

Carter, I. (1999) *A Measure of Freedom*, Oxford: Oxford University Press.

Castells, M. (1996) *The Rise of Network Society*, Oxford: Blackwells.

Central Statistical Office (1992) *Annual Abstract of Statistics*, London: HMSO.

Centre for Venture Philanthropy, home page, www.pcf.org/pcfsite/stratphil/stratphillinks/ definitions.html.

Chadeau, A. and Roy, C. (1986) "Relating Households Final Consumption to Household Activities: Subsidiarity or Complementary Between Market and Non-Market Production," *The Review on Income and Wealth* 32(4).

Chandler, A. D. and Takashi, H. (1990) *Scale and Scope: The Dynamics of Industrial Capitalism*, Cambridge, MA: Belknap Press.

Chang, C. and Tuckman, H. (1996) "The Goods Produced by Nonprofit Organizations," *Public Financial Quarterly* 24(1): 25–43.

Chang-Ho, L. (2002) "Volunteerism in Korea," *Journal of Volunteer Administration* 20(3): 10–11.

Charnovitz, S. (1997) "Two Centuries of Participation: NGOs and International Governance," *Michigan Journal of International Law* 18: 183–286.

Chatfield, C. (1997) "Intergovernmental and Nongovernmental Associations to 1945," in J. Smith, C. Chatfield, and R. Pagnucco (eds.) *Transnational Social Movements and World Politics: Solidarity Beyond the State*, Syracuse, NY: Syracuse University Press.

Chaves, M. (2003) "Religious Authority in the Modern World," *Society* 40(March/April): 38–40.

—— (2002) "Religious Congregations," in L. M. Salamon (ed.) *The State of Nonprofit America*, Washington, DC: The Brookings Institution.

Chesterman, M. (1979) *Charities, Trusts and Social Welfare*, London: Weidenfeld & Nicholson.

Chesterton, G. K. (1922) *What I Saw in America*, New York: Dodd, Mead & Co.

Clark, J. (2003) *Worlds Apart: Civil Society and the Battle for Ethical Globalization*, London: Earthscan, and Boomfield, CT: Kumarian.

—— (2001) "Trans-national Civil Society: Issues of Governance and Organisation," Issues paper prepared as background for a seminar on Transnational Civil Society (June 1–2, 2001), London School of Economics.

—— (1991) *Democratizing Development: The Role of Voluntary Agencies*, London: Earthscan, and West Hartford, CT: Kumarian Press.

—— (1972) "Organizational Structure, Environment, and Performance: The Role of Strategic Choice," *Sociology* 6: 1–22.

413

Clark, J. and Themudo, N. (2004) "The Age of Protest: Internet Based 'Dot-causes' and the 'Anti Globalization' Movement," in J. Clark (ed.) *Globalizing Civic Engagement: Civil Society and Transnational Action*, London: Earthscan.

Clark, P. and Wilson, J. (1961) "Incentive Systems: A Theory of Organizations," *Administrative Science Quarterly* 6: 129–66.

Clarke, G. (1998) "Nongovernmental Organisations and Politics in the Developing World," *Political Studies* 46: 36–52.

Clemens, E. S. (1993) "Organizational Repertories and Institutional Change: Women's Groups and the Transformation of the US Politics 1890–1920," *American Journal of Sociology* 98(4): 755–98.

Clotfelter, C. T. (1992) *Who Benefits From the Nonprofit Sector?*, Chicago, IL: University of Chicago Press.

Clotfelter, C. T. and Ehrlich, T. (eds.) (1999) *Philanthropy and the Nonprofit Sector in a Changing America*, Bloomington and Indianapolis, IN: Indiana University Press.

Cnaan, R., Handy, A., and Wadsworth, M. (1996) "Defining Who is a Volunteer: Conceptual and Empirical Considerations," *Non-profit and Voluntary Sector Quarterly* 25(3): 364–83.

Cobb, C., Halstead, T., and Rowe, J. (1995) *The Genuine Progress Indicator*, San Francisco, CA: Redefining Progress.

Coble, R. (1999) "The Nonprofit Sector and State Governments: Public Policy Issues Facing Nonprofits in North Carolina and Other States," *Nonprofit Management & Leadership* 9(3): 293–313.

Cohen, J. L. (1999) "Trust, Voluntary Association and Workable Democracy: The Contemporary Sources of American Distrust," in M. E. Warren (ed.) *Democracy and Trust*, Cambridge: Cambridge University Press.

Cohen, J. L. and Arato, A. (1997) *Civil Society and Political Theory*, Cambridge: Cambridge University Press.

Cohen, R. and Rai, S. M. (eds.) (2000) *Global Social Movements*, London: Athlone Press.

Coing, H. (1981) "Remarks on the History of Foundations and Their Role in the Promotion of Learning," *Minerva* 19(2): 271–81.

Coleman, J. S. (1990) *Foundations of Social Theory*, Cambridge, MA: Harvard University Press.

Coleman, J. S., Katz, M. E., and Menzel, H. (1966) *Medical Innovation: A Diffusion Study*, Indianapolis, IN: Bobbs-Merrill.

Comaroff, J. L. and Comaroff, J. (1999) *Civil Society and the Political Imagination in Africa: Critical Perspectives*, Chicago, IL: University of Chicago Press.

Commission of the European Communities (1997) *Promoting the Role of Voluntary Organizations in Europe*, Luxembourg: Office for Official Publications of the European Communities.

Commission on Foundations and Private Philanthropy (1970) *Foundations, Private Giving, and Public Policy*, Chicago, IL: University of Chicago Press.

Commission on the Future of the Voluntary Sector (1996) *Meeting the Challenge of Change: Voluntary Action in the 21st Century*, London: NCVO.

Coon, H. (1938) *Money to Burn*, London, New York, and Toronto: Longmans, Green.

Coser, L. (1965) "Foundations as Gatekeepers of Contemporary Intellectual Life," in L. Coser (ed.) *Men of Ideas*, New York: The Free Press.

—— (1956) *The Functions of Social Conflict*, Glencoe, IL: The Free Press.

Council on Civil Society, cosponsored by the Institute for American Values and the University of Chicago Divinity School, home page, www.americanvalues.org.

Council on Foundations (ed.) (1993) *Evaluation for Foundations*, San Francisco, CA: Jossey-Bass.

Covington, S. (1994) *Community Foundations and Citizen Empowerment: Limited Support for Democratic Renewal*, Washington, DC: NCRP.

Curti, M. E. (1961) "Tradition and Innovation in American Philanthropy," Proceedings of the American Philosophical Society, 105(April): 145–56.

Daft, R. (1997) *Management,* Fort Worth, TX: Harcourt Brace College.

Dahrendorf, R. (2001) Goodman Lecture 2001, London: National Council of Voluntary Organisations.

—— (1991) "Die gefährdete Civil Society," in K. Michalski (ed.) *Europa und die Civil Society,* Stuttgart: Castelgandolfo-Gespräche.

—— (1995) "Über den Bürgerstatus," in B. Van Den Brink and W. Van Reijen (eds.) *Bürgergesellschaft, Recht und Demokratie,* Frankfurt: Suhrkamp.

—— (1959) *Class and Class Conflict in Industrial Society,* London: Routledge & Kegan Paul.

Darcy de Oliveira, M. and Tandon, R. (1994) "An Emerging Global Civil Society," in *Citizens: Strengthening Global Civil Society,* Washington, DC: CIVICUS, World Alliance for Citizen Participation.

Dasgupta, P. (1993) *An Inquiry into Well-being and Destitution,* Oxford: Clarendon Press.

Dasgupta, P. and Serageldin, I. (eds.) (2000) *Social Capital: A Multifaceted Approach,* Washington, DC: The World Bank.

Davis Smith, J. (1998) *The 1997 National Survey of Volunteering,* London: Institute of Volunteering Research.

Dawson, S. (1996) *Analysing Organisations,* London: Macmillan.

Day, J. and Wengler, J. (1998) "The New Economics of Organisation," *McKinsey Quarterly* 1: 4–18.

Day, J., Mang, P., Richter, A., and Roberts, J. (2001) "The Innovative Organisation: Why New Ventures Need More Than a Room of Their Own," *McKinsey Quarterly* 2: 20–31.

Deacon, B., Hulse, M., and Stubbs, P. (1997) *Global Social Policy: International Organisations and the Future of Welfare,* London: Sage.

Deakin, N. (2001) *In Search of Civil Society,* London: Palgrave.

—— (chair) (1996) *Meeting the Challenge of Change: Voluntary Action Into the 21st Century,* London: NCVO.

—— (1995) "The Perils of Partnership: The Voluntary Sector and the State, 1945–1992," in J. D. Smith, C. Rochester, and R. Hedley (eds.) *An Introduction to the Voluntary Sector,* London: Routledge.

Dees, J. G., Emerson, J., and Economy, P. (2001) *Enterprising Nonprofits,* New York: John Wiley & Sons.

Defourny, J. and Develtere, P. (1999) *The Social Economy: The Worldwide Making of a Third Sector,* Liège: Centre d'Economie Sociale.

Deguchi, M. (2001) "The Distortion Between Institutionalised and Noninstitutionalised NPOs: New Policy Initiatives and Nonprofit Organisations in Japan," in H. K. Anheier and J. Kendall (eds.) *Third Sector Policy at the Crossroads: An International Nonprofit Analysis,* London: Routledge.

DeLaMar, R. (2000) "Volunteerism in Brazil: A Society Redefines Its Concept of Service," *Volunteer Leadership* (Spring): 26–8.

Delsen, L. (1995) *Atypical Employment: An International Perspective, Causes, Consequences, and Policy,* Groningen: Wolters-Noordhoff.

Deming, W. E. (2000) *Out of Crisis* (2nd edn), Cambridge, MA: MIT Press.

Desai, M. (1994) "Measuring Political Freedom," Discussion Paper 10, London: Centre for the Study of Global Governance, London School of Economics.

Desai, M. and Redfern, P. (eds.) (1995) *Global Governance: Ethics and Economics of the World Order,* London and New York: Pinter.

Deutsch, K. W. (1963) *The Nerves of Government,* New York: The Free Press.

Development Co-operation Directorate, Organisation for Economic Co-operation and Development (OECD) (2001) *Partnerships in Statistics for Development in the 21st Century,* Paris: OECD. Available online: www.paris21.org.

Development Initiatives (2000) "Global Development Assistance: The Role of NGOs and Other Charity Flows," Somerset: Development Initiatives, July (mimeo).

415

Diamond, L. (ed.) (1997) *Consolidating the Third Wave Democracies: Themes and Perspectives*, Baltimore, MD: Johns Hopkins University Press.

Diani, M. and McAdam, D. (eds.) (2003) *Social Movements and Networks*, Oxford: Oxford University Press.

Diener, E. and Suh, M. (eds.) (1999) *Subjective Well-being in Global Perspective*, Cambridge: MIT Press.

Dilulio, J. J. (1998) "The Lord's Work: The Church and Civil Society," in E. J. Dionne Jr. (ed.) *Community Works: the Revival of Civil Society in America*, Washington, DC: The Brookings Institution.

DiMaggio, P. J. (forthcoming) "Culture and the Nonprofit Sector," in W. Powell and R. S. Steinberg (eds.) *The Nonprofit Sector: A Research Handbook Second Edition*, New Haven, CT, and London: Yale University Press.

DiMaggio, P. J. and Anheier, H. K. (1990) "A Sociological Conceptualization of Non-Profit Organizations and Sectors," *Annual Review of Sociology* 16: 137–59.

DiMaggio, P. J. and Powell, W. W. (1983) "The Iron Cage Revisited: Institutional Isomorphism and Collective Rationality in Organizational Fields," *American Sociological Review* 48(2): 147–60.

Ding, Y., Jiang, X., and Qi, X. (2003) *China*, Makati City, Philippines: Asia Pacific Philanthropy Consortium.

Dingle, A. (eds.) (2001) *Measuring Volunteering: A Practical Toolkit*, Washington, DC: Independent Sector and United Nations Volunteers. Available online: www.independentsector. org/programs/research/toolkit/IYVToolkit.PDF (accessed February 15, 2001).

Dionne Jr., E. J. and Chen, M. H. (2001) *Sacred Places, Civil Purposes: Should Government Help Faith-Based Charity?*, Washington, DC: The Brookings Institution.

Dionne Jr., E. J. and DiIulio Jr., J. J. (eds.) (2000) *What's God Got to Do With the American Experiment?*, Washington, DC: The Brookings Institution.

Douglas, J. (1987) "Political Theories of Nonprofit Organization," in W. W. Powell (ed.) *The Nonprofit Sector: A Research Handbook*, New Haven, CT, and London: Yale University Press.

Douglas, J. and Wildavsky, A. (1980–1) "Big Government and the Private Foundations," *Policy Studies Journal* 9: 1175–90.

Dowie, M. (2001) *American Foundations: An Investigative History*, Cambridge, MA, and London: MIT Press.

Drucker, P. F. (1998) *The Drucker Foundation Self-Assessment Tool: Participant Workbook*, San Francisco, CA: Jossey-Bass.

—— (1990) *Managing the Non-Profit Organization: Principles and Practices*, New York: HarperCollins.

—— (1954) *The Practice of Management*, New York: Harper.

Duncan, R. (1979) "What is the Right Organizational Structure?," *Organizational Dynamics* (Winter): 59–80.

Durkheim, E. (1984) *The Division of Labour in Society* [De la Division du Travail Social] (2nd edn), Basingstoke: Macmillan.

—— (1933) *The Division of Labor in Society*, New York: The Free Press.

Economic Planning Agency, Japan (1998) *Economic Analysis of Private Nonprofit Activity Organisations*, Tokyo: Economic Planning Agency.

Economist, The (2000) "Special Article: NGOs: Sins of the Secular Missionaries," London: January 29, 354(8155): 25–8.

Edelman Public Relations (2000) Survey on NGOs and the Trust Void. Available online: www.edelman.com/.

Edgecomb, E., Klein, J., and Clark, P. (1996) *The Practice of Microenterprise in the U.S.: Strategies, Costs, and Effectiveness*, Washington, DC: Aspen Institute.

Edwards, B. and Foley, M. (1998) "Civil Society and Social Capital Beyond Putnam," *American Behavioral Scientist* 42(1): 124–39.

—— (1997) "Social Capital, Civil Society and Contemporary Democracy," *American Behavioral Scientist* (Special Issue) 40(5).

Edwards, B., Foley, M. W., and Diani, M. (2001) *Beyond Tocqueville: Civil Society and the Social Capital Debate in Comparative Perspective*, Hanover, NH: University Press of New England.

Edwards, M. (2004) *Civil Society*, Cambridge: Polity Press.

—— (1999) "Legitimacy and Values in NGOs and Voluntary Organizations: Some Sceptical Thoughts," in D. J. Lewis (ed.) *International Perspectives on Voluntary Action: Reshaping the Third Sector*, London: Earthscan.

Edwards, M. and Gaventa, J. (eds.) (2001) *Global Citizen Action*, Boulder, CO: Lynne Riener.

Edwards, M. and Hulme, D. (1996) "Too Close for Comfort? The Impact of Official Aid on Nongovernmental Organizations," *World Development* 24(6): 961–73.

—— (eds.) (1995) *Beyond the Magic Bullet: NGO Performance and Accountability in the Post-Cold War World*, London: Macmillan.

Edwards, M., Hulme, D., and Wallace, T. (1999) "NGOs in a Global Future: Marrying Local Delivery to Worldwide Leverage," *Public Administration and Development* 19: 177–86.

Ehling, M. and Schmidt, B. (1999) "Ehrenamtliches Engagement. Erfassung in der Zeitbudget-erhebung des Statistischen Bundesamtes und Möglichkeiten der Weiterentwicklung," in E. Kistler, H. H. Noll, and E. Priller (eds.) *Perspektiven gesellschaftlichen Zusammenhalts. Empirische Befunde, Praxiserfahrungen, Meßkonzepte*, Berlin: Edition Sigma.

Eisner, R. (1994) *The Misunderstood Economy: What Counts and How to Count It*, Boston, MA: Harvard Business School Press.

Elias, N. (1994) *The Civilizing Process*, Oxford: Blackwell.

Elkington, J. (1998) *Cannibals With Forks: The Triple Bottom Line of 21st Century Business*, Gabriola Island, BC: New Society Publishers.

Emanuele, R. and Simmons, W. O. (2002) "More than Altruism: What Does the Fringe Benefit Say About the Increasing Role of the Nonprofit Sector?," *Mid-American Journal of Business* 17(2).

Emerson, J. and Twersky, F. (1996) *New Social Entrepreneurs: The Success, Challenge and Lessons of Nonprofit Enterprise Creation*, San Francisco, CA: The Roberts Foundations.

Emerson, R. M. (1962) "Power-Dependence Relations," *American Sociological Review* 27(1): 31–40.

Employment and European Social Fund (1999) *Employment in Europe 1999*, European Commission, Employment and Social Affairs.

Enquettekommission des Deutschen Bundestages (2002) *Zivilgesellschaft und bürgerschaftliches, Engagement*, Berlin: Deutscher Bundestag.

Esping-Andersen, G. (1990) *The Three Worlds of Welfare Capitalism*, Princeton, NJ: Princeton University Press.

Etzioni, A. (1996) *The New Golden Rule*, New York: Basic Books.

—— (1975) *A Comparative Analysis of Complex Organizations*, New York: The Free Press.

—— (1971) *The Active Society: A Theory of Societal and Political Processes*, London: Collier-Macmillan.

European Commission (1997) Communication from the Commission on Promoting the Role of Voluntary Organisations and Foundations in Europe, COM 97/241, Luxembourg: Office for Official Publications of the European Communities.

—— (1995) European System of Accounts, Luxemberg: Eurostat.

Eurostat (2000) *Survey on Time-Use—Activity Coding List*, Final draft, www.un.org/Depts/unsd/timeuse/tusresource_manuals/eurostat_man.pdf (accessed February 20, 2001).

Evers, A. (1995) "Part of the Welfare Mix: The Third Sector as an Intermediate Area between Market Economy, State and Community," *Voluntas* 6(2): 159–82.

Falk, R. (1999) *Predatory Globalisation: A Critique*, Cambridge: Polity Press.

417

Farley, R. (ed.) (1995) *The State of the Union America in the 1990s*, New York: Russell Sage Foundation (two volumes).

Feigenbaum, S. (1980) "The Case of Income Redistribution: A Theory of Government and Private Provision of Collective Goods," *Public Finance Quarterly* 8(1): 3–22.

Feldstein, M. S. (1971) *The Rising Cost of Hospital Care*, Washington, DC: Information Services Press.

Ferguson, A. (1995 [1767]) *An Essay on the History of Civil Society* (edited by Fania Oz-Salzberger), Cambridge: Cambridge University Press.

Ferguson, R. F. and Dickens, W. T. (eds.) (1999) *Urban Problems and Community Development*, Washington, DC: The Brookings Institution.

Ferlie, E. (ed.) (1996) *The New Public Management in Action*, Oxford: Oxford University Press.

Fine, A. H., Thayer, C. E., and Coghlan, A. (1998) *Program Evaluation Practice in the Nonprofit Sector*, Washington, DC: Aspen Nonprofit Research Fund. Available online: www.nonprofit research.org/usr_doc/Fine.pdf.

Fischer, D. (1983) "The Role of Philanthropic Foundations in the Reproduction and Production of Hegemony: Rockefeller Foundation and the Social Sciences," *Sociology* 17: 206–33.

Fischer, H. (ed.) (1998) *Yearbook of International Humanitarian Law*, The Hague, The Netherlands: T. M. C. Asser Instituut.

Fisher, J. (1993) *The Road from Rio: Sustainable Development and the Non-governmental Movement in the Third World*, Westport, CT: Praeger.

Fitzherbert, L. and Richards, G. (2001) *A Guide to the Major Trusts Vol. 1, The Top 300 Trusts*, London: Directory of Social Change.

Fitzherbert, L., Addison, D., and Rahman, E. (1999) *A Guide to the Major Trusts* (1990–2000 edn), London: Directory of Social Change.

Fleishman, J. L. (1999) "Public Trust in Not-for-Profit Organisations and the Need for Regulatory Reform," in C. T. Clotfelter and T. Ehrlich (eds.) *Philanthropy and the Nonprofit Sector in a Changing America*, Bloomington and Indianapolis, IN: Indiana University Press.

Florini, A. M. (ed.) (2000) *The Third Force: The Rise of Transnational Civil Society*, Washington, DC: Carnegie Endowment for International Peace.

Florini, A. M., Senta, K., and Kokusai, N. (2000) *The Third Force: The Rise of Transnational Civil Society*, New York and Tokyo: Carnegie Endowment for International Peace and Japan Center for International Exchange.

Flynn, P. and Hodgkinson, V. (eds.) (2001) *Measuring the Impact of the Nonprofit Sector*, New York: Plenum/Kluwer.

Folmer, H. and Tietenberg, R. (eds.) (1999) *The International Yearbook of Environmental and Resource Economics 1999/2000: A Survey of Current Issues*, Cheltenham: Edward Elgar.

Forbes, D. P. (1998) "Measuring the Unmeasurable: Empirical Studies of Nonprofit Organisation Effectiveness," *Nonprofit and Voluntary Sector Quarterly (NVSQ)* 27(2): 159–82.

Foreman, K. (1999) "Evolving Global Structures and the Challenges Facing International Relief and Development Organizations," *Nonprofit and Voluntary Sector Quarterly* 28(4) (Supplement): 178–97.

Forsythe, D. (ed.) (2000) *Human Rights and Comparative Foreign Policy*, Tokyo and New York: United Nations University Press.

Foundation Center (2003) *Foundation Yearbook 2003*, New York: Foundation Center.

—— (2002) *International Grant-Making*, New York: Foundation Center.

—— (2001) *Foundation Yearbook 2001*, New York: Foundation Center.

—— (2000–3) *Foundation Giving Trends*, New York: Foundation Center.

Fowler, A. (2000) *The Virtuous Spiral: A Guide to Sustainability of NGOs in International Development*, London: Earthscan.

—— (1995) "Assessing NGO Performance: Difficulties, Dilemmas and A Way Ahead," in M. Edwards and D. Hulme (eds.) *Non-Governmental Organisations Performance and Accountability: Beyond the Magic Bullet*, London: Earthscan.

418

Freedom House (FH) (2001) Country Ratings, www.freedomhouse.org/ratings/index.htm.

Freeman, R. (1997) "Working for Nothing: The Supply of Volunteer Labour," *Journal of Labour Economics* 15(1): S140–S166.

Friedman, T. (2000) *The Lexus and the Olive Tree*, New York: Anchor Books.

Friends of the Earth International, home page, www.foei.org.

Frumkin, P. (2002) *On Being Nonprofit: A Conceptual and Policy Primer*, Cambridge, MA: Harvard University Press.

—— (1997) "Three Obstacles to Effective Foundation Philanthropy," in J. Barry and B. Manno (eds.) *Giving Better, Giving Smarter: Working Papers of the National Commission on Philanthropy and Civic Renewal*, Washington, DC: National Commission on Philanthropy and Civic Renewal.

Frumkin, P. and Andre-Clark, A. (2000) "When Missions, Markets and Politics Collide: Values and Strategies in the Nonprofit Human Services," *Nonprofit and Voluntary Sector Quarterly* 29(1): 141–63.

Fukuyama, F. (1995) *Trust: Social Virtues and the Creation of Prosperity*, New York: Simon & Schuster.

Fundacao Oriente (1992) *Guia das Fundacoes Portuguesas*, Lisbon: Romos Afonso & Moita.

Futter, V. (2002) *Nonprofit Governance and Management*, Chicago, IL: American Bar Association.

Gaberman, B. (1999) Speech to "Philanthropy Australia" conference, Sydney.

Galaskiewicz, J. and Bielefeld, W. (2001) "The Behaviour of Non-profit Organizations," in H. K. Anheier (ed.) *Organizational Theory and the Non-profit Form: Proceedings of a Seminar Series at the LSE Centre for Civil Society Report No. 2.*, London: Centre for Civil Society, London School of Economics and Political Science.

—— (1998) *Nonprofit Organizations in an Age of Uncertainity: A Study of Organizational Change*, New York: Aldine de Gruyter.

Galtung, J. (1992) "Theory Formation in Social Research: A Plea for Pluralism," in E. Oyen (ed.) *Comparative Methodology: Theory and Practice in International Social Research*, London: Sage.

Garonzik, E. (1997) "Foundation Funding: Venture Capital for Civil Society," in Civicus (ed.) *Sustaining Civil Society: Strategies for Resource Mobilization*, Washington, DC: Civicus.

Gaskin, K. (1999) *VIVA in Europe. A Comparative Study of the Volunteer Investment and Value Audit*, London: Institute for Volunteering Research.

Gaskin, K. and Smith, J. D. (1997) *A New Civic Europe? A Study of the Extent and Role of Volunteering*, London: The National Centre for Volunteering.

Gellner, E. (1994) *Conditions of Liberty: Civil Society and Its Rivals*, London: Hamish Hamilton.

General Accounting Office (1990) *Nonprofit Hospitals: Better Standards Needed for Tax Exemption*, Washington, DC: General Accounting Office.

Gibelman, M. and Gelman, S. (2001) "Very Public Scandals: Nongovernmental Organizations in Trouble," *Voluntas* 12(1): 49–66.

Giddens, A. (2000) *The Third Way and Its Critics*, Cambridge: Polity Press.

—— (1998) *The Third Way: The Renewal of Social Democracy*, Cambridge: Polity Press.

Gidron, B. and Katz, H. (2001) "Patterns of Government Funding to Third Sector Organizations as Reflecting a De-Facto Policy and Their Implications on the Structure of the Sector in Israel," *International Journal of Public Administration* 24(11): 1133–60.

Gidron, B., Bar, M., and Katz, H. (2003) *The Israeli Third Sector—Between Welfare State and Civil Society*, New York: Kluwer Academic/Plenum.

Glaeser, E. L., Laibson, D., and Sacerdote, B. (2000) *The Economic Approach to Social Capital*, National Bureau of Economic Research Working Paper No. 7728, Harvard Institute of Economic Research. Available online: post.economics.harvard.edu/hier/2001papers/2001list.html.

Glasius, M. (2002) "Expertise in the Cause of Justice: Global Civil Society Influence on the Statute for an International Criminal Court," in M. Glasius, M. Kaldor, and H. K. Anheier (eds.) *Global Civil Society 2002*, Oxford: Oxford University Press.

Glasius, M. and Kaldor, M. (2002) "The State of Global Civil Society: Before and After September 11," in H. Anheier, M. Glasius, and M. Kaldor (eds.) *Global Civil Society 2002*, Oxford: Oxford University Press.

Glasius, M., Kaldor, M., and Anheier, H. K. (eds.) (2002) *Global Civil Society 2002*, Oxford: Oxford University Press.

Glennerster, H. (2000) *British Social Policy Since 1945* (2nd edn), London: Blackwell.

Gobin, C. (1997) "The Mirage of a Social Europe," *Le Monde Diplomatique* (November), www.monde-diplomatique.fr/en/1997/11/europe (accessed January 15, 2001).

Goldschmidt-Clermont, L. and Pagnossin-Aligisakis, E. (1995) *Measures of Unrecorded Economic Activities in Fourteen Countries (United Nations Development Programme, Human Development Report Office)*, Occasional Paper 20, www.undp.org/hdro/oc20a.htm (accessed February 20, 2001).

Gomez, P. and Zimmermann, T. (1993) *Unternehmensorganisation: Profile, Dynamik, Methodik*, Frankfurt: Campus.

Gonella, C., Pilling, A., and Zadek, S. (1998) *Making Values Count: Contemporary Experience in Social and Ethical Accounting, Auditing and Reporting*, London: Association of Chartered Certified Accountants.

Gramsci, A. (1971) *Selections from the Prison Notebooks* (edited and translated by Quintin Hoare and Geoffrey Nowell Smith), London: Lawrence & Wishart.

Gray, B. H. and Schlesinger, M. (2002) "Health," in L. M. Salamon (ed) *The State of Nonprofit America*, Washington, DC: The Brookings Institution.

Greenpeace Spain, home page, www.greenpeace.es.

Greenpeace USA, home page, www.greenpeaceusa.org.

Greiner, L. (1972) "Evolution and Revolution as Organizations Grow," *Harvard Business Review* 50: 37–46.

Grigoryan, S. (2002) "Volunteering and Volunteer Management in Armenia," *Journal of Volunteer Administration* 20(3): 12–13.

Grønbjerg, K. A. (1998) "Markets, Politics and Charity: Nonprofits in the Political Economy," in W. W. Powell and E. S. Clemens (eds.) *Private Action and the Public Good*, New Haven, CT: Yale University Press.

—— (1994) "Using NTEE to Classify Non-profit Organizations: An Assessment of Human Service and Regional Applications," *Voluntas* 5: 301–28.

—— (1993) *Understanding Nonprofit Funding: Managing Revenues in Social Services and Community Development Organizations*, San Francisco, CA: Jossey-Bass.

Grunewald, M. H. (1995) "The Regulatory Future of Contingent Employment: An Introduction," *Washington and Lee Law Review* 52(3): 725–53. Available online: www.wlu.edu/~lawrev/abs/grunewald.htm (accessed January 15, 2001).

Habermas, J. (1992) *Faktizität und Geltung*, Frankfurt: Suhrkamp.

—— (1991 [1962]) *The Structural Transformation of the Public Sphere: An Inquiry into a Category of Bourgeois Society* (translated by Thomas Burger, with the assistance of Frederick Lawrence), Cambridge, MA: MIT Press.

—— (1985) *Die neue Unübersichtlichkeit*, Frankfurt: Suhrkamp.

Hackman, J. R. and Oldham, G. R. (1975) "Development of the Job Diagnostic Survey," *Journal of Applied Psychology* 60: 159–70.

Hall, M. (2001) "Measurement Issues in Surveys of Giving and Volunteering and Strategies Applied in the Design of Canada's National Survey of Giving, Volunteering and Participation," in *Non-profit and Voluntary Sector Quarterly* 30(3): 515–27.

Hall, M. and Banting, K. (2000) "The Nonprofit Sector in Canada: An Introduction," in K. Banting (ed.) *The Nonprofit Sector in Canada: Roles and Relationships*, Kingston, Canada: School of Policy Studies, Queen's University.

Hall, P. D. (2003) *A Historical Overview of Philanthropy, Voluntary Associations, and Nonprofit Organizations in the United States, 1600–2000*, Boston, MA: Hauser Center for Nonprofit Organizations, John F. Kennedy School of Government, Harvard University.

—— (1992) *Inventing the Nonprofit Sector and Other Essays on Philanthropy, Voluntarism, and Nonprofit Organizations*, Baltimore, MD: Johns Hopkins University Press.

Halman, L. (2001) *The European Values Study: A Third Wave. Source Book of the 1999/2000 European Values Study Surveys*, Tilburg, the Netherlands: Tilburg University Press.

Halpern, D. (1999) *Social Capital: The New Golden Goose?*, London: Institute for Public Policy Research.

Hammack, D. C. (ed.) (1998) *Making the Nonprofit Sector in the United States*, Bloomington and Indianapolis, IN: Indiana University Press.

Handy, C. (1990) *Understanding Voluntary Organizations: How to Make Them Function Effectively*, London: Penguin.

—— (1989) *The Age of Paradox*, Boston, MA: Harvard Business School Press.

Hannan, M. T. and Carrol, G. R. (1995) "An Introduction to Organizational Ecology," in G. R. Carroll and M. T. Hannah (eds.) *Organizations in Industry: Strategy, Structure and Selection*, New York: Oxford University Press.

Hannan, M. T. and Freeman, J. (1977) "The Population Ecology of Organizations," *American Journal of Sociology* 82: 929–64.

Hansmann, H. (1996) *The Ownership of Enterprise*, Cambridge, MA: Harvard University Press.

—— (1990) "The Economic Role of Commerical Nonprofits: The Evolution of the Savings Bank Industry," in H. K. Anheier and W. Seibel (eds.) *The Third Sector: Comparative Studies of Nonprofit Organizations*, Berlin and New York: DeGruyter

—— (1987) "Economic Theories of Non-profit Organisations," in W. W. Powell (ed.) *The Nonprofit Sector: A Research Handbook*, New Haven, CT: Yale University Press.

—— (1980) "The Role of Non-Profit Enterprise," *Yale Law Journal* 89(5): 835–901.

Harvard Center for International Development (CID) World Bank DataMart (2000) home page, paradocs.pols.columbia.edu:8080/datavine/MainFrameSet.jsp.

Hasenfeld, Y. H. (ed.) (1992) *Human Services as Complex Organizations*, London: Sage.

Havel, V. (1985) *The Power of the Powerless: Citizens Against the State in Central-Eastern Europe*, London: Hutchinson.

Havens, J. J. and Schervish, P. G. (2001) "The Methods and Metrics of the Boston Area Diary Study," *Non-profit and Voluntary Sector Quarterly* 30(3): 527–50.

Hawrylyshyn, O. (1977) "Towards a Definition of Non-Market Activities," *The Review on Income and Wealth* (Series) 23(1).

Health Charities Coalition of Canada, home page, www.healthcharities.ca.

Hedberg, B., Nyston, P., and Starbuck, W. (1976) "Camping on Seesaws: Prescriptions for a Self-designing Organization," *Administrative Science Quarterly* 21: 41–65.

Hegel, G. W. F. (1991 [1820]) *Elements of the Philosophy of Right* (edited by Allen W. Wood, translated by H. B. Nisbet), Cambridge: Cambridge University Press.

Held, D., McGrew, A., Goldblatt, D., and Perraton, J. (1999) *Global Transformations: Politics, Economics and Culture*, Cambridge: Polity Press.

Henley Centre (1998) *Planning for Social Change 1998*, London: The Henley Centre.

Herberts, K. (2001) "Finland," in A. Schluter, V. Then, and P. Walkenhorst (eds.) *Foundations in Europe, Society, Management and Law*, London: Directory of Social Change.

Herman, R. (ed.) (1994) *The Jossey-Bass Handbook of Nonprofit Management and Leadership*, San Francisco, CA: Jossey-Bass

Herman, R. and Renz, D. (1997) "Multiple Constituencies and the Social Construction of Nonprofit Effectiveness," *Nonprofit and Voluntary Sector Quarterly (NVSQ)* 26: 185–206.

Herzog, R. (1997) "Zur Bedeutung von Stiftungen in unserer Zeit," in Bertelsmann Stiftung (ed.) *Operative Stiftungsarbeit*, Gütersloh: Verlag Bertelsmann Stiftung.

421

Himmelstein, J. L. (1997) *Looking Good and Doing Good: Corporate Philanthropy and Corporate Power*, Bloomington and Indianapolis, IN: Indiana University Press.

Hirschman, A. (1982) *Shifting Involvements: Private Interest and Public Action*, Princeton, NJ: Princeton University Press.

Hirst, P. and Thompson, G. (1999) *Globalization in Question: The International Economy and the Possibilities of Governance*, Cambridge: Polity Press.

Hobbes, T. (1990 [1650]) *Leviathan* (edited by Richard Tuck), Cambridge: Cambridge University Press.

Hodgkinson, V. A. and Foley, M. (eds.) (2003) *The Civil Society Reader*, Hanover, NH, and London: University Press of New England.

Hodgkinson, V. A. and Weizman, M. (1993) *Non-profit Almanac: Dimensions of the Independent Sector*, Washington, DC: Independent Sector.

Hodgkinson, V. A., with Nelson, K. E., and Sivak Jr., E. D. (2002) "Individual Giving and Volunteering," in L. M. Salamon (ed.) *The State of Nonprofit America*, Washington, DC: The Brookings Institution.

Hodgkinson, V. A., Wetzman, M. S., Toppe, C. M., and Naga, S. M. (1996) *The Non-profit Almanac: Dimensions of the Independent Sector 1996–1997*, San Francisco, CA: Jossey-Bass.

—— (1992) *The Non-profit Almanac: Dimensions of the Independent Sector 1992–1993*, San Francisco, CA: Jossey-Bass.

Hogwood, B. W. and Gunn, L. (1984) *Policy Analysis for the Real World*, Oxford: Oxford University Press.

Home Office (1998) *Getting it Right Together: Compact on Relations Between Government and the Voluntary Sector in England*, London: Stationery Office.

Hood, C. (1995) "Contemporary Public Management: A New Global Paradigm?," *Public Policy and Administration* 10(2): 104–17.

—— (1991) "A New Public Management For All Seasons?," *Public Administration* 69(1): 3–19.

Hopkins, B. R. (1992) *The Law of Tax-Exempt Organizations* (6th edn), New York: John Wiley & Sons.

—— (1987) *The Law of Tax-Exempt Organizations* (5th edn), New York: John Wiley & Sons.

Hopkins, M. (1999) *The Planetary Bargain: Corporate Social Responsibility Comes of Age*, London: Macmillan.

Hopkins, M. and De Colle, S. (1999) *Towards an Human Development Index for Corporations*, Background Paper for the 1999 Human Development Report.

Horch, H. D. (1992) *Geld, Macht und Engagement in freiwilligen Vereinigungen*, Berlin: Duncker & Humblodt.

Howell, J. and Pearce, J. (2001) *Civil Society and Development: A Critical Exploration*, Denver, CO: Lynne Rienner.

Huber, E., Ragin, C., and Stephens, J. D. (1993) "Social Democracy, Christian Democracy, Constitutional Structures, and the Welfare State," *American Journal of Sociology* 99(3): 711–49.

Hudson, A. (2000) "Making the Connection: Legitimacy Claims, Legitimacy Chains and Northern NGOs' International Advocacy," in D. J. Lewis and T. Wallace (eds.) *New Roles and Relevance: Development NGOs and the Challenge of Change*, Hartford, CT: Kumarian.

Hudson, B. A. and Bielefeld, W. (1997) "Structures of Multinational Nonprofit Organisations," *Nonprofit Management and Leadership* 8(1): 31–49.

Hudson, M. (2003) *Managing at the Leading Edge: New Challenges in Managing Nonprofit Organisations*, London: Directory of Social Change.

—— (1999) *Managing Without Profit: The Art of Managing Third-sector Organizations*, London: Penguin.

Huizinga, J. (1954) *The Waning of the Middle Ages*, New York: Doubleday.

Hulme, D. and Edwards, M. (1997) *NGOs, States, and Donors: Too Close for Comfort?*, London: Macmillan in association with Save the Children.

Human Rights in Development Yearbook (1998) The Hauge: Kluwer Law International.

Huntington, S. P. (1991) *The Third Wave: Democratization in the Late Twentieth Century*, Norman, OK: University of Oklahoma Press.

Ilchman, W. F. and Burlingame, D. F. (1999) "Accountability in a Changing Philanthropic Environment: Trustees and Self-Government at the End of the Century," in C. T. Clotfelter and T. Ehrlich (eds.) *Philanthropy and the Nonprofit Sector in a Changing America*, Bloomington and Indianapolis, IN: Indiana University Press.

Independent Sector, home page, www.independentsector.org.

Independent Sector (2002) Giving and Volunteering in the United States 2001, Washington, DC: Independent Sector (7th biennially report; see www.independentsector.org/GandV/default. htm).

Inglehart, R. (1997) *Modernization and Postmodernization: Cultural, Economic, and Political Change in 43 Societies*, Princeton, NJ: Princeton University Press.

Inglehart, R. and Baker, W. (2000) "Modernization, Cultural Change, and the Persistence of Traditional Values," *American Sociological Review* 65: 19–51. InterAction website: www. interaction.org (accessed January, 2004).

Inglehart, R., Basañez, M., and Moreno, A. (1998) *Human Values and Beliefs: A Cross-Cultural Sourcebook: Political, Religious, Sexual, and Economic Norms in 43 Societies: Findings from the 1990–1993 World Values Survey*, Ann Arbor, MI: University of Michigan Press.

Institute for Volunteering Research, home page, www.ivr.org.uk/institute.htm.

International Center for Not-for-Profit Law (ICNL) (1998a) *The Tax Treatment of Non-governmental Organizations: A Survey of Best Practices from Around the World*, Washington, DC: ICNL. Avaliable online: www.icnl.org/gendocs/TAXPAPER.htm.

—— (1998b) *Integrity, Good Governance, and Transparency: Rules for Self-Regulation*, Washington, DC: ICNL. Available online: www.icnl.org/gendocs/selfreq.htm.

—— (1998c) *Checklist for NPO Laws*, Washington, DC: ICNL. Available online: www.icnl.org/ gendocs/cheklist.htm.

International Center for Not-for-Profit Law (ICNL) and the World Bank (1997) *Handbook on Good Practice for Laws Relating to Nongovernmental Organizations*, Washington, DC: ICNL (see also www.icnl.org/handbook/).

International Federation of Red Cross and Red Crescent Societies (IFRC) (1999) *Strategy 2010: Learning from the Nineties and Other Supporting Documents*, Geneva: IFRC.

International Network on Strategic Philanthropy, home page, www.insp.efc.be, accessed 2004.

Itoh, S. (2003) "Japan," in T. Yamamoto (ed) *Civil Society in Asia Pacific Philanthropy Consortium*, Makati City, Philippines: Asia Pacific Philanthropy Consortium.

James, E. (1989) *The Non-Profit Sector in International Perspective*, New York: Oxford University Press.

—— (1987) "The Non-Profit Sector in Comparative Perspective," in W. W. Powell (ed.) *The Non-Profit Sector: A Research Handbook*, New Haven, CT: Yale University Press.

—— (1986) "Cross Subsidization in Higher Education: Does it Pervert Private Choice and Public Policy?," in D. C. Levy (ed.) *Private Education: Studies in Choice and Public Policy*, New York: Oxford University Press.

—— (1984) "Benefits and Costs of Privatized Public Services: Lessons from the Dutch Educational System," *Comparative Education Review* 28: 605–25.

—— (1983) "Why Nonprofits Grow: A Model," *Journal of Policy Analysis and Management* 2(3): 350–66.

—— (1982) "The Private Provision of Public Services: A Comparison of Holland and Sweden," Program on Non-Profit Organizations Working Paper No. 60, Yale University.

James, E. and Rose-Ackerman, S. (1986) "The Nonprofit Enterprise in Market Economies," in J. M. Montias and J. Kornai (eds.) *Economic Systems*, New York: Harwood Academic Publishers.

423

Jenkins, C. (forthcoming) "Nonprofit Organizations and Political Advocacy," in W. W. Powell and R. S. Steinberg (eds.) *The Nonprofit Sector: A Research Handbook* (2nd edn), New Haven, CT and London: Yale University Press.

Jensen, L. (2003) *The Rhetorical Dimensions of Charitable Choice: Causal Stories, Problem Definition, and Policy Outcomes*, Boston, MA: University of Massachusetts.

Johns Hopkins University, Center for Civil Society Studies, Baltimore, MD, home page, www.jhu.edu~ccss.

Kaldor, M. (2003) *Global Civil Society: An Answer to War*, Cambridge: Polity Press.

Kaldor, M., Anheier, H. K., and Glasius M. (2003a) *Global Civil Society 2003*, Oxford, New York: Oxford University Press.

—— (2003b) "Global Civil Society in an Era of Regressive Globalisation," in M. Kaldor, H. K. Anheier, and M. Glasius (eds.) *Global Civil Society 2003*, Oxford: Oxford University Press.

Kandil, A. (1998) "The Nonprofit Sector in Egypt," in H. K. Anheier and L. M. Salamon (eds.) *The Nonprofit Sector in the Developing World*, The Johns Hopkins Nonprofit Series, Manchester: Manchester University Press.

Kanter, R. M. (1983) *The Change Masters*, New York: Simon & Schuster.

Kanter, R. M. and Summers, D. S. (1987) "Doing Good While Doing Well: Dilemmas of Performance Measurement in Nonprofit Organisations and the Need for a Multiple Constituency Approach," in W. W. Powell (ed) *The Nonprofit Sector: A Research Handbook*, New Haven, CT: Yale University Press.

Kaplan, A. E. (1999) *Giving USA*, New York: AAFRC Trust for Philanthropy.

Kaplan, R. S. and Norton, D. P. (2001) *The Strategy-Focused Organization: How Balanced Scorecard Companies Thrive in the New Business Environment*, Boston, MA: Harvard Business School Press.

Karatnycky, A. and the Freedom House Survey Team (2001) *Freedom in the World: The Annual Survey of Political Rights & Civil Liberties, 2000–2001*, New York: Freedom House.

Karl, B. D. and Karl, A. W. (1999) "Foundations and the Government: A Tale of Conflict and Consensus," in C. T. Clotfelter and T. Ehrlich (eds.) *Philanthropy and the Nonprofit Sector in a Changing America*, Bloomington and Indianapolis, IN: Indiana University Press.

Karl, B. D. and Katz, S. N. (1987) "Foundations and the Ruling Class," *Daedalus* 116(1): 1–40.

—— (1981) "The American Private Foundation and the Public Sphere, 1890–1930," *Minerva* 19(2): 236–69.

Kaufmann, D., Kraay, A., and Zoido-Lobatón, P. (1999a) "Governance Matters," World Bank Policy Research Working Paper 2196, Washington, DC: World Bank. Available online: www.worldbank.org/wbi/governance/pubs/govmatters.htm.

—— (1999b) "Aggregating Governance Indicators," World Bank Policy Research Working Paper 2195, Washington, DC: World Bank. Available online: www.worldbank.org/wbi/governance/pubs/aggindicators.htm.

Kaul, I., Grunberg, I., and Stern, M. (eds.) (1999) *Global Public Goods: International Cooperation in the 21st Century*, Oxford: Oxford University Press.

Keane, J. (2001) "Global Civil Society?," in H. K. Anheier, M. Glasius, and M. Kaldor (eds.) *Global Civil Society 2001*, Oxford: Oxford University Press.

—— (1998) *Civil Society: Old Images, New Visions*, Cambridge: Polity Press.

Keck, M. E. and Sikkink, K. (1998) *Activists Beyond Borders: Advocacy Networks in International Politics*, Ithaca, NY: Cornell University Press.

Keirouz, K. S., Grimm Jr., R. T., Steinberg, R. (1999) "The Philanthropic Giving Index: A New Indicator of the Climate for Raising Funds," *Nonprofit and Voluntary Sector Quarterly* 28(4): 491–9.

Kendall, J. (2003) *The Voluntary Sector: Comparative Perspectives in the UK* (1st edn), London and New York: Routledge.

Kendall, J. and Anheier, H. K. (1999) "The Third Sector and the European Union Policy Process: An Initial Evaluation," *Journal of European Public Policy* 6(2): 283–307.

Kendall, J. and Knapp, M. (2000) "Measuring the Performance of Voluntary Organisations," *Public Management* 2(1): 105–32.

—— (1996) "The Voluntary Sector in the UK," in L. M. Salamon and H. K. Anheier (eds.) *The Johns Hopkins Nonprofit Series, Volume 8*, Manchester: Manchester University Press.

Kennedy, S. S. (2003) *Charitable Choice: First Results from Three States*, Indianapolis, IN: Center for Urban Policy and the Environment, School of Public and Environmental Affairs, Indiana University-Purdue University.

Kettl, D. (2000) *The Global Public Management Revolution: A Report on the Transformation of Governance*, Washington, DC: The Brookings Institution.

—— (1997) "The Global Revolution in Public Management: Driving Themes and Missing Links," *Journal of Policy Analysis and Management* 16(3): 446–62.

—— (1993) *Sharing Power: Public Governance and Private Markets*, Washington, DC: The Brookings Institution.

Kidron, M. and Segal, R. (1995) *State of the World Atlas* (5th edn), London: Penguin.

Kieser, A. and Kubicek, H. (1983) *Organisation*, Berlin: deGruyter.

Kiger, J. (1954) *Operating Principles of the Larger Foundations*, New York: Russell Sage Foundation.

Kingma, B. R. (2003) "Public Good Theories of the Nonprofit Sector: Weisbrod Revisted," in H. K. Anheier and A. Ben-Ner (eds.) *The Study of the Nonprofit Enterprise: Theories and Approaches*, New York: Kluwer Academic/Plenum.

Knapp, M. R. J., Hardy, B., and Forder, J. (2001) "Commissioning for Quality: Ten Years of Social Care Markets in England," *Journal of Social Policy* 30(2): 283–306.

Knoke, D. (1981) "Commitment and Detachment in Voluntary Associations," *American Sociological Review* 46(2): 141–58.

Kochen, M. (ed.) (1989) *The Small World*, Norwood, NJ: Ablex Press.

Koch-Weser, C. (1999) "Foundations in the Developing World," in Bertelsmann Foundation (ed.) *The Future of Foundations in an Open Society*, Gütersloh: Bertelsmann Foundation.

Konrad, G. (1984) *Anti-Politics*, London: Quartet Books.

Korten, D. (1995) *When Corporations Rule the World*, West Hartford, CT, and San Francisco, CA: Kumarian Press and Berrett-Koehler Publishers, Inc.

—— (1990) *Getting to the 21st Century: Voluntary Action and the Global Agenda*, West Hartford, CT: Kumarian Press.

Kotler, P. and Andreason, A. (1991) *Strategic Marketing for Nonprofit Organizations*, Englewood Cliffs, NJ: Prentice Hall.

Kovach, H., Neligan, C., and Burall, S. (2003) *The Global Accountability Report: Power without Accountability?*. Available online: www.oneworldtrust.org.

Kramer, R. (2000) "A Third Sector in the Third Millennium?," *Voluntas* 11(1): 1–23.

—— (1990) "Change and Continuity in British Voluntary Organizations, 1976 to 1988," *Voluntas* 1(2): 33–60.

—— (1987) "Voluntary Agencies and the Personal Social Services," in W. W. Powell (ed.) *The Nonprofit Sector: A Research Handbook*, New Haven, CT: Yale University Press.

—— (1981) *Voluntary Agencies in the Welfare State*, Berkeley, CA: University of California Press.

Krashinsky, M. (1998) "Does Auspice Matter? The Case of Day Care for Children in Canada," in W. W. Powell and E. S. Clemens (eds.) *Private Action and the Public Good*, New Haven, CT: Yale University Press.

Kriesberg, L. (1997) "Social Movements and Global Transformation," in J. Smith, C. Chatfield, and R. Pagnucco (eds.) *Transnational Social Movements and Global Politics: Solidarity Beyond the State*, Syracuse, NY: Syracuse University Press.

Kumar, S. (1996) "Accountability: What Is It and Do We Need It?," in S. Osborne (ed.) *Managing in the Voluntary Sector*, London: Thomson.

Kumar, S. and Nunan, K. (2002) *A Lighter Touch: An Evaluation of the Governance Project*, York: Voluntary Action Camden.

Kurczewski, J. (1997) "Poland," in L. M. Salamon (ed.) *International Guide to Nonprofit Law*, New York: John Wiley & Sons.

Kurschner, D. (1996) "The 100 Best Corporate Citizens," *Business Ethics* (May/June): 24–35.

Kuti, E. (1996) "The Nonprofit Sector in Hungary," in L. M. Salamon and H. K. Anheier (eds.) *The Johns Hopkins Nonprofit Series*, Manchester: Manchester University Press.

Ladd, E. C. (1994) *The American Ideology: An Exploration of the Origin, Meaning, and Role of American Political Ideas*, Storrs, CT: Roper Center for Public Opinion Research.

Lake, K., Reis, T., and Spann, J. (2000) "From Grantmaking to Change Making: How the W. K. Kellogg Foundation's Impact Services Model Evolved to Enhance the Management and Social Effects of Large Initiatives," *NonProfit and Voluntary Sector Quarterly* 29(1): 41–68.

Landim, L. (1998) "The Nonprofit Sector in Brazil," in H. K. Anheier and L. M. Salamon (eds.) *The Nonprofit Sector in the Developing World, The Johns Hopkins Nonprofit Series*, Manchester: Manchester University Press.

—— (1997) "Brazil," in L. M. Salamon and H. K. Anheier (eds.) *Defining the Nonprofit Sector*, Manchester: Manchester University Press.

Landry, C. (2000) *The Creative City: A Toolkit for Urban Innovators*, London: Comedia, Earthscan.

Lansey, J. (1997) "Membership Participation and Ideology in Large Voluntary Organisations: The Case of the National Trust," *Voluntas* 7(3): 221–40.

Laumann, E. and Knoke, D. (1987) *The Organizational State: Social Choice in National Policy Domains*, Madison, WI: University of Wisconsin Press.

Laver, M. and Hunt, W. B. (1992) *Policy and Party Competition*, New York and London: Routledge.

Lawrence, P. and Lorsch, J. (1967) *Organization and Environment: Managing Differentiation and Integration*, Boston, MA: Harvard Business School.

Leat, D. (1999) "British Foundations: The Organisation and Management of Grantmaking," in H. K. Anheier and S. Toepler (eds.) *Private Funds, Public Purpose*, New York: Kluwer/ Plenum.

—— (1992) *Trusts in Transition: The Policy and Practice of Grant-making Trusts*, York: Joseph Rowntree Foundation.

—— (1988) *The Voluntary Sector and Accountability*, London: NCVO.

Leete, L. (forthcoming) "Paid Employment in the Non-Profit Sector," in W. W. Powell and R. Steinberg (eds.) *The Non-Profit Sector Research Handbook*, New Haven, CT, and London: Yale University Press.

—— (2000) "Wage Equity and Employee Motivation in Nonprofit and For-profit Organizations," *Journal of Economic Behavior and Organization* 43(4): 423–46.

Lefort, C. (1986) *The Political Forms of Modern Society: Bureaucracy, Democracy, Totalitarianism* (edited and introduced by John Thompson), Cambridge: Polity Press.

Le Grand, J. (1999) "Competition, Collaboration or Control? Tales from the British National Health Service," *Health Affairs* 18: 27–37.

Leslie, F. (2002) *Charitable Giving in Canada*, Toronto: Canadian Centre for Philanthropy.

Letts, C. W., Ryan, W. P., and Grossman, A. (1999) *High Performance Nonprofit Organizations: Managing Upstream for Greater Impact*, New York: John Wiley & Sons.

—— (1997) "Virtuous Capital: What Foundations Can Learn From Venture Capitalists," *Harvard Business Review* 2(March/April): 36–44.

Lewin, K. (1999 [1948]) *Resolving Social Conflicts, Selected Papers on Group Dynamics*, New York: Harper.

Lewis, D. J. (2001) *The Management of Non-governmental Development Organisations: An Introduction*, London: Routledge.

—— (1998) "Development NGOs and the Challenge of Partnership: Changing Relations Between North and South," *Social Policy and Administration* 32(5): 501–12.

Lewis, D. J. and Sobhan, B. (1999) "Routes of Funding Roots of Trust? Northern NGOs, Southern NGOs, Donors, and the Rise of Direct Funding," *Development in Practice* 9(1–2): 117–29.

Lewis, J. (1999) "Reviewing the Relationship Between the Voluntary Sector and the State in Britain in the 1990s," *Voluntas: International Journal of Voluntary and Nonprofit Organizations* 10(3): 255–70.

Lewis, J. P. (1987) *Strengthening the Poor: What Have We Learned?*, New Brunswick, NJ: Transaction Books.

Light, P. C. (2002) *Pathways to Nonprofit Excellence*, Washington, DC: The Brookings Institution.

—— (2000) *Making Nonprofits Work: A Report on the Tides of Nonprofit Management Reform*, Washington, DC: The Brookings Institution.

Lijphart, A. (1994) *Electoral Systems and Party Systems: A Comparative Study of Twenty-Seven Democracies, 1945–1990*, Oxford: Oxford University Press.

Lindblom, C. (1968) *The Policy-Making Process*, Englewood Cliffs, NJ: Prentice Hall.

Lindeman, E. C. (1988 [1936]) *Wealth and Culture*, Reprint, Society and Philanthropy Series, New Brunswick, NJ, and Oxford: Transaction Books.

Lindenberg, M. (1999) "Declining State Capacity, Voluntarism, and the Globalization of the Not-For-Profit Sector," *Nonprofit and Voluntary Sector Quarterly* 28(4) (Supplement): 147–67.

Lindenberg, M. and Bryant, C. (2001) *Going Global: Transforming Relief and Development NGOs*, Bloomfield, CT: Kumerian Press.

Lindenberg, M. and Dobel, J. P. (1999) "The Challenges of Globalization for Northern International Relief and Development NGOs," *Nonprofit and Voluntary Sector Quarterly* 28(4) (Supplement): 2–24.

Linz, J. J. and Stepan, A. (1996) *Problems of Democratic Transition and Consolidation*, Baltimore, MD: Johns Hopkins University Press.

Lipschutz, R. D. with Mayer, J. (1996) *Global Civil Society and Global Environmental Governance: The Politics of Nature from Place to Planet*, New York: SUNY Press.

Lipset, S. M. (1996) *American Exceptionalism: A Double-Edged Sword*, New York: Norton.

Lipsky, M. and Smith, S. R. (1989–90) "Nonprofit Organizations, Government, and the Welfare State," *Political Science Quarterly* 104(4): 625–48.

Listening Post Project (2003), home page, www.jhu.edu/listeningpost.

Local Initiatives Support Corporation, home page, www.lisc.org.

Locke, E. A. (1991) "The Motivation Sequence, the Motivation Hub and the Motivation Core," *Organizational Behaviour and Human Decision Processes* 50: 288–99.

Logan, D. (2002) *Corporate Citizenship: Defining Terms and Scoping Key Issues*, London: Corporate Citizenship Company.

Lundström, T. and Wijkström, F. (1997) *The Nonprofit in Sweden*, Manchester: Manchester University Press.

Lyons, M. (2001) *The Third Sector: The Contribution of Nonprofit and Corporate Enterprise in Australia*, Sydney: Allen & Unwin.

Lyons, M., Hoking, S., and Hems, L. (1999) "Australia," in L. M. Salamon, H. K. Anheier, R. List, S. Toepler, S. W. Sokolowski, and Associates (eds.) *Global Civil Society*, Baltimore, MD: Center for Civil Society Studies, Institute for Policy Studies, Johns Hopkins University.

Lynn, P. (1997) "Measuring Voluntary Activity," *Non-Profit Studies* 2(1): 1–11.

McAdam, D. (ed.) (1996) *Opportunities, Mobilization Structures and Framing Processes*, Cambridge: Cambridge University Press.

McAdam, D., Tarrow, S., and Tilly, C. (2001) *Dynamics of Contention*, Cambridge: Cambridge University Press.

McCarthy, K. (2003) *American Creed: Philanthropy and the Rise of Civil Society 1700—1865*, Chicago, IL: University of Chicago Press.

427

—— (1989) "The Gospel of Wealth: American Giving in Theory and Practice," in R. Magat (ed.) *Philanthropic Giving: Studies in Varieties and Goals*, New York and Oxford: Oxford University Press.

MacDonald, D. (1956) *The Ford Foundation: The Men and the Millions*, New York: Reynal & Co.

Macdonald, L. (1994) "Globalizing Civil Society: Interpreting International NGOs in Central America," *Millennium* 23(2): 267–85.

McGreogor, D. (1960) *The Human Side of Enterprise*, New York: McGraw-Hill.

McIlnay, D. P. (1998) *How Foundations Work*, San Francisco, CA: Jossey-Bass.

McKeown, L. (2002) *Volunteering in Canada*, Toronto: Canadian Centre for Philanthropy.

McLaughlin, K., Osborne, S. P., and Ferlie, E. (eds.) (2002) *New Public Management: Current Trends and Future Prospects*, London: Routledge.

McLean, I. and Johnes, M. (2000) *Aberfan: Government and Disasters*, Cardiff: Welsh Academic Press.

McMenamin, B. (1996) "Trojan Horse Money," *Forbes* 158(14): 123–6.

McMullen, K. and Brisbois, R. (2003) "Coping with Change: Human Resource Management in Canada's Non-profit Sector," CPRN Research Series on Human Resources in the Non-profit Sector, No. 4, Ottawa, ON: Canadian Policy Research Networks Inc.

Madison, J. (1961) *The Federalist Papers*, New York: Penguin.

Magretta, J. (2002) *What Management Is: How it Works and Why it's Everyone's Business*, New York: The Free Press.

Mahoney, C. and Estes, C. (1987) "The Changing Role of Private Foundations: Business as Usual or Creative Innovation?," *Journal of Voluntary Action Research* 16(4): 22–31.

Mansfield, J. (1997) "On the Contested Nature of the Public Good," in W. W. Powell and E. Clemens (eds.) *Private Action and the Public Good*, New Haven, CT: Yale University Press.

March, J. G. and Olsen, J. P. (1979) *Ambiguity and Choice in Organizations* (2nd edn), Bergen: Universitetsforlaget.

Margo, R. (1992) "Foundations," in C. T. Clotfelter (ed.) *Who Benefits from the Nonprofit Sector?*, Chicago, IL: University of Chicago Press.

Maw, N. N. G (1999) "Overview," in S. Crainer (ed.) *Financial Times Handbook of Management*, London: Pitman.

Mayntz, R. (1963) *Soziologie der Organization*, Reinbek: Rowolt.

Melnick, G., Keeler, E., and Zwanziger, J. (1999) "Market Power and Hospital Pricing: Are Nonprofits Different?," *Health Affairs* 18(3): 167–73.

Meyer, J., Boli, J., and Ramirez, F. (1997) "World Society and the Nation State," *American Journal of Sociology* 103: 144–81.

Meyer, M. and Zucker, L. (1989) *Permanently Failing Organizations*, Thousand Oaks, CA: Sage.

Michels, R. (1962) *Political Parties: A Sociological Study of the Oligarchical Tendencies of Modern Democracy*, New York: The Free Press

Michnik, A. (1985) "The New Evolutionism," in *Letters from Prison and Other Essays*, Berkeley, CA, and London: California University Press.

Micklethwait, D. and Wooldridge, A. (1996) *The Witch Doctors: Making Sense of Management Gurus*, New York: Random House.

Middleton, M. (1987) "Nonprofit Boards of Directors: Beyond the Governance Function," in W. W. Powell (ed.) *The Nonprofit Sector: A Research Handbook*, New Haven, CT: Yale University Press.

Minkoff, D. (1997) "Producing Social Capital: National Social Movements and Civil Society," *American Behavioral Scientist* 40(5): 606–19.

Mintzberg, H. (1983) *Structures in Fives: Designing Effective Organizations*, Englewood Cliffs, NJ: Prentice Hall

—— (1979) *The Structuring of Organizations*, Englewood Cliffs, NJ: Prentice Hall.

Mitchell, N. and McCormick, J. (1988) "Economic and Political Explanations of Human Rights Violations," *World Politics* 40(4): 476–98.

Moore Jr., B. (1967) *Social Origins of Dictatorship and Democracy: Lord and Peasant in the Making of the Modern World*, Boston, MA: Beacon Press.

Moore, M. H. (2000) "Managing for Value," *Nonprofit and Voluntary Sector Quarterly* 29(1): 183–204.

MORI (1994) *Giving to Charity: A Survey of Public Attitudes and Behaviour*, Research study conducted for ICFM.

Morley, E., Vinson, E., and Hatry, H. P. (2001) *Outcome Measurement in Nonprofit Organizations: Current Practices and Recommendations*, Washington, DC: Independent Sector.

Moskowitz, M. and Levering, R. (1993) *The Best 100 Companies to Work For in America*, New York: Penguin.

Moulton, L. and Anheier, H. K. (2000) "Public–Private Partnerships in the United States: Historical Patterns and Current Trends," in S. P. Osborne (ed.) *Public–Private Partnerships: Theory and Practice in International Perspective*, London: Routledge.

Moveon Peace, home page, peace.moveon.org/peace.php3.

Mulgan, G. (2000) "Government and the Third Sector: Building a More Equal Partnership," in H. K. Anheier (ed.) *Third Way—Third Sector*, Report No. 1, London: Centre for Civil Society, London School of Economics.

Murray, V. (2000) "Evaluating the Impact of Public–Private Partnerships: A Canadian Experience," in S. P. Osborne (ed.) *Public–Private Partnerships: Theory and Practice in International Perspective*, London: Routledge.

Nagai, A., Lerner, R., and Rothman, S. (1994) *Giving for Social Change: Foundations, Public Policy and the American Political Agenda*, Westport, CT: Praeger.

Naidoo, K. and Tandon, R. (1999) "The Promise of Civil Society," in K. Naidoo and B. Knight (eds.) *Civil Society at the Millennium*, West Hartford, CT: Kumarian Press.

Najam, A. (2000) "The Four-C's of Third Sector-Government Relations: Cooperation, Confrontation, Complementarity, and Co-optation," *Nonprofit Management and Leadership* 10(4): 375–97.

—— (1996) "Understanding the Third Sector: Revisiting the Prince, the Merchant, and the Citizen," *Nonprofit Management & Leadership* 7(2): 203–19.

Nanus, B. and Dobbs, S. M. (1999) *Leaders Who Make a Difference: Essential Strategies for Meeting the Nonprofit Challenge*, San Francisco, CA: Jossey-Bass.

National Commission on Civic Renewal, *The Index of National Civic Health*, College Park, Maryland.

National Low Income Housing Coalition, home page, www.nlihc.org/advocates/.

Naughton, J. (2001) "Contested Space: The Internet and Global Civil Society," in H. K. Anheier, M. Glasius, and M. Kaldor (eds.) *Global Civil Society 2001*, Oxford: Oxford University Press.

NCRP (National Committee for Responsive Philanthropy) (1991) *California Community Foundation and the Disadvantaged: No Focus, Marginal Impact*, Washington, DC: NCRP.

Nell-Breuning, O. V. (1976) "Das Subsidiaritätsprinzip," *Theorie und Praxis der sozialen Arbeit* 27: 6–17.

Nelson, R. R. and Krashinsky, M. (1973) "Public Control and Organization of Day Care for Young Children," *Public Policy* 22(1): 53–75.

Nielsen, W. (1972) *The Big Foundations*, New York: Columbia University Press.

"Nonprofit Employment Data Project," Johns Hopkins University, Baltimore, MD: Center for Civil Society Studies, available online: www.jhu.edu/~ccss/research/employ.html.

North, D. (1990) *Institutions, Institutional Change and Economic Performance*, Cambridge and New York: Cambridge University Press.

O'Connell, B. (1999) *Civil Society: The Underpinnings of American Democracy*, Hanover, NH: University of New England Press.

Odendahl, T. (1990) *Charity Begins at Home*, New York: Basic Books.

—— (1987) "Independent Foundations and the Wealthy Donors: An Overview," in T. Odendahl (ed.) *America's Wealthy and the Future of Foundations*, New York: Foundation Center.

O'Donnell, G. and Schmitter, P. (1986) *Transitions from Authoritarian Rule: Tentative Conclusions about Uncertain Democracies*, Baltimore, MD: Johns Hopkins University Press.

Offe, C. and Fuchs, S. (2002) "A Decline of Social Capital? The German Case," in R. D. Putnam (ed.) *Democracies in Flux: The Evolution of Social Capital in Contemporary Society*, New York: Oxford University Press.

Office of National Statistics (ONS) (2001) *Household Satellite Account — Volunteering HHP8–2001–08, 09, 11*, London: Office of National Statistics.

Olasky, M. (1992) *The Tragedy of American Compassion*, Washington, DC: Regnery Gateway.

Oliver, D. T. (1999) "Nonprofits Rake in Billions in Government Funds," *Human Events* 55(36): 9–18.

Olson, M. (1965) *The Logic of Collective Action*, Cambridge, MA: Harvard University Press.

O'Neill, K. (1999) "Internetworking for Social Change: Keeping the Spotlight on Corporate Responsibility," Discussion Paper No. 111, Geneva: United Nations Research Institute for Social Development.

O'Neill, M. (2002) *Nonprofit Nation: A New Look at the Third America* (2nd edn), San Francisco, CA: Jossey-Bass.

—— (2001) "Research on Giving and Volunteering: Methodological Considerations," *Non-Profit and Voluntary Sector Quarterly* 30(3): 505–14.

O'Regan, K. and Oster, S. (2002) "Does Government Funding Alter Nonprofit Governance? Evidence from New York City Nonprofit Contractors," *Journal of Policy Analysis and Management* 21(3): 359–79.

Organisation for Economic Co-operation and Development (OECD) (2003) *OECD Health Data 2003: A Comparative Analysis of 30 Countries*, Paris: OECD.

—— (1997) *Geographical Distribution of Financial Aid to Developing Countries*, Paris: OECD.

—— (1995) *Income Distribution in OECD Countries*, Social Policy Studies No 18, Paris: OECD.

—— (various years) *Development Assistance Committee, Development Assistance*, Paris: OECD

Ortmann, A. and Schlesinger, M. (2003) "Trust, Repute, and the Role of Nonprofit Enterprise," in H. K. Anheier and A. Ben-Ner (eds.) *The Study of the Nonprofit Enterprise Theories and Approaches*, New York: Kluwer Academic/Plenum.

Osborne, D. and Gaebler, T. (1992) *Reinventing Government: How the Entrepreneurial Spirit is Transforming Government*, Reading, MA: Addison-Wesley.

Osborne, S. P. (1998) "Organizational Structure and Innovation in U.K. Voluntary Social Welfare Organizations: Applying the Aston Measures," *Voluntas* 9(4): 345–62.

Oster, S. (1995) *Strategic Management for Nonprofit Organizations*, New York and Oxford: Oxford University Press

Ostrander, S. A. (1993) "Diversity and Democracy in Philanthropic Organisations: The Case of the Haymarket People's Fund," in D. R. Young, R. M. Hollister, and V. A. Hodgkinson (eds.) *Governing, Leading and Managing Nonprofit Organizations*, San Francisco, CA: Jossey-Bass.

Ostrander, S. A. and Schervish, P. G. (1990) "Giving and Getting: Philanthropy as a Social Relation," in J. Van Til (ed.) *Critical Issues in American Philanthropy: Strengthening Theory and Practice*, San Francisco, CA: Jossey-Bass.

Ostrower, F. (1995) *Strategic Management of Nonprofit Organizations*, New York: Oxford University Press.

Ostrower, F. and Stone, M. M. (forthcoming) "Governance: Research Trends, Gaps, and Future Prospects," in W. W. Powell and R. S. Steinberg (eds.) *The Nonprofit Sector: A Research Handbook* (2nd edn), New Haven, CT, and London: Yale University Press

Otlet, P. (1924) "Tableau de l'Organisation Internationale. Rapport general a la Conference des Associations Internationales," Geneva (UIA publication number 114).

Ott, J. S. (ed.) (2001) *The Nature of the Nonprofit Sector*, Boulder, CO: Westview Press.

Ouchi, W. G. (1991) "Markets, Bureaucracies and Clans," in G. Thompson, J. Frances, R. Levacic, and J. Mitchell (eds.) *Markets, Hierarchies and Networks*, London: Sage.

Oz-Salzberger, F. (1995) "Introduction," in F. Oz-Salzberger (ed.) *Adam Ferguson: An Essay on the History of Civil Society*, Cambridge: Cambridge University Press.

Padgett, J. F. and Ansell, C. K. (1993) "Robust Action and the Rise of the Medici, 1400–1434," *The American Journal of Sociology* 98(6): 259–61.

Pankoke, E. (1994) "Zwischen Enthusiasmus und Dilletantismus. Gesellschaftlicher Wandel freien Engagements," in L. Vogt and A. Zwingerle (eds.) *Ehre*, Frankfurt: Suhrkamp.

Park, T. (1994) "Non-profit Foundations in Korea," in K. Jung (ed.) *Evolving Patterns of Asia-Pacific Philanthropy*, Seoul: Yonsei University Institute of East and West Studies.

Passey, A., Tonkiss, F. Hems, L., and Fenton, N. (2000) *The United Kingdom Voluntary Sector Almanac*, London: NCVO Publications.

Paton, R. C. (1998a) *Performance Measurement, Benchmarking and Public Confidence*, London: Charities Aid Foundation.

—— (1998b) "The Trouble With Values," in D. Lewis (ed.) *International Perspectives on Voluntary Action: Rethinking the Third Sector*, London: Earthscan.

Perotin, V. (2001) *The Voluntary Sector, Job Creation and Social Policy: Illusions and Opportunities*, Geneva: International Labour Review.

Perrow, C. (2001) "The Rise of Nonprofits and the Decline of Civil Society," in H. Anheier (ed.) *Organisational Theory and the Non-profit Form*, London: Centre for Civil Society, Report 2, London School of Economics.

—— (1986) *Complex Organizations: A Critical Essay*, New York: Random House

Peterson Commission (1970) *Foundations, Private Giving and Public Policy: Recommendations of the Commission on Foundations and Private Philanthropy*, Chicago, IL, and London: University of Chicago Press.

Pfeffer, J. (1992) *Managing with Power: Politics and Influence in Organizations*, Boston, MA: Harvard Business School Press.

—— (1981) *Power in Organizations*, Marshfield, MA: Pitman.

Pfeffer, J. and Salancik, G. (1978) *The External Control of Organizations: A Resource Dependence Perspective*, New York: Harper & Row.

Pharaoh, C. (1996) "The Growth of Community Trusts and Foundations," in CAF (ed.) *Dimensions of the Voluntary Sector*, West Malling, Kent: Charities Aid Foundation.

Pharoah, C. and Siederer, N. (1997) "Numbers, Income, Assets: New Numbers," in C. Pharoah and M. Smerdon (eds.) *Dimensions of the Voluntary Sector*, West Malling, Kent: Charities Aid Foundation.

Pharr, S. J. and Putnam, R. D. (eds.) (2000) *Disaffected Democracies: What's Troubling the Trilateral Countries?*, Princeton, NJ: Princeton University Press.

Picarda, H. (1977) *Law and Practice Relating to Charities*, London: Butterworth.

Pierson, C. (1991) *Beyond the Welfare State?*, University Park, PA: Pennsylvania State University Press.

Pifer, A. (ed.) (1984) *Philanthropy in an Age of Transition*, New York: Foundation Center.

Pinter, F. (2001a) "Funding Global Civil Society Organisations," in H. K. Anheier, M. Glasius, and M. Kaldor (eds.) *Global Civil Society 2001*, Oxford: Oxford University Press.

—— (2001b) "The Role of Foundations in the Transformation Process in Central and Eastern Europe," in A. Schlüter, V. Then, and P. Walkenhorst (eds.) *Foundations in Europe: Society, Management and Law*, London: Directory of Social Change.

Plowden, W. (2001) *Next Steps in Voluntary Action*, London: Centre for Civil Society, London School of Economics and NCVO.

Porter, M. E. and Kramer, M. R. (1999) "Philanthropy's New Agenda: Creating Value," *Harvard Business Review* (November/December): 121–30.

Posavac, E. J. and Carey, R. G. (1997) *Program Evaluation: Methods and Case Studies*, Upper Saddle River, NJ: Prentice Hall.

Potucek, M. (2000) "An Uneasy Birth of the Czech Civil Society," *Voluntas* 11(2): 107–21.

Powell, W. W. (1990) "Neither Market nor Hierarchy: Network Forms of Organization," *Research in Organizational Behavior* 12: 295–336.

—— (ed.) (1987) *The Non-profit Sector: A Research Handbook*, New Haven, CT: Yale University Press.

Powell, W. W. and Clemens, E. S. (eds.) (1998) *Private Action and the Public Good*, New Haven, CT: Yale University Press.

Powell, W. W. and DiMaggio, P. J. (eds.) (1991) *The New Institutionalism in Organizational Analysis*, Chicago, IL: University of Chicago Press.

Powell, W. W. and Friedkin, R. (1987) "Organizational Change in Nonprofit Organizations," in W. W. Powell (ed.) *The Nonprofit Sector A Research Handbook*, New Haven, CT, and London: Yale University Press.

Powell, W. W. and Owen-Smith, J. (1999) "Universities as Creators and Retailers of Intellectual Property: Life-Sciences Research and Commercial Development," in B. Weisbrod (ed.) *To Profit or Not to Profit: The Commercial Transformation of the Nonprofit Sector*, New York: Cambridge University Press.

Powell, W. W. and Smith-Duerr, L. (1994) "Networks and Economic Life," in N. J. Smelser and R. Swedberg (eds.) *The Handbook of Economic Sociology*, Princeton, NJ: Princeton University Press.

Powell, W. W. and Steinberg, R. S. (eds.) (forthcoming) *The Nonprofit Sector: A Research Handbook* (2nd edn), New Haven, CT, and London: Yale University Press.

Power, M. (1999) *The Audit Society: Rituals of Verification*, Oxford; New York: Oxford University Press.

Preston, A. E. (1989) "The Nonprofit Worker in a Forprofit World" *Journal of Labor Economics* 7(4): 438–63.

Prewitt, K. (1999) "The Importance of Foundations in an Open Society," in Bertelsmann Foundation (ed.) *The Future of Foundations in an Open Society*, Gütersloh: Bertelsmann Foundation.

Priller, E., Zimmer, A., and Anheier, H. K. (1999a) "Der Dritte Sektor in Deutschland," *Aus Politik und Zeitgeschichte* 99(9): 12–21.

Priller, E., Zimmer, A., Anheier, H. K., Toepler, S., and Salamon, L. M. (1999b) "Germany," in L. M. Salamon, H. K. Anheier, R. List, S. Toepler, S. W. Sokolowski, and Associates (eds.) *Global Civil Society: Dimensions of the Nonprofit Sector*, Baltimore, MD: Johns Hopkins Center for Civil Society Studies.

Princen, T. and Finger, M. (1994) *Environmental NGOs in World Politics: Linking the Global and the Local*, London and New York: Routledge.

Probst, G. (1987) *Selbstorganisation*, Berlin: Duncker & Humblodt.

Prochaska, F. K. (1990) "Philanthropy," in F. M. L. Thompson (ed.) *The Cambridge Social History of Britain 1750–1950, Vol. 3*, Cambridge: Cambridge University Press.

Pugh, D., Hickson, D., Hinings, C., and Turener, T. (1969) "The Context of Organizational Structures," *Adminsitrative Science Quarterly* 14: 91–114.

—— (1968) "Dimensions of Organizational Structure," *Administrative Science Quarterly* 13: 65–91.

Putnam, R. (ed.) (2002) *Democracies in Flux*, New York and Oxford: Oxford University Press.

—— (2000) *Bowling Alone*, New York: Simon & Schuster.

Putnam, R., Leonardi, R., and Nanetti, R. (1993) *Making Democracy Work: Civic Traditions in Modern Italy*, Princeton, NJ: Princeton University Press.

Quadagno, J. (1990) "Theories of the Welfare State," *Annual Review of Sociology* 13: 109–28.

Ragin, C. (1998) "Comments on 'Social Origins of Civil Society'," *Voluntas: International Journal of Voluntary and Nonprofit Organizations*, 9(3): 261–70.

Rainey, H. and Bozeman, B. (2000) "Comparing Public and Private Organizations: Empirical Research and the Power of the A Priori," *Journal of Public Administration Research and Theory* 10(2): 447–69.

Rees, S. (1998) *Effective Nonprofit Advocacy*, Working Paper Series, Aspen, CO: Aspen Institute.

Reeves, T. C. (1969) *Freedom and the Foundation: The Fund for the Republic in the Era of McCarthyism*, New York: Albert K. Knopf.

Reichard, C. (2001) "New Approaches to Public Management," in K. König and H. Siedentopf (eds.) *Public Administration in Germany*, Baden-Baden: Nomos.

Reis, T. and Clohsey, S. J. (2001) "Unleashing New Resources and Entrepreneurship for the Common Good: A Philanthropic Renaissance," in A. Schluter, V. Then, and P. Walkenhorst (eds.) *Foundations in Europe, Society, Management and Law*, London: Directory of Social Change.

Renz, L. (1997) *International Grant Making: A Report on US Foundations*, New York: Foundation Center.

—— (various years) *Foundation Giving. Yearbook of Facts and Figures on Private, Corporate and Community Foundations*, New York: Foundation Center.

Richard, S. W. (1998) *Organizations: Rational, Natural, and Open Systems*, Upper Saddle River, NJ: Prentice Hall.

Ridings, D. (1999) "The Legitimization of Foundation Work," in Bertelsmann Foundation (ed.) *The Future of Foundations in an Open Society*, Gütersloh: Bertelsmann Foundation.

Rimel, R. W. (1999) *Strategic Philanthropy: Pew's Approach to Matching Needs with Resources*, Philadelphia, PA: Pew Charitable Trust.

Ritchey-Vance, M. (1991) *The Art of Association: NGOs and Civil Society in Brazil*, Arlington, VA: Inter-American Foundation.

Rochefort, D. A. and Cobb, R. W. (1994) "Problem Definition: An Emerging Perspective," in D. A. Rochefort and R. W. Cobb (eds.) *The Politics of Problem Definition: Shaping the Policy Agenda*, Kansas, KS: University of Kansas.

Roelefs, J. (1984/5) "Foundations and the Supreme Court," *Telos* 62: 59–87.

Roemer, M. (1993) "National Health Systems Throughout the World," *Annual Review of Public Health* (14): 335–53.

—— (1973) *The Nature of Human Values*, New York: The Free Press.

Rokeach, M. (1968) *Beliefs, Attitudes and Values*, San Francisco, CA: Jossey-Bass.

Romanelli, E. (1991) "The Evolution of Organisational Forms," *Annual Review of Sociology* 17: 79–103.

Rose-Ackerman, S. (1996) "Altruism, Nonprofits and Economic Theory," *Journal of Economic Literature* 34: 701–28.

Rosenberg Jr., C. (1996) "Wealthy and Wise: How You and America Can Get the Most Out of Your Giving," *Public Administration Review* 56(3): 222–4.

Rudney, G. (1987) "Creation of Foundations and Their Wealth," in T. Odendahl (ed.) *America's Wealthy and the Future of Foundations*, New York: Foundation Center.

Rueschemeyer, D., Huber, E., and Stephens, J. D. (1992) *Capitalist Development and Democracy*, Chicago, IL: University of Chicago Press.

Ruhm, C. J. and Borkoski, C. (2000) *Compensation in the Non-Profit Sector*, Working Paper Series No. 7562, Cambridge: National Bureau of Economic Research.

Ryan, W. P. (1999) "The New Landscape for Nonprofits," *Harvard Business Review* 77(1): 127–36.

Sachße, C. (1994) "Subsidiarität: Zur Karriere eines sozialpolitischen Ordnungsbegriffes," *Zeitschrift für Sozialreform* 40(1): 717–31.

Saguaro Seminar (2000) *Social Capital Community Benchmark Survey*, Cambridge, MA: Harvard University Press.

Salamon, L. M. (2003) *The Resilient Sector: The State of Nonprofit America*, Washington, DC: The Brookings Institution.

—— (ed.) (2002a) *The State of the Nonprofit America*, Washington, DC: The Brookings Institution, in collaboration with the Aspen Institute.

—— (2002b) *The Tools of Government: A Guide to the New Governance*, New York: Oxford University Press.

—— (1999) *America's Nonprofit Sector: A Primer*, New York: Foundation Center.

—— (1997a) *Holding the Center: America's Nonprofit Sector at a Crossroads*, New York: The Nathan Cummings Foundation.

—— (1997b) *The International Guide to Nonprofit Law*, New York: John Wiley & Sons.

—— (1995) *Partners in Public Service: Government–Nonprofit Relations in the Modern Welfare State*, Baltimore, MD: Johns Hopkins University Press.

—— (1994) "The Rise of the Nonprofit Sector," *Foreign Affairs* 73(3): 111–24.

—— (1992a) "Foundations as Investment Managers: Part I. The process," *Nonprofit Management and Leadership* 3(2): 117–37.

—— (1992b) *America's Nonprofit Sector: A Primer*, New York: Foundation Center.

Salamon, L. M. and Anheier, H. K. (1999) "Civil Society in Comparative Perspective," in L. M. Salamon, H. K. Anheier, R. List, S. Toepler, and S. W. Sokolowski, and Associations (eds.) *Global Civil Society: Dimensions of the Nonprofit Sector*, Baltimore, MD: Johns Hopkins Center for Civil Society Studies.

—— (1998a) "The Third Route: Government–Nonprofit Collaboration in Germany and the United States," in W. W. Powell and E. S. Clemens (eds.) *Private Action and the Public Good*, New Haven, CT: Yale University Press.

—— (1998b) "Social Origins of Civil Society: Explaining the Nonprofit Sector Cross-Nationally," *Voluntas: International Journal of Voluntary and Nonprofit Organizations* 9(3): 213–47.

—— (eds.) (1997) *Defining the Non-profit Sector: A Cross-National Analysis*, Manchester: Manchester University Press.

—— (1996) *The Emerging Nonprofit Sector: An Overview*, Manchester: Manchester University Press.

—— (1992a) "In Search of the Nonprofit Sector I: The Question of Definitions," *Voluntas* 3(2): 125–51.

—— (1992b) "In Search of the Nonprofit Sector II: The Problem of Classification," *Voluntas* 3(3): 267–309.

Salamon, L. M. and Flaherty, S. L. Q. (1997) "Nonprofit Law: Ten Issues in Search of Resolution," in L. M. Salamon (ed.) *The International Guide to Nonprofit Law*, New York: John Wiley & Sons.

Salamon, L. M. and Sokolowski, S. W. (2003) *Toward a Civil Society Index: Measuring the Dimensions of the Civil Society Sector*, Working Paper of the Johns Hopkins Center for Civil Society Studies, Baltimore, MD: Johns Hopkins Center for Civil Society Studies.

Salamon, L. M. and Tice, H. (2003) "Measuring Nonprofit Institutions in National Accounts," *OECD Statistics Newsletter* (April).

Salamon, L. M. and Toepler, S. (2000) *The Influence of the Legal Environment on the Development of the Nonprofit Sector*, Working Paper No. 17, Center for Civil Society Studies, Baltimore, MD: Johns Hopkins Center for Civil Society Studies.

Salamon, L. M., Hems, L., and Chinnock, K. (2000) *The Nonprofit Sector: For What and For Whom?*, Working Paper No. 37, Comparative Nonprofit Sector Project, Baltimore, MD: Johns Hopkins Center for Civil Society Studies.

Salamon, L. M., Sokolowski, S. W., and List, R. (2003) *Global Civil Society: An Overview*, Baltimore, MD: Johns Hopkins Center for Civil Society Studies.

Salamon, L. M., Anheier, H. K., List, R., Toepler, S., Sokolowski, S. W., and Associates (1999a) *Global Civil Society: Dimensions of the Non-profit Sector*, Baltimore, MD: Johns Hopkins University, Institute for Policy Studies, Center for Civil Society Studies.

—— (1999b) *The Emerging Sector Revisited: A Summary—Revised Estimates*, Baltimore, MD: Johns Hopkins University, Institute for Policy Studies, Center for Civil Society Studies.

Salm, J. (1999) "Coping with Globalization: A Profile of the Northern NGO Sector," *Nonprofit and Voluntary Sector Quarterly* 28(4) (Supplement): 87–103.

Sargent, A. and Kaehler, J. (1999) "Returns on Fundraising Expenditures in the Voluntary Sector," *Nonprofit Management and Leadership* 10(1): 5–19.

Schambra, W. A. (1997) "Building Community Top-down or Bottom-up?: Local Groups are the Key to America's Civic Renewal," *The Brookings Review* 15(4): 20–3.

Schlesinger, A. (1944) "Biography of a Nation of Joiners," *American Historical Review* 50 (October): 1–25.

Schlesinger, M. (1998) "Mismeasuring the Consequences of Ownership: External Influences and the Comparative Performance of Public, For-Profit, and Private Nonprofit Organizations," in W. W. Powell and E. S. Clemens (eds.) *Private Action and the Public Good*, New Haven, CT: Yale University Press.

Schlesinger, M., Bradford G., and Bradley, E. (1996) "Charity and Community: The Role of Nonprofit Ownership in a Managed Health Care System," *Journal of Health Politics* 21(4): 697–751.

Schlueter, A., Then, V., and Walkenhorst, P. (eds.) (2001) *Foundations in Europe: Society, Management and Law*, London: Directory of Social Change.

Scholte, J. (1999) "Globalisation Prospects for a Paradigm Shift," in M. Shaw (ed.) *Politics and Globalisation*, London: Routledge.

Schultze, C. (1977) *The Public Use of Private Interest*, Washington, DC: The Brookings Institution.

Schuppert, G. F. (2003) "Gemeinwohlverantwortung und Staatsverständnis," in H. K. Anheier and V. Then (eds.) *Zwischen Eigennutz und Gemeinwohl: Neue Formen und Wege der Gemeinnützigkeit*, Gütersloh: Bertelsmann Foundation.

Schwartz, P. (1991) *The Art of the Long View*, New York: Doubleday.

Schwarz, P. (1992) *Management in Nonprofit Organisationen*, Bern: Haupt.

Schwarz, P., Purtschert, R., and Giroud, C. (1999) *Das Freiburger Management-Modell für Nonprofit-Organisationen*, Bern: Haupt.

Seibel, W. (1996) "Successful Failures: An Alternative View of Organizational Coping," *American Behavioral Scientist* 39(18): 1011–24.

—— (1994) *Funktionaler Dilettantismus. Erfolgreich scheiternde Organisationen im "Dritten Sektor" zwischen Markt und Staat*, Baden-Baden: Nomos.

—— (1990) "Government/Third Sector Relationships in a Comparative Perspective: The Cases of France and West Germany," *Voluntas* 1: 42–61.

Selle, P. and Strømsnes, K. (1998) "Organised Environmentalists: Democracy as a Key Value," *Voluntas* 9(4): 319–43.

Sen, A. (1981) *Poverty and Famines: An Essay on Entitlements and Deprivation*, Oxford: Clarendon Press.

Shaw, M. (2000) *Theory of the Global State: Global Reality as an Unfinished Revolution*, Cambridge: Cambridge University Press.

Shelbourn, G. C. (1994) *International Charitable Giving: Laws and Taxation*, London: Dordrect.

Silk, T. (ed.) (1999) *Philanthropy and Law in Asia*, San Francisco, CA: Jossey-Bass.

Simon, H. (1976) *Administrative Behaviour* (4th edn), New York: The Free Press.

Simon, J. G. (1996) "The Regulation of American Foundations: Looking Backward at the Tax Reform Act of 1969," *Voluntas* 6(3): 243–54.

Simon, K. (1999) *The Role of Law in Encouraging Civil Society*, Washington, DC: ICNL. Available online: www.icnl.org/ gendocs/Arabconf.htm.

—— (1997) *Legal Principles for Citizen Participation: Toward a Legal Framework for Civil Society Organizations*, Washington, DC: CIVICUS.

Sirianni, C. and Friedland, L. (2001) *Civic Innovation in America: Community Empowerment, Public Policy, and the Movement for Civic Renewal*, Berkeley, CA: University of California Press.

Skocpol, T. (2002) "From Membership to Advocacy," in R. Putnam (ed.) *Democracies in Flux*, Oxford: Oxford University Press.

—— (1992) *Protecting Soldiers and Mothers: The Political Origins of Social Policy in the United States*, Cambridge, MA: Belknap Press of Harvard University Press.

Skocpol, T. and Fiorina, M. P. (eds.) (1999) *Civic Engagement in American Democracy*, Washington DC, New York: The Brookings Institution, Russell Sage Foundation.

Skocpol, T., Ganz, M., and Munson, Z. (2000) "A Nation of Organizers: The Institutional Origins of Civic Voluntarism in the United States," *American Political Science Review* 94(3): 527–49.

Smillie, I. (1995) *The Alms Bazaar: Altruism Under Fire: Non-Profit Organizations and International Development*, London: Intermediate Technology Publications.

Smillie, I. and Hailey, J. (2001) *Managing for Change: Leadership, Strategy and Management in Asian NGOs*, London: Earthscan.

Smith, J. A. and Borgmann, K. (2001) "Foundations in Europe: The Historical Context," in A. Schluter, V. Then, and P. Walkenhorst (eds.) *Foundations in Europe, Society, Management and Law*, London: Directory of Social Change.

Smith, J. D. (1998) *The 1997 National Survey of Volunteering*, London: The National Centre of Volunteering.

Smith, J. D., Chatfield, C., and Pagnucco, R. (eds.) (1997) *Transnational Social Movements and Global Politics: Solidarity Beyond the State* (1st edn), Syracuse, NY: Syracuse University Press.

Smith, S. R. (2002) "Social Services," in L. M. Salamon (ed.) *The State of Nonprofit America*, Washington, DC: The Brookings Institution.

Smith, S. R. and Lipsky, M. (1993) *Nonprofits for Hire: The Welfare State in the Age of Contracting*, Cambridge, MA: Harvard University Press.

Smyth, J. (2000) *The Guide to UK Company Giving*, London: Directory of Social Change.

Social Watch (2000) *Social Watch 2000*, Social Watch. Available online: www.socialwatch. org/2000/eng/chartings/stepsforward.htm; and www.socwatch.org.uy/2000/eng/chartings/methodology.htm (for methodology).

Sokolowski, S. W. (2000) *Civil Society and the Professions in Eastern Europe Social Change and Organizational Innovation in Poland*, New York: Kluwer Academic.

—— (1996) "Show Me the Way to the Next Worthy Deed: Toward a Microstructural Theory of Volunteering and Giving," *Voluntas* 7(3): 259–78.

Sombart, W. (1976 [1906]) *Why Is There No Socialism in the United States?*, White Plains, NY: International Arts and Science Press.

Stanfield, S. (ed.) (1995) *Nonprofit Organizations and Social Justice*, San Francisco, CA: Jossey-Bass.

Starbuck, W. and Dutton, W. (1973) "Designing Adaptive Organizations," *Journal of Business Policy* 3(4): 21–8.

Steinberg, R. (2003) "Economic Theories of Nonprofit Organizations: An Evaluation," in H. K. Anheier and A. Ben-Ner (eds.) *The Study of the Nonprofit Enterprise*, New York: Kluwer Academic/Plenum.

—— (1993) "Public Policy and the Performance of Nonprofit Organizations: A General Framework," *Nonprofit and Voluntary Sector Quarterly* 22(1): 13–31.

Steinberg, R. and Weisbrod, B. A. (1998) "Pricing and Rationing by Nonprofit Organizations with Distributional Objectives," in B. A. Weisbrod (ed.) *To Profit of Not to Profit: the Commercial Transformation of the Nonprofit Sector*, Cambridge: Cambridge University Press.

Stepan, A. (1988) *Rethinking Military Politics: Brazil and the Southern Cone*, Princeton, NJ: Princeton University Press.

Steuerle, E. and Hodgkinson, V. (1999) "Meeting Social Needs: Comparing the Resources of the Independent Sector and Government," in E. Boris and E. Steuerle (eds.) *Nonprofits and Government: Collaboration and Conflict*, Washington, DC: Urban Institute Press.

Stewart, D. M., Kane, P. R., and Scruggs, L. (2002) "Education and Training," in L. M. Salamon (ed) *The State of Nonprofit America*, Washington, DC: The Brookings Institution.

Stiglitz, J. (1998) Wider Lecture, January, Helsinki.

Strachwitz, R. (1999) "Foundations in Germany and Their Revival in East Germany After 1989," in H. K. Anheier and S. Toepler (eds.) *Private Funds, Public Purpose: Philanthropic Foundations in International Perspective*, New York: Kluwer Academic/Plenum.

—— (1998) "Operative and fördernde Stiftungen: Anmerkungen zur Typologie," in Bertelsmann Stiftung (ed.) *Handbuch des Stiftungsmanagements*, Wiesbaden: Gabler.

Strachwitz, R. and Toepler, S. (1996) "Traditional Methods of Funding: Endowments and Foundations," in L. Doyle (ed.) *Funding Europe's Solidarity*, Brussels: AICE.

Strategy Unit (2002) *Private Action, Public Benefit: A Review of Charities and the Wider Not-For-Profit Sector*, London: Cabinet Office.

Stuart, J. (ed.) (2003) *The 2002 NGO Sustainability Index for Central and Eastern Europe and Eurasia*, Washington, DC: USAID.

Tannenbaum, R., Weschler, I. R., and Massarik, F. (1961) *Leadership and Organization: A Behavioral Science Approach*, New York: McGraw-Hill.

Tarrow, S. (1996) "Making Social Science Work Across Space and Time: A Critical Reflection on Robert Putnam's Making Democracy Work," *American Political Science Review* 90(2): 389–97.

Taylor, F. W. (1967) *The Principles of Scientific Management*, New York: Norton.

Tempel, E. R. (ed.) (2003) *Hank Rosso's Achieving Excellence in Fund Raising* (2nd edn), San Francisco, CA: Jossey-Bass.

Terry, L. D. (1998) "Administrative Leadership, New Managerialism, and the Public Management Movement," *Public Administration Review* 58(3): 194–200.

Tew, E. S. (1963) "Location of Intenational Organizations," *International Organizations* 8: 492–3.

Titmuss, R. (1973) *The Gift Relationship: From Human Blood to Social Policy*, London: Penguin.

de Tocqueville, A. D. (1969 [1835]) *Democracy in America*, New York: Vintage Books.

Toepler, S. (1999) "Operating in a Grantmaking World: Reassessing the Role of Operating Foundations," in H. K. Anheier and S. Toepler (eds.) *Private Funds, Public Purpose: Philanthropic Foundations in International Perspective*, New York: Kluwer Academic/Plenum.

—— (1998) "Foundations and their Institutional Context: Cross-evaluating Evidence from Germany and the United States," *Voluntas: International Journal of Voluntary and Nonprofit Organizations* 9(2): 153–70.

—— (1996) *Das gemeinnützige Stiftungswesen in der modernen demokratischen Gesellschaft*, Munich: Maecenata.

Toepler, S. and Anheier, H. K. (2004) "Organizational Theory and Nonprofit Management: An Overview," in A. Zimmer and E. Priller (eds.) *Future of Civil Society: Making Central European Nonprofit-Organizations Work*, Wiesbaden: VS Verlag für Sozialwissenschaften.

Tracey Garey Changemakers, home page, www.changemakers.net/.

Transparency International (TI) (1999–2000) The 2000 Corruption Perceptions Index (CPI). Available online: www.transparency.org/cpi/2000/cpi2000.html.

Troyer, T. (2000) *The 1969 Private Foundation Law: Historical Perspectives on its Origins and Underpinnings*, Washington, DC: Council on Foundations.

Tullock, G. (1965) *The Politics of Bureaucracy*, Washington, DC: Public Affairs Press.

Ullman, C. F. (1998) "Partners in Reform: Nonprofit Organizations and the Welfare State in France," in W. W. Powell and E. S. Clemens (eds.) *Private Action and the Public Good*, New Haven, CT, and London: Yale University Press.

UNCSD (1996) *Indicators of Sustainable Development Framework and Methodology*, New York: United Nations.

UNDP (1990–2000) *Human Development Reports 1990–2000*, New York: United Nations. See also www.undp.org/hdro/.

Union of International Associations (2002/3) *Yearbook of International Associations, Guide to Global Civil Society Networks, Volume 5*, Munich: Saur.

United Nations (UN) (1993) *System of National Accounts*, New York: United Nations. See also www.un.org/Depts/unsd/sna/sna1-en.htm.

United Nations Statistics Division (2002) *Handbook on Nonprofit Institutions in the System of National Accounts*, New York: United Nations Statistics Division.

United Way of America, Alexandria, VA, home page, www.unitedway.org.

Unwin, J. and Westland, P. (1997) *Local Funding: The Impact of the National Lottery Charities Board*, London: Association of Charitable Foundations.

Uphoff, N. (1995) "Why NGOs Are Not a Third Sector: A Sectoral Analysis with Some Thoughts on Accountability, Sustainability and Evaluation," in M. Edwards and D. Hulme (eds.) *Beyond the Magic Bullet: NGO Performance and Accountability in the Post-Cold War World*, London: Earthscan.

—— (1988) "Assisted Self-Reliance: Working With, Rather than For, the Poor," in J. P. Lewis (ed.) *Strengthening the Poor: What We Have Learned*, Brunswick, NJ: Transaction Books.

USAID (2000) Bureau for Europe and Eurasia, Office of Democracy and Governance, *The 1999 NGO Sustainability Index*, Washington, DC: USAID. Available online for 1998, 1999, 2000: www.usaid.gov/regions/europe_eurasia/dem_gov/ngoindex/index.htm.

—— (1995) *Foreign Assistance: Private Voluntary Organizations' Contributions and Limitations*, Washington, DC: USAID.

—— (1998–2003) *Report of Voluntary Agencies Engaged in Overseas Relief and Development Registered with the U.S. Agency for International Development*, Washington, DC: USAID.

U.S. Census Bureau (various years) *Statistical Abstract of the United States*, Washington, DC: Government Printing Office.

van der Ploeg, T. (1999) "A Comparative Legal Analysis of Foundations: Aspects of Supervision and Transparency," in H. K. Anheier and S. Toepler (eds.) *Private Funds and Public Purpose, Philanthropic Foundations in International perspectives*, New York: Kluwer Academic/ Plenum.

Van der Vijver, F. and Leung, K. (1997) *Methods and Data Analysis for Cross-Cultural Research*, Thousand Oaks, CA: Sage.

Van Deth, J. W. and Scarbrough, E. (eds.) (1995) *The Impact of Values*, Oxford: Oxford University Press.

Van Deth, J. W., Maraffi, M., Newton, K., and Whitely, P.F. (eds.) (1999) *Social Capital in Europe*, London: Routledge.

Verba, S., Schlozman, K. L., and Brady, H. (1995) *Voice and Equality: Civil Voluntarism in American Politics*, Cambridge, MA: Harvard University Press.

Vianna Jr., A. (2000) "Civil Society Participation in World Bank and Inter-American Development Bank Programs: The Case of Brazil," *Global Governance* 6(4): 457–72.

Vidal, A. C. (2002) "Housing and Community Development," in L. M. Salamon (ed.) *The State of Nonprofit America*, Washington, DC: The Brookings Institution.

Vincent, J. and Pharoah, C. (2000) *Patterns of Independent Grant-Making in the UK, Dimensions 2000*, Volume 3, West Malling: Charities Aid Foundation.

Volkhart, F. H. (2001) "The Roles of NGOs in Strengthening the Foundations of South African Democracy," *Voluntas* 12(1): 1–15.

Voluntas (2000) *Ten Years After: The Third Sector and Civil Society in Central and Eastern Europe* 11(2) (June): 103–06. J. Kendall, H. K. Anheier, and M. Potůček, Special Issue, New York: Plenum/Kluwer.

Von Till, J. (1978) *Mapping the Third Sector*, New York: Foundation Center.

Voss, K. (1993) *The Making of American Exceptionalism: The Knights of Labor and Class Formation in the Nineteenth Century*, Ithaca, NY: Cornell University Press.

Wagner, A. (1997) "Der Nonprofit Sektor in der Schweiz," in C. Badelt (ed.) *Handbuch der Nonprofit Organisationen*, Stuttgart: Poeschl.

Wallace, T. (2000) "Development Management and the Aid Chain: The Case of NGOs," in D. Eade (ed.) *Development and Management*, Oxford: Oxfam.

Wapner, P. (1996) *Environmental Activism and World Civic Politics*, New York: SUNY Press.

Warren, M. E. (ed.) (1999) *Democracy and Trust*, Cambridge: Cambridge University Press.

Weaver, W. (1967) *U.S. Philanthropic Foundations*, New York: Harper & Row.

Weber, M. (1978) *Economy and Society*, Berkeley, CA: University of California Press.

—— (1935 [1905]) *The Protestant Ethic and the Spirit of Capitalism*, New York: Scribner's.

—— (1924) *The Theory of Social and Economic Organization*, New York: The Free Press.

Weffort, F. (1989) "Why Democracy?," in Alfred Stepan (ed.) *Democratizing Brazil: Problems of Transition and Consolidation*, New York: Oxford University Press.

Weick, K. (1995) *Sensemaking in Organizations*, Thousand Oaks, CA: Sage.

Weisbrod, B. A. (1998a) "The Nonprofit Mission and Its Financing: Growing Links Between Nonprofits and the Rest of the Economy," in B. A. Weisbrod (ed.) *To Profit or Not to Profit: The Commercial Transformation of the Nonprofit Sector*, New York: Cambridge University Press.

—— (ed.) (1998b) *To Profit or Not to Profit: The Commercial Transformation of the Nonprofit Sector*, Cambridge and New York: Cambridge University Press.

—— (1998c) "Modeling the Nonprofit Organization as a Multiproduct Firm: A Framework for Choice," in B. A. Weisbrod (ed.) *To Profit or Not to Profit: The Commercial Transformation of the Nonprofit Sector*, Cambridge and New York: Cambridge University Press.

—— (1988) *The Non-profit Economy*, Cambridge, MA: Harvard University Press.

—— (1977) *The Voluntary Nonprofit Sector*, Lexington, MA: D. C. Heat & CO.

Weitzman, M. S., Jalandoni, N. T., Lampkin, L. M., and Pollak, T. H. (2002) *The New Nonprofit Almanac and Desk Reference: The Essential Facts and Figures for Managers, Researchers, and Volunteers* (1st edn), San Francisco, CA: Jossey-Bass.

Wells, H. G. (1906) *The Future in America*, New York: Harper & Brothers.

Whitaker, B. (1979) *The Foundations: An Anatomy of Philanthropic Societies*, New York: Pelican Books.

—— (1974) *The Philanthropoids*, New York: William Morrow.

The White House (1999) *The Third Way: Progressive Governance for the 21st Century*, Washington, DC, April 25.

Williams, R. (1998) "Know Thy Critics," *Foundation News and Commentary* (May/June): 25–9.

Williamson, O. (1975) *Markets and Hierarchies: Analysis and Antitrust Implications*, New York: The Free Press.

Wilson, J. and Musick, M. (1997) "Who Cares? Toward an Integrated Theory of Volunteer Work," *American Sociological Review* 62: 694–713.

Wolch, J. R. (1990) *The Shadow State: Government and Voluntary Sector in Transition*, New York: Foundation Center.

Wolff, E. N. (1995) *Top Heavy: A Study of the Increasing Inequality of Wealth in America*, A Twentieth Century Report, New York: The Twentieth Century Fund Press.

Wolpert, J. (1995) "Delusions of Charity," *American Prospect* 23 (Fall 1995): 86–8.

World Bank (1998/2000) *World Development Indicators*, Washington, DC: World Bank. See also www.worldbank.org/data/working/def8.html (for definitions of indicators).

—— (1999) *Worldwide Governance Research Indicators Dataset*. Available online: www.worldbank.org/ wbi/governance/datasets.htm#dataset.

—— (1997) *Handbook on Good Practices for Laws Relating to Non-Governmental Organizations*, Discussion Draft, Washington, DC: World Bank Environment Department.

—— (various years) *World Development*, Washington, DC: World Bank.

World Values Study Group (2000) *World Values Survey, 1981–1984, 1990–1993 and 1995–97 CD Rom, Cumulative File for the First 3 Waves*, Ann Arbor, MI: Institute for Social Research, Inter-university Consortium for Political and Social Research.

World Wildlife Fund USA, home page, www.worldwildlife.org/.

Wuthnow, R. (2002) "Bridging the Privileged and the Marginalized," in R. Putnam (ed.) *Democracies in Flux*, Oxford: Oxford University Press.

—— (2000) *Linkages Between Faith-Based Nonprofits and Congregations*, Working Paper, Washington, DC: Aspen Institute.

—— (1998) *Loose Connections: Joining Together in America's Fragmented Communities*, Boston, MA: Harvard University Press.

—— and Hodgkinson, V. A. (eds.) (1990) *Faith and Philanthropy in America: Exploring the Role of Religion in America's Voluntary Sector*, San Francisco, CA: Jossey-Bass.

Wyszomirski, M. J. (2002) "Arts and Culture," in L. M. Salamon (ed) *The State of Nonprofit America*, Washington, DC: The Brookings Institution.

Yamamoto, T. (ed.) (1998) "The Nonprofit Sector in Japan," in L. M. Salamon and H. K. Anheier (eds.) *The Johns Hopkins Nonprofit Series*, Manchester: Manchester University Press.

Yamauchi, T., Shimizu, H., Sokolowski, S. W., and Salamon, L. M. (1999) "Japan," in L. M. Salamon, H. K. Anheier, R. List, S. Toepler, S. W. Sokolowski, and Associates (eds.) *Global Civil Society Dimensions of the Nonprofit Sector*, Baltimore, MD: Johns Hopkins Center for Civil Society Studies.

Yeo, S. (2002) *Membership and Mutuality: Proceedings of a Seminar Series Organised at the LSE Centre for Civil Society*, Report No 3, London: Centre for Civil Society, London School of Economics.

Ylvisaker, P. N. (1987) "Foundations and Nonprofit Organizations," in W. W. Powell (ed.) *The Nonprofit Sector: A Research Handbook*, New Haven, CT: Yale University Press.

Young, D. R. (2003) "Entreprenuers, Managers, and the Nonprofit Enterprise," in H. K. Anheier and A. Ben-Ner (eds.) *The Study of the Nonprofit Enterprise Theories and Approaches*, New York: Kluwer Academic/Plenum.

—— (2000) "Alternative Models of Government-Nonprofit Relations: Theoretical and International Perspectives," *Nonprofit and Voluntary Sector Quarterly* 29(1): 149–72.

—— (1998) "Commercialism in Nonprofit Social Service Associations: Its Character, Significance, and Rationale," in B. A. Weisbrod (ed.) *To Profit or Not to Profit: The Commercial Transformation of the Nonprofit Sector*, New York: Cambridge University Press.

—— (1992) "Organizing Principles for International Advocacy Associations," *Voluntas* 3(1): 1–28.

—— (1983) *If Not For Profit, For What? A Behavioural Theory of the Nonprofit Sector Based on Entreprenuership*, Lexington, KY: Lexington Books.

Young, D. R. and Salamon, L. M. (2003) "Commercialization, Social Ventures, and for-profit Competition," in L. M. Salamon (ed.) *The State of Nonprofit America*, Washington, DC: The Brookings Institution, pp. 423–46.

Young, D. R. and Steinberg, R. S. (1995) *Economics for Nonprofit Managers*, New York: Foundation Center.

Young, D. R., Bania, N., and Bailey, D. (1996) "Structure and Accountability: A Study of National Nonprofit Associations," *Nonprofit Management and Leadership* 6(4): 347–65.

Young, D. R., Koenig, B. L., Najam, A., and Fisher, J. (1999) "Strategy and Structure in Managing Global Associations," *Voluntas* 10(4): 323–43.

Yuki, G. A. (1989) *Leadership in Organizations*, Englewood Cliffs, NJ: Prentice Hall.

Zadek, S. and Raynard, P. (1996) *Accounting for Change: The Practice of Social Auditing*, London: New Economics Foundation (mimeo). (See New Economics Foundation and Traidcraft plc in UK).

Zerubavel, E. (1991) *The Fine Line: Making Distinctions in Everyday Life*, New York: The Free Press.

Zimmer, A. (2001) "Corporatism Revisited: The Legacy of History and the German Nonprofit Sector," in H. K. Anheier and J. Kendall (eds.) *Third Sector Policy at the Crossroads: An International Nonprofit Analysis*, London: Routledge.

—— (1996) *Vereine—Basiselement der Demokratie*, Opladen: Leske & Budrich.

Zimmer, A. and Priller, E. (2003) "Der Dritte Sektor zwischen Markt und Mission," in D. Gosewinkel, D. Rucht, W. Van Den Daele, and J. Kocka (eds.) *Zivilgesellschaft—national und transnational*, Berlin: Sigma, pp. 105–28.

Index

Numbers in italic type indicate pages containing relevant figures, tables, and maps; numbers in bold indicate pages containing relevant boxed text.

442

449